AFRICAN HISTORICAL DICTIONARIES
Edited by Jon Woronoff

Historical Dictionary of the Republic of Guinea-Bissau

Third Edition

Richard Andrew Lobban, Jr.
and
Peter Karibe Mendy

African Historical Dictionaries No. 22

The Scarecrow Press, Inc.
Lanham, Md., & London
1997

SCARECROW PRESS, INC.

Published in the United States of America
by Scarecrow Press, Inc.
4720 Boston Way
Lanham, Maryland 20706

4 Pleydell Gardens, Folkestone
Kent CT20 2DN, England

British Cataloguing-in-Publication Information Available

Library of Congress Cataloging-in-Publication Data
Lobban, Richard.
    Historical dictionary of the Republic of Guinea-Bissau / Richard
Andrew Lobban, Jr. and Peter Karibe Mendy.—3rd ed.
        p.   cm.—(African historical dictionaries ; no. 22)
    Includes bibliographical references.
    ISBN 0-8108-3226-7 (alk. paper)
    1. Guinea-Bissau—History—Dictionaries.   2. Guinea-Bissau—
Bibliography.   I. Mendy, Peter Karibe Michael.   II. Title.
III. Series.
DT613.5.L62   1996
966.57—dc20   96-24815
                                                            CIP

ISBN 0-8108-3226-7 (cloth : alk. paper)

♾ ™ The paper used in this publication meets the minimum
requirements of American National Standard for Information
Sciences—Permanence of Paper for Printed Library Materials, ANSI
Z39.48–1984.
Manufactured in the United States of America.

DEDICATION

The third edition of the *Historical
Dictionary of the Republic of Guinea-Bissau*
is dedicated to:
Awara, Kaiysa, Ywina, Josina, and Nichola
for their appreciation of ROOTS

Contents

Illustrations

Maps

Photographs

Editor's Foreword to the Third Edition

Guinea-Bissau is not one of Africa's largest countries, nor its most populous, nor its most prosperous. But it has carved a very special place in African history through a long and bloody struggle for independence. How it was before colonization, how it was colonized, how it escaped colonialism, and what has happened since independence are therefore of special interest to students of African affairs. So is another recent event in which this country hopefully will be a trend-setter, namely the move toward enhanced democracy.

Unfortunately, since the republic is somewhat peripheral and not that easy to visit and because Portuguese is spoken, less is known about Guinea-Bissau than most African states. That is why we are particularly pleased that this *Historical Dictionary of Guinea-Bissau* is not only an updating but an expansion of the previous edition. Like its predecessor, there is an extensive chronology, a lengthy list of acronyms, a wide range of entries on significant persons, places, and events, ethnic groups, political parties and government institutions and a very comprehensive, select bibliography.

This third edition of the *Historical Dictionary of Guinea-Bissau* is co-authored by Richard Lobban, and Peter Karibe Mendy, with contributions by Susan Hurley-Glowa. Dr. Lobban, Professor of anthropology, and Director of the Program of African and Afro-American Studies at Rhode Island College, wrote the first and co-authored the second edition. One of the few Americans to have seen Guinea-Bissau during the struggle for independence, he visited the liberated zones in 1973, returned in 1975 and 1993 and has followed events closely ever since. He has written extensively on the area, including co-authorship of the latest edition of the *Historical Dictionary of Cape Verde*. Dr. Mendy is Deputy Director of Guinea-Bissau's National Institute of Studies and Research (INEP). Among his main interests are the history of the resistance to colonialism and the emergence of political pluralism. His latest book, *Colonialismo Português Em Africa: A*

Tradição de Resistência Na Guiné-Bissau (1879–1959) has just appeared in 1994. Ms. Hurley-Glowa is a Brown University doctoral student researching Crioulo ethnomusicology.

Series Editor
Jon Woronoff

Authors' Foreword to the Third Edition

It is hard to believe that eight years have passed since writing the second edition of this book, but when Jon Woronoff contacted me again and asked if I would like to update and enlarge the past version, I happily agreed. Joshua Forrest, co-author of the second edition, had begun new directions in research and writing, so I thought about adding other features to the present edition. In the intervening years my historical studies of Guinea-Bissau had deepened through regular teaching of a course on this subject, but having shifted some of my fieldwork to other parts of Africa I felt strained to write comfortably about the current situation in Guinea-Bissau. Luckily, Peter Karibe Mendy was convinced to join the third edition to make up for my shortcomings. Our new partnership has been very rich. Mendy is keen to acknowledge the central role of his parents for inspiring his quest for the study of Guinea-Bissau and its people.

I believe that it is important to have more Guineans contributing directly to writing their own history. Mendy has added very substantially to the modern political entries and to the history of the towns and cities of Guinea-Bissau and the anti-colonial resistance. At the same time, Guinea-Bissau is about to follow Cape Verde in holding its first multi-party elections and this book permits Mendy to describe the new political parties and processes in Guinea-Bissau.

While we are so grateful to all of those who have contributed in the past and present, we take responsibility for what is written here.

Richard Lobban, Pawtuxet Village, Rhode Island
Peter Mendy, Alto Bandim, Bissau

Acknowledgments

A great number of individuals and events have contributed to the history of Guinea-Bissau: generations of Africans, the Portuguese explorers and settlers, thousands of forced laborers, colonists, and nationalists. This collective process of history making has given us the material for our history writing.

I would like to thank the governments of Guinea-Bissau and Cape Verde for permitting travels to Guinea-Bissau in 1973, 1975, and 1993 and to Cape Verde in 1975, 1992, and 1995. The first edition of this book was assisted by a grant from the Rhode Island College Research Fund which helped meet some of the costs of typing and duplication. The first edition was also assisted by Raymond Almeida, José Aica, and Linda Zangari.

For the second edition of the book, Jon Woronoff and I agreed that it was time to write separate books on each country. So I was pleased to have Marilyn Halter as my co-author for the second edition of the *Historical Dictionary of Cape Verde*, and Joshua Forest for the co-author of the second edition of the *Historical Dictionary of Guinea-Bissau*. Some elements of Halter's writing carry on in the third edition of the Cape Verde book with Marlene Lopes. In some cases, material developed for the Cape Verde books has relevance to Guinea-Bissau and it continues here with editing and updating. I want to express my gratitude for Halter's earlier collaboration, which is not continuing here because of her many writing and teaching demands at Boston University. The second edition of the Cape Verde book received significant input on Cape Verdean ethnomusicology from Peter Manuel.

The third edition of the Guinea-Bissau book also credits the former role of Joshua Forrest as the co-author of the second edition. His doctoral research on the politics of Guinea-Bissau in the 1980s added that dimension to the book. His research has most recently appeared in his book on Guinea-Bissau (published by Westview Press).

Events in Guinea-Bissau have moved on from the coup of

President Vieira in 1980 and have reached plural democracy as was the case in Cape Verde. Because of these changes I again sought someone with knowledge of the current situation in Guinea-Bissau, while my own research took me further into the past—expanding the book in both directions. The search for a new colleague was gratefully assisted by George Brooks at the University of Indiana who suggested that I contact Peter Karibe Mendy. Indeed, the dictionary format of this work can not reveal the degree to which the several, and very important, works of George Brooks have added to my understanding of the Senegambian region. I am most grateful to benefit from his published works, correspondence, and broad knowledge, especially on the American connections to the Upper Guinea coast and to neighboring Cape Verde.

The third edition of the Guinea-Bissau book received financial backing from the West Africa Research Association which generously supported research and travel in Cape Verde, Senegal, and Gambia in 1992 and by the Rhode Island College Faculty Research Fund. The New Bedford Public Library and the American Antiquarian Society have been helpful in providing information about the early American Consuls to Cape Verde. In Cape Verde I am especially appreciative of the support and assistance of José Maria Almeida at the Arquivo Histórico Nacional and the access I was given to the 19th-century slave registries. Marlene Lopes at the Cape Verdean Studies Special Collection of Adams Library has also been vital in this ongoing research. The bibliography has been typed and edited by Bernadette Doyle and Robert Tanue Wuelleh of Rhode Island College; these important services have been a great help in bringing this book together. My gratitude to all of these individuals, institutions, and their staffs is very great indeed.

Peter Karibe Mendy is exceedingly grateful to Isaac Monteiro, coordinator of the Centre for Socio-Economic Studies (CESE) of INEP, Aristides Gomes, researcher of CESE, and Fafali Koudawo, researcher of the Centre for the Study of Contemporary History (CEHC) of INEP for their valuable opinions and great encouragement. He is also much indebted to the staff of the Public Library, especially to Diamantino Queiros and Francelino Correia, for their generous help and enormous patience. Moreover, he would like to express his deepest gratitude to his family, especially Awara, Kaiysa and Ywina, for the tremendous comprehension and unfailing moral support. Peter Mendy and Richard Lobban are both very grateful to Harriet McGuire for her very high level of enthusiastic support and important logistical aid in getting the manuscript across the Atlantic.

Peter Manuel's earlier role continues in the third edition of the Guinea-Bissau and Cape Verde books, but it is Susan Hurley-Glowa who has very substantially expanded the specific entries on ethnomusicology in the third editions of both Cape Verde and Guinea-Bissau books.

Thanks also to Carolyn, Josina, and Nichola Fluehr-Lobban for putting up with my late hours and late arrivals to meals during the many months that passed while working on this project.

Abbreviations and Acronymns

ADB	African Development Bank
AGBEPSF	Associação da Guiné-Bissau para Educação e Promoção da Saude Familiar
AID	Agency for International Development
AIDS	Acquired Immune Deficiency Syndrome (SIDA)
ANP	Assembléia Nacional Popular (People's National Assembly)
BNG	Banco Nacional da Guiné-Bissau (National Bank of Guinea-Bissau)
BNU	Banco Nacional Ultramarino (Overseas National Bank)
CEAO	Communauté Economique de l'Afrique Occidentale (West African Economic Community)
CECEP	Comissariado de Estado de Coordenação Econômica e Plano
CEI	Casa dos Estudantes do Império
CEL	Comité Executívo da Luta (Executive Committee of the Struggle)
CIDAC	Amilcar Cabral Center for Information and Documentation
CIPM	Centro de Instrução Político Militar
COM	Comissão das Organizações das Mulheres
CONCP	Conferência das Organizações Nacionalistas das Colônias Portuguesas
CSL	Conselho Superior da Luta (High Council of the Struggle)
CUF	Companhia União Fabril
DGS	Direção Geral de Segurança
ECA	(UN) Economic Commission for Africa
ECOWAS	Economic Community of West African States
FAO	(UN) Food and Agricultural Organization
FARP	Forças Armadas Revolucionárias do Povo
FD	Frente Democrática
FDS	Frente Democrática Social

FLG	Frente de Libertação da Guiné
FLGC	Frente de Libertação da Guiné Portuguesa e Cabo Verde
FLING	Frente de Luta Pela Independência Nacional da Guiné-Bissau
FRAIN	Frente Revolucionária Africana para a Independência Nacional das Colônias Portuguesas
FRELIMO	Frente de Libertação de Moçambique
FUL	Front Uni de Libération (de Guinée et du Cap Vert)
GADCVG	Grupo de Acção Democrática de Cabo Verde e da Guiné
IBRD	International Bank for Reconstruction and Development
IDA	International Development Association
IFAD	International Fund for Agricultural Development
IMF	International Monetary Fund
INEP	Instituto Nacional de Estudos E Pesquisa (National Institute for Studies and Research
JAAC	Juventude Africana Amilcar Cabral
JIU	Junta de Investigações Ultramar
LDGH	Liga Guineense de Direitos Humanos
MAC	Movimento Anti-Colonialista
MFA	Movimento das Forças Armadas
MFDC	Mouvement des Forces Démocratiques de la Casamance
MING	Movimento para Independência Nacional da Guiné Portuguesa
MLG	Movimento de Libertação da Guiné
MLGCV	Mouvement de Libération de la Guinée "Portugaise" et des Îles du Cap Vert
MLICV	Mouvement de Libération des Îles du Cap Vert
MpD	Movimento para Democracia
MPLA	Movimento Popular de Libertação de Angola
MUDe	Movimento de Unidade para a Democracia
NATO	North Atlantic Treaty Organization (OTAN)
OAU	Organization of African Unity
PAICV	Partido Africano da Independência de Cabo Verde
PAIGC	Partido Africano da Independência da Guiné e Cabo Verde
PCD	Partido da Convergência Democrática
PDP	Partido Democrático do Progresso
PIDE	Polícia Internacional e de Defesa do Estado
PP	Pioneiros do Partido
PRD	Partido para Renovação e Desenvolvimento

PRS	Partido da Renovaçâo Social
PUSD	Partido Unido Social Democrata
PVDE	Polícia de Vigilância e Defesa do Estado
RDAG	Rassemblement Démocratique Africaine de la Guineé
RGB-MB	Resistência da Guiné-Bissau/Movimento Bâfata
SIDA	Swedish International Development Agency
UCID	União Caboverdeana para A Independência e Democracia
UDCV	União Democrática de Cabo Verde
UDEMU	União Democrática das Mulheres
UDG	União Democrática da Guiné
UGEAN	União Geral dos Estudantes da Africa Negra
UGTGB	União Geral dos Trabalhadores da Guiné-Bissau
UN	United Nations (ONU)
UNCTAD	UN Conference on Trade and Development
UNDP	UN Development Program
UNGP	União dos Naturais da Guiné Portuguesa
UNTG	União Nacional dos Trabalhadores da Guiné
UPG	União Popular da Guiné
UPICV	União das Populações das Ilhas de Cabo Verde
UPLG	União Popular para Libertação da Guiné
URGP	Union des Ressortissants de la Guinée
USAID	United States Agency for International Development
WADB	West African Development Bank (BOAD)
WHO	World Health Organization

Introduction

Guinea-Bissau is unusual among West African countries because much of its history is closely tied to that of the Cape Verde Islands by virtue of the common Portuguese administration. The two lands were linked, to unequal degrees, for more than five hundred years. The Portuguese began to visit and settle in both countries from the middle of the fifteenth century to the third quarter of the twentieth century. For tens of thousands of Guinean captives, abducted from their homes and villages for much of this period, Cape Verde was a final destination, or a transit port to the New World.

Similarly Cape Verdean traders, often known as *lançados* (outcastes), were not only the commercial agents linking the two lands and peoples, but also created much of Crioulo culture and people. The Crioulo language emerged in the 15th and 16th centuries as a mixture of Portuguese and various African languages. This process synthesized social groups such as the *grumêtes* (armed soldier-traders), the *tangomãos* (interpreters), and the Mandinka-based *Dyulas* (long distance traders). Indeed, the Crioulo majority of Cape Verde produced a number of the significant leaders in the movement for independence of Guinea-Bissau in 1975. As a consequence of these deep linkages, this book offers numerous references to Cape Verde. For greater depth and detail the reader is referred to the third edition of the *Historical Dictionary of Cape Verde* (Richard Lobban and Marlene Lopes, Scarecrow Press, 1995). Several common subject entries link these two works.

However, in this book Lobban and Mendy have an Afro-centric focus and look at the same realities from a Guinean point of view. The reader is also encouraged to read Andrew F. Clark and Lucie Colvin Phillips's parallel work on Senegal (Scarecrow Press, 1994) and the second edition of Thomas O'Toole's book on Guinea-Conakry (Scarecrow Press, 1987) since the histories of these other two nations often relate to Guinea-Bissau as well.

But make no mistake: Guinea-Bissau (former Portuguese

Guinea) has a history very much its own. It was settled long before the Portuguese arriyed; Cape Verde's settlement is only colonial. The many African languages of Guinea-Bissau are still spoken there; Cape Verde has largely extinguished African languages except as some lexical survivals in Crioulo. A large group of Guineans are Muslims; hardly any Cape Verdeans follow this faith. The history of Guinea is intimately tied to the great events of African regional history, including the major state formation of Ghana and Mali, migrations, architecture, agricultural patterns, and a spirit of Islamic revival. Cape Verde only felt the echos of these processes as slaves from the defeated forces were brought into its society and economy. The most significant recent event was the war of national liberation which was fought in the forests of Guinea but had a Cape Verdean leadership that brought independence to Cape Verde with hardly a shot being fired there.

Nomenclature

The name "Guinea" has at least two possible origins. It may be derived from a corruption of the word "*Aguinaou*," as the general Berber reference for the "Land of the Blacks" (which is geographically and conceptually parallel to the term "*Bilad as Sudan*" in Arabic). The Portuguese and Spanish had intensive centuries of occupation by Moors and Berbers long before the Portuguese descended upon the West African coast in the fifteenth century. At that time, the Portuguese were the only European power in maritime exploration of that region, and they applied the term "Guinea" to the entire region from Senegal to Angola. Later it was differentiated into Upper and Lower Guinea coasts and finally to Portuguese Guinea as their domain shrunk over the centuries amidst regional pressure from French and English colonialism.

Alternatively, the term may be a corruption of the empire of "Ghana" famed for its gold and for sparking Portuguese interest in the region. As the years went on, the "gold of Guinea (Ghana)" became synonymous for the region, and the English used the term as a reference to their currency. Later the word "guinea" became applied to other parts of the world, such as New Guinea, which was the home of non-Western dark-skinned people.

The term Guinea-Bissau is used in this book as the modern referent to Portuguese Guinea (Guiné-Portuguesa) which was of approximately the same size except for early colonial border adjustments in the Casamance regions. For simplicity, we have used the term Guinea-Bissau to transcend all historical periods, even though its territory has been reduced. The term Guinea-Bissau is also used to differentiate this territory from Guinée-Conakry, neighboring to the south but having had a colonial experience with the French. The Republic of Guinea-Bissau is the official English translation of the name of this nation. The adjective, Guinean, refers to an inhabitant of this country unless otherwise specified.

The terminology for the island Republic of Cape Verde is used to distinguish it from the westernmost Cap Vert region of Senegal for which the archipelago is named. The long-lasting desert-like ecology of the Cape Verde Islands testifies that the islands were named by the early Portuguese explorers in reference to the much greener coast, and not for any "green" in the islands.

Location and Climate

The Republic of Guinea-Bissau (having an area of 36,125 square kilometers) lies between 12° 40' north and 10° 52' north latitude and between 13° 38' west and 16° 43' west longitude. Generally, the climate is hot and tropical, although there are two distinct seasons. From June to November is the hot and rainy season during which the bulk of the annual 198–centimeter rainfall occurs. The recent Sahelian droughts have diminished the amount of rain in the north and have resulted in uneven rainfall and poorer harvest elsewhere.

Early History

The earliest human occupation of the West African savanna probably dates back to the times of *Homo erectus* or perhaps even *Homo africanus*; however, the forested regions closer to the coast may not have seen human occupation until much later, perhaps by 9,000 BC when small groups of hunting and fishing peoples moved into these regions. There is the possibility that the West African savanna, especially along the Niger valley, supported small-scale millet or sorghum agriculture perhaps by 4,000 BC. The relative success of the savanna farmers placed some pressure on the coastal and forest peoples, which began a long process of their southwestward migration and dispersal. In any case, the archaeology of West Africa is only in its early phases.

The rise of the medieval states of Ghana, and later Mali, had an even more pronounced effect on the forested interior regions as well as the coastal peoples. Guided by Islamic religious and economic values, both medieval states supplied captives for the Arab-based trans-Saharan slave export trade to serve the markets of North Africa. The peoples of modern Guinea-Bissau were particularly involved and disturbed during the formation of Mali's tributary kingdoms which served its regional requirements for captives, gold, and other local resources.

As camel transport across the desert was increased and iron technology became more widespread after the time of Christ, the process of regional economic transformation was intensified. Crops from southeast Asia, such as bananas and sugar cane, which were well suited to the West African tropics added variety to the coastal means of livelihood. The expansion of trade by the Empire of Ghana and the deeper introduction of Islam to the savanna in about the ninth century lay the basis for the penetration of the forest on a greater scale by people from the interior at the expense of the coastal hunters and gatherers.

By the eleventh century, the Almoravids had briefly conquered Ghana only to have it re-established in 1205 by the Susu (Soninke), of whom modern descendants are found in southern coastal Guinea-Bissau. The Susu re-conquest was maintained for only thirty years, at which point the Keita dynasty of Mali founded its powerful military and trade organization in 1235. The main thirteenth century influence of Mali which was felt directly and profoundly in Guinea-Bissau was the creation and subsequent expansion of the secondary, semi-autonmous kingdom of Kaabu, which soon had the effect of either assimilating the interior Senegambians or driving them further toward the coast. In this way, the agricultural Senegambians who may have displaced the former hunters and gatherers were themselves displaced by the more dominant rulers of Kaabu, the local representatives of Mali.

The Golden Age of Exploration

The Portuguese developed an interest in Africa and its valuable resources partly from a desire to push Moorish influence out of Iberia. The best example of this was Prince Henry's conquest of Ceuta in 1415 and other early fifteenth-century Portuguese moves to explore, conquer, and claim portions of northwest Africa.

Throughout the fifteenth century, Portuguese *barcas* and *caravelas* pushed ever further down the west African coast, reaching Cape Bojador in 1434, the Senegal River mouth in 1445, and the exploration of the estuaries and islands of Senegambia in 1446 by Captains Gil Eannes and Nuño Tristão. By 1456 some of the Cape Verde Islands were first noted for the Portuguese, although it is possible that Phoenician or Malian sailors, or Lebou fishermen had been there before the Portuguese, but these claims can not yet be proven. By 1460, António de Noli and Diogo Gomes claimed official discovery of the Cape Verde Islands for King Afonso V of Portugal. Almost immediately the Portuguese began to arrive on São Tiago, Fogo, and other Cape Verde islands, although their presence on the coast was confined to a few small fortified enclaves.

The Rise of the Euro-African Slave Trade

From these early days of exploration one may also date the initial instances of Portuguese slaving and African resistance. At first, only dozens of slaves were captured, but by the mid-fifteenth century there were already hundreds of Africans annually exported and forced to work in Europe or the Canaries. The settlement of the Cape Verde islands gave rise to the slave plantation system there. By the last third of the fifteenth century about 500 to 1,000 slaves reached the islands annually. Some of these slaves were exported to Portugal or other Atlantic islands from Cape Verde.

The subsequent discovery and settlement of the New World triggered an intensification of the slave trade in the sixteenth century, resulting in growing European competition to the point where Portugal was no longer able to meet the demand. The Portuguese crown issued slave trade monopolies on the coast, but other European marauders and African and Luso-African middlemen sought their own private gains in this tragic but lucrative business. By 1580 Portugal itself came under the rule of the Spanish crown, and English, Dutch, and Spanish slavers and pirates eroded Portuguese control and influence on the West African coast by attacking and looting Portuguese forts and trading posts.

Portuguese penetration and knowledge of the African interior was quite superficial at the time. However, their slave trading intensified commercial competition among African slavers and slave merchants, who desired to acquire firearms from the Portuguese in order to conduct effective slave raids and protect themselves from other slave raiders. As a result, a long cycle of interior slave wars was generated and persisted for centuries, causing notable state formation in some cases and fear and insecurity in others.

This situation was beneficial to the Portuguese who cared little about the origins of those destined to serve as domestic servants or plantation labor. For example, when asked by Malian leaders in 1534 to help them defend against attacks by emergent Songhai, the Portuguese declined, because their influence was weak and slaves would be generated irrespective of which side won. Slaves were driven on foot to the coast bearing heavy wooden coffles or in light river craft. Long-distance Dyula traders kept a watchful eye until their captives reached the coast to be exchanged for guns, rum, cloth, glassware, knives, and tin goods. While a "captaincy" system prevailed in the relatively secure Cape Verde, the Portuguese presence in Guinea was mainly at fortified enclaves at such places as Cacheu and Bissau. Thus their hold on the African continent was marginal, but the economic, political, and military forces they unleashed had a deep and extensive effect in the interior.

The seventeenth century saw even greater growth of the slave trade, but the relative portion of slaves transported on Portuguese ships and from the Upper Guinea coast had slowed. Indeed, one of Portugal's main objectives in Guinea-Bissau and Cape Verde at this time was just to protect itself against the frequent attacks and encroachments of other European powers. Attempts were made at military consolidation and commercial restraint in Guinea-Bissau, but in general, Portugal's rule on the coast remained rather undisciplined and precarious. Generally it depended upon good relations with Kaabu rulers in the interior and Pepel communities along the coast. However, relations frequently broke down between the Portuguese and African communities. Even though slaving constituted a primary interest of the Portuguese and *lançado* traders, the Guineans were engaged in small-scale agriculture and craft production of sufficient scope to generate local markets and continue long distance trade networks with which the Portuguese could not interfere.

During the eighteenth century the Portuguese perpetuated the regional political economy of the slave trade. But, during this century, the centers of slave trading shifted further to Angola, much further down on the Lower Guinea coast. The Portuguese crown and the Marquis de Pombal tried to reassert their monopoly over Cape Verdean commerce and made some short-lived endeavors to revitalize the slave trade in Guinea-Bissau by granting special trade rights to two Brazilian states needing plantation labor. Meanwhile, poorer Cape Verdeans often escaped drought and economic hardships by joining crews of whaling and packet ships or working in São Tomé. French attacks continued in the islands, while the British began a protracted campaign to wrest Bolama from Portuguese control on the coast.

The early nineteenth century saw the widespread abolition of the European slave trade, but the Portuguese were especially slow to respond. American, and especially New England, merchant ships continued to acquire slaves from the Portuguese on the coast and in the islands. Sometimes commerce with Americans even exceeded that with Portugal. The salt, hides, wax, and slave trade went on. As before, a central Portuguese concern was not administrative or commercial reform, which was difficult given their involvement with slavery, but simply the defense of their territories from British and French expansion. The slave trade drew to a close as the export of palm and coconut products, dyes, ivory, and hides came to wield greater importance in the international market than slaves, who were marginal to the cash exchange system. The American "Africa Squadron" based in Cape Verde made some formal but ineffective efforts to repress the slave system along the coast as well.

Throughout most of the nineteenth century, the Portuguese were still restricted to their fort-protected coastal settlements. The Mandinka of Kaabu continued to control the eastern portion of the interior. Thus Kaabu served as an important barrier to the inland expansion of the Portuguese, and as much of Kaabu's economic strength lay in its own role in the slave trade, the state entered into a sharp decline when this trade was curtailed so that it was quite vulnerable to Muslim Fula insurgency and repeated invasions from the Futa Jallon region as well as local revolts against Mandinka rule. The decisive fall of Kaabu to the Fula in 1867 gave the Portuguese an opportunity to divide and conquer both peoples and insert their own native *regulo* chiefs to assist in military control and "native" administration. The Balanta, Pepels, and other coastal Senegambian people did their best to protect themselves from the Fula-Mandinka warfare.

The Rise of Colonialism in Guinea-Bissau

During the last quarter of the nineteenth century, especially after the Berlin Conference of 1884 to 1885, and the formal delineation of the African territorial claims of Portugal, France and the other dominant European powers, the Portuguese unleased a series of brutal colonial "pacification" drives against the peoples of the coast and interior. In a move toward military security and bureaucratic efficiency, the administration of Guinea-Bissau was separated from Cape Verde in 1879 for the first time in four centuries of Portuguese presence.

The frequent "pacification" campaigns carried out between the 1880's and 1936 by the small colonial army were unable, at first, to suppress the endless revolts, mutinies, and tenacious resistance of local peoples except for the Fula, whose leadership was sometimes allied with the Portuguese in the wars of "pacification" and colonial administration. The hiring of Senegalese mercenaries combined with the ruthless military raids of Teixeira Pinto.

The overthrow of the Portuguese monarchy in 1910 gave some hope for reform to the Republicans, who were themselves toppled in 1926 by Portuguese fascists; all hope was then lost. Intensified colonial exploitation was the result in Guinea-Bissau, which saw low wages or forced labor to produce exportable cash crops such as peanuts, palm oil, and coconuts. Inevitably this heavy burden of colonial rule was to generate an anti-colonial liberation movement.

The Colonial Heritage and the Challenge of National Integration

Effective Portuguese rule in what is today's Guinea-Bissau only goes back to the early part of this century. It was not until 1915 that the mainland was finally "pacified." This was after centuries of attempts to create at least an informal colony, followed by decades of desperate efforts to fulfill the Berlin Conference requirement of "effective colonial occupation." But even with the final conquest of the mainland, Portuguese sovereignty would not be established on the adjacent Bijagos archipelago until 1936. The tradition of resistance continued during the brief period of effective colonial domination, in the form of passive defiance, but later culminated in eleven years of armed struggle for national liberation.

Ever since the arrival of Portuguese *caravelas* in the territory, Portugal had claimed its mission to be that of bringing "civilization" and salvation to otherwise "primitive" and *gentio* (heathen) peoples. The evangelizing/civilizing mission was always presented as the crux of Portuguese colonial philosophy. From the onset, territorial aggrandizement and economic exploitation was equated with the fulfillment of an evangelical duty—the duty, as former ideologue, Minister of the Colonies, and Prime Minister of the fascist *Estado Novo* (New State) dictatorship in Portugal Marcelo Caetano, put it, ". . . to extricate them from the darkness of paganism and save their soul" (1).

The highly exaggerated "historic function" of Portugal was given legal expression in the very important Colonial Act of 1930, which formally established the *Estado Novo* regime in "Portuguese Africa." The act boldly proclaimed that it was "the organic essence of the Portuguese Nation" to realize "the historic function of possessing and colonizing overseas dominions and civilizing the indigenous populations therein contained"(2).

Colonial Policies

The Portuguese policy of assimilation was considered an integral part of the Portuguese colonial doctrine and was inextricably linked to the *missão civilizadora* (civilizing mission). Predicated on the ardent belief in the "natural superiority" of Portuguese culture, it was (like the French policy of assimilation practiced in Senegal and based on the "natural superiority" of French culture) a blatant display of racial arrogance and chauvinism.

Considered "inherently inferior," the *indigenas* (natives) of the African colonies of Guinea-Bissau, Angola, and Mozambique, but not Cape Verde, had to be dragged gradually from their "primitive" and "savage" condition and "civilized" in the image of the Portuguese. The process involved the destruction of traditional societies, the inculcation of Portuguese culture, and the integration of "detribalized" and "lusitanianized" *assimilados* into Portuguese society. The *missão civilizadora* was to be realized through work and education.

In Guinea-Bissau, as in Angola and Mozambique, but not in Cape Verde, the dual system of education which was established entailed a duplication of the metropolitan primary and secondary school systems, on the one hand, and a not so elaborate arrangement for a basic program of instruction on the other. The former, called *ensino primario elementar e complementar*, and the responsibility of the colonial state, was intended for the *civilizados* of the urban centers; it rigidly followed the same curricula as those of the metropolitan primary and secondary schools. The latter, designated *ensino primario rudimentar* (or *ensino de adaptaçâo* after 1956), and the responsibility of the Catholic Missions, was devised to teach the *indigenas* "to speak, read, write and calculate in Portuguese" as well as "to inculcate in them work habits and aptitudes conducive to the abandonment of idleness and the preparation of future rural workers and craftsmen"(3).

Notwithstanding this duality, however, the education of both *civilizados* and *indigenas* was aimed at creating and expanding a reservoir of willing and able collaborators, with minimal education and training but with strong interests in the maintenance of *Pax Lusitana*. Basically, it was practical and functional and not intended, as Cardinal Manual Gonçalves Cerejeira, the Patriarch of Lisbon, made explicit in 1960, to create an African intelligentsia. The type of schools needed in "Portuguese" Africa, the Cardinal pointed out, were "schools . . . to teach the natives to write, to read and to count, but not make them doctors"(4). The obvious racist assumptions of the *missão civilizadora* in general, and the policy of assimilation in particular, should not obfuscate the very important economic aspect of Portuguese colonial domination.

The Anti-Colonial Resistance

In 1956, the Partido Africano da Independência de Guiné e Cabo Verde (PAIGC) was formed to make a series of peaceful nationalist appeals to the Portuguese and international organizations to set a timetable for independence, as was the case in many contemporary African countries. The Portuguese response came in the form of a massacre of striking Bissau dockworkers in 1959 which impelled the PAIGC toward a path of armed liberation struggle. The nationalist war (1963 to 1974) was led by the party founder and noted African revolutionary, Amilcar Cabral. This war was linked to parallel struggles in Angola and Mozambique. Ultimately, the several wars put so much pressure of the Salazar and Caetano governments that it was brought down on 25 April 1974. Soon afterward, on 24 September 1974, Portugal recognized the independence of Guinea-Bissau, which had been declared a year earlier in the liberated zones. The Portuguese granted independence to Cape Verde on 5 July 1975.

After independence, both countries were ruled by a unitary PAIGC, until November 1980 when João "Nino" Vieira overthrew Guinea-Bissau's President Luís Cabral. In 1981, Cape Verde withdrew from PAIGC membership; the relationship between Praia and Bissau is still not fully healed. Despite some challenges to the authority of "Nino," he has held on to power for the remaining years. During this time he has presided over two startling transformations in Guinea-Bissau. In the case of modernizing the economy and moving from the state-controlled system which he inherited, there have been major structural adjustments and a rather liberal "open door" policy in trade. On the political side, he has moved the nation from a constitutional one-party state to one in which multi-party democracy and elections have taken place. Although he finally managed to win the first national election after two rounds, it was sharply and broadly contested. President Vieira now appears to be in firm and newly legitimated power which is backed by his party, the army, and state bureaucracy.

Development and Economics

Despite the very important economic and political reforms, Guinea-Bissau remains remarkably poor and underdeveloped. It has had a steady trade deficit and public debt. Both imports and exports are still heavily from and to Portugal and not from or to other African countries. The GNP has only risen slightly in the last ten years. High infant mortality and low life expectancy are still serious problems. Under colonial rule, the exploitation of both human and natural resources was the main objective, and infrastructure was built to serve those ends. Guinea's colonial legacy left it impoverished and with few resources for economic development, and many of these were damaged or destroyed by the war. Today it has resumed agricultural production which results in some surplus of cash crops. Yet most farming systems in Guinea-Bissau have been, and continue to be, organized around food production. Some is sold through government channels, while other products are exchanged in private sales or even smuggled into neighboring countries.

Guinea-Bissau's development potential still needs expansion and improvement of basic infrastructure of roads, bridges, ferries, motorized vessels, and improvements in telecommunications and port facilities. Without such improvements the flow of goods and services will not be easy and regular. Extensive technical training of local personnel is equally required to take advantage of the many development projects offered from abroad.

At the same time, the government must continue to facilitate free market exchange so production may be rewarded by higher prices. Then, more favorable exchange and improved transport can stimulate increased production and export of local products, such as fruits, seafoods, rice, livestock, hides, and timber which can, in turn, reduce the trade deficit. However, augmented agricultural production will also depend upon government provision of agricultural credit for the purchase of seeds, tools, plows, fertilizers, and other agricultural equipment.

The large number of rivers in Guinea-Bissau offer some potential for hydro-electric power generation. There is also an enormous potential for small-scale domestic and foreign fishing with a sustainable yield put at up to 200,000 tons. Government efforts to stimulate foreign investment in fishing contracts and local fish processing could be significant.

There are several mineral deposits in Guinea-Bissau with development potential including bauxite, phosphates, diamonds, and gold, but all await improved infrastructure and investment. Most promising are the proven reserves of off-shore oil. Despite some contentious disputes with Senegal and Guinea-Conakry, one expects these resources to be more productive than in the past.

Industrial production still lags in Guinea-Bissau and only small-scale industries such as light mechanical repair, and soap, match, and beer production seem stable. The lack of industry worsens the balance of payment problems and serves to keep many Guinean workers involved with agricultural pursuits rather than interested in developing industrial skills. Conceivably, the free-market atmosphere may inspire local capitalists, but to date it seems that those with accumulated wealth are more inclined to invest in speculative real estate or agricultural schemes. There is still no university in Guinea-Bissau.

Finally, the government will have to address the imbalance in state spending from the urban-based public sector and toward the countryside. Indeed, the ratio of energy consumption in Bissau relative to the rest of the country is 24:3, and well over half of the budgetary spending is devoted to the salaries of civil servants, of whom the vast majority reside in the Bissau area or a few other towns. This reflects the urban-biased colonial legacy and the personal interests of critically placed public sector employees and will therefore continue to be difficult to combat.

For Guinea-Bissau the end of colonial rule and the attainment of political independence is still a primary achievement which should be celebrated. Resumption of agricultural self-sufficiency and export and its record as a nation of peace and security are notable achievements. Most of all, since the last edition of this book, the signal success in conducting fair, peaceful, and democratic elections within a free and open economy must be the concluding notes of optimism for the coming century.

Notes for the Introduction

1. Ferreira, Eduarto De Sousa. *Portuguese Colonialism in Africa: The End of an Era*. Paris: Unesco Press, 1974, p. 112.
2. Robinson, R. A. H. *Contemporary Portugal*. London: George Allen and Unwin, 1979, p. 96.
3. Ferreira Rosa, M. "Ensino Rudimentar para Indígenas em Angola, e na Guiné Portuguesa," *Boletim Cultural da Guiné Portuguesa*, VI (24): 1951: 842.
4. Robinson, *op. cit.*, p. 101.

Historical Chronology for Guinea-Bissau

The long history and varied cultures of Guinea-Bissau are rooted in the great African empire building, migration, and ethnogenesis of the diverse Senegambian, Mande, and Fula peoples as well as their links to Berbers, Moors, and Jews. Thus this chronology begins long before the written history of Guinea, which emerged in the context of Portuguese colonialism on the broader Upper Guinea coast. During and after the colonial portion of Guinea's history, it shared a common administration with the Cape Verde Islands from 1460 to 1879. These ties were renewed from 1975 to 1980 but were since severed. These two lands have been linked by colonialism, the slave trade, commerce, language, culture, and politics. The formation of Guinea-Bissau was much influenced by neighboring African peoples, and Europeans, especially Portuguese. Ancient state formation, maritime innovation, Portuguese exploration, Islamic *jihads*, the discovery and settlement of the New World (especially Brazil), slavery, colonialism, and nationalism have all contributed to the creation of the people and the history of Guinea-Bissau.

Before the Christian Era

6000 BC Wetter climate in the Sahara supports hunting economies.
5000 BC Saharan hunters noted in rock paintings.
4000 BC Emergence of domestic livestock in the African savanna?
3500 BC Dessication of the Sahara; emergence of savanna crops.
3000 BC Ancestral Berbers become Saharan pastoralists.
2000 BC Expansion of savanna agriculture.
1700 BC Introduction of horses and chariots to Africa.
1500 BC Rise of small settled communities in the savanna.
1000 BC Interaction of Sahelian and Berber (Saharan) peoples. Sahelian crops penetrate the West African forests.

700's BC   Phoenicians establish trade posts on Atlantic coast of Portugal and Morocco and trade with Saharan Berbers.

600–300 BC   Herodotus states that Phoenicians, sailing for Pharoah Necho II, circumnavigated Africa on a three-year voyage during which they presumably passed the coast of Guinea-Bissau.

500's BC   Phoenicians trade on the Moroccan coast. Camels are used in the Saharan trade. Iron technology develops at Nok, Nigeria. Senegambian people incorporate southeast Asian food crops. Jewish presence in North Africa and Sahara.

535 BC   Greeks restricted from the Atlantic by the Phoenicians in ships of more than thirty meters, some with crews of over 200.

445 BC   According to *De Situ Orbis* by Pomponius Melo and the *Chronicles of Spain* by Florio do Campo (1541), which were reported by André Donelha in 1625, the Phoenician captain Hanno sailed from Cadiz to navigate the coast of Africa as far as the Red Sea on a five year voyage. On this epic trip he passed the "Fortunate Islands" (the Canaries), on to "some small islands" (the Hesperias, presumably the Cape Verde Islands). A few days later he reached the Gorgon Dorcades (Bijagós?) Islands which were inhabited by "hairy, swift, monstrous, wild women [daris; chimpanzees?] who could not be subdued even with bonds." These islands were two days sailing from the mainland at a place called Corno das Hesperias (the West Horn), [presumably Cap Vert in Senegal] where the coast began to turn toward the east. He also reached "Cerne" and a land having a smoking volcano [Fogo Island?].

300 BC   Iron working expands in West African Sahel.

200 BC   Romans control most of Iberia. The Soninke at Kumbi Saleh.

147 BC   According to Pliny, a Roman named Polybius may have reached Cap Vert in Senegal.

113 BC   According to Pomponius Mela, a Greek named Eudoxes sailed from the Red Sea to pass the Cape of Good Hope and Cap Vert (Senegal) and reach the Pillars of Hercules (Gibraltar).

100 BC   According to Strabo (based on Posidonius) a Greek named Eudoxes, from Cyzicus, sailed from Cadiz around Africa. Increased trans-Saharan trade by horse and camel.

69 BC   Romans reported in central Sahara.

46 BC   Caesar's victory over Numidia.

The Christian Era

ca. 100 AD   During reign of Trajan, Roman expedition reaches the Fezzan.

115 AD   Jewish revolt in Cyrenaica put down and Jews disperse further into the Sahara and Maghreb.

200's–300's AD   Foundation of a savanna state by the Mandingo (Soninke) who later led to the empire of ancient Ghana.

300's AD   Camels are central for Saharan trade of the Berbers, who are influenced by Judaic traditions. The first Jews migrate from Africa to Portugal. Berber and Jewish traders in the Sahel may have contributed to the formation of the savanna kingdoms through the sixteenth century.

313 AD   Christianity accepted by Roman Emperor Constantine.

411–660   Suevi and Visigoth presence in Portugal.

428 AD   Vandals cross at Gibraltar to North Africa.

439 AD   Vandals occupy Carthage.

476 AD   Fall of the Roman Empire.

533–535   Under Justinian, Byzantine Christians defeat the Vandals and occupy North Africa.

The Islamic Era

570 AD   Birth of Muhammad, the Muslim Prophet.

622 AD   Twenty kings of Ghana had already ruled by the founding year of the Muslim religion.

700's AD   Possible construction of the megalithic stone circle sites in Gambia and central Senegal. Iron working reaches the Senegal River valley.

711 AD   Muslim Moors cross the Straits of Gibraltar to begin their occupation of the Iberian peninsula.

750 AD   Origins of Gao, Songhai.

770 AD   The Arab Al Fazari notes the "Land of Gold" in reference to the Soninke kingdoms of Ghana and Waram.

800 AD   Berbers introduce Islam to the West African Sahel. Tekrur is the first state to be fully converted to Islam.

900 AD   Savanna peoples expand south and west to the forest regions.

990 AD   Fall of Tekrur in Senegal.

1000's   Moors reportedly travel to Cape Verde for salt.

1010   King of Gao accepts Islam.

1033   Sanhaja Berbers led by Yahia ibn Ibrahim make *haj* to Mecca.

1050 Berbers under Abdullah ibn Yasin, with allies from Futa Toro, begin attacks on Ghana and bring Islam to the West African Sahel. Barmandama becomes the first Muslim king of Mali.

1054 Almoravids under Yahya ibn Umar take the town of Awdoghast in ancient Ghana. The Dia dynasty of Gao is established.

1056–87 Reign of Abu Bakr who leads Berbers against the Soninke.

1065 The Spanish Arab Al-Dakru wrote of Tunka Manin, the King of Ghana. This non-Muslim king allowed Muslim merchants to live in a separate trading town outside his royal compound.

1076 Almoravids take Kumbi Saleh to complete their conquest of ancient Ghana, which becomes a Muslim state by conquest.

1086 The Sultan of Kanem accepts Islam.

1094 Death of the Spanish Arab Abu Ubaid Al-Bakri who published early geographical accounts of Northwest Africa.

1100's Moors reported to have sailed west of Morocco for "100 days in wide ships" until they reached the land of *Mu-lan-pi* (the New World?). Almoravids still control half of Iberia. Birth of Al-Idrisi, the famed Moorish geographer of the western Sudan.

1135 Almoravid rule of Ghana ends; independent Ghana is reestablished.

1143 The Portuguese Crown gains its independence from Spain, which falls under two centuries of the Muslim Almohad dynasty.

1151 Arabs visit Canaries, according to Al-Idrisi.

1154 Publication of Al-Idrisi's Book of Roger, an early and accurate regional geography.

1200's Muslims of Futa Toro take over Diara, formerly part of Ghana.

1203 Sumanguru Kante seizes Kumbi Saleh, another remnant of Ghana.

1230 Rise of the Empire of Mali with increased attacks against Ghana by the Muslim Emperor Sundiata Keita.

1232–1492 In Spain, only Granada remains under Muslim rule.

1240 Ghana continues its decline. In the battle of Kangaba, the Soninke leader Sumanguru is killed; his followers retreat to Futa Toro.

1245 Sundiata is established as the Mansa Mari-Djata I of Mali.

1248–1279 Reign of Portuguese King Afonso III.

1249 Final explusion of the Moors from Portugal.

ca. 1250 Formation of the Mandingo kingdom of Kaabu in Guinea-Bissau. Kaabu is a tributary state to the expanding Empire of Mali. Senegambians are pushed toward coast or assimilated.

1252 Europe shifts currency standard from silver to gold. This increases Portugal's interest in Mali as a source of gold.

1255 Mansa Ulli continues the expansion of the Empire of Mali. He was the first Mansa to make the *haj*. Gao emerges as a rival.

1270 Death of Mansa Ulli of Mali.

1279–1325 Reign of King Diniz of Portugal.

1291 Genoan brothers Ugolino and Guido Vivaldi attempt African circumnavigation but are lost near the Canaries.

1295–96 Franciscan monk Raymond Lull writes *Arbor Scientiae*, a book of early cartography, navigation, and instrument making.

1299 Mansa Sakura of Mali is killed on his return from *haj*.

ca. 1300 Mansa Muhammad of Mali was reported by Arab historian Umari to have sent 200 ships with men and 200 with supplies to the New World. They returned and another 1,000 were reportedly sent. Columbus was later asked to investigate this report. Wolof kingdoms emerge in coastal Senegal.

1304 Birth of Ibn Battuta in Tangiers.

1312–37 Reign of Mansa Kankan Musa, the great Emperor of Mali. During his reign, and of his brother Sulayman (1337–1360), Islam expands and many great mosques are constructed, notably at Jenne and Timbuktu. This period is associated with an influx of Arab merchants and scholars who earned Mali's wide reputation for education and wealth in Europe and Africa. The effects of Malian expansion are directly felt in Guinea and all the way to the Senegambian coast.

1320 Map of Genoan Petrus Vesconte shows Africa as circumnavigable.

1320's Majorcan maps depict interior of Africa as a "Land of Gold."

1324 Famed *haj* of Mansa Musa of Mali.

1325–57 Reign of Portuguese King Alfonso IV.

1325–1433 Timbuktu is the main trading town of Mali, which absorbs Gao during reign of Mansa Musa.

1330's Mali is shown on maps of Jewish cartographers.

1332 Musa I reigns in Mali; Tuareg Berbers pay him tribute.

1337 Death of Mansa Musa; start of reign of Mansa Sulayman.

1340 Songhai founded.

1348–50 Black Plague arrives in Lisbon. Jews are "blamed."

ca.1350 Arabs had visited the Canary Islands according to the *Libro del Conoscimiento* showing the islands with Arabic names.

1352–53 Abu Abdallah Muhammad Ibn Battuta visits Mali from Tangiers. Malian Ambassador is stationed in Fez.

1357 King Alfonso IV dies during an epidemic of the Black Plague.

1360–74 Death of Mansa Sulayman; reign of Mansa Mari-Djata II.

1368/69 Death of Ibn Battuta in Fez.

1370 Medici Atlas published.

1374–87 Reign of Mansa Musa II.

1375 Atlas of Abraham Cresques, a Moorish Jew from Majorca, shows correct detail of the Moroccan coast and the Malian interior before the time of Prince Henry. The maps, compasses, and reports of gold stimulate Portuguese maritime exploration. Mali begins long decline under threat of Gao to the east and Tuaregs from the north.

1380 and **1385** publication of Atlantic charts by Guillermo Sollen.

1383–1435 Period of Portuguese gold shortage stimulates African exploration. Recurrent epidemics of the Black Plague in Portugal.

1384 Royal House of Avis rules in Portugal after two years of war.

1385–1433 Reign of Portuguese King João I.

1387 Death of the Jewish cartographer Abraham Cresques.

1387–88 Reign of Mansa Magha II, but his succession was much disputed by Sandahi in 1388–1389 and Mahmed in 1390.

1390 Mahmed ascends the throne as Mansa Magha III.

1391 Pogroms against Andalusian Jews.

The Age of Maritime Exploration

1394 Birth of Prince Henry, "The Navigator," who built the "think tank" for navigators at Sagres.

1400 Susu (Soninke) begin their dominance in Futa Jallon. The Diallo branch of the Fula established at Masina.

1403 Early Genoese map of North Africa.

1406 Death of the great Muslim scholar Ibn Khaldun.

1413 Ansêlme d'Isalquier from Toulose reaches Gao across the Sahara.

1415 The forces of Prince Henry capture Ceuta. Timbuktu and Jenne are main centers of Islamic teaching in the Sahel.

1418 João Gonçalves Zarco visits the Canary Islands, which had been known to the Romans and probably to the Phoencians.

1419 Zarco credited with discovering the Madeira Islands.

1420 Prince Henry uses maps of Jaffuda Cresques. The "Golden Age" of Portuguese maritime exploration begins in earnest.

1424 Zarco colonizes Madeira; Prince Henry sends 2,500 men in 120 ships to occupy the Canaries.

1427 Azores Islands are explored and later settled by Portuguese.

1430's Sugarcane planted in Madeira. The Plaguereturns to Portugal.

1431–33 Tuaregs attack and finally seize Timbuktu.

1433–38 Reign of Portuguese King Edward.

1434 Sailing for Prince Henry, Gil Eannes and Alfonso Gonçalves Baldaia reach Cape Bojador in *barcas*, and oared gallies.

1436 Portuguese fail in their attempt to take Tangiers; Portuguese sailors reach Cape Blanco, Morocco.

1438–1481 Reign of Alfonso V, but there is a sustained rebellion for the first three years of his reign.

The Era of The Slave Trade

1441 The first African slaves are captured by the Portuguese Nuño Tristão and Antão Gonçalves at Rio do Ouro in Morocco.

1443 Prince Henry claims trade south of Cape Bojador for the Crown.

1444–1445 Portuguese Captains Lançarote and Diniz Dias reach Cap Vert at Senegal. 235 slaves brought back to Portugal. Other Africans resist and flee or are killed.

1444–1460 At least several hundred slaves are exported from Portugal to Spain each year.

1446 Navigator Alvaro Fernandes is probably the first Portuguese in Guinea. Some 1,000 Africans are captives in Portugal.

1447 Genoan António Malfante crosses Sahara to reach Tuat.

Nuño Tristão killed somewhere along the Senegambian coast.

1448 At least 1,000 slaves shipped to Portugal from Africa.

1449 Anti-Jewish riots in Portugal.

1450's to **1480's** Portuguese fail to make overland route to Timbuktu. 800–1,000 slaves brought back to Portugal each year. Beafadas defeat Fulas at Braço.

1453 Azurara writes his *Crónica dos Feitos da Guiné*.

1454–56 Venetian Luís de Cadamosto and Genoan Antioniotto Usodimare sail for Portugal on coasts of Morocco and Upper Guinea.

1455, 8 January, Pope Nicolau V issues *Bull Romanus Pontifex*. Portuguese establish slave trading *feitoria* at Arguim in Morocco. The Portuguese Diogo Gomes and Venetian Alvise Cadamosto trade with the Wolof of Senegal. Cadamosto travels to Madeiras and along the Gambia River.

July, the Genoese António de Noli may have been the first European to sight the eastern Cape Verde Islands.

1456, May, Cadamosto may have sighted some of the Cape Verde Islands. Islam is accepted by Sultan of Zaria. Pope Calisto III issues *Bull Inter Coetera* to guide explorers.

1458 Last major episode of the Black Plague in Portugal. Timbuktu is conquered by Songhai (Gao).

1460 The Portuguese explorers, Diogo Gomes, Diogo Afonso, and the Italian De Noli brothers, António and Bartolomeo, "discover" the Sotavento Islands in the Cape Verde Archipelago. Early settlement begins soon afterward. Death of Prince Henry.

1462, 17 January, Diogo Afonso is the first Portuguese on Santo Antão, where he celebrates the first mass. De Noli brothers and their nephew Rafael De Noli intensify their efforts to settle Riberia Grande, Sâo Tiago.

19 September, Crown grants capitancy in Cape Verde Islands to Diogo Afonso. Sugar cane production begins in 1460's.

1464–1492 Reign of Sunni Ali expands the Songhai empire.

1466, 12 June, Royal charter grants early Portuguese settlers in Cape Verde the right to trade in African slaves and other goods from the coast, except at Argium, which is reserved for the King. Many settlers return to Portugal. The first Franciscans arrive.

1468 First contract for the export of *urzela* from Cape Verde.

1468–1474 Crown grants five year trade monopoly to Fernão Gomes, upon his payment of 200,000 reis/years, if he explores 100 leagues of the coast east of Sierra Leone each year.

1469 Florentine trader Bendetto Dei crosses the Sahara to Timbuktu.

1470 Fernão Gomes discovers São Tomé.

1471 First crossing of the Equator by Portuguese sailors.

1472 Limits placed on Cape Verdean coastal free trade.

1473 Portuguese reach Benin. Songhai conquers Jenne of Mali. Spanish-Jewish astronomers Abraham Zacuto and José Vizinho formulates early nautical declination tables.

1475–79 Luso-Spanish war.

1475–1600 Portuguese slaving concentrated on the Upper Guinea coast.

1476 Spanish attack Cape Verde and capture *capitão* António De Noli.

1479 **4 September**, Spain and Portugal sign Papal Treaty of Alçacovas to bring peace and demarcate their territories north or south of a line near the Tropic of Cancer. This allows Portuguese exploration of the African coast and control of Al-Mina gold.

1480 Start of the Spanish Inquisition and the expulsion of Jews.

1481 **12 December**, Azambuja left Portugal with 10 caravels, 500 soliders, 100 workmen, and building materials to construct the fort at Al-Mina. Mansa Mamadu is ruling in Mali.

1481–1495 Death of King Alfonso V; Rise of João II.

1482 Combined population of Sao Tiago and Fogo estimated at 1,608 "Whites," 400 freed slaves, and 13,700 slaves.

1482–83 Columbus serves on Azambuja mission to construct Al-Mina. Diogo Cão reaches Congo for the first time.

1483 French sailors reach the Cape Verde Islands.

1486 Benin sends its ambassador to Portugal.

1488 Wolof royalty of Senegal received in Lisbon.

1489 **30 May**, Crown grants land in Cape Verde to the Duke of Beja. Portuguese fail in expedition to Jolof and Mali Empire.

1490's Coli Tenguella (I) mobilizes the Denianke in Futa Toro to revolt against Askia the Great of Songhai.

The Rise of the Inquisition

1492 The Rise of the Spanish Inquisition. Thousands of Moors and Jews are expelled from Spanish Granada, tens of thousands flee to Portugal. Some Jews allowed to remain upon payment of large ransoms. Jewish children are seized and baptized by force. King João II sends 700 Jews to São

Tomé, still others sent to Guinea and Cape Verde. The Jewish exodus to the Upper Guinea coast sows the seeds of *lançado*/Crioulo culture.

12 October, Christopher Columbus reaches the Bahamas. Sunni Ali dies; Askia Muhammad follows as ruler of Songhai.

1493 4 May, Pope Alexander VI issues Papal Bull *Inter Caetera* to demarcate Portuguese and Spanish New World claims as east or west of a line 100 leagues west of the Cape Verde Islands. The second voyage of Columbus has a free Black crew member.

1494 7 June, Treaty of Tordesillas adjusts the above treaty so that Portugal claims lands east of a line placed at 370 leagues west of Cape Verde (i.e. Brazil), and Spain has lands further west.

1495–1521 The death of Portuguese King João II begins the reign of King Manuel and the "Golden Age" of Portugal.

1496 December to November 1497 Portugal orders the expulsion of Jews.

1497 Vasco da Gama stops at Cape Verde on his epoch voyage to India. He reaches Sal Island on 22 July and São Tiago on 27 July. Forcible conversion and baptism of 20,000 Iberian Jews.

1498 Christopher Columbus visits Cape Verde 27 June–4 July.

1499–1500 Amerigo Vespucci, sailing as a Spanish pilot, stops in Cape Verde Islands at Fogo. Da Gama stops in May 1499 on return from India and destroys one of his ships to prevent it from falling into Moorish hands.

1500 Pedro Alvares Cabral leaves two ships in Cape Verde. *Lançados* are mentioned in a Crown letter to João de Castro Burgales.

1501–02 Vespucci sails by Cape Verde Islands for second time.

1502–03 Da Gama probably stops again in Cape Verde on his way to and from India. Columbus reaches North American mainland.

1503–04 Vespucci stops in Cape Verde Islands for third time. Da Gama probably stops in Cape Verde on return from India.

1504 Slaves from São Tomé reach Cape Verde for export.

1505–08 Duarte Pacheco Pereira writes his great book on global navigation, *Esmeraldo de Situ Orbis*, which also reports on products and wealth from the Guinea coast.

1506 Death of Christopher Columbus. Publication of *Regimento do Cruzeiro do Sol* provides astrological charts below the

Equator. About 2,000 "New Christians" killed in Lisbon pogrom.

1506–1510 Valentim Fernandes writes about the Cape Verde Islands and the Mande, Susu, and Fula peoples along the Guinea coast.

1508 First legislation is published to control the activities of the *lançados* of Guinea and Cape Verde.

1510 The *capitania* system is established in the Cape Verde Islands, "requiring" a regular supply of slaves from the coast.

1511 Coli Tenguella (I) is killed by the Songhai army. Captives from this war against Futa Toro are sold to the Portuguese.

1512 Crown orders that all slaves from Guinea go directly to Lisbon.

1513–1515 2,966 slaves taken from the peoples of the Guinea coast are sold in São Tiago for domestic use and export.

1514 Expansion of the export slave trade from the Cape Verde Islands for the production of cotton and urzella.

1515 King Manuel grants royal trade license to Novos Cristãos of São Tiago. Maize is introduced to Cape Verde Islands from Brazil.

1517 Crown forbids Cape Verdean merchants to trade at Sierra Leone. Sugar cane plantations begin in São Tiago.

1518 First direct shipment of African slaves to the New World. Crown orders *lançados* to abandon coastal trade.

1519–1522 First global circumnavigation by the Portuguese Captain Magelhâes (Magellan).

1521–1557 Death of Portuguese King Manuel; start of the reign of King João III. The first African slaves arrive in Cuba.

1526 Leo Africanus publishes his *Description of Africa*.

1528 Askia the Great is deposed by his son Musa.

1530's French and *lançado* merchants displace Portugal in Senegal.

1531 The Inquisition expands to Portugal, and in the next 200 years thousands are executed, tortured, and imprisoned. A great earthquake in Portugal is "blamed" on the Jews.

1532 King João III claims the Bijagós Islands which he grants to his brother, Prince Dom Luís.

1533 Ribeira Grande, the capital town of São Tiago is elevated to the status of "city" with its own Diocese having political and religious jurisdiction extending to the Guinea coast. Genoese monopoly expands Cape Verdean sugar cane plantations which call for more agricultural slaves.

1534 Ambassador of Mali visits Portugal for help against Songhai. The Portuguese respond by mediating between Mali and Tekrur.

1537 French loot six ships in Cape Verdean waters.

1538 The first African slaves are sent to Brazil. The Portuguese fail in attempt to conquer Canhabaque in Bijagós.

1540's Englishman William Hawkins trades on the Guinea coast.

1542 French raid the Cape Verde Islands. Portugal forcibly converts about 60,000 Jews.

1545 Expanded settlement of southern Cape Verde Islands.

1546 Songhai finally defeats the Empire of Mali. Many former tributary states of Mali (e.g. Kaabu), gain full independence.

1548 Early settlement of Santo Antão calls for more slaves.

1549 Hans Stade stops in Cape Verde and notes that the Portuguese there are "rich in Black Moorish slaves."

1549–1582 Songhai expands further under the reign of Askia Dawud.

1550 Cape Verde census shows 13,700 slaves. The Portuguese ship an average of 8,000 to 10,000 slaves from Angola annually. Portuguese traders present at the Bambuk gold fields.

1550's Dutch seize Portuguese *feitorias* at Arguim, Gorée, and Al-Mina. English continue to erode the control of Portuguese slave trade. Substantial numbers of slaves are exported to Brazil. European trade with *lançados* and coastal West African Dyulas is well established. Portuguese make heavy use of *degredados* as galley rowers.

1552 3,000 slaves reported on Madeira (about ten percent of the population), for sugar cane production under the control of wealthy Portuguese, Genoese, Venetians, and *Novos Cristâos*.

1555 Father Fernando Oliveira, probably a Capuchin, publishes a strong criticism of the slave trade in Guinea.

1556 Approximate start of the construction of the cathedral of Ribeira Grande, in São Tiago.

1557–1578 Reign of Portuguese King Sebastião; Cardinal Henrique becomes the Inquisitor General of Portugal.

1559 Coli Tenguella (II) leads the Denianke dynasty in Futa Toro.

1560 The father of André Donelha buys three Mané slaves who inform him of wars against the Manés and Sapes. One Sape king took refuge with *tangomãos* at Cacheu, another fled to São Tiago.

1560's Expansion of English slaving on the West Coast of Africa.

1562 John Hawkins loots six Portuguese ships and deepens the English challenge to the Portuguese claims to the Guinea coast.

1563–1564 John Hawkins and Francis Drake ship African slaves.

1564 The hereditary *capitão* of São Tiago dies; the *capitania* system reverts to being a Portuguese crown province.

1565 Drake loots eleven ships in Portuguese waters.

1566 John Lovell, Francis Drake, and John Hawkins sailing for England loot fourteen Portuguese ships in Guinean and Cape Verdean waters. French pirates attack Portuguese in Madeiras.

1567 John Lovell loots Portuguese slavers at sea. John Hawkins raids Cacheu River and makes overland attack on Pepels of Cacanda.

1570's–1600's An annual average of 3,000 African captives are shipped largely from Guinala in Guinea-Bissau by the *lançados* and *tangomâos*; about half of the slaves are sent to Brazil.

1572 The town of Riberia Grande in Cape Verde has a population of 1,500, including merchants, adventurers, *lançados*, and slaves.

1574 André Donelha travels from São Tiago to Portudal, Cacheu, Rio Grande, and Sierra Leone. Cape Verde Governor General António Velho Tinoco visits the ports of Cacheu and Guinala.

1576 The Cape Verde Islands changed from semi-autonomous *capitanias* to directly-ruled *provincias*.

1578 King Sebastião killed in combat in Morocco; Cardinal Henrique becomes the King of Portugal.

1580's Cacheu is reported to have 700–800 Christians "between white and black."

1580–1640 King Henrique is toppled. Portugal comes under the rule of the Spanish Hapsburg Kings, but Cape Verde continues as a major slave entrepot, under Portuguese and *lançado* control, threatened by the Dutch, French, and English.

1581 André Donelha visits Guinala noting eight slave ships from São Tiago and at least ten others owned by *tangomâos*.

1582 The population of Fogo and São Tiago includes 13,700 slaves, and 600 whites.

1584 André Donelha sails up the Gambia to Cantor and visits Cacheu.

1585 The English pirate Francis Drake attacks Cape Verde and loots the São Tiago towns of Praia, Santa Catarina, and Ribeira Grande with his force of 600 men, on 16–17 November. This contributes to the Portuguese decision to improve the island defenses.

1588 The *feitor* of Cacheu, Lopes Cardoso (a Portuguese born in Cape Verde) convinces Cacanda Pepels to accept the construction of a *casa forte*, which allows *lançado* independence from Pepels and the start of a *capitania* system subordinate to Cape Verde. The English defeat the Spanish Armada.

1590 Pepels attack the Cacheu fort but are repelled by the *lançados*, who celebrate their victory by renaming the *casa forte*, "Nossa Senhora do Vencimento."

1590's Dutch intensify trade efforts along Guinea coast.

1591 Foreigners are forbidden to trade in *Guiné do Cabo Verde*. The Songhai army is defeated by the Moroccans at Tondibi.

1594 Andre Alvares de Almada, a Cape Verdean *mestiço* slave trader publishes his Tratado Breve dos Rios de Guiné do Cabo Verde.

1596 Birth of the historian Abdel Rahman as-Sadi in Timbuktu.

1600–1650 About 4,000 slaves from Upper Guinea coast were exported annually to Brazil and elsewhere (about 200,000 for this period). The population of São Tiago and Fogo includes about 1,500 free people and 14,000 slaves.

1601 The Crown gives Portuguese Jews the right to settle and trade on the Guinea coast.

1604 Only 30,000 *Novos Cristãos* remain in Portugal. First Jesuit mission established in Cape Verde; Jesuit Father Baltasar Barreira travels to the Guinea coast.

1607 February, Second group of Jesuits reach Cape Verde.
March, Jesuits go to Bissau.

1608 Father Barreira returns to São Tiago from Portudal and Cacheu.

1609 The Portuguese typically export about 3,000 slaves annually. Jesuit priests Gomes and Dias visit Cacheu from São Tiago.

1609–1612 1,468 slaves imported to Cape Verde from Guinea, but 8,110 slaves were re-exported to the New World, Canaries, and Spain.

1610 Jesuit Gomes revisits Cacheu.

1611 19 November, King Felipe writes to Father Barreira noting that Guineans "need" to be conquered; that the Portuguese who lived in Portudal and Senegambia should observe

Crown rules about the sale of iron; that foreigners should be excluded from trade; and that the *capitania* should be strengthened at Cacheu.

1614 João Tavares de Sousa appointed as first *feitor* at Cacheu and São Domingos River in Guinea.

1615 Baltasar Pereira de Castello-Branco made *feitor*, *capitão*, and magistrate of Cacheu, Rio Grande, and São Domingos.

1616 Father Manuel Alvares writes his *Descriçâo Geográfica da Serra Leôa*, where he dies in the following year.

1617 More than 2,000 African captives shipped from Cacheu.

1618 English Company of Adventurers is chartered for trade in gold and slaves. The Company builds a fort on James Island in the River Gambia to rival the Portuguese in Casamance and Guinea.

1619 Slave traders allowed to pay Crown tax directly at Cacheu and bypass the slave tax paid in the Cape Verde Islands.

1620 Royal order sends Portuguese women *degredados* to Cape Verde to "extinguish the mulattoe race."

1621 Portugal loses Rufisque, Portudal, and Joal to the Dutch.

1625 Publication of André Donelha's, *Account of Sierra Leone and the Rivers of Guinea of Cape Verde*.

1627 Catholic Church opposes the Jesuit mission.

1628–42 Jesuit mission moves its mission to the Guinea coast.

1630–54 Dutch attack Portuguese interests in West Africa and Brazil.

1636 First African slaves exported to Rhode Island by Portuguese and especially English slave traders.

1637 Dutch West India Company seizes Al-Mina from Portuguese, ending their control of 155 years.

1638 Portuguese lose trade center at Arguim to Dutch. French become established on the Senegal River.

1639–42 Severe famine in Senegambia.

1640's New World sugar production demands more slaves.

1640 Portugal reclaims monarchy from Spain.

1641 Portugal and Holland sign a non-aggression pact, but many Dutch violations continue. Locust plague on Senegambian coast. Gonçalo Gambôa de Ayala nominated *capitão-mor* of Cacheu and expands Portuguese trade centers at Farim and Ziguinchor.

1643 Most traders at Ziguinchor are Cape Verdean *lançados*.

1647 Capuchin mission opens in Cape Verde.

1650 João Carreiro Fidalgo appointed as *capitão-mor* of Cacheu. He arrives with two *caravelas* of fifty men each as well as canons and arms with the intention to intimidate the local population and build a fort, but this is not successful.

1650–70's About 7,500 slaves exported to Brazil each year or about 150,000 for this period. Sugar production and the slave economy of Madeira decline. The Wolof and Bambara are in cycles of regional warfare to produce slaves or defend themselves from attacks by slavers.

1650–1879 Guinea-Bissau administered from Cape Verde, especially to produce slaves for Brazil and South American plantations and mines. Period of great insecurity in Senegambia.

ca. 1650 *Tarikh as-Sudan* written in Timbuktu, by Mahmoud Kati, the Chronicler for Askia the Great.

1652 Praia replaces Ribeira Grande as the capital of Cape Verde.

1655 Dutch attack Fogo. Death of Abdel Rahman as-Sadi.

1658 Franciscan mission established in Guinea.

1659 French establish settlement at St. Louis in Senegal.

1660 Formation of English Royal Adventurers in Africa.

1661 English rebuild Fort James in Gambia.

1664 1,280 soldiers defend Riberia Grande, which is five percent White; ninety-five percent Black and Mestiço.

1665 Abdel Rahman as-Sadi publishes posthumously the *Tarikh As-Sudan* first written by Mahmoud Kati.

1669–92 Economic depression in Portugal.

1672 Formation of the English Royal African Company.

1676 Formation of Companhia de Cacheu, Rios e Comércio da Guiné to provide taxes and slaves for the Portuguese Crown, and approve the *capitão-mor*, who is António de Barros Bezerra and the main share holder of the company, which failed in 1682.

1677 French take Gorée from Dutch.

1679 *Regulos* near Cacheu revolt against *lançado* traders. French *Compagnie du Senegal* exports slaves to the West Indies.

1680 Formation of Companhia Africano do Cabo Verde e Cacheu.

1680's Major expansion of French activity in *Guiné do Cabo Verde*.

1682 *Capitão-mor* Bezerra imprisoned in São Tiago for embezzlement. He is replaced by José Gonçalves de Oliveira as the new *capitão-mor* of Cacheu. The *Companhia Pará e Maranhão* is formed to export 10,000 slaves annually to Brazil.

1684 Revolt at Cacheu led by *mestiça* trader Bibiana Vaz and her "seditious group" which holds *capitão-mor* de Oliveira as a captive in Farim for fourteen months until he escapes. A poorly enforced law is passed to improve conditions in slave ships.

1685 *Code Noir* by Louis XIV, encouraged baptism and religious worship by slaves while expanding the slave trade at Bissau.

1686 Spanish Capuchins write anti-slavery manifesto in Bissau.

1686–87 The representative of the French slave trading *Compagnie du Senegal*, Michel De La Courbe travels to Bissau.

1687, 23 January, Cape Verdeans forbidden to sell *panos* to foreigners, in an effort by the Crown to keep their control of the slave trade and limit the coastal commerce of lançados.

2 April, Cape Verde Governor Carvalho da Costa visits Cacheu.

14 September, Vitoriano Portuense is made Bishop of Cape Verde. De La Courbe, now the French commander of Gorée, visits Bolama and calls for French occupation. António de Barrosa Bezerra reappointed as *capitão-mor* of Cacheu.

1688, 17 April, Bishop Portuense assumes position of Governor of Cape Verde and Guinea.

1689–93 French slave traders active in Cacheu and Casamance under De La Courbe.

1690 Formation of Companhia do Cacheu e Cabo Verde to control regional trade in slaves and ivory. This company failed in 1696, and economic stagnation returned to the region. Bishop Portuense of Ribeira Grande stages raids on his priests who are sleeping with their slave concubines, a widespread practice which added to the Crioulo population.

1694–95 Bishop Portuense visits Cacheu, Bissau, Farim, and Geba. While in Bissau he baptizes the King, Bacompol Có, as "Dom Pedro," whose eldest son, Batonto is sent to Lisbon to be baptized with the King of Portugal as his godfather.

1695 Alluvial gold discovered in Brazil increases demand for slaves for mining.

1695 Construction begins on a small *feitoria* (*Nossa Senhora da Conceiçao*) in Bissau (subordinated to Cacheu) to serve the interests of the Companhia de Cacheu e Cabo Verde under a mandate by King Pedro II.

1696 José Pinheiro da Camara is appointed as *capitão-mor* of Bissau. The Bishop of Cape Verde, Vitoriano Portuense, makes his second visit to Guinea to establish a small convent with about five African disciples. This effort later led to the construction of the Church of Our Lady of Candelária in Bissau. Upon the death of King Bacompolo Có, Incinha Te becomes the King of Bissau. The *presídio* of Farim is established.

1697 Widespread Pepel revolt is organized by Incinha Te against the Portuguese. Mandinkas of Farim also revolt.

1698 *Capitão-mor* José Pinheiro is arrested by Incinha Te, King of Bissau. Pinheiro dies in custody. Rodrigo de Oliveira da Fonseca appointed as *capitão-mor* of Bissau.

1698–99 French slave traders seek protected commerce in Bissau.

1698–1708 Rhode Islanders build 103, ships largely for the "Triangle Trade." The New England colonies are importers of Caribbean molasses to produce rum for barter for slaves from Guinea.

1700–1850 The height of the slave trade.

1700 The Portuguese Crown allows trade with foreigners, especially the French, at Bissau. Cathedral at Ribeira Grande completed.

1701 The *capitania* fort at Bissau is abandoned because of African resistance.

1703 Portugal enters war against Spain. Portugal signs the Treaty of Metheun with England to formalize their economic ties.

1705 Growth of indigo production in Cape Verde requires more slaves.

21 January, Bishop Portuense dies in São Tiago.

1706 *Companhia do Cacheu e Cabo Verde* formally closed.

1707–1708 King João V orders the fort at Bissau to be destroyed and its artillery sent to Cacheu.

1712 May, the French under Jacques Cassard loot São Tiago.

1713 French increase trade with the Wolof and Tekrur in Senegal.

1718 French seek permission from the Pepels to build fort at Bissau.

1720 Increased production of *urzella* in the Cape Verde Islands.

1723 French ship is lost bringing fort building supplies to Bissau.

1724 The Portuguese *capitão-mor* of Cacheu convinces Pepels not to allow French to build their fort.

1725 Fula Islamic revival begins in Futa Toro and Futa Jallon and brings the Denianke dynasty to an end. The Fula spirit of regional *jihad* encourages the Fula of Guinea-Bissau to resist the authority of the Mandinka kingdom of Kaabu.

1738   Cape Verdean Governor petitions the king to liberalize the trade in *panos* and allow their sale to foreigners.

1743   Ribeira Grande reported in ruins, only twenty "whites" in Cape Verde. Many slaves seek freedom and flee into the São Tiago interior.

1747   The Portuguese baptize the King of Bissau to regain control.

1747–1758   Prolonged drought in Senegambia and Cape Verde.

1750   King João V dies, succeeded by José I and his important Prime Minister, the Marquis de Pombal (Sebastião José de Carvalho), who brings "reforms," weakening feudalism and ending the Inquisition. The Treaty of Madrid redefines New World borders. Locust plague in Guinea-Bissau and the Gambia.

1750's   Merchants of Grão Pará and Maranhão (Brazil) call for an increase in its slave imports from Guinea for sugar, cotton, rice, and cacao production and are authorized by the Crown to form a slave trading and commercial company.

1753   Portuguese raise their flag over Bolama Island and claim sovereignty. Pepel leader Palan Cá both attacks and collaborates with the Portuguese efforts to rebuild a fort at Bissau to expand the slave trade to Brazil. Nicolau de Pina Araújo appointed as *capitão-mor* of the recreated *capitania* of Bissau.

1754   Representative of the *capitania* of *Grão Pará* is sent to the Portuguese king to discuss the formation of a *Companhia*.

1755, 7 June, Companhia Geral do Grão Pará e Maranhão is formed by the Marquis de Pombal to import slaves for a twenty-year period. The *Companhia* monopolizes the Cape Verdean/Guinean economy and essentially assumes their administration. Slaves are registered and sold through Ribeira Grande, whose Governor reports directly to the Crown. The *Companhia* has its own fleet of forty-one cargo and war ships.

1756–1763   The "Seven-Years War" recalls French and reduces their activity near Bissau.

1758   Portuguese governor of Cape Verde hopes to use the new fort to resist Pepel attacks.

1764   Cape Verde Governor notes deplorable state of island defenses.

1765   Construction begins on the new Fortaleza of São José de Bissau. For ten years many Cape Verdean and Pepel lives are lost in this project through epidemics and military clashes.

1768 Portugal abolishes distinction between "Old" and "New" (Jewish) Christians (i.e., *lançados*).

1770 The official capital of Cape Verde and Guinea is transferred to Praia from Ribeira Grande.

1775 Emergence of the Imamate of Futa Toro. Completion of the fort of São José de Bissau.

1776 The American Revolutionary War begins and Americans increase imports of rice and cotton from Maranhão, which requires more slaves from Guinea. Slaves are generated as the revivalist Fula Muslims complete the formation of the Imamate of Futa Toro and bring an end to the Denianke lineage in Futa Toro.

1777 End of the administration by the Marquis de Pombal.

1778 The *Companhia do Grão Pará e Maranhão* ends and is replaced by Comércio Exclusivo.

1780–1786 Operation of the *Companhia do Comércio da Costa d'Africa*.

1780's About 2,200 slaves exported annually from Senegambia.

1786 Drought in Gambia and Guinea-Bissau.

1788 Futa Djallon is formed as a Fula theocracy. The Imamy of Futa Toro prohibits regional transshipment of slaves, but the demand for slaves on the coast thwarts this policy.

1791 Freetown established in Sierra Leone for slaves repatriated by the English as the Abolition movement intensifies.

1792 The English, led by Phillip Beaver, settle on Bolama without permission from the Bijagós people, who attack and hold English hostages who are ransomed at prevailing slave prices.

1793 French Revolutionary assembly abolishes slavery. English withdraw from Bolama under Bijagós pressure.

1800's European nations begin the abolition of the slave trade, which declines but continues at Bissau and Cacheu until mid century.

1804 Independence of Haiti.

1807 Portuguese royal family flees to Brazil to escape Napoleon. England abolishes slavery.

1808 United States prohibits the slave trade, but not slave ownership.

1810 Treaty between Portugal and Britain has secret provision giving the British control of Bissau and Cacheu for fifty years.

1812 British export slaves from Upper Guinea to Cape Verde for secret sales to American slave shippers during war between the two nations. This region supplies about ten to twelve percent of all African slaves at this period; the majority go to Cuba.

1813 **24 April**, Honório Pereira Barreto born of Cape Verdean ancestry in Cacheu.

1814 English try to take Bolama from Portugal. Famine in Cape Verde.

1815 Treaty of Vienna between England and Portugal orders Portugal to curb its slave trade north of the Equator.

1817–1820 Nine Rhode Island ships seized by Federal courts for illegal African slave trading.

1820's Jewish Miguelistas flee to Cape Verde and the Guinea coast. Their role in regional commerce continues mainly in hides, wax, ivory, gold, and commodities other than slaves.

1820 Liberal revolution in Portugal.

1821 Cape Verde and Guinea-Bissau are given one representative to the Portuguese King.

1822 Brazil becomes independent of Portugal.

1824–1825 Pepel and Portuguese forces clash at Cacheu.

1825 Portuguese Governor in Praia raises money for famine relief by sales of Crown-owned *urzella*; he is removed from office.

1826 Timbuktu in Mali falls under Fulani control.

1827 British occupy Bolama and liberate its slaves.

1828 French advance into the "Portuguese" Casamance at the Island of Joque (*Ilheu dos Mosquitos*).

1830 English protest Portuguese military occupation of Bolama.

1831–1833 Portuguese signed treaty with Felupes of Bolor. Severe famine in Cape Verde Islands kills 30,000.

1832 The Prefecture of Cape Verde and Guinea is created, with Guinea a subordinated district and Bissau its capital.

1834 Britain abolishes slavery in its colonies and pressures others to follow. The Society for the Abolition of Slavery established in Paris. Honório Barreto is appointed as the Provedor (Purveyor) of Cacheu. The population of Cape Verde is put at 51,854 free persons and 3,974 slaves.

1836 Portuguese "officially" abolish the slave trade, but in Guinea and Cape Verde it continues. The French occupy Karabane and Sedhiou on the Casamance, putting more pressure on the Portuguese. The judge of the *praça* of Bissau is assassinated.

1837 Honório Pereira Barreto is appointed Governor of *Guiné-Portuguesa*, but is still subordinate to Cape Verde.

1837–1859 Governor Barreto claims Bolama and Canhabaque as under Portuguese authority. Guinean economy declines as the abolition movement intensifies, and resistance to slavery increases by the inhabitants of the area. Barreto repeatedly protests French occupation of the Casamance.

1838 The English remove the Portuguese flag at Bolama, where they free about 200 slaves owned by José Caetano Nozolini of Bissau. The English begin their first coal dump in Mindelo.

1842 Treaty between Britain and Portugal abolishes the slave trade in all overseas possessions. Pepel and *grumete* uprising in Bissau. The first Cape Verdean printing press publishes the first *Boletim Oficial do Governo Geral de Cabo Verde*.

1843 The United States African Squadron is based in Cape Verde for the "suppression" of the American slave trade. Mutiny in Bissau.

4 June, The Anglo-Portuguese *Comissão Mixta* signs accord in Boa Vista to abolish slavery.

1843 Fula *jihad* against Mandinka in Casamance region initiates a half century of regional strife.

1844 Pepel uprising in Bissau suppressed by international naval intervention. Manjaco attacks on Cacheu.

1846 Pepel uprising in Bissau. Mandinka and *grumete* uprising in Farim. Peanuts are first exported from Bolama.

1848 Formal abolition of slavery in French colonies. Reports of slaves still being purchased by French at Sedhiou in Casamance.

1852 Unification of Districts of Bissau and Cacheu.

1853 French intervention in Bissau. Treaty signed with the Pepels.

1854 Mandinka uprising in Geba. Portugal frees state-owned slaves.

1856 Church-owned Portuguese slaves emancipated, as well as those born of a slave mother. Manjacos and Pepels attack Cacheu. Portuguese sign treaty with Bijagós leaders. Cape Verdean settlement established at Buba.

1858 Portuguese decree calls for the end of slavery in twenty years. British steam warship liberates Portuguese slaves in Bolama. Portugal and Britain meet on Bolama ownership issue.

1860 British claim that Bolama is a part of Sierra Leone.

1860's–1870's Growth of "legitimate" trade in palm oil and peanuts.

1861 The Africa Squadron recalled from Cape Verde for military needs in the United States as the American Civil War begins. Attack on Cacheu by Manjacos and Pepels.

1862–1863 Timbuktu falls under Tukulor control.

1863 American President Lincoln abolishes slavery in the United States. The Tuaregs force the Tukulors out of Timbuktu.

1863–1866 Famine in Cape Verde kills 30,000 and causes large scale emigration.

1865 Abolition of slavery in the Dutch Colonies.

1866 Seminary opens in São Nicolau.

1867, September, Yellow fever epidemic on Senegambian coast. The Fula-led *jihad* ends the Mandinka kingdom of Kaabu at the battle of Kansala.

1868 The British assault Bolama, and Portugal protests strongly. BNU branch opens in Cape Verde.

1869 All forms of slavery abolished in the Portuguese Empire. The Suez Canal opens, diverting Cape Verdean sea traffic.

1870 **21 April**, American President U.S. Grant arbitrates the Luso-British conflict over Bolama in favor of Portugal. Britain accepts and withdraws their claim. Portugal seizes Nalu lands near Tombali.

1871 A *grumete* assasinates Governor of Guinea, Telles Caldeira in Cacheu; this is followed by widespread "punitive" measures.

1875 Portuguese Decree calls for ex-slaves in Cape Verde to work for two more years after 1878 for their ex-masters.

1878 Felupes attack Bolor garrison. The Portuguese counter with "punitive" campaign ending in the famed "disaster" at Bolor. This causes the Portuguese to separate the administration of Guinea-Bissau from Cape Verde. French campaigns against Futa Jallon.

1879 **18 March**, "Autonomous" *Guiné-Portuguesa* has its first capital at Bolama with Lt. Col. Agostinho Coelho the first Governor. He launches "pacification" campaigns in Bissau, Buba, and Nhacra to try to assert control.

1879–1891 Clashes continue between *Fulas Pretos* and *Fulas Forros*, which are exploited by the Portuguese. The Fulas of Bololo are led by *regulo* Mamadu Paté who fights with the Fulas of Forrea led by *regulo* Bacar Guidali.

1880's Portugal ruled by the "liberal" Bragança monarchy.

1880 **7 February**, *Boletim Oficial do Governo de Guiné-Portuguesa* begins publication.

December, Portuguese sign treaty with Bakari Demba of Firdu.

1881 Lt. Capt. Pedro Inácio Gouveia appointed Governor of Guinea. Futa Fulas attack Buba. Portuguese attack Futa Forros and sign treaty with Fulas of Labé.

1882 Portuguese defeat Beafadas at Jabada and attack the fortified Fula village of Mamadu Paté, and Bakar Kidali capitulates. The Portuguese seize about 200 prisoners (mostly women and children) and many livestock. Construction begins on the Dakar-St. Louis railroad (including Guinean workers).

1883 The new *conselho* of Bissau unites Bolama, Cacheu, and Bololo.

March, Dansa (cousin of Musa Molo) leads Fula force to sack the Portuguese settlement at São Belchoir (near Geba) and to take twelve *Cristãos* as captives.

5 April, Treaty of "Peace, Friendship and Obedience" is signed between the Portuguese and Adju Pumol, Majaco ruler of the Guinean islands of Jeta and Pecixe; the treaty is not respected by his subjects.

June, Portuguese attack Balantas of Nhacra.

13 October, Publication of *A Fraternidade* appears in Bolama to support drought relief in Cape Verde.

1884 Angolan soldiers in the Portuguese army are defeated by Pepels at Cacanda. Judge of Cacheu, Joãquim Rodrigues, is assassinated. Manjacos of Caió sack the Portuguese sloop *Honório Barreto*. Fulas defeat the Beafadas at Buduco in Guinala. Portuguese attack Pepels, Beafadas, and Mandinkas.

Colonial Partition

1884–85 The Berlin Congress provides for the partition of the African continent, making boundaries which largely remain today. The condition of "effective" occupation is set, which results in the "Scramble for Africa." Americans are observers; no Africans are invited.

1885 Francisco Paula Gomes Barbosa becomes Governor of Guinea.

1886 **12 May**, Luso-French border accord signed; Portugal withdraws its claims to Ziguinchor in exchange for Nalu territory in Cacine. Bacar Guidali is killed by Mamadu Paté who becomes the *regulo* of Forrea. The Portuguese and Beafadas fight at Bijante. Musa Molo attacks the Beafadas, and Mandinkas at Geba, Buba, and towns in the Casamance. The Portuguese and 4,000 Beafada and Mandinka irregulars counter-attack, and after one month of operations, Musa Molo is defeated at the battle of Fancá in

Mansomine; his army flees to the Casamance. Col. José Eduardo de Brito becomes Governor of Guinea.

3 December, Portuguese sign treaty with Alfa Yaya of Labé. Samory Touré proclaims his theocratic state of Dyula. Slavery is abolished in Cuba.

1887   3 April, Portuguese sign treaty with Firdu leaders Bakari Demba and Musa Molo.

31 August, Luso-French Accord is ratified. The French occupy Conakry. Eusébio Castelo do Vale becomes Governor of Guinea.

1888   Rear Admiral Francisco Teixeira da Silva becomes Governor of Guinea; soon followed by Joãquim da Graça Correia e Lança.

Febuary–May, mission establishes Franco-Portuguese borders. Slavery abolished in Brazil.

1889–1890   Brussels Anti-Slavery Conference forbids import of arms and spiritous liquors in Africa twenty degrees north of the Equator and twenty-two degrees south.

1889–1890   Two month rebellion of Beafadas, Mandinkas, and Fulas (of Musa Molo) in Geba and Ganadu.

1890's   Guineans continue to resist the Portuguese efforts at colonialization of the interior lands. Military repression directed against Moli Boia who is backed by the French in the Casamance. Uprising at Geba by Pepel and *grumete* alliance. Mamadu Paté resumes attacks at Buba, and Musa Molo renews his attacks at Farim.

1891   19 April, Portuguese launch two-month campaign under Capt. Joaquim António Carmo de Azevedo with an artillery battery against the Pepels at Intim and Antula, near Bissau. This ends with the deaths of four white officers including the Commander, three sergeants, forty-one soldiers, and many African auxiliaries. Luís Augusto de Vasconcelos e Sá becomes Governor of Guinea. Start of the Seven Years' War of Samory Touré and the French.

1892   Military administration established in Guinea with a major increase in troops to try to crush the widespread uprisings. Cape Verde and Guinea become "autonomous districts." Samory Touré establishes his second Dyula Empire.

1893   Joint Pepel and Balanta attack on the Fort *São José* in Bissau. Fodé Kaba allies with French to defeat the Diolas of Casamance.

1894   The Portuguese led by Col. Luís A. de Vasconcelos e Sá, launch a major counterattack against the Pepels and Balantas. This war results in the signing of an "Act of

Submission" on 22 July, which is not widely accepted by the Pepels. The French and Musa Molo wage war on the Upper Casamance against the forces of Bamba Dalla.

1895 Lt. Capt. Eduardo João da Costa Oliveira becomes the Governor of Guinea. French attack the Balantas in the Casamance.

1897–1898 Portuguese attack Manjacos in Caió and Mandinkas in Oio. The colonial forces, supported by Fula *regulo* Mamadu Paté and Beafada *regulo* Infali Sonco, are soundly defeated at Oio.

1899 French attack Banyun of Casamance.

1900 Portuguese fail to subjugate the Bijagós people at Canhabaque. First Pan-African Congress held in London. First Luso-French demarcation campaign begins.

1901 *Concelho* of Bissau re-established. Portuguese seek to "pacify" the Mandinkas at Oio and Felupes at Jufunco. Second demarcation campaign begins.

1902 Report of slave market still existing on Karabane Island at the mouth of the Casamance. Portuguese "defeat" Mandinkas at Oio. Third demarcation campaign begins.

1903 Campaign against Felupes of Arame. Introduction of "hut tax."

1904 Rebellion in Cacheu region suppressed by the Portuguese, whose forces are defeated by Mandinkas at Farim. Fourth and Fifth (final) demarcation campaigns begin.

1905 Campaign against Felupes of Cacheu.

1906–1909 Continuing resistance in Geba area by the Beafada leader, Infali Sonco, who blocks communications between Bissau and Bafata. Tax revolts break out among the Felupes in Cacheu region, the Balantas at Gole, and the Pepels near Bissau.

1907 Portuguese launch major campaign against the Bijagós of Formosa Island and against Infali Sonco and his allies in the central region of Guinea.

1908 Major military campaign led by 1st Lt Oliveira Muzanty with large numbers of reinforcements from Mozambique and Portugal is put against the Balantas, Mandinkas, and Pepels. Pepels resist at Intim and Bandim and counterattack at Bissau. Infali Sonco retreats to Oio.

1909 Balanta attack at Gole blocked by Portuguese forces and the mercenary soldiers led by the Senegalese Abdul Injai.

1909–1925 Nineteen "pacification" campaigns are waged in Guinea-Bissau and are noted for excessive brutality, especially by the forces of Abdul Injai.

1910 Portuguese monarchy overthrown, starting a period of great Republican political instability. Creation of *Liga Guineense*.

1911 "Native" Labor Regulations allowing for forced labor are approved by Lisbon.

1912 February, the Balantas of Bissau and the Baiotes of Cacheu revolt against the Portuguese and *grumetes*. Arrival of Capt. João Teixeira Pinto, who is later charged with atrocities.

1913 British report continuing secret slave trade in Guinea-Bissau, which the Portuguese dismiss as being just "captured rebels." Teixeira Pinto and Adbul Injai attack Oio. Blaise Diagne becomes the first African elected to the French National Assembly.

December, Manjacos massacre Portuguese tax brigade at Churoenque.

1914 Portuguese troops quartered in Bissau's *Fortaleza de São José* as a reserve in World War One. Major "pacification" campaign led by Abdul Injai and Capt. João Teixeira Pinto against Manjacos, Balantas, and Pepels meets strong resistance. Uprising of Baiotes.

1915 Continuation of campaigns to establish control beyond the small confines of the *fortaleza* of *São José* in Bissau. These meet resistance by the *grumetes* of Bissau and Pepels of Intim, Bandim, and Biombo. Given the brutality of the campaign, Teixeira Pinto is removed from his position and is sent to Mozambique, where he is killed fighting against the Germans. Abdul Injai is appointed as *regulo* of the Oio. *Liga Guineense* is dissolved.

1917 Russsian revolution creates a bipolar political world in which the Soviet Union supports the anticolonial forces in Africa. Major military campaigns in the Bijagós, especially Canhabaque. Organic Charter of Guinea divides the population into *indigenas* and *civilizados*.

1918 Campaigns against the Felupes.

1919 Campaign in Mansabá, Oio against Abdul Injai who disregarded Portuguese authority. Injai is exiled to Cape Verde.

1920 *Liga Africana* established in Lisbon, thus begining a sense of unity of Africans in the Portuguese colonies.

1924 **17 August**, Journal *Pro-Guiné* starts publication to represent the Republican Democratic Party. It is closed after ten issues.

12 September, Birth of Amilcar Cabral.

1925 Major Portuguese campaign at Canhabaque in Bijagós Islands.

1926 28 May, Republicans overthrown and Portuguese fascism rises under General Gomes da Costa. Locust plague in West Africa.

1928–1930 António de Oliveira Salazar consolidates fascist power in Portugal.

1930–1933 Salazar formulates *Estado Novo* as the blueprint for Portuguese fascism and colonialism.

1931 Month-long revolt in Guinea-Bissau is led by deported politicians and local colonial officials who were opposed to the Salazar government. Pepels and Mancanhas clash in Bissau.

1933 Felupe uprising at Jufunco in Cacheu area. Portuguese (*Estado Novo*) Constitution approved along with the Organic Charter for their Colonial Empire.

1934 Felupe uprising at Baseor in Cacheu area.

1935 Felupe uprising at Susanna in Cacheu area. Major Portuguese campaign in the Bijagós Islands, especially at Galinhas and Canhabaque.

1939 *Fortaleza de São José* declared a national Portuguese monument.

1940 Guinea-Bissau's Catholic diocese is separated from Cape Verde.

1941 During World War Two, Portuguese troops are quartered in Bissau's *Fortaleza São José* and in the Cape Verde Islands. The colonial capital of Guinea is moved from Bolama to Bissau.

1945 Formation of PIDE from PVDE. Anti-fascist revolt by Henrique Galvão. For the first time, the Pan African Conference (Manchester) calls for the complete independence of Africa.

1946 Publication of the first *Boletim Cultural da Guiné-Portuguesa*.

1947 17 December, First publication of *Arauto*, a Catholic Church bulletin in Guinea. Henrique Galvão reports about the abhorent labor conditions in Portuguese Africa.

1949 Opening of Tarrafal prison in Cape Verde Islands for political opponents of Lisbon. Amilcar Cabral lives in Praia.

1950 Third Pan-African Congress held in London; representatives of *Liga Africana* present.

1951 Status of Guinea changes from "colony" to "overseas province."

1952 Amilcar Cabral moves to Bissau.

1953 Amilcar Cabral conducts Guinea's first agricultural census.

1954 Creation of MING. British journalist Basil Davidson reveals patterns of slavery and contract labor in Portuguese African colonies.

1955 Portugal is admitted to the United Nations.

1956, 19 September, the PAIGC is formed in Bissau.

1957 Portuguese Communist Party endorses anti-colonial parties. The Gold Coast becomes independent Ghana.

1958 Anti-colonial Congress held in Accra. The MLG is formed. Guinée-Conakry becomes independent. *Liceu* Honório Barreto is the first high school in Bissau.

1959 Amilcar Cabral is supported by the British Communist Party. The MLGCV is formed in Dakar to launch a propaganda struggle.

January, Anti-colonial Congress in Tunis; FRAIN is formed to link the PAIGC with the MPLA. Formation of the UPICV.

3 August, Pidjiguiti massacre; PAIGC changes tactics.

1961 Formation of the CONCP, which replaces FRAIN.

13–17 July, the MLGCV and PAIGC merge to become the FULGPICV which later is simplified to just PAIGC. FLING carries out armed raids at Susanna and nearby areas. Henrique Galvão seizes ocean liner to protest Portuguese colonial policy in Africa. 50,000 killed in Angolan war. *Indigenato* system is offically abolished in all Portuguese colonies.

1962 Amilcar Cabral says that the PAIGC is a party of "soliders for the United Nations."

1963 OAU formed in Addis Ababa, Ethiopia.

1963–1974 Period of the nationalist war in Guinea-Bissau.

1963, 21 July, Secret meeting in Dakar raised issue of expanding the war to the Cape Verde Islands. Never implemented.

1964 18 January, New Series of *Boletim Oficial* begins in Guinea.

13–17 February, First National Congress of the PAIGC inside Guinea at Cassacá. Divisions inside the PAIGC are eliminated or repressed.

1964–1965 FLING conducts raids in Guinea-Bissau to rival the PAIGC.

1965 Américo Tomas re-elected as Portuguese President. Gambia becomes independent. The PAIGC is selected for OAU support over FLING. The MLGCV seeks support from the American Embassy in Dakar and American support groups in New York.

1966 War expands in Guinea with mortars, bazookas, small canons, and 75mm recoilless rifles.

1968 19 February, PAIGC attacks Bissalanca Airport at Bissau. PAIGC gains initiative in the war. The PAIGC moves closer to the Soviet Union and the Portuguese Communist Party, but it maintains an independendent political line.

26 September, Caetano replaces incapacitated Salazar.

1969, 3 February, FRELIMO President Eduardo Mondlane assassinated.

1970, 1 July, Amilcar Cabral and associates meet the Pope in Rome.

1971 The PAIGC starts campaign of nationalist wall slogans in Cape Verde.

1972, April, United Nations Special Mission visits liberated territories and takes testimony about colonial atrocities and judges the extent of PAIGC territorial control.

21 September, big anti-colonial demonstration in Praia. DGS/PIDE broadens powers to resist insurgencies.

The Independence Era

1973, 81,000 refugees from Guinea-Bissau have fled to Senegal.

20 January, Assassination of Amilcar Cabral in Conakry;

31 January, Titina Sila, Member of PAIGC's CSL, killed by the Portuguese in combat in the North Front.

February, PAIGC units launch attacks, especially at Farim.

March, intensified use of SAM–7's against Portugal's air force in Guinea-Bissau. Portugal loses some twenty aircraft. PAIGC units attack Catio, Cadique, and Guidage.

April, PAIGC attacks at Guidage.

May, PAIGC attacks at Catio, Bula, Guidage.

25 May, "Operation Amilcar Cabral" captures the Portuguese fort at Guiledge with heavy losses in life and war material.

June, PAIGC attacks at Gadamael.

18–22 July, Second Congress of the PAIGC in Medina Boé.

24 September, First Peoples National Assembly at Medina Boé, with UN observers present, declares the independence of the State of Guinea-Bissau. Gen. António Spinola relieved of his command of the war.

2 November, United Nations General Assembly calls on Portugal to cease all military activity in Guinea-Bissau.

6 November, PAIGC units attack Bula and Bafata.

19 November, Guinea-Bissau admitted as the forty-second member of the OAU.

1974, 25 April, Fall of fascist/colonial Portugal following the revolt of the *Movimento das Forças Armadas* led by Gen. Vasco Gonçalves. MFA restores democracy to Portugal and promises decolonization. Discussions begin on Luso-Guinean cooperation.

1 May, political prisoners released from Tarrafal, Cape Verde. PAIGC adopts policy of mass mobilization in Cape Verde.

19 May, Big demonstrations in Mindelo; Portuguese troops fire on demonstrators in Praia.

6 June, PAIGC wins referendum in Cape Verdean decolonization.

3 July, flag of the PAIGC recognized in Cape Verde.

July, Struggle in Lisbon between the neo-colonialist position of Spinola and the decolonization position of Vasco Gonçalves.

August, PAIGC and MFA have meetings in Algiers and London to arrange for troop withdrawal in Bissau.

September, Spinola meets Mobutu in Sal to discuss Angola. Spinola blocks Pedro Pires from flying to Sal from Bissau. Spinola prevented from landing in Bissau. 150 Rightist Portuguese marines transferred from Guinea-Bissau in early withdrawal provoke incidents in São Vicente over decolonization. They are sent back to Lisbon. PAIGC influence spreads quickly and widely, but Spinola still blocks the discussion of independence for Cape Verde.

12 September, JAAC formed.

14 September, Portugal recognizes independent Guinea-Bissau.

22 September, 3,000 soldiers from Bissau return to Lisbon.

29 September, General Strike in Cape Verde. Spinola seeks to arrest PAIGC members and block the arrival of any more. Silvino da Luz, already in Cape Verde, goes into hiding.

30 September, Spinola toppled by leftists in the MFA.

13 October, Pedro Pires returns to Cape Verde.

15 October, the last of 30,000 Portuguese troops leave Guinea.

19 October, Luís Cabral and Aristides Pereira enter Bissau.

October, The UDCV and UPICV oppose the PAIGC and seek an independent Cape Verde.

1 November, the MFA endorses the PAIGC as the sole party for decolonization. The UPICV and UDCV oppose the unity of Guinea-Bissau and Cape Verde.

7 November, major negotiations between the PAIGC and the MFA result in a plan for independence in six months and a jointly supervised electoral referendum without the UDCV and UPICV.

9 December, PAIGC militants take over Radio in São Vicente.

1975, 15 April, the MFA accepts the new Cape Verdean ANP.

11 May, coup by Spinola fails in Lisbon.

20–26 June, PAIGC delegation of Fidelis Cabral de Almeida and José Araujo goes to Cascais, Portugal.

24–25 June, The CSL of the PAIGC decides in Bissau to make a Council of Unity of the two states of Guinea-Bissau and Cape Verde. The PAIGC gives "total respect to the principles of free choice, democracy, and sovereignty of the people." The CSL notes the blood and glorious sacrifices of our glorious people, the eternal glory of Amilcar Cabral, and the patriotism of Cape Verde.

5 July, Cape Verde becomes independent.

12 July, São Tomé and Príncipe become independent.

1976 Flora Gomes releases film *Le Retour de Cabral*.

1 July, Nationalization of Cape Verde bank, ports, and airline.

30 October, Law in Cape Verde allows detention powers.

1977 Guinea-Bissau serves as transit point for Cuban troops going to Angola. 300 Cubans in Bissau for police training. Educational reforms in Guinea-Bissau to eliminate colonial influences and increase technical and practical skills. Law passed to allow the military to try political crimes. PAIGC institutes repressive measures against dissidents.

15–20 November, Third Party Congress of PAIGC

1978 Contingent of FARP to serve as guard for the Angolan President. PAIGC "shuffle" blocks dissidents seeking liberalization. UCID grows from PAIGC dissidents.

1979, February, Manuel Faustino and José Veiga leave the PAIGC and government with criticism about lack of internal democracy.

April, Expulsion/defection of members of PAIGC National Council.

May, Guinea and Cape Verde cancel joint military exercise.

1980, 7 October, Constitution put into effect granting the leading role of the PAIGC as the sole party for the state.

7–10 October, Extraordinary session of the ANP of Guinea-Bissau grants wide-ranging powers to the President.

14 November, Guinea-Bissau President Luís Cabral overthrown and jailed by João Vieira in Bissau. António Buscadini and Otto Schacht are killed; Vasco Cabral is injured. Rafael Barbosa is freed from jail, speaks on the radio, and is quickly rearrested. The constitution of Guinea-Bissau is suspended.

21 November, João Vieira discovers 500 bodies in mass graves.

31 December, Pedro Pires notes that the Guinea-Bissau coup is a loss of security for the PAIGC in Cape Verde.

1981 Bissau declares "The Year of National Concord."

1 January, democratic elections in Senegal.

19 January, the PAICV becomes the ruling party of Cape Verde. Political unity between Guinea and Cape Verde is suspended.

17 February, President Vieira has state visit to Conakry.

20 February, student protesters beaten and expelled from school in Bissau.

14 March, President Vieira has state visit to Senegal.

14 May, President Vieira visits Conakry for its 34th anniversary.

30 July, short-lived coup in Gambia put down by Senegalese.

31 August–1 September, UCID opposition leaders arrested in Cape Verde. Several are held under poor conditions without charge.

8–14 November, Extraordinary PAIGC Congress makes Vieira the new Secretary General.

15 November, Senegal and Gambia agree to form Confederation.

16 December, PAIGC frees Luís Cabral and others arrested in November 1980 coup. Cabral goes to exile in Cuba.

31 December, coup in Ghana.

1982 Bissau declares the "Year of Production and Productivity."

17 May, Victor Saude Maria becomes Prime Minister.

8 June, Guinea-Bissau and Cape Verde re-establish diplomatic relations. The "Group of Five" Luso-phone African nations have summit conference in Praia.

1983 Bissau declares the "Year of Action, Not Words."

9 March, World Bank backs Guinean economic stabilization plan.

10 April, President Vieira has state visit to Liberia.

23 July, First Cape Verdean ambassador accepted in Bissau.

18–20 December, The "Group of Five" meet in Bissau.

1984 Bissau declares the "Year of Rigorous Discipline and Institutionalization."

7 January, Emergency PAIGC meeting to discuss Senegalese-Guinean dispute over oil rights in Casamance region.

8–12 January, Dispute continues with controversial crashes of two military planes in Bissau, which killed three people.

March, Prime Minister Maria charged in plot and placed under arrest.

7 November, Senegal and Guinea agree to international arbitration of dispute. The "Group of Five" meet in Maputo.

1985, 12 March, Arbitration of Senegal-Guinean dispute held in Geneva.

17 October, Abortive military coup in Guinea-Bissau is attempted by Minister of Justice Paulo Correia and former Attorney General Viriato Pâ. Finally fifty are arrested. The "Group of Five" meet in Sao Tomé.

1986, Bissau declares the "Year of Reinforcing National Unity."

7–9 January, the INEP research institute in Bissau holds international conference on state formation in Luso-phone Africa.

25 March, Minister of Tourism and Commerce Mario Cabral and Police Inspector Abubacar Djaló are arrested for a role in the October 1985 plot, but they are later released.

April, President Vieira states his plan to introduce democracy.

4 April, the ANP plans to expel PAIGC members involved in plot.

5 June, Military court tries fifty-two alleged coup plotters for role in 1985 attempt including Correia and Pâ as leaders.

12 July, One dozen opponents of the PAIGC are sentenced to death; four were later freed, others sentenced to prison terms.

17 July, six death sentences are commuted, but despite appeals from the international community, six death sentences are carried out, including those against: Paulo Correia, Viriato Pâ.

27 July, the Resistência da Guiné-Bissau/Movimento Ba-fatá formed in Lisbon by Domingos Fernandes Gomes.

9–14 November, IVth Congress of the PAIGC confirms Vieira as Secretary General.

15 November, the first Faculty of Medicine opened in Bissau. The "Group of Five" meet in Luanda.

1987 Bissau declares the "Year of Production."

1989, 10 June, Guinean patrol boat fires on Senegalese fishing vessel in Guinea's exclusive economic zone.

31 July, Geneva court rules in favor of Senegal; Bissau rejects the judgement.

August, relations deteriorate between Senegal and Guinea.

24 September, Portuguese organize and run Guinean TV network.

1990 Bissau declares the "Year of Stability."

1 January, Guinean navy seizes Senegalese fishing trawlers.

19 January, amnesty given to sixteen alleged ploters in 1985 coup.

27–28 January, Pope John Paul II visits Bissau.

1 March, Opening of the *Banco Internacional da Guiné-Bissau*, the first commercial bank since 1974. March, the MpD in Cape Verde initiates opposition to the PAICV.

20 March, Rafael Barbosa forms the *Frente Democratica Social*.

11 April, Senegalese Navy fires on and seizes a Soviet ship flying the Guinean flag.

13 April, Guinea calls for release of Soviet ship.

28 April, Guinea threatens armed conflict over territorial and maritime disputes with Senegal.

29 April–8 May, Extraordinary meeting of the ANP approves new constitution allowing for multi-party opposition to the PAIGC.

April–May, small clashes between the MFDC and Senegalese.

2 May, Senegalese forces penetrate and withdraw from northern Guinea-Bissau without incident.

19 May, Senegalese troops penetrate near Cacheu region and have small clashes with Guinean forces with some casualties.

31 May, Guinea-Bissau mediates accord between Senegal and the MFDC.

August–September, forty killed in fifteen day period between MFDC and Senegalese army in Casamance.

2 September, PAIGC adopts policy of transition to pluralism.

13–21 September, the PAICV and MpD plan the transition to democratic pluralism in Cape Verde.

8–12 October, President Vieira has state visit to Taiwan.

15 October, eight killed in MFDC attacks in the Casamance.

20–23 November, International Conference seeks to protect the historical features of Bolama.

December, 100 deaths in the last six months with MFDC. Flora Gomes's *Mortunega* wins bronze prize in Carthage film festival. Mozambique and Ivory Coast legalize political opposition. São Tomé passes referendum for multi-party Constitution.

1991, 13 January, The MpD defeats the PAICV in Cape Verde elections.

14 January, Pedro Pires resigns as Prime Minister.

17 January, José Mascarenhas Monteiro defeats Aristides Pereira in Presidential elections in Cape Verde. March, demonstrations in Mali force multi-party democracy.

18 April, FD founded by Aristides Celso Menezes Fernandes.

5 May, PAIGC in Bissau follows the PAICV and abolishes the Constitutional provision which establishes the Party as "the leading political force in the state and society." This moves the PAIGC in Bissau toward political pluralism.

30 June, 121 PAIGC militants appeal for democracy.

4 July, Statute passed by the National Assembly to allow for the right of democratic opposition.

20 July, the *Liga Guineense de Proteçao Ecológica* formed by Aladje Bubacar Djaló in Bissau.

2 August, PCD formed in Bissau.

August, Military promises elections in Togo after twenty-four years.

September, Multi-party Constitution approved in Guinea-Bissau.

18 November, FD legalized.

15 December, The MpD wins *conselho* elections in the Cape Verde.

26 December, FDS legalized.

27 December, PCD legalized. Opposition wins elections in São Tomé and Príncipé.

1992 February, Ghana plans for multi-party elections.

31 April, Peace Accords negotiated in Cacheu, Guinea-Bissau between Senegalese and the MFDC seccessionist movement.

24 May, FLING legalized in Guinea-Bissau.

25 June, MpD allows electoral rights to overseas Cape V Verdeans.

5 July, PAICV calls rally to support the existing flag, which has been redesigned by the MpD.

24 July, New Cape Verdean flag officially adopted. The former PAIGC/PAICV flag is abolished.

August, Multiparty Commission of Transition is created.

7 August, PDP legalized.

26 August, Angola changes constitution to accept plural democracy and to drop the term 'Peoples' from the name of the Republic of Angola.

29 September, multi-party assembly elections in Angola.

9 October, PRD legalized.

1993 Election violence in Casamance region of Senegal sends at least 17,000 refugees into refugee camps in northern Guinea-Bissau.

24 January, National Electoral Commission approved to register the new political parties and supervise elections in Guinea-Bissau.

17 March, alleged coup of Amadu Mané kills Major Robalo de Pina of the Rapid Intervention Force.

17 April, PRD leader João da Costa jailed as alleged member of the above "coup."

13 September, Guinea-Bissau will establish relations with Israel and South Africa.

September, LGPE becomes the twelfth legal opposition party.

14 October, Senegalese-Guinean dispute resolved in accord providing a 50:50 share for fishing resources; and 85:15 for oil resources. Intense discussion raised over Bissau's wisdom in accepting this minority share.

1994, 6 February, Aristides Menezes, leader of the FDP, the first opposition party in Guinea, dies in Lisbon of illness.

27 March, provisional date for first democratic, multi-party elections, which are postponed.

19 June, second provisional date for elections.

3 July, first multi-party elections held in Guinea-Bissau. 'Nino' Vieira wins 46.20% of the Presidential vote; Koumba Yala wins 21.88%; Domingos Fernandes Gomes wins 17.44%. A run-off election is required according to law. The PAIGC gets sixty-two seats in the Peoples National Assembly (ANP); the RGB-MB gets eighteen seats; the PRS gets twelve seats (qq.v.).

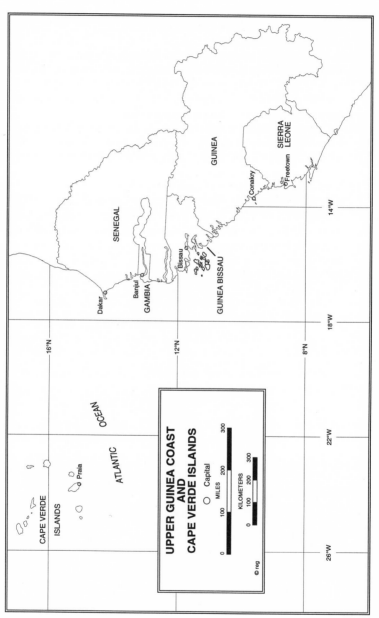

Map 1. Upper Guinea Coast and Cape Verde Islands

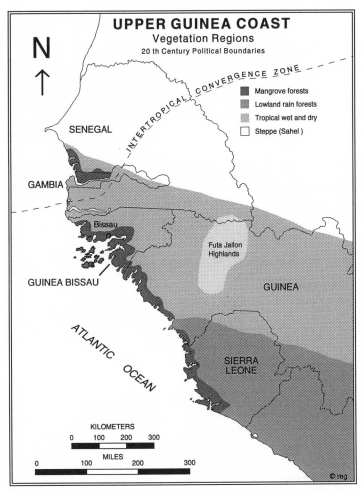

UPPER GUINEA COAST
Vegetation Regions
20 th Century Political Boundaries

N ↑

INTERTROPICAL CONVERGENCE ZONE

- ■ Mangrove forests
- ▨ Lowland rain forests
- ▨ Tropical wet and dry
- □ Steppe (Sahel)

SENEGAL

GAMBIA

Bissau

GUINEA BISSAU

Futa Jallon
Highlands

GUINEA

ATLANTIC OCEAN

SIERRA
LEONE

KILOMETERS
0   100   200   300

MILES
0   100   200   300

© reg

Map 2. Upper Guinea Coast: Vegetation Regions

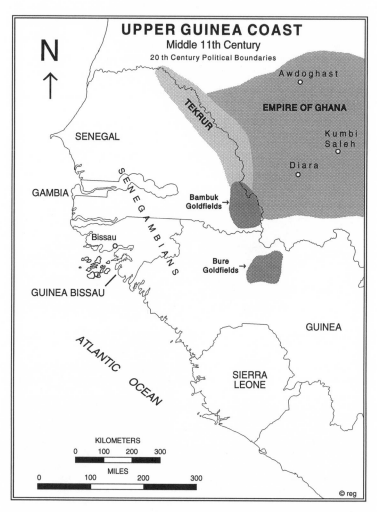

Map 3. Upper Guinea Coast: Middle 11th Century

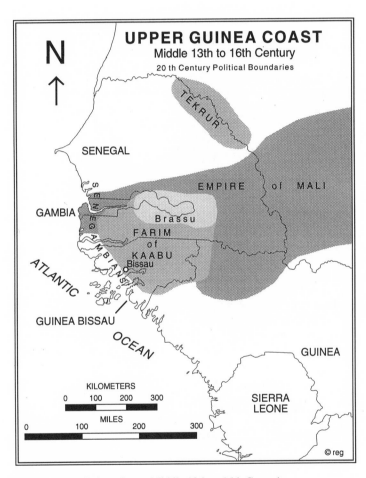

Map 4. Upper Guinea Coast: Middle 13th to 16th Centuries

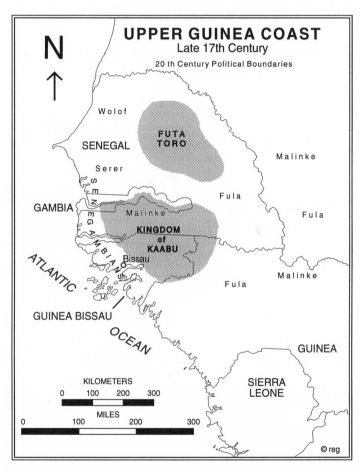

Map 5. Upper Guinea Coast: Late 17th Century

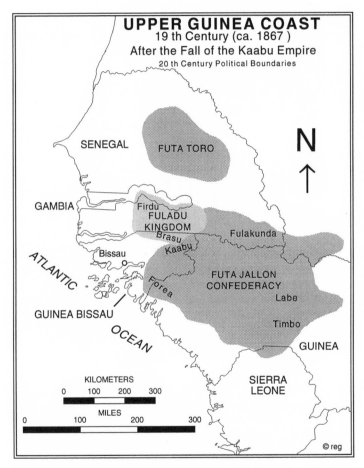

UPPER GUINEA COAST
19 th Century (ca. 1867)
After the Fall of the Kaabu Empire
20 th Century Political Boundaries

N
↑

SENEGAL

FUTA TORO

GAMBIA

Firdu
FULADU
KINGDOM
Brasu
Kaabu
Fulakunda

Bissau

ATLANTIC

Forea

GUINEA BISSAU

OCEAN

FUTA JALLON
CONFEDERACY
Labe

Timbo

GUINEA

SIERRA
LEONE

KILOMETERS
0   100   200   300

MILES
0   100   200   300

© reg

Map 6. Upper Guinea Coast about 1867

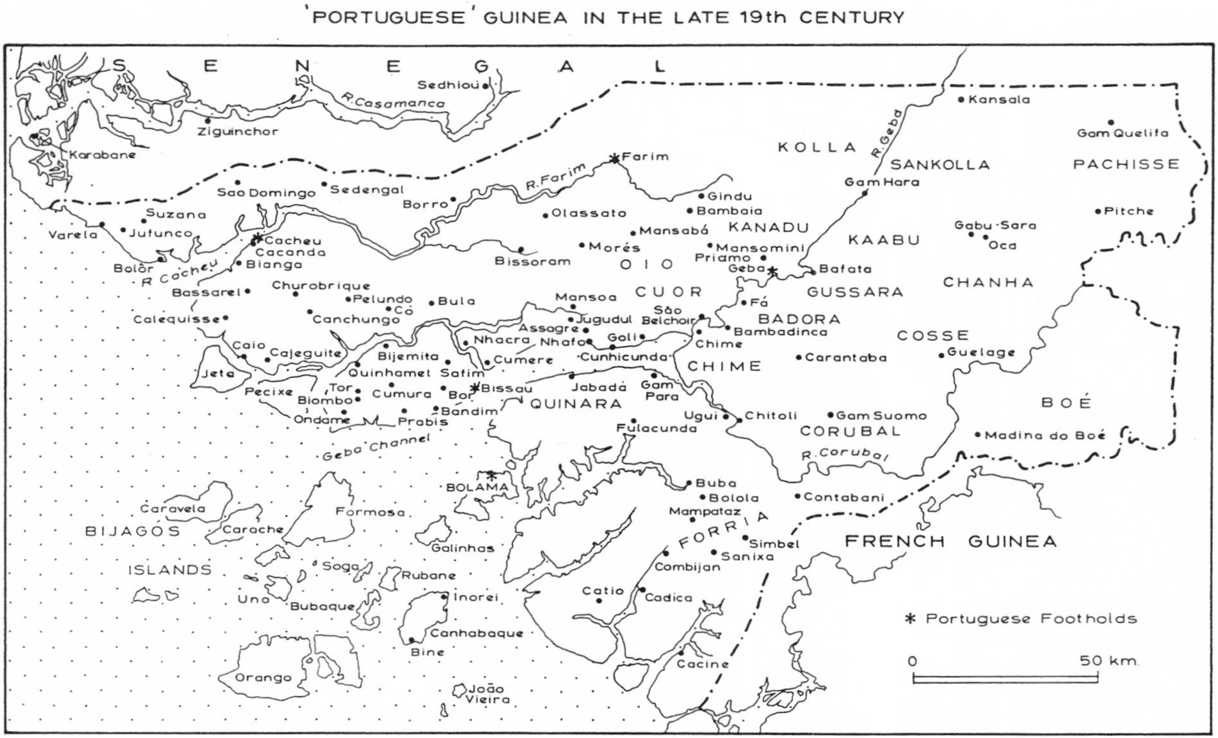

'PORTUGUESE' GUINEA IN THE LATE 19th CENTURY

Map 7. 'Portuguese' Guinea in the Late 19th Century

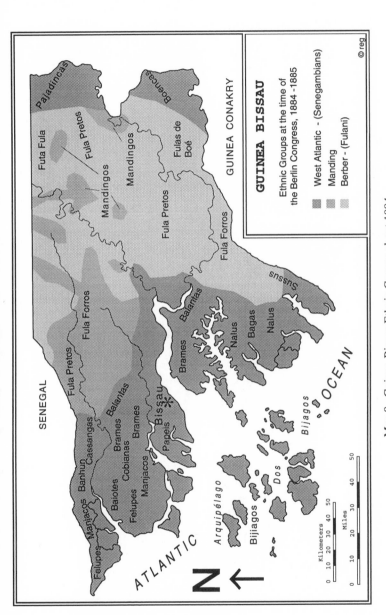

Map 8. Guinea-Bissau Ethnic Groups about 1884

GUINEA BISSAU

Ethnic Groups at the time of
the Berlin Congress, 1884-1885

West Atlantic - (Senegambians)

Manding

Berber - (Fulani)

© reg

SENEGAL

GUINEA CONAKRY

ATLANTIC

OCEAN

Felupes
Manjacos
Banhun
Cassangas
Baiotes
Cobianas
Felupes
Manjacos
Brames
Balantas
Brames
Papeis
Bissau
Fula Pretos
Fula Forros
Balantas
Brames
Nalus
Bagas
Nalus
Sussus
Fula Forros
Fula Pretos
Pajadincas
Futa Fula
Fula Pretos
Mandingos
Mandingos
Mandingos
Fula Pretos
Fulas de
Boé
Boencas

Arquipélago
Bijiagos
Dos
Bijiagos

Kilometers
0 10 20 30 40 50

Miles
0 10 20 30 40 50

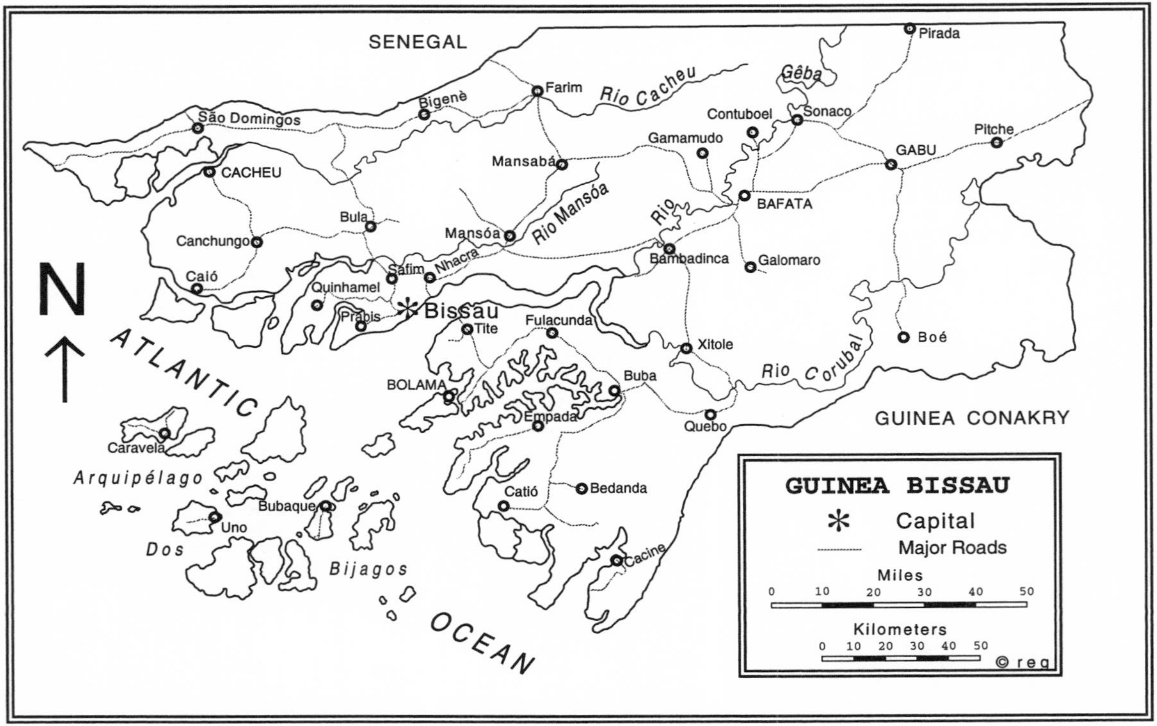

Map 9. Guinea-Bissau: Modern Cities and Towns

Map 10. West Africa Section of Barbarie, Egypte, Nigritie, Guinee, Nubie, Abissinie, by Robert De Vaugondy, Paris, 1780.

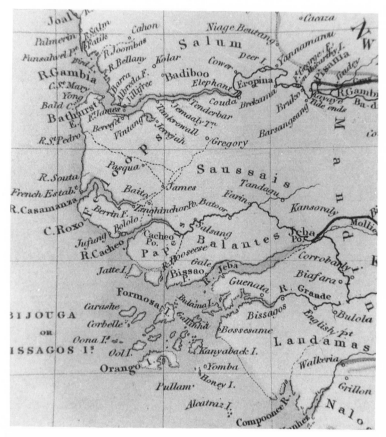

Map 11. West Africa. Published by the Society for the Diffusion of Useful Knowledge, ca. 1850.

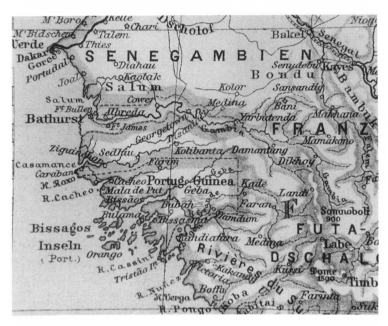

Map 12. Ober-Guinea und West Sudan, Meyers, Bibliographisches Institut Leipzig, ca. 1886.

The Dictionary

A

ABDUL INJAI (ABDOUL NDAIYE). During the colonial wars of 'pacification,' the Portuguese were able to recruit African mercenaries for military service. One of the best known of the late nineteenth and early twentieth century was Senegalese-born Wolof (q.v.) Abdul Injai who served in some of the many punitive missions of Oliveira Musanty and Teixeira Pinto (q.v.) from 1905–1915. These destructive wars were focused mainly against the coastal Senegambian people and the *grumetes* (q.v.). Abdul Injai was involved in the central Guinea-Bissau campaign in 1909 against Infali Sonko (q.v.) and against the Balantas, Mandinkas, Manjacos, and Pepels (q.v.). In 1907, as a result of his attacks in Oio, Abdul Injai was appointed as the *regulo* (q.v.) of Cuor in that region. His harsh rule finally earned him disfavor even with the Portuguese, who sent a military force against him in 1919. He was arrested and deported to the Cape Verde Islands where he died. His collaboration with colonialism came, in later years, to be a metaphor for betrayal.

ABDUL RAHMAN AL-SADI (28 May 1596–?). Al-Sadi was born into an educated Muslim family in Timbuktu, Mali (q.v.) about five years after the Moroccan invasion which brought an end to the Songhai (q.v.) state. For sixty years he was able to record important events of this period. Al-Sadi is the author of *Tarikh As-Sudan*, which, with Alfa Mahmoud Kati's (q.v.) *Tarikh Al-Fettash*, ranks as one of the key documents of the medieval savanna. Al-Sadi's work deals not only with Songhai and the Moroccan invasion, but also with Tuareg, Fula (q.v.), Malian, and Bambara societies, as well as details about trade, politics, religion, and military events. The first draft of this great work of thirty-eight chapters was completed in about

1629 while Al-Sadi held administrative posts which gave him access to key information. He was probably a colleague of Kati, another great savanna chronicler in the mid seventeenth century. While some have found shortcomings in grammar, precision, and style, there are few works which play such a key role in the historiography of this region at the time.

ADMINISTRADOR. The *administrador* was a colonial offical who was the head of a *circunscriçõe* within the *Regime do Indigenato* (q.v.). The *administrador* had the regional power under the Labor Code to recruit by force anyone who could not otherwise provide taxable employment.

AFRICA SQUADRON. From 1843 to 1859 the United States Navy officially sought to curtail the trade in African slaves by establishing the Africa Squadron, a fleet of sailing 'cruisers' used to further the anti-slavery mission by boarding suspected ships and seizing their human cargoes. The Squadron was supposed to function jointly with British ships sailing under similar orders.

This effort had its roots in the 1819 Anglo-American treaty which was an early step toward curbing the slave trade. Officially, the organization of the Squadron continued this earlier policy. Britain had officially abolished the trade in its colonies in 1833, but British slavers were still active. The British portion of the Squadron was based in Sierra Leone. Nevertheless, the British and Americans had not fully healed the wounds of the American Revolution and of the War of 1812, so they were still unable to fully agree to mutual inspection of each other's ships. As a consequence the Squadron was partly shackled in its conception.

Further limitations on its mission had been proposed by United States Senator James DeWolfe of Bristol, Rhode Island. The DeWolfe family, especially James' brother George, was not disinterested; this prominent Rhode Island family had gained great wealth from the slave trade during the preceding years. According to the historian George Brooks, James De-Wolfe was also the father-in-law of a brother of Matthew Perry who was the first Commander of the United States Africa Squadron based in Cape Verde. In 1843, the Secretary of the Navy was Abel B. Upshur who was from the southern States, as were most of his successors. As a result, Upshur assigned poorly-equipped ships carrying only eighty guns for this assignment. If the fifty-one guns of the *USS Constitution,* which sailed with the Squadron in 1853, are subtracted, it is easily seen how inadequate the Squadron was to the job assigned. In addition, a large ship such as the *Constitution* was hardly what was needed to pursue fast, small ships into the West African river systems.

Not surprisingly, Upshur insisted on the conservative policy which gave the highest priority to the protection of American lives, commerce, and ships. This approach added to the limitations on the possible actions of the Squadron captains. Thus, with a structural bias toward southern and slave-trading influences, it is not surprising to learn that the Africa Squadron was largely ineffective.

Moreover, by this time, much of the slaving had moved from the Upper Guinea coast to the Lower Guinea coast at the Slave Coast (Nigeria) and was far from Cape Verde. Given the distances involved, it was rare that more than two ships were actually sailing the very long coast at any point. Those intending to load slaves could either wait until the Squadron cruisers had departed the area, or they could fly the Portuguese flag to circumvent the 1842 protocol which allowed American cruisers to board only American flag ships. There were some instances of Africa Squadron cruisers seizing American slave ships which sailed under the Portuguese flag.

Some of these cruisers were based in São Vicente, others were at São Tiago, such as the cruisers *Preble* and *Jamestown*. During the 1843–45 command of the Squadron by Captain William Perry, only one slaver was reported captured, and this was later freed by a New Orleans court. In Sepember 1844, Perry sailed the *Preble* to Bissau as a show of force to protect American goods and merchants during a local uprising.

For the next decade, under the commands of Commodores Crabbe, George C. Read, Isaac Mayo, and others, no more than one slaver was seized each year. During its sixteen years of operation only nineteen slavers were actually brought to trial; of these, four were released and the others received small fines or light jail terms for the captains. When the Squadron ended in 1859, there were ships carrying 113 guns, but the inflated prices for slaves (given their relative scarcity) still made smuggling irresistably profitable. Brooks points out that even as late as the period between 1859 and 1862, New York still outfitted 170 slaveships, on the very eve of the Civil War with the American South over this issue. This number of slave ships was far more than those from Europe or Cuba at this time.

The long-lasting toleration of slavery was finally reversed only in 1859, when relations with Britain were improved and the slave system was more aggressively opposed by Lincoln to undermine the slave system in the south. After the start of the American Civil War the Africa Squadron was transferred to naval picket duty to blockade southern ports. The Emancipation Proclamation, and the defeat of the Confederacy, brought the formal practice of the slave trade to its extinction by the mid 1860's. *See*: SLAVERY; GUINEA-BISSAU: AMERICAN (USA) RELATIONS.

AFRICANUS, LEO (Al-Hassan ibn Muhammad Al-Wazzan Az-Zayyati ca. 1494–). Leo Africanus is the name by which the famed Moorish geographer is better known. He was probably born in Fez, Morocco to a family of Spanish Arabs exiled after the Spanish Inquisition began in 1492. He traveled as far as Turkey, Songhai (q.v., during the reign of Askia Muhammad) and to Bornu, Wadai, and Egypt. Captured by Sicilians in 1518, he was given protection by Pope Leo X in Rome who valued this traveler's reports. It was in this connection that he gained the name Leo of Africa (Africanus). His work *Description of Africa* was written in Italian and was completed in 1526 but probably not published until 1550. By 1556 translations appeared in Latin and French. These works became the classic, detailed source on medieval Sudanic African empires, such as Mali (q.v.), for many years. This primary data and his incorporation of earlier scholarship added to Portuguese enthusiasm for exploration along the Upper Guinea coast.

AGRICULTURE. Agriculture represents the foundation of Guinea's economic (q.v.) structure, with 87.89 percent of the population involved in agricultural production. Land shortage is not a problem in most areas; many families continue to extend their land holdings or rice fields. While land tenure systems vary notably from region to region, they continue to be regulated by the peasants themselves without outside interference. Unlike other Portuguese colonies, Guinea-Bissau had only a tiny handful of large plantations, and these were placed under state authority after independence. Labor forms vary from individual family units, to collective labor teams, to small units organized by sex or by age group, to single individuals who are at times assisted by task specific mutual aid groups.

Of the major cash crops, eighty percent of the rice is cultivated by the Balantas (q.v.) in the south, while most of the peanuts are grown in the Fula and Mandinka (.v.) dominated regions of Bafatá and Gabu (.v.). However, most peasant farms practice multicropping, integrating various combinations of food and cash crops on their land: rice, millet, *fonio* grain, and beans are a common combination. Other widely cultivated food crops include manioc, sorghum, white potatoes, yams, maize, sugar cane, and numerous types of tropical fruits. Of these food crops, those which are not consumed by the household are bartered or sold in the local market. This is also the case with products culled from trees or wild fruits, palm nuts for oil (q.v.), and wine, cashew nuts, and coconuts.

The anti-colonial war had a massively destructive impact on agricultural production for two reasons: first, up to a quarter of the rural producers fled the country, and many more were forced away from their lands and onto colonially controlled *aldeamentos* (q.v.). This meant that not only a large proportion of the rural work force was displaced, but that extensive soil erosion occurred due to the non-use of arable lands; erosion was especially severe where lands were bombed by the Portuguese. Secondly, much arable land was lost due to the destruction by bombing of numerous riverine dikes. These dikes are necessary to prevent the influx of ocean salt from the riverines onto the rice fields and arable land plots, as salt destroys the arability of the land.

After independence, agricultural and livestock (q.v.) production was hindered by the delayed return of peasant refugees, by the painstaking efforts involved in rejuvenating arable lands damaged by ocean salt and by bombings, and by the lack of governmental assistance provided to peasants in rebuilding the riverine dikes. As a result, less than half the acreage farmed in 1963, before the beginning of the war, is presently under cultivation.

Peanut production, which was revived after the war, fell to 20,000 tons in the drought year of 1980, recovered to 30,000 tons in 1981 and 1982, but then is estimated to have dropped severely in 1983. Rice production was 29,000 tons in 1972 (during wartime); 67,000 tons in 1975; 45,000 in 1976; 30,000 in 1977; 60,000 in 1978; dropped to 34,000 in 1980; rose to 80,000 in 1981 and to 100,000 tons in 1982. Drought (q.v.) and inconsistent rainfall usually accounted for such production fluctuations in the 1970's, although this has been less of a problem since 1980. Marketing opportunities also account for some of the variation in production levels.

Many representatives of the complex of West African crops

may be found in Guinea-Bissau. This complex underlies the establishment of the major Sahelian states of West Africa. Grains include fonio, sorghum, and millet, some Guinea yam, and okra. Calabash gourds, papayas, mangoes, and watermelons are also important. Sudanic or Sahelian crops with commercial usages also include cotton, oil palm, and sesame, with special note given to kola nuts which have been significant as a trade item and in social relations as an offering among elders.

Millet is one of the more important grains in this complex of traditional Sahelian crops, as it is widely considered to be at the foundation of the independent evolution of agriculture in this region in antiquity. There are various names and a confusing taxonomy but one may distinguish bulrush millet (*Pennisetum typhoideum*), which is also known as pearl millet, from sorghum (*Sorghum vulgare*), also known as *durra*. These are all known as *milho* in Portuguese, with local distinctions in terminology by varying color of the grains. These tall grasses resemble American corn (*Zea mays*) at a distance, but bulrush millet grains grow in clusters like a cattail but not on a unified cob. By contrast sorghum grains grow in a tuft formation. Bulrush millet is very hardy and requires little rainfall, while sorghum is more often irrigated but may be grown as a dry land crop.

Very many of the important West African crops are, in fact, native to the Americas and were only introduced in the sixteenth century. Chief among these is maize or American corn, which is well suited to rainy areas or to places cultivated by irrigation. Lima and haricot beans are common American legumes now frequently found in Guinean foods. The diet also includes American crops such as pineapples, pumpkins, squash, tomatoes, and papaya. Native American crops of great importance to Africa also include: cocoa, red pepper, and tobacco. *See* ECONOMICS ENTRIES.

ALDEAMENTO. Fortified village system used by the Portuguese military in Guinea-Bissau to concentrate rural populations behind barbed wire to deny the PAIGC access to the people. In a non-military context the *aldamento* was a Portuguese equivalent of their *encomienda* or *hacienda* system in which extensive land holdings were sold and operated with the people who lived on those lands. Thus it was a system something between outright slavery (q.v.) and sharecropping.

ALFA. This is a generic title of respect among Fula (q.v.) speakers. Among the most famed title holders in Guinea were

Alfa Mahmoud, Alfa Molo, and Alfa Yaya (qq.v.). Traditionally it was used only among select religious or political leaders, but it has become more widely applied in recent decades.

ALFA MAHMOUD KATI (ca. 1525–1593). Kati was one of the main chroniclers of the Songhai (q.v.). He is one of several important Muslim historians of Soninke (q.v.) origin. It is from Kati and several others that we have the early records of the western Sahel. His sometimes title, *Alfa* (q.v.), indicates the respect he was shown by his contemporaries. Evidently he also served as a qadi, or scholar of Islamic jurisprudence, during the time of the Empire of Songhai, especially during the reign of Askia Ishaq II (1588–1591). His most prominent work is his *Tarikh al Fettash* which chronicles the main leaders of Songhai such as Askia Mohammad (1492–1528) and Askia Daoud (1549–1582), as well as its rival Tekrur (q.v.). This is often considered the foundation of the modern history of the Sahel.

ALFA MOLO EGUE BALDE of JIMARA (?- 1881). An elephant hunter of the Bande family of Futa Jallon (q.v.). Alfa Molo led the successful movement against King Janke Walli of the Mandinka state of Kaabu (q.v.) in 1867, thus creating Fuladu (q.v.), the first Fula (q.v.) state in the region between Futa Toro and Futa Jallon (q.q.v.). Fuladu ruled over Kaabu in Guinea-Bissau, as well as the headwaters of the Casamance (q.v.) and the Gambia Rivers. This conquest of Kaabu was achieved as a local sequel to the earlier *jihad* of Al-Haj Al-Mami Umar Tall (q.v.) of Futa Jallon. The success of Alfa Molo was due, in part, to the support he received from the *Qadriyia* brotherhood headed by Alfa Yaya (q.v.), who remained as the higher regional authority.

Alfa Molo was the son of the Al-Mami of Timbo (a Fula province of Futa Jallon). The Islamic history of Timbo can be traced back to at least 1740 when its mosque was first constructed. Its most famous leader was Alfa Karamoko of Timbo (1685–1775) who was a seventh generation Fula immigrant to Futa Jallon.

One of the nineteenth century Al-Mamis of Timbo married a Kaabu princess named Kumancho Sane. Around the time of Alfa Molo's conquest of Kaabu, he also married into the royal family of Kumba Wude but this may have taken place as a result of the conquest. This marriage resulted in at least two sons, Dikori and Musa Molo (q.v.). Upon the death of Alfa

Molo he was replaced by his brother Bakari Demba, until Demba was overthrown in 1893 by Alfa Molo's son Musa Molo who continued the line of Fula dominance.

In establishing the hegemony of the new Fula state, Alfa Molo came into conflict with other Fulas, and the Dumbuya lineage of the Mandinka led by Fodé Kaba, occupying slave trade routes in the Casamance and regions north of the Gambia River. Indeed, Alfa Molo had killed the father of Fodé Kaba in this commercial and political rivalry in about 1870. After his death by disease in 1881 in Guinea-Bissau, Fulas elsewhere in the country staged local revolts. Strong measures taken by Musa Molo temporarily renewed the Fula state, but after 1931 there was no effective, legitimate king.

ALFA YAYA of LABÉ. Alfa Yaya was the chief representative of Fula power in Futa Jallon (.v.), whose rise in power was simultaneous with French penetration from the coast. Although Alfa Yaya had a nominally pro-French position, he sought to use French rule to consolidate his own position, especially between 1891 and 1896. Alfa Yaya's opportunism led to a revolt by his son, resulting in a decisive battle in which Alfa Yaya crushed his opposition. Alfa Yaya was largely responsible for bringing the last wave of Islam into Kaabu (q.v.) in Guinea-Bissau and to Kakande in Boke just over the border in Guinea-Conakry. In signing a French accord on 10 February 1897 he served French interests by the reconquest of other regions of Futa Jallon including Timbu. Based on these divisions, the French administration of Labé was separated from that of Timbo on 18 December 1898.

In 1904 the relationship between Alfa Yaya and the French had soured in a series of jurisdictional disputes including the severance of a portion of Labé province to be transferred to Portuguese control in Guinea-Bissau. Seeing his power being eroded, Alfa Yaya planned an armed revolt against the French, but a spy revealed the plans, leading to Alfa Yaya's arrest and deportation to Dahomey in 1905. After his release in 1910 he made another attempt to organize resistance in 19ll, but this too was blocked by arrest and deportation to Port Etienne where he died.

AL-IMAMI UMAR(U) TALL. See TALL, AL-HAJ AL-IMAMI UMAR.

AL-IMAMI SAMORI TOURE. See TOURE, AL-IMAMI SAMORI.

ARAUJO, JOSÉ EDUARDO F. (15 March 1933–20 January 1992). After his secondary education, Araujo entered the Faculty of Law in the University of Lisbon while in his twenties. He returned to Praia in 1958 but only to travel on to Dakar and Conakry to join his comrades in the PAIGC (q.v.). He long served as a PAIGC militant in many high-ranking capacities, including political commissar of the permanent commission of the southern national committee in Guinea-Bissau during the armed struggle. Araujo was also the head of the PAIGC information section in Conakry and was a member of the Executive Committee of the Struggle, CEL (q.v.), in charge of production. After the reorganization of the CEL, Araujo became Minister of the General Secretariat. Araujo was a member of the team that negotiated for Cape Verdean independence in 1975.

Following independence he became the Organizational Secretary for the PAIGC and a trouble-shooting Minister without portfolio, as well as the Minister of Education and Culture. When he discovered that the 1992 annual celebration of National Heroes Day had a diminished role for Amilcar Cabral (q.v.), he became so upset that he was stricken with a heart attack and died that same day. Araujo is buried in Varzea cemetery in Praia.

ARMAZÉNS DO POVO, (People's Stores). During the period of the nationalist war, the PAIGC had two main points in its economic program. On the one hand, it sought to halt the Portuguese use of Guinean exports and to force a heavier reliance on imports, thereby raising the economic costs of continuing colonialism. On the other hand, the PAIGC aimed at launching a small scale export and import economy for the liberated zones. The system of People's Stores operated to address these two points and improve the market system in the liberated zones. Imported items included textiles, machetes, hoe blades, blankets, salt, sugar, cigarettes, tobacco, bicycles, pots, sewing machines, string, matches, flash lights, soap, needles, thread, paper, sandals, buttons, and fish nets, to name a number of the more popular items. By 1973 about thirty-two People's Stores were in operation in many areas of the countryside and in the frontier regions.

This integrated economic system strictly excluded cash but determined fixed exchange equivalents for agricultural produce and other items generated in Guinea-Bissau. For example, one kilogram of rice could be exchanged for one kilogram of sugar or for clothing which could be tailor made at the larger People's Stores. Three kilograms of rice would be worth a pair of trousers. A pair of women's shoes was equivalent to 15 kgs. of rice, or 1 meter of crocodile skin could be converted to 2 kgs. of rice. Although rice was the main staple exchanged, exports of the People's Stores also included peanuts, palm oil, ivory, hides, honey, beeswax, kola nuts, palm nuts, sesame seeds, and corn. The export of kola nuts was the greatest export earner by value, but rice was the major export by volume, which, in 1971, represented 668,511 kgs. In the late 1960's and early 1970's exports generally increased with the export high in 1971 put at about 4.25 million *escudos* ($145,000 U.S.). While this sum was not large in absolute terms, the bulk of trade through the People's Stores was by barter with no cash flow. The degree to which the needs of the people of Guinea-Bissau could be met through the People's Stores denied an additional market to the colonial economy.

The embryonic People's Stores system, developed during the struggle, underwent major expansion in the post-independence period to provide for the state distribution and regulation of basic commodities. Until being dismantled through the sweeping privatization measures, there were more than 125 People's Stores. The system had incorporated the former Casa Gouveia commercial chain operated for Portuguese interests. *See* AGRICULTURE; ECONOMICS; ECONOMICS; LIVESTOCK; OIL PALM; PEANUTS; RICE.

ARMED FORCES. *See* FORÇAS ARMADAS.

ARMÉE DE LIBERATION NACIONALE GUINÉENE (ALNG). The armed branch of the Frente de Luta Pela Independência Nacional da Guiné-Bissau (q.v., FLING), formed shortly after 1962. There is little evidence about the strength of the ALNG, but it saw combat only on the rarest of occasions and exclusively in the area of Guinea-Bissau near the western Casamance.

ASKIA MOHAMMAD. Ruler of Songhai (1493–1528). *See* SONGHAI.

ASSEMBLÉIA NACIONAL POPULAR (ANP), People's National Assembly. The ANP was first constituted in the liberated territories between August and October 1972, a year before the end of the armed phase of the independence struggle. The population involved selected 273 regional councillors who, in turn, elected 91 of their peers to serve as National Assemly deputies. Both voting procedures consisted of yes/no balloting for a single candidate who had been previously selected by the party in the course of discussions with the local populace. The 91 elected deputies were combined with 21 deputies appointed by the party and five representatives of the party youth group to form a total ANP of 120 delegates. The ANP passes laws, ratifies decrees, and can revise the constitution. At the first meeting of the ANP on 24 September 1973 in the liberated zones of Guinea-Bissau (during the war) it adopted the Constitution and elected officers and ministers for the Council of State. At this meeting, acting as the President of the ANP, 'Nino' Vieira proclaimed the independence of Guinea-Bissau.

In April 1975 the ANP held its first meeting after liberation. In December 1976 the same electoral procedures were repeated, but membership of the second ANP was expanded to 147, with two thirds selected by the party. This ANP was disbanded immediately following the 1980 *coup d'état* of N. Vieira, but a third ANP, with 150 members, was formed through elections held in March and April 1984.

The People's National Assembly is officially the highest political body in Guinea-Bissau, but in fact, from 1972 to 1979 and since 1984, it convened and continues to meet only once a year for several days and does not wield substantial political power, most of which lies with top level party and state structures. With the introduction of multi-party democracy, a 100–member ANP is planned. *See* APPENDIX: OFFICIALS OF GUINEA-BISSAU.

ASSIMILADOS. With the Colonial Act of 1930, just prior to the onset of Salazar's rule and while he was Minister of the Colonies, the status of *assimilado* was assigned to those *indigenas* in the Portuguese African colonies whose cultural standards of literacy, education, financial position, or other criteria would entitle them to fuller rights as Portuguese citizens. This designation was to elevate a very select few from the classification of *indigena*, also described in the Act of 1930, which applied to the vast majority of the African colonial populations, making them wards of the State who were denied their civil rights including the right to vote. This Act relegated them to the lowest paying jobs and inferior schools and subjected them to a head tax, restricted movement, and more severe and arbitrary punishment within the criminal justice system.

Because Cape Verdeans have some cultural similarity to the Portuguese, they were considered to be *assimilados* and therefore were citizens of Portugal and entitled access to Portuguese state schooling. Consequently, they tended to be somewhat better educated than other peoples of Lusophone Africa, and many participated in Portuguese colonialism as public administrators and civil servants throughout the other colonies. However, a close examination of the reality of the *assimilados'* political and economic position reveals a situation of discriminatory policies, limited civil rights, and inequality of opportunity.

The status of *assimilado* was offered to those Africans in the colonies who wanted recognition, empowerment, and social mobility. On the other hand, anyone of European ancestry, no matter how high or low their station, had no need to aspire to assimilation, as it was a birth right. Africans, and, to a lesser degree, Cape Verdeans, needed education, property, and unquestioned obedience to a state which negated their being and cultural history. There were many who were willing to pay even this price, but as this struggle for a new legitimacy advanced some of those who resisted found a new resolve to go their own way. Foremost among these was Amilcar Cabral (q.v.) who suggested that the price might include "class suicide" and that national liberation was, above all, "an act of cultural liberation." Overall, the small numbers of *assimilados* show that this policy was never meant to transform the entire population. *See* REGIME DO INDIGENATO.

AZAMBUJA, DIEGO DA. Portuguese knight under the reign of Dom João II (1477, 1481–95) who was charged with West African coastal exploration, trading for gold, and the rapid construction of the São Jorge Al-Mina fortress on the Gold Coast. Materials and specialist craftsmen were brought from Portugal in December 1481 in ten caravels with some 500 soldiers. The project was completed by the end of 1482 to guard the Portuguese trade in slaves and gold until the arrival of the Dutch in the 1630's. The gold from Al-Mina and elsewhere on the Guinea coast was vital in the financing of the Portuguese economy and explorations of the period.

AZURARA, GOMES EANES DE. A well-known fifteenth century chronicler for Prince Henry (q.v.). Although written in support of the architects of the great age of Portuguese exploration and expansion, the works of Azurara are considered a basic source in the documentation and chronology of this period. He wrote of the 1415 Ceuta campaign in the "Key to the Mediterranean." In 1453 he wrote "Crónica de Guine" which described some of the earliest seizing of Africans and African resistance to the predations of the early slavers.

B

BA. *See* TENGUELLA, COLI.

BADIUS. Badius are so-called as a corruption of the Portuguese 'vadios' (meaning vagrants or wanderers). They are the African origin peasantry of Cape Verde and especially of the interior of São Tiago and Fogo islands. They are descended primarily from runaway slaves and have retained a certain degree of cultural distinctiveness in their customs, folklore, religious practices, and dialect of *Crioulo*. Living in remote regions and maintaining a social distance from the rest of the population during the centuries of colonial rule, the *badius* were the least assimilated to Portuguese culture by comparison with other Cape Verdeans. They were viewed as the primary representatives of an African heritage and, as such, have historically been denigrated by the colonial authorities and looked down upon by other Cape Verdeans. African *funco* house styles, *pano* (q.v.) cloth weaving, mortar and pestle grinding, African dance patterns, and many other traits continue to affirm the *badiu* linkage with the people of the Upper Guinea coast.

The few known instances of slave and peasant rebellions in Cape Verde were usually among the *badiu* populations, giving them a certain notoriety in popular mythology that has engendered a mixture of disdain and admiration toward this so-called 'primitive' social group. Perhaps becuse of the threat that they once posed to the colonial authorities in resisting assimilation, the *badius* were more likely to have been recruited for contract labor, and they provided the backbone of forced emigration to the cacão plantations in the Portuguese islands of São Tomé and Príncipe.

BAFATÁ. Bafatá is the capital town of the eastern region of the same name. It is the second largest city in Guinea-Bissau and one of the most important commercial centers, with a population of about 46,300 people (1991 Census), composed mainly of Fulas and Mandinkas (qq.v.). At the confluence of the rivers Geba (q.v.) and Colufe, it is about 153 kilometers from Bissau (q.v.). Bafatá means, in the Mandinka language, both 'death of river' and 'river is full,' an allusion to a kind of estuary. On the most elevated part of the country is the birthplace of the famous Amilcar Cabral (q.v.). It was here, two years before this African revolutionary was born, that his father, Juvenal Cabral (q.v.), a primary school teacher, made a passionate plea to the visiting Governor Jorge Frederico Velez Caroco, on 2 April 1922, for the provision of more schools and the development of education in the colony.

Bafatá started as a tiny *tabanca* (village) founded, according to oral tradition, by Malam Santi, a decorated Mandinka veteran of Portuguese 'pacification' campaigns, from nearby Geba. The settlement was of little importance until the headquarters of the Residency of Geba, established on 3 September 1906, was transferred there from the old and decaying *presídio* of Geba (some twelve kilometers to the west) in 1907. It was this year that the campaign against Infali Sonco (q.v.), the rebellious Beafada (q.v.) ruler of Cuor, whose realm was now part of the recently established residency, was launched. The important role played by the notorious Senegalese mercenary Abdul Injai (q.v.) resulted in his nomination as *regulo* (q.v.) (Portuguese-appointed 'native' ruler) of Cuor by Governor João Augusto de Oliveira Muzanty. Shortly after the end of the campaign, which resulted in Sonco abandoning his territory, Vasco de Sousa Calvet de Magalhães, a veteran of the war against the rebellious African ruler as well as many 'pacification' campaigns, became the new resident.

Bafatá is said to owe its urbanization to this man, who was known locally as "Comandant Djaingol," which in the Fulbe language means 'Commandant Fire' (an allusion to the fiery or bad-tempered nature of this colonial official). With forced labor, he supervised the construction of public buildings, the port, the Moorish style central market, and *inter alia*, the bridge over the river Colufe (thereby connecting the town to Bambadinca, an important commercial center about thirty kilometers southwest).

In 1917, with a population of around 1,000 inhabitants (about half of them Europeans, Lebanese, and *Civilizados*), Bafatá acquired the status of a town. With the final 'pacification' of the mainland in 1915, great efforts were made to consolidate Portuguese sovereignty economically, by means of a policy of strict official control of internal commerce through a series of regulations effectively concentrating a large proportion of the domestic trade into officially-designated *centros comerciais* (trading centers). Peanuts (known locally as *mancarra*), cotton, and rubber were the main items of trade before the protracted armed liberation struggle paralyzed trading activities. Bafatá became the second principal trading center, with a large population of Lebanese who began to arrive in notable numbers at the beginning of the century and who, by 1950, owned half of the commercial establishments there. Local branches of particularly large Portuguese and French trading companies like *Companhia União Fabril* (CUF, [q.v.] represented locally as *Casa Gouveia*), *Barbosa e Comandita,* and *Compagnie Français de l'Afrique Occidentale* (CFAO) were established there.

Although today there are no branches of European or other foreign trading houses, trade is still very important and has, since the liberalization of the economy in the late 1980's, been growing steadily. It remains an important center for artisan activities such as basket weaving, cloth weaving, shoemaking, ropemaking, pottery manufacture, the production of batiks and, among other things, wood sculpting. It is where the country's only modern factory producing high quality bricks and rooftiles is located.

BAGAS. The Bagas are a village-living, early Senegambian (q.v.) people found in the southwestern coastal area of Guinea-Bissau and adjacent Guinea-Conakry. The Bagas certainly pre-date the Susus (q.v.) who came to dominate the region and generally assimilate the Bagas. The Susus had been expelled from interior regions in Fula jihads of the eighteenth and nineteenth centuries.

BAIOTES. A numerically small group of the Diola (q.v.) cluster of the Senegambian (q.v.) littoral people. Their concentration is in the southern Casamance area and in northwestern Guinea-Bissau, around the town of Suzanna, as well as on both banks of the Cacheu River (q.v.) adjacent to the ocean. The Baiotes are related to the Felupes (q.v.), the other member of the Diola cluster. The Baiotes depend on rice (q.v.) cultivation and have acephalous political organization, although there are instances of local petty chiefs. They and the Felupes were especially exposed and vulnerable to Mandinka (q.v.) and *lançado* (q.v.)

slavers. Particularly high numbers of these people were exiled as slaves.

BALAFON. The music (q.v) of Guinea-Bissau often includes the *balafon* or xylophone played by the Mandinka (q.v.) people throughout the Western Sahel. The name originates from the words *"bala"* (wood) and *"fo"* (to speak) and refers to a family of instruments including some with just a few keys to wooden xylophones with seventeen to twenty-two keys. The keys are made from the wood of African rosewood trees and divide the octave into seven equidistant pitches. The *griots* (q.v.) of West Africa often use the *balafon* or *kora* (a stringed instrument) in their performances.

Because of the remarkable similarity between xylophones in Africa and those in Southeast Asia, it has been proposed that the instrument originated in Asia and was carried across the Indian Ocean to East Africa beginning about 1,000 B.C. The use of the xylophone gradually diffused along the trade routes and was eventually taken up by people all over Africa including the Mandinka. (S. Hurley-Glowa).

BALANTAS (Balantes). The Balantas are the largest single ethnic group of Guinea-Bissau. The Balantas are members of the Senegambian (q.v.) cultural stock, Atlantic sub-family of the Niger-Congo (q.v.) language stock. The Balanta people are generally egalitarian in socio-political organization, but some areas have local chiefs. Today they are found mainly in areas nearer the coast, although they once occupied the interior until the Mandinka (q.v.) expansion, which drove the acephalous Senegambians to the coastal areas. Large Balanta concentrations are in the central northern area west of Farim (q.v.) and northeast of Bissora and in coastal southern areas in the hinterland around Catio. They are, in short, located both north and south of the River Geba (q.v.). Virtually all Balanta are non-Islamic rice (q.v.) cultivators.

Numerous campaigns of subjugation were directed against the Balanta in the periods 1883–1885, 1891–1910 and 1912–1915 until they were brought under nominal Portuguese control. As one of the most oppressed groups in Guinea-Bissau, the Balanta were particularly heavily involved in the nationalist struggle between 1963 and 1974. The 1950 census counted 146,300 people as Balanta or 29.1 percent of the total population. In 1960 the population of Balanta was estimated at 250,000, but the 1979 population census sets the figure at 200,874, representing 27.2 percent of the total population.

BALDE. *See* ALFA MOLO EGUE BALDE; MUSA MOLO.

BAMBARAS. A relatively large member of the Mandinka (q.v.) concentrated on the Upper Niger in Mali (q.v.), where they are often occupied as slightly Islamized fishing people. In the third quarter of the seventeenth century the Bambaras revolted against the rule of Mali (q.v.) and created the two independent states of Segou and Kaarta which absorbed the local remnants of the Empire of Mali. Between 1670 and 1810 the Bambaras controlled Djenne, and they briefly held Timbuktu. The Bambara influence declined after this period and from 1854 to 1861 Fula (q.v.) jihads destroyed the Bambara states. In Guinea-Bissau there are very small concentrations of these animistic peoples in the vicinity of Gabú (q.v.).

BANA. Adriano Gonçalves, commonly known as "Bana," is one of the best known recording artists from Cape Verde, whose music is popular in Guinea-Bissau. He was born 11 March 1932 in Mindelo, São Vicente and has been singing for fifty years. Since 1959, he has been featured in forty-five recordings, six CD's, and four films. A giant of a man at nearly two meters tall, he has a deep, resonant voice that is much admired and imitated, and his interpretations of *mornas* and *coladeras* have set the standard for years to come. Since 1959, Bana has lived and worked in France and Holland, finally moving to Portugal in the seventies. Over the years, he opened several clubs in Lisbon that became Cape Verdean meeting points, with music and cuisine from the islands. His most recent restaurant is called Monte Cara. In quasi-retirement now, Bana has finally moved back to Mindelo and has opened a nightclub there where he and others regularly perform Cape Verdean music. (S. Hurley-Glowa).

BANCO NACIONAL ULTRAMARINO (BNU, Overseas National Bank). The BNU was a major Portuguese banking organization set up in Lisbon in 1864 and in Cape Verde in 1868. A branch of the BNU was first established in Guinea-Bissau in Bolama (q.v.) in 1903. The BNU monopolized banking in Guinea-Bissau during the colonial period.

The BNU Board of Directors was in intimate association with the colonial administration, having two former colonial secretaries as well as major shareholders associated with the *Companhia União Fabril* (CUF) (q.v.) and its overseas linkages. In addition, the BNU had significant association with finance capital in Paris, Madrid, and London. Net profit during a typical colonial year (e.g., 1963) was some $3 million USD with dividends commonly at nine percent from colonial investments. The BNU was also associated with the major insurance firm, *Companhia de Seguros a Mundial*. In Guinea-Bissau the BNU was represented by the *Sociedade Comercial Ultramarina*, which was second only to the "Casa Gouveia" Corporation, an affiliate of CUF in Guinea which was owned by António da Silva Gouveia who dominated trade and commerce in Guinea. With such connections, the BNU had a central role in Guinean economics (q.v.) including agriculture, transport, petro-chemicals, oil-processing and rice-processing in Guinea-Bissau and Cape Verde. After independence there were deep divisions between Lisbon and Bissau over the terms of repatriating BNU capital. Guinea-Bissau nationalized the BNU in February 1975 and renamed it the Banco Nacional da Guinea-Bissau (BNG). The BNG was originally established as the BNU, and ended the *escudo* currency which was replaced by the new *peso* of Guinea.

BANYUNS (BANHUNS, BAINUK). This very small Senegambian (q.v.) group is closely related to the Casangas (q.v.) and the Cobianas and may be found in the southern Casamance (q.v.) area, just to the northeast of Cacheu (q.v.). It seems clear that the ancestors of the Banyun were living far more extensively in the same region even well before the fourteenth century expansion of Mali (q.v.). At this earlier time they were found on both banks of the Gambia and most of northern and northeastern Guinea-Bissau. During the period of Mandinka (q.v.) expansion the Banyuns were pushed toward the coast and were largely absorbed by the Diolas, Manjacos, and Balantas (qq.v.). The small numbers of Banyun are the dispersed remnants from the centuries of slavery (q.v.), Mandinka (q.v.) dominance and acculturation, and nineteenth century Fula (q.v.) jihads. While the Banyuns are acephalous, agricultural animists, the related Casangas (q.v.) developed a secondary kingship structure with a capital at Brikama.

To regional Muslims, the term Banyun came to connote a perjorative "infidel." As such, in times of a regional war or jihad, the Banyun were often seized as prisoners of war who were sold as slaves to *lançados* (q.v.) along the coast. The

Banyuns and Casangas were known as skilled weavers and dyers. In the late sixteenth century the Casangas became active slave hunters and expanded into Banyun territory, assimilating many of these people. The term Casamance (q.v.) is said to be derived from Kassa-Mansa, the Casanga ruler at Brikama. The more the Casangas expanded, the more the Banyun were decimated and dispersed.

BARBOSA, RAFAEL PAULA (1924–). Barbosa was born in Safim, near Bissau (q.v.) of a Guinean mother and Cape Verdean father. He was employed in Bissau as a public works foreman when he and Amilcar Cabral (q.v.) and several others joined to form the PAIGC (q.v.) in 1956. Barbosa operated under the nom de guerre of Zain Lopes as the President of the Central Committee of the PAIGC until his arrest on 13 March 1962 by the Portuguese in Bissau (where he was carrying out his revolutionary activities). He was initially tortured and then released by the Portuguese on 3 August 1969 after seven years of imprisonment. His confinement led him to compromising positions from the viewpoint of the PAIGC which expelled him from the party in April 1970. He had still been considered the President of the PAIGC until February 1964.

After winning state power, the PAIGC charged Barbosa with high crimes against the state and party, having implicated him in the assassination of Amilcar Cabral. At the conclusion of his trial on 8 October 1976, he was sentenced to death for his anti-PAIGC and pro-Spinola (q.v.) statements and activities. On 4 March 1977, his death sentence was commuted to fifteen years at hard labor. In the move toward democratization Barbosa has reappeared as the leader of the Frente Democrática Social (q.v.).

BARRETO, COL. HONÓRIO PEREIRA. (24 April 1813–1859). Barreto, born in Cacheu (q.v.), was the son of a Cape Verdean official (João Pereira Barreto) of the Cacheu garrison and a well connected Afro-Portuguese businesswoman who also dealt in slaves (Rosa de Carvalho Alvarenga) from the *presídio* of Ziguinchor. (q.v.) Educated in Lisbon from a very young age, Honório Barreto was a passionate Lusophile, despite being, in his own words, "a man of color." With a new administrative reorganization which created the *Prefeitura de Cabo Verde e Costa da Guiné* in 1832, he was nominated in 1834 at the young age of twenty-one, *provedor* (purveyor) of the Concelho of Cacheu, which was a subdivision of the Comarca (District) of

Guinea, now headquarted in Bissau (q.v.) due in part to the strategic and defensive limitations of Cacheu. Three years later, Barreto was Governor of the District of Guinea, zealously defending Portugal's "historical rights of discovery and conquest." He is believed to be the first Governor of Guinea of Cape Verdean origins.

Immediately, he launched a protracted and bitter war of words against the French 'usurpers' in the Casamance. But at the same time, he was also much troubled about the conditions of the *praças*, *presídios*, and *gentios insolentissimos* ("very uppity pagans"). His famous work, *Memoria Sobre O Etado Actual de Senegambia Portugueza* (1843), is not only the most scathing criticism of Portuguese administration in the "possession" of Guinea, but it is among the best contemporary accounts of the nature of the Luso-Guinean encounter.

According to Barreto, in Cacheu, as elsewhere in Guinea, the *gentios insolentissimos* generally dominated the Portuguese with "insults, injuries and even murders" (H. P. Barreto 1843:6). He complained bitterly that here the Portuguese remained not only subjected to the "unreasonable demands" and tax exactions of the local rulers but indeed to a differential treatment vis à vis other Europeans. Specifically, all Portuguese ships entering the Port of Cacheu were obliged to pay to each of the two local rulers double the amount of duty the French and the English were charged.

BATTUTA, IBN. This great Muslim traveler and geographer gave much information and inspiration about Africa and the Middle East to the Medieval world. In 1355 he delivered a series of lectures in Grenada which sparked great interest among the Portuguese, Spanish, and Moors, such as Abdul Rahman Al-Sadi and Leo Africanus (qq.v.), about the riches of Sahelian Africa.

BATUKO, BATUCO, BATUQUE. *Batuko* is a music and dance *genre* performed by women (q.v.) of rural *badiu* (q.v.) communities of São Tiago. Of all the musics of Cape Verde, *batuko* has the strongest resemblance to traditions from mainland Africa in its dance style, rhythmic organization, and call-and-response structure. *Batuko* is generally performed by a group of women who sit in a semi-circle with rolled-up *panos* (q.v.) held between their thighs. They beat contrasting rhythmic patterns on these *panos*, creating a polyrhythmic texture through the juxtaposition of twos against threes with beats called *bam-bam* and *rapica*. One person acts as the leader, beginning and ending songs in a call-and-response style common in African music. *Batuko* song lyrics cover a wide range of topics but are usually limited to only a few phrases that are repeated at length by the leader and chorus. Songs can be either improvised on the spot by the group leader or have a fixed melody and text. Group members sing choruses, beat rhythms on their *panos*, and take turns as solo dancers. Dancers stand in the middle of the semi-circle and begin by moving slowly to the music, gradually picking up energy and speed leading to a climax of activity called *tchabeta*, signified by the dancer's rapid hip movements and the strong singing and energetic pounding on the *panos* by the rest of the group. During the dance, attention is focused on the hips, which are accentuated by a low-slung *panos* tied around them. The hips gyrate in rapid, staccato movements that are sexually suggestive. At the end of each song, the dancer selects the next dancer by giving her the *pano* or placing it around her.

There are several folk theories about the origins of *batuko*. One suggests that *batuko* came about when colonial lords offered guests their pick of female slaves for sexual pleasure during a visit. The *batuko* dance was thought to be a way of displaying the charms of the various women to aid the guests in making a selection. A second theory maintains that *batuko* evolved as a means for women to cope with the loss of their men—through death, departure to work abroad, or simple desertation for other women. Some say that *badiu* women dance to purge themselves of their grief and that a night of singing and dancing until dawn brings inner peace and happiness.

In communities with active ensembles, girls learn to perform *batuko* at an early age and are taught that it is something to be taken seriously. Some of the best dancers are very young girls, although women of all ages, even women in their seventies and eighties, are valued ensemble members. As life styles are changing in Cape Verde, fewer young women from the villages in the interior are learning *batuko* and the tradition may become extinct in coming years. (S. Hurley-Glowa).

BAUXITE. *See* COMPANHIA LUSITANA DO ALUMINIO DA GUINE E ANGOLA; MINERALS.

BEAFADAS (Biafadas). This formerly non-Islamic Senegambian (q.v.) group once occupied the Kaabu (q.v.) area until their

fourteenth or fifteenth century expulsion and major acculturation by the Mandinkas (q.v.). At these earlier dates, the Beafadas ranged from the coast near Bolama (q.v.) through a broad
central region and even beyond the northeast corner of modern
Guinea-Bissau. Subsequently, the Beafadas acquired many
Mandinka characteristics, including the system of secondary
kingship, especially in the sixteenth century and thereafter
when they were tributaries to the Empire of Mali (q.v.). Probably in the seventeenth or eighteenth centuries, during the
period of intense slave wars, the Beafadas were pushed, or
retreated, further westward to the coast as refugees from
Kaabu (q.v.).

In the nineteenth century the Beafadas successfully resisted
the incursions of the Fulas of Futa Jallon (qq.v) and forced
them to divert to the northeast of the Beafada territory. The
period of Portuguese colonial penetration was met by numerous instances of Beafada resistance (q.v.) in the period 1880–
1882, 1886, 1900, and in the period 1907–1908 before they were
considered "pacified."

During these retreats or migrations, the Beafadas drove a
wedge in the Balanta (q.v.) population already resident there.
Today there are very few Beafadas in any part of eastern
Guinea-Bissau, and their much smaller numbers are mainly in
the Fulacunda-Buba area on the south bank of the Rio Grande
(Geba, q.v.). Another small group of Beafadas are found in the
area near the border with Guinea-Conakry at Guiledge (q.v.).

BEAVER, PHILLIP. *See* BOLAMA.

BERLIN CONGRESS. In the winter of 1884–1885 the major
European powers of the time met in Berlin to organize the
colonial partition of Africa. The Congress was dominated by
France and England, but claims to African territory were made
by Portugal (q.v.), Germany, Italy, Spain, and Belgium. This
meeting, called for by Portugal, launched the 'scramble for
Africa' which triggered an era of military conquest and subjugation by European powers in order to support their claims of
effective occupation and control which generated prolonged
African resistance (q.v.).

The basic configuration of modern African national boundaries has largely descended from the Berlin Congress, with
various local adjustments made throughout the colonial era.
Before the Congress, the European ruling classes had, in
general, neglected Africa as too expensive for permanent set-

tlement, and there was remarkably little knowledge of the people and resources of the interior at that time. The age of European exploration of Africa was taking place mainly in the period just prior to and after the Berlin Congress. Many of the present African conflicts have roots in the arbitrary borders drawn a century ago.

BEZERRA, ANTÓNIO DE BARROS. Bezerra was appointed as the Captain-Major of Cacheu (q.v.) in about 1676 after the formation of the *Companhia de Cacheu, Rios e Comércio da Guiné*. He was a seasoned Portuguese trader of thirty-five years' experience in the region and a principal shareholder of the *Companhia*. He was a bellicose man who, upon assuming office, immediately set about implementing the monopolization and entrenchment plans for Cacheu. Viewing the objectives of the Portuguese as bold challenges to their power and privileges, the local rulers naturally became restless. The attempt to restrict trade was also much resented by the local African, Afro-Portuguese, and Portuguese traders, for whom it meant diminished profits or even bankruptcy. The uncompromising stance of the local rulers, as well as the hostility, particularly of the independent-minded Afro-Portuguese traders, brought about the arrest of Captain-Major Bezerra, and his subsequent imprisonment in São Tiago, in 1682, just before the expiration of the *Companhia*'s contract at Cacheu. Though the Captain-Major was apparently a victim of the Governor of Cape Verde's anti-corruption measures, the dissolution of the monopoly company itself was attributed mainly to the lack of control in Cacheu. Bezerra was subsequently replaced by Captain-Major José Gonçalves de Oliveira.

BIJAGOS (BIDYOGOS, BIJAGOS, BIJEGAS, BISSAGOS, BO-JAGOS, BUJAGOS). This ethnic stock is the principal group which occupies the islands of the same name on the Atlantic coast of Guinea-Bissau (11°15'N; 16° 05'W). The Bijagós archipelago must not be confused with the Cape Verde archipelago, since both were offshore islands under Portuguese colonial administration. The main islands include Bubaque, Canhabaque, Caravela, Carache, Formosa, Grande, Orango, and Soga. The Bijagós people are animists with petty chiefdoms probably derived from the adjacent mainland, since they have certain affinities with the Diolas, Cocolis, Nalus, Pajadincas, and Pepels (qq.v.). At present their economy is largely derived from fishing and palm products.

The fiercely independent Bijagós peoples were not "pacified" by the Portuguese until as late as 1936 and were distinguished among the peoples of Guinea-Bissau for the persistence of their opposition to foreign penetration and colonial rule. Their earliest resistance can date to the very first Portuguese exploration in the fifteenth century. A Portuguese attack on Canhabaque in the Bijagós likewise failed in 1550. The Bijagós people are famed for their *almadias* (large, ocean-going canoes holding up to seventy people). These fast-moving vessels enabled them to conduct liberal raids on the coast with little fear of retaliation during the time of slavery (q.v.). During the seventeenth and eighteenth centuries, Portuguese slavers could sometimes take advantage of the Bijagós' rivalries with other Senegambians (q.v.) who were captured and traded to the Portuguese arriving in the Bijagós Islands with a healthy respect for Bijagós autonomy.

In the period 1840 to 1850 the Bijagós again mounted a stiff resistance (q.v.) against European intrusion, and they were certainly not under effective Portuguese control. The British and French called on the Portuguese to suppress these people, but the Portuguese were unable to meet this request. In 1849 the British and French organized a joint 'punitive' raid on the islands with three ships and more than fifty soldiers. After meeting with strong opposition they too withdrew. Additional recorded instances of largely unsuccessful attempts to suppress the Bijagós "tax revolts" occurred in 1900, 1906, during the Teixeira Pinto (q.v.) campaigns of 1913–1915, in 1917, 1918, 1924, and in 1936 with the subjugation of the people of Canhabaque. The relative isolation of the Bijagós from mainland scrutiny made the twentieth-century colonial experience a reign of terror.

Finally under colonial rule, the Bijagós were not only subject to the diverse colonial taxes and the *Regime do Indigenato* (q.v.), but they were subject to heavy abuses in forced 'native' labor for the harvesting of palm fruits which were grown throughout the archipelago, but especially at Bubaque and Caravela. The fruits produced both palm kernels and palm oil. The *Companhia Agricola e Fabril da Guiné* was central to this Bijagós industry. An Englishman, Isaac Thomas Hawkins, started this enterprise in 1920 at the *tabanca* of Am-maquina ('place of the machine') in Soga to extract palm oil from palm kernels. Generally the company was quite successful and persisted throughout the period of twentieth-century colonial rule. Acting upon this model, other Europeans created the

Sociedade Agricola do Gambiel, the *Companhia Agricola de Fá*, and the *Companhia Estrela de Farim*.

According to the elders of Eticoba, five years after the establishment of the palm *fabrica*, the enterprise was sold by Hawkins to a German group which closed the operation at Soga and built a new *fabrica* on Bubaque. The renewed form began functioning in 1925 with some Portuguese participation and a monopoly on all kernel and oil production in the Bijagós archipelago including the additional islands of Eguba, Rubane, and Enu.

It was an extremely rigid and repressive system. Forced labor was the means used to build the *fabrica*, to supply the palm fruits, and to work the machinery for extracting palm oil and for crushing the palm nuts.

In Soga, as in Bubaque, Formosa, Caravela, and Carache, the forced recruitment of the tree climbers who cut the palm fruits affected all island *tabancas*. The palm fruits are known as *chabeu* (in Crioulo). For the system to function, the labor needs of the *fabrica* would be transmitted to the colonial authorities, who would pass the requests on to the collaborating *regulos* (q.v.) and *chefes de tabancas*, who would, in turn produce the required number of tree climbers. According to the *homens grandes* of Formosa, the *chefes de posto* in Abu would receive orders from his superior, the *administrador* (q.v.) of the Bijagós region, in Bubaque, for every *tabanca* on the island (today there are fourteen) to send five healthy men to Bubaque to gather *chabeu* for the *fabrica*. This request would be passed on to the *authoridades gentilicas* who finally used over zealous *cipaios* (African strongarm enforcers) who would enormously facilitate the request even if sadistic maltreatment was needed to accomplish the recruitment.

The "contract" between the *fabrica* and forced laborers could last as little as one month, but it could be extended to two, three, or six months or an entire season (January to August). Most lasted only a month or two, since another objective was to involve as many Bijagós people in wage employment as possible so that they could meet their tax 'obligations' which were to be paid in cash. The same labor force system also applied in the much smaller *fabrica* in Caravela, while a still smaller and much later *fabrica* in Formosa apparently used a "freely" contracted labor force.

Nevertheless, it should also be pointed out that not all the workers of the *fabricas* in Bubaque and Caravela were recruited by force. Other groups like the Manjacos and Pepels (qq.v.) from the mainland voluntarily went to such islands as Bubaque, Formosa, and Caravela to cut *chabeu*, probably motivated by the requirement to pay colonial taxes and the need to acquire money to purchase material goods and fulfill certain social obligations. As a result, such seasonal migrations to the Bijagós sometimes became permanent and led to a significant population of Pepels in Formosa.

However, the fact remains that most Bijagós were forcefully recruited, and their standard requirement was to gather fifty *chabeus* each day. Those not meeting this requirement were liable to severe punishment by the *cipaios*.

Wages also varied considerably. According to the *homens grandes* of Soga, payment was never received in the form of money. The laborers were only given food, a blanket, and tobacco leaves. The money which they earned was simply kept by the colonial authorities to pay the *imposto de capitação* (head tax). Koya, the *regulo* of Bubaque, pointed out that the *chabeu* gatherers on that island were paid between fifty to sixty *escudos* monthly. The *homens grandes* of the *tabanca* of Ancadaque (in Formosa) maintained that the "contracted" laborers were paid sixty *escudos* a month plus food and a blanket at the end of their "contract".

It appears that the significant role of the palm nut industry in the Bijagós undermined traditional activities such as rice cultivation, the production of palm wine and other food crops, hunting, fishing, and canoe-building.

As a result of these oppressive conditions, the history of the Bijagós is also a history of resistance. Most often this was passive defiance without clearly stated political objectives, but they were nevertheless manifestations of the profound dissatisfaction with the colonial order. Perceived as such, the Portuguese endlessly resorted to brutal repression to maintain the forced labor system and the colonial tax structure.

One of the most common of protest against forced labor, particularly after "pacification," was withdrawal to the thickly forested areas or to islands such as Canhabaque. Responding to this tactic, the Portuguese turned to collective punishment of the families of those who took flight and the *autoridades gentilicas* would be charged with curbing acts of resistance to the colonial order.

Protest against the payment of the myriad colonial taxes also took the form of withdrawal and evasion, which were increasingly difficult to manage as the colonial system tightened. Consequently the tactics were modified to include lying and deceiving the colonial officials and concealing everything from them since the colonial authorities would seize livestock, food, and other valuables in lieu of unpaid taxes.

BIKER, JUDICE JOAQUIM. First Lieutenant Biker served in the colonial military in Guinea-Bissau and participated in the war of "pacification" in the Biriban area. Later, when he served as the Governor of Guinea-Bissau, he became well known for his 1903 documentation of the slave labor conditions in São Tomé (q.v.). Biker's articles unleashed a major political scandal showing that 2–4,000 "contract laborers" went to São Tomé each year, but few ever returned to Cape Verde and Angola where they originated. These tumultuous early years in the twentieth century saw the overthrow of the Portuguese monarchy and the brutal "pacification" campaigns of Major João Teixeira Pinto (q.v.).

BISSAU. Capital city of the Republic of Guinea-Bissau at the broad estuary of the Geba (q.v.) River on the north shore (11° 51'N; 15° 35'W). Bissau is situated on what was until about the 1960's an island—the channel which separated it from the mainland, called the *Canal do Impernal*, has since dried up. The island's excellent geographic position on the Geba channel made it easily reached by ocean-going vessels. Its fine natural harbor on the east coast was an added attraction. The area has long been occupied by a concentration of Pepel people.

The first European to reach the area remains uncertain, but it has been established by internationally respected Portuguese historians like the late Avelino Teixeira da Mota, who spent a long time in the territory as a colonial official, that the Portuguese explorer Nuño Tristão (q.v.) never reached, and was not killed, in the region. Tristão was enthusiastically involved in slavery (q.v.), but he is said to have died, during his fourth voyage of "discovery" in 1446, somewhere between the rivers Sine and Saloum (q.v.) and Gambia, the victim of a hail of poison-tipped arrows of some "unfriendly natives," who also killed all but two members of the landing party of twenty-one men. It was the same year that another Portuguese explorer, Alvaro Fernandes, reached Varela Point, on the extreme north-west coast of the country, making him perhaps the first European to reach modern Guinea-Bissau. In any case, a decade later, two European explorers, the Portuguese Diogo Gomes (q.v.) and the Venetian Alvise Cadamosta (q.v.), on separate voyages, dropped anchor in the Rio Geba (q.v.) region on the mouth of which the island of Bissau is located and also noted some off-shore islands (e.g., in the Bijagós [q.v.] archipelago).

In the sixteenth century Bissau became a modest coastal base for a number of slave-trading *lançados*, *grumetes* (qq.v.), and other Luso-Africans and continued in this capacity through the late nineteenth century. These brazen entrepreneurs busied themselves with the slave trade, fully exploiting the "trades" of the Rio Grande de Buba (q.v.), as well as the rivers Corubal, Geba, and Mansoa (qq.v.). Unlike the situation in Cacheu (q.v.), avaricious activities were pursued here with no interference from Portuguese or European authorities. The local Pepel rulers, strong believers in free trade, had steadfastly refused to allow the building of forts or stockaded settlements anywhere on the island. Consequently, there was no representative of the Portuguese Crown here pretending to enforce Portugal's loudly-proclaimed 'exclusive rights' over the whole region.

As the activities of the *estrangeiros* (foreigners) intensified during the seventeenth century, due to the increased demand for African captives for the plantations of the Americas, the Portuguese naturally became alarmed. The French, in particular, had a trading factory on the island which was doing a bustling trade in slaves, ivory, and wax in the 1680's. It was during this time that three Spanish Capuchin missionaries, who kept a church in the tiny port settlement of Bissau, protested strongly to the king of Portugal, in a letter dated 14 April 1686, about the never-ending 'tribal wars' fomented by the *lançados* and their *grumete* allies for the procurement of captives in response to the European demand. By the end of that year, the Capuchins were replaced by Portuguese Franciscan friars.

The zealousness of the Franciscan missionaries resulted in the conversion of the reigning Pepel King of Bissau, Bacompolo Co, who hitherto had adamantly refused to allow any fort building in his realm. Baptized as *Dom Pedro*, the king somehow granted the Portuguese permission to fortify Bissau. The second *Companhia de Cacheu e Cabo Verde*, a monopolistic company founded on 3 June 1690 with the principal objective of supplying slaves to the Spanish Indies, was entrusted with supervising the building of the fort of *Nossa Senhora da Conceição*. Two years later, on 15 March 1692, the Captaincy of Bissau was established but subordinated to that of Cacheu; its Captain-Major, however, was not nominated until four years later, on 1 March 1696. Following attacks by European powers and virtual anarchy in the slave trade, Bissau was designated as a Captaincy-General in 1692 in order to strengthen the

Portuguese monopoly coordinated from the Cape Verde Islands. This was designed to establish a more meaningful coastal presence between Cacheu to the north and Bolama (q.v.) to the south. By 1696 Bissau town held a fort, church, and hospital and controlled trade on the Geba and Corubal Rivers. The trade remained largely in the hands of sometimes independent *lançados*.

Although the projected fort was built, the serious conflict provoked by the Portuguese attempt to determine events in Bissau led, in 1707, to the extinction of the *capitania*, the demolition of the fort, and the abandonment of the island to the *estrangeiros*. About a dozen Portuguese settlers were assigned there each year in the early eighteenth century; later this number was raised to forty per year. A high death rate from tropical diseases and frequent attacks by neighboring Africans on ports and forts strongly discouraged expanded colonization.

By the mid-eighteenth century, alarmed yet again by the activities of the French in particular, the Portuguese were making strenuous efforts to return to Bissau. Meanwhile France was heavily engaged in a number of wars in Europe, (from about 1744 to the end of the Seven Years' War, 1756–1763). This greatly reduced French activity around Bissau, so the Portuguese seized the opportunity and went all out to reoccupy and build a fort in the port of Bissau. On 9 February 1753, supported by a number of European merchant vessels anchored at the port, they overcame the fierce resistance of the local Pepel inhabitants and landed soldiers, craftsmen, slaves, degredados, and forced laborers from Cape Verde and Portugal and also war and building materials. The Captaincy of Bissau was hastily re-established and a Captain-Major appointed shortly afterwards. For the next two years, however, the hit-and-run guerilla warfare tactics of the Pepels frustrated the building of the second fort of Bissau.

The *Companhia Geral do Grão Para e Maranhão*, founded on 7 June 1755 to address the serious shortage of slaves in those two provinces in Brazil, was given the responsibility of erecting the third fort of Bissau as well as maintaining the few *praças* and *presídios* in the region. Ten years later, with an army of more than two thousand slaves and forced laborers from Cape Verde, as well as scores of convicts from Portugal, work on the fort began. For another ten years, in spite of the continuous high death toll from malaria, yellow fever, and scurvy and the ceaseless harassment of the Pepels, the Portuguese pressed on with the construction of the fort of *São José de Bissau*. Under the constant protection of Portuguese warships, the imposing fort was finally completed in August 1775.

But until its dissolution in February 1778, the *Companhia Geral do Grão Para e Maranhão* used *São José* primarily as a depot to store African captives before shipment to the slave markets of the Americas. The fort itself did not radically alter Pepel-Portuguese relations. The local rulers continued to demand and receive *daxas* from the Portuguese and other Europeans until the establishment of *Pax Lusitana* in the early twentieth century.

During the early years of the nineteenth century, the economy of Bissau, based on the slave trade, suffered a dramatic decline with Portugal's abolition of the traffic in 1815 and the patrols of the British Navy (based in Freetown, Sierra Leone) and the American Anti-Slavery Africa Squadron (q.v.) (based in Cape Verde). The gradual shift to 'legitimate trade' meant a slow recovery, but this was greatly affected by the almost permanent state of insecurity, due to the centuries-old dispute between the local rulers and the Portuguese over the questions of sovereignty and independence. In the meanwhile, the settlement steadily grew with the establishment of a few European and Cape Verdean traders and agents of European commercial houses. On 21 June 1885, the Bissau Municipal Council was created, the first such institution in the territory that today is Guinea-Bissau. Four years later, Bissau was elevated to the category of a town. It was in the same year, 1859, that the famous Honório Pereira Barreto (q.v.), the overzealous Cacheu-born African defender of Portuguese colonial interests in the region, died and was buried in the municipal cemetery. In 1869 Bissau became one of four administrative *comunas* in order to create a more effective local administration, although the Governor's residence was still at Geba, a small town much further east in the interior. In that year, Bissau became known as the capital of the District of Guinea. Its population was a mere 573 inhabitants, made up of 391 native Africans, 166 Cape Verdeans, and 16 Europeans. When the administration of Guinea-Bissau was fully separated from Cape Verde in 1879, the capital was transferred to Bolama.

The isolated nature of the European presence was also apparent in 1911 when the Intim and Bandim Pepel people refused to give over some land for a sports field just outside of the northwest part of the city. Even at this relatively late date, the insecurity of the town, and the competing interest of Cacheu and Bolama, kept its population small. Bissau only gained the status of a "city" in 1917. An epidemic of the bubonic plague in 1922 spurred a modest improvement of the urban sanitation system.

As a small colonial city, the worldwide depression of the 1920's and 1930's slowed its development still more. Indeed, the first three decades of the twentieth century saw almost continuous resistance (q.v.) by the Pepels in the Bissau area, and there were few advantages to life in Bissau. Probably because of its advantageous geographical location and fine natural harbor, the colonial capital was moved from Bolama to Bissau on 9 December 1941. Celebrations of the fifth century since Portuguese 'discovery' of Guinea also seemed to stimulate additional urban planning and growth. However, this only cemented colonial values into urban patterns of racial and class segregation into African, Cape Verdean, European, and Lebanese (q.v.). While the population of Bissau is overwhelmingly African, the ethnic groups represented by the 1950's and 1960's were drawn from most parts of the country, and the original Pepel majority was no longer even half of the people of the city.

Another phase in increasing the ethnic diversity of Bissau took place at the Pijiguiti (q.v.) dockyards on 3 August 1959, leading to building a broad, multi-ethnic nationalist movement. The Pijiguiti massacre, as it became known, caused the leadership of the nascent PAIGC to determine that a path of armed struggle, rather than negotiation, would be necessary to achieve independence. Bissau itself was attacked in 1968 and June 1971 during the nationalist war (1963–1974). The population of Bissau rose from approximately 25,000 to 80,000 in the course of the war as a result of the dislocation of the rural populations due to military activity. After independence in 1974, there was some discussion about moving the capital to a central place in the interior, but it remains at Bissau. The population of Bissau in 1979 was put at 109,214, which was more than 13 percent of the whole country. According to the 1991 population census it has almost doubled to some 197,610 individuals or about 20 percent of the present national population.

It is mostly composed of young migrants attracted to city life but dependent upon salaried relatives. The city today incorporates formerly independent settlements like *Antula*, *Bandim* and *Intim* and is rapidly spreading out. It is where the overwhelming majority of the country's industrial units are located and, consequently, where the nation's salaried workforce is concentrated. Regarding urban development, some progress has been made toward port expansion, piped water systems, and electric power, but major difficulties remain in the areas of adequate housing, sufficient supplies of fuel oil for electric power, spare parts for the electric and water systems, and employment.

BOLAMA. Centuries before the arrival of the Portuguese, the island of Bolama, strategically located (11° 35' N, 15° 28' W) between the Areias and Bolola (q.v.) channels (near the mouths of the rivers Geba and Rio Grande de Buba/Bolola, q.v.), was a territory controlled by the Beafadas (q.v.), who were pushed from the interior to the southern littoral areas by the Mandinka (q.v.) invaders and rulers of the Kingdom of Kaabu (q.v.). Their settlement here meant displacement of the original inhabitants who, with only the sea in front of them, found themselves forced to flee to the offshore Bijagós (q.v.) islands. When the Portuguese arrived, probably in 1446, Bolama was separated from the mainland by a narrow channel. It is not clear if Bolama was inhabited at this time. What is certain, however, is that it was coveted and claimed by both the Beafadas and the Bijagós of especially Canhabaque Island, and whatever hostility may have existed between these two groups was fully exploited by Europeans and Africans in the era of the transatlantic slave trade. Beafadas commonly became the victims of the marauding raids of the Bijagós.

With fine ports and anchorages, fertile soils, and a rich flora and fauna, Bolama was also coveted by the Europeans. During the early 1640's, as a result of glowing reports about its suitability for colonization, a recommendation was made for the main Portuguese settlement at Cacheu (q.v.) to be transferred there but to no avail. In 1669, the island was reported to be uninhabited, the Beafadas inhabitants having apparently fled because of the predatory raids of the Bijagós. Almost twenty years later in 1687, La Courbe, the French Commandant of the Senegalese island of Gorée (seized from the Dutch in 1677), visited the place and noted that it was uninhabited. Thus Bolama had great strategic importance in France's southward thrust for spheres of influence in West Africa. With the interest of the French aroused, André Brue, Director-General of the Gorée-based *Compagnie des Indes*, landed there in 1700 and recommended the establishment of a commercial base but once again to no avail, due mainly to inability to mobilize the required financial resources.

During the eighteenth century, which witnessed the zenith of the systematic exploitation of the region for captives for slave labor in the Americas, the Portuguese in *Guiné do Cabo Verde* ("Guinea of Cape Verde," or the Upper Guinea Coast) were increasingly challenged by the Dutch, French, and English. Confined to a few trading posts in the coastal area roughly corresponding to that of modern Guinea-Bissau and especially threatened by French expansionism, the Captain-Major of Bissau (q.v.), Francisco Roque Sottomayor, raised the Portuguese flag over Bolama and planted a *padrão* (stone monument bearing the arms of Portuguese monarchs) in 1753, thus formally claiming sovereignity to this good defensive position on riverways to the interior. This act was not followed by any permanent occupation, and the island remained uninhabited and was claimed by both the Beafadas and the Bijagós. This reflected Portugal's weak position in the area, a weakness to be made more apparent by the British attempt forty years later to establish a white settler colony on Bolama, with virtually no resistance from the local Portuguese.

On 25 May 1792, one of two ships which together carried a total of 275 settlers from England, dropped anchor at Bolama without prior authorization from either the Beafada or the Bijagó authorities. Nine days later, a surprise attack by Bijagó warriors from Canhabaque Island left a casualty count of ten men killed or injured and six women and children taken as hostages (to be ransomed later). Although afterwards the leader of the expedition, a naval officer called Phillip Beaver, was able to 'purchase' the island from both rulers of the Beafadas and the Bijagós, the settlement was nevertheless abandoned by the end of November 1793, not because of pressure from the Portuguese authorities, but indeed because of the exceedingly high death toll among the settlers, as well as the hostility of the Bijagós of Canhabaque who regularly exploited Bolama's rich soils and forest.

During the 1820's and 1830's, American colonization societies also manifested interest in Bolama as a prospective site for the settlement of emancipated African Americans. Notwithstanding the strong recommendations, the projected settlement was never realized. Besides the fact that the promoters could not mobilize the required funds to finance the venture, the island was the subject of a bitter dispute between Great Britain and Portugal over the question of ownership, a quarrel which would later involve the United States of America.

The earlier 'purchase' of Bolama by Phillip Beaver, leader of the ill-fated British colonization attempt, formed the basis of Great Britain's claim of sovereignity, a claim which Portugal, an old ally, relentlessly challenged. Especially from the late 1830's to the late 1850's, when the Portuguese (who also "purchased" Bolama from both rulers of the Beafadas and the Bijagós) tried to maintain a semblence of control among the small resident population of Portuguese, Cape Verdean, and Luso-African (slave) traders, the dispute entailed several occupations by troops of both countries, each involving the cutting down of flag poles and the raising up of national flags.

The conflict was complicated by the fact that the British Government, having abolished the transatlantic slave trade in 1808 and eager to promote "legitimate commerce," had taken the enormous responsibility of policing the West African coast. This meant frequent visits to Bolama, ostensibly in search of slave traffickers.

For example, on 9 December 1838, sailors from the British Royal Navy brig *Brisk* descended upon the tiny port settlement of Bolama, seized over 200 slaves from the plantation of the notorious Cape Verdean slave trader Caetano Nozolini, cut down the mast from which the Portuguese flag flew, and raised the Union Jack (the British Flag). As soon as they left, the Portuguese pulled down the British flag and raised their own. Four months later, the *Brisk* returned; again her sailors cut down the Portuguese flagpole, destroyed the local barracks, and sacked and burned properties of Caetano Nozolini. The "violence of the English" was repeated in 1842; five years later, in 1847, it included seizure of a number of slaves belonging to Nozolini's wife, *Nhanha* Aurelia Correia, another notorious slave trader and apparently the daughter of a Bijagó "queen" and a Cape Verdean adventurer.

In 1857, as a result of the protracted conflict, a despondent Governor of the territory, the Cacheu-born Honório Pereira Barreto (q.v.), suggested to the Lisbon authorities that since Portugal did not exercise any sovereignity over the island, 'for fear of the English,' a deal should be made with the British, giving them the *presidio* of Ziguinchor (which the French were posed to grab) in exchange for Bolama. Even if the Portuguese would have taken the suggestion seriously, the British had other plans; in 1860, they incorporated Bolama and the Bissagós Islands in their colony of Sierra Leone. And so, for almost a decade, a bitter diplomatic war raged between Lisbon and London.

The long-standing Anglo-Portuguese dispute over Bolama was eventually sent to United States President Ulysses S. Grant for final arbitration. On 21 April 1870, the American President ruled in favor of Portugal and six months later the Governor-General of Cape Verde took formal possession of the island. Until the advent of the post-independence period, a *praça* (square) and a statue of Ulysses S. Grant commemorated this act in the city of Bolama. After this arbitration Bolama became one of four *comunas* in Guinea-Bissau.

Nine years after the famous arbitration verdict, the territory of Guinea-Bissau became separated (on 18 March 1879) from the administration of Cape Verde. The Portuguese hastily fixed the first capital of their newly proclaimed colony of *Guiné Portuguesa* at Bolama. The first governor, Lieutenant-Colonel Agostino Coelho, immediately set about creating a new administrative structure shortly after assuming office. He built a new meteorological station and set up a press to publish the official news-sheet *Boletim Oficial da Guiné Portuguesa* and other official publications. With the tiny settlement of Bolama a place where the few resident traders could still recall the frequent assault of the Bijagós, the principal preoccupation of the new Governor became the question of "effective occupation," a condition which predated that set by the 1884–1885 Berlin Conference. Coelho, therefore, quickly attended to the deployment of the small military force at his disposal. For the next fifty years or so, Bolama would be the launching pad for Portugal's desperate "pacification campaigns" on the mainland as well as in the Bijagós islands.

Meanwhile, the small capital of *Guiné Portuguesa* grew and expanded. As *mancarra* (peanuts), rubber, wax, hides, and ivory gradually replaced slaves as the principal items of trade during the second half of the nineeenth century, cultivators, gatherers, and traders gravitated to the island and the surrounding region (the adjacent mainland and the nearby Galinhas Island) to exploit the fertile soils and the rich forests. Officially, peanuts became the country's main export from Bolama in 1846. Peanuts were first exported, unofficially, from about 1835 when they were shipped from Galinhas island, together with cotton and probably slaves, by the dynamic *Nhanha* Aurelia Correia. Today peanuts are overtaken by fish and cashew nuts.

In 1903, the Portuguese monopolist bank, *Banco Nacional Ultramarino* (BNU), which had the exclusive right to issue banknotes in the territory, opened a branch in the town, and ten years later, the town was elevated to the category of a city. Magnificent public buildings and fine houses were built, giving the capital an air of prosperity.

But Bolama's economic importance had waned by the turn of the century. The "golden age" of the *pontas* (agro-commercial establishments, [q.v.] where cash crops like *mancarra* were grown and such products as hides, rubber, and wax were traded) in the Rio Grande region had come to an abrupt end. The internecine wars which raged among the Fulas, and between these and other ethnic groups like the Beafadas, during the last quarter of the nineteenth century had a disastrous effect. The instability which ensued resulted in the abandonment of numerous *pontas* dotted along the fertile banks of the Rio Grande and its tributaries. With the Portuguese unable to guarantee security of life and property, as the ceaseless assualts of the Fulas and Beafadas killed defenseless Manjacos who worked the fields and destroyed shops and farm machinery, agricultural production slumped. Especially after the "pacification" of the mainland in 1915, the focus of attention turned to the peaceful eastern and northern regions of the country, where the colony's major cash crops were being produced and gathered, with Bissau, accessible by river and road transport, the main port and commercial heartbeat of the territory. Bolama languished into decadence.

With the final establishment of *Pax Lusitana* in 1936, following the defeat of the defiant Bijagós of Canhabaque, the peace and tranquility whch reigned attracted a few foreign enterprises such as Pan American Airlines, which opened an office in the capital in 1940 and began immediately to use regularly the island's excellent bay as a stop for its famous "clipper" seaplanes. The new burst of activity was short-lived. With the intensification of World War II, the departure of especially French and German traders, and the transfer of the capital to Bissau in December 1941, Bolama languished into yet more decadence. In July 1942, the *Banco Nacional Ultramarino* (q.v.) closed its branch and moved to the new capital, and three years later Pan American Airlines also closed its office and ceased operations from the territory altogether.

A museum of colonial architecture, the city of Bolama is today in the final stages of decadence, with abandoned houses and public buildings ruined and falling apart. The effort to preserve historic sites as national monuments has so far come to nothing.

BOLANHAS (BALANA, BULAÑA). *Bolanhas* are essentially riverine marshes typical of coastal Guinea. Given proper drainage and tidal irrigation, the *bolanhas* are well suited for rice agriculture (q.v.).

BOLOLA. Bolola, an old Beafada (q.v.) kingdom and port, is also referred to as Balola. It is located upstream from the kingdom of Buguba/Biguba on the Rio Grande de Buba, formerly the Rio Grande de Bolola. The ruler of the kingdom was a subject of the Mandinka (q.v.) Mansa of Kaabu (qq.v.). During the sixteenth and seventeenth centuries, the port, which was close to the modern town and port of Buba, attracted a large number of *lançados* (q.v.) and slave traders because of the cheaper price offered for captives. It was also here, in 1636, that the Portuguese (mostly Afro-Portuguese) from the port and fortified village of Porto da Cruz in the Beafada kingdom of Guinala settled. Among the new settlers was the family of Francisco de Lemos Coelho, a slave trader and author of the now classic *Descrição da Costa da Guiné desde Cabo Verde a Serra Leoa con todas as ilhas e rios que os brancos navegam*, written in 1669 (edited by Damião Peres and published by the Academia Portuguesa de História in 1953 as *Duas Descrições Seiscetistas da Guiné*.) Francisco de Lemos Coelho travelled extensively in the region between the 1640's and the 1660's. According to Coelho, the fort which was built by his relative Captain Cristovão de Melo was abandoned in the late 1640s after de Melo returned to Portugal.

With the gradual ending of the Atlantic slave trade during the second half of the nineteenth century, Bolola's economic survival was largely secured by the spill-over effect from nearby Buba. The status of Buba as the principal trading center of the whole territory was due to the establishment of numerous *pontas* (q.v.) in the Rio Grande area and the commercialization of *mancarra* (groundnuts or peanuts), as well as being an important caravan stop along the centuries-old trade routes linking the coast to the interior and different ecological zones in the region. Consequently, Bolola stagnated with Buba's decline as a result of the protracted civil wars which raged furiously in Forrea (an extensive former Beafada territory which included the Rio Grande region) from about 1878 to 1890.

Bolola's stagnation was greatly facilitated by the intense quarrel between Bakar Quidali (or Guidali), ruler of Forrea, and his subordinate chief, Mamadú Paté (q.v.), the ruler of the chieftancy of Bolola. This bitter conflict culminated in the 'betrayal' of Quidali by Paté, when the forces of Alfa Yaya (q.v.), the Almami (supreme political and religious leader) of the Futa Jallon (q.v.) Confederation, were mobilized to stop the chaos and disruption to economic activities (particuliarly the closing of the route for caravans from Futa Jallon passing through Forrea, (q.v.). Beside this goal, Paté also had the ambition to spread Islam, and thus he invaded Forrea in 1886. Facing defeat after successfully defending his stronghold for three days, Bakar Quidali chose suicide and Mamadú Paté became the new ruler.

Mamadú Paté reigned in Forrea from 1887 until his death in 1890. His successor, Mamadú Paté Coiada, soon found himself in serious conflict with the new ruler of Bolola, Cherno Kali. Opposed to the never-ending exactions and violence of Paté Coiada, Kali organized a united front of Beafada and Fula (q.v.), led by him and Bakar Indjai, the Beafada ruler of Cubisseco, to wage war against his superior. But although Paté Coiada and his army were soundly defeated at the battle of Rumague in 1885, the bloody conflict did not result in overthrowing the ruler of Forrea nor in the recovery of lost territories by the Beafadas.

Meanwhile, Bolola, like other settlements in the area, languished as the inhabitants increasingly abandoned their homes to escape the violence and extortions which continued to some extent during colonial rule. Today, the settlement is a small sleepy village of little importance.

BOLOR. Situated on the mouth of the river Cacheu, Bolor is in the territory of the Felupes (q.v.). Bolor was acquired by the Portuguese in 1831 and was immediately fortified with six pieces of artillery in order to control access to the river. Denominated a *presídio*, Bolor was subordinated to the *praça* of Cacheu (q.v.). The trade of Bolor included wax, hides, and rice (which was exported in large quantities to Cacheu, whose inhabitants were largely dependent upon it). Besides its strategic importance, Bolor was also hailed as the healthiest place in the whole territory, with apparently very hospitable inhabitants who were said to adore ''whites'' and were ''by nature'' averse to war.

Before long, this *presídio* was also in the familiar state of decadence of the Portuguese 'possessions' in the region. Already in 1843, the energetic Luso-African governor of Guinea, Honório Pereira Barreto (q.v.), was bitterly complaining that there were no vestiges of fortification left anywhere; apparently, the Portuguese military presence was limited to a detachment of three ill-armed, raggedy soldiers. Such weakness is reflected in the Felupe assault on the *presídio* in 1878 and, with the Portuguese determination to "teach the *gentios* a lesson," the "disaster" of Bolor took place shortly afterward.

The motives behind that attack on the *presídio* of Bolor by the Felupes of nearby Jefunco in September 1878 are not clear. Portuguese historians like João Barreto put emphasis on a long-standing rivalry between the inhabitants of Bolor and those of Jefunco. The latter apparently wanted access to Cacheu through the territory of the former, who would not yield. Irrespective of the motives, the Portuguese in Cacheu readily perceived that attack on the *presídio* as an attack on Portuguese sovereignty, especially with the cutting down of the mast from which the Portuguese flag flew.

Although there were no casualties, the incident nevertheless so enraged the Portuguese authorities that a delegation was immediately sent to Bolor. The Jefunco ruler was summoned to appear and give an explanation for the assault. Refusing adamantly, he stressed that he was the *senhor* of the region, thus making sovereignty a fundamental issue. Still exhilarated by the decisive victories over the Manjacos (q.v.) of Cacanda, Bianga, and Churo, near Cacheu, in 1871, the Portuguese resolved to "punish" the *gentios* and "pacify" the territory once and for all. A force of over 100 regular soldiers and a large number of African auxiliaries left Cacheu for Bolor, followed by the Governor of Guinea, António José Cabral Vieira.

On 29 December 1878, as a part of the expeditionary force was disembarking on a beach at Bolor, they were greeted by a rain of poison-tipped arrows from awaiting Felupe warriors. Two Portuguese officers and over fifty regular soldiers and African auxiliaries died. The rest of the force, including the Governor, still on board vessels preparing to disembark, hastily weighed anchor and headed for Cacheu, full sail. The massacre left the Portuguese resentful and revengeful but unable for decades to muster sufficient strength to launch a punitive campaign.

The so-called "disaster" of Bolor was a great blow to Portuguese national pride and imperial ambitions. Apparently, it also had the effect of jolting the Lisbon authorities into paying more attention to the "affairs of Guinea." This came to entail the "independence" of Guinea from the administration of Cape Verde on 18 March 1879, even though in reality Guinea consisted of a few *praças* and *presídios* (the supposed islands of Portuguese sovereignty on the mainland). In fact, for centuries the Portuguese were subjected to the much-reported "insults" and "abuses" of the *gentio* inhabitants, including the payment of taxes and duties to the native authorities, and Guinea was thereby not effectively controlled by Cape Verde.

It was not until 1901 that the Portuguese were able to organize a punitive "pacification" campaign against the Felupes of Jefunco. Supported by two gunboats, the expedition actually resulted in the destruction of a number of villages around Bolor, the killing of a few people, and the establishment of a fragile *Pax Lusitania*, to be strengthened by periodic police operations which lasted up to the late 1930's. Otherwise, Bolor remained, and remains, a relatively unimportant settlement.

BRAMES. These representatives of the Senegambian (q.v.) stock, Atlantic sub-family, are located in the area between Canchungo and Bula on the right bank of the Mansoa River. Related to the Pepel and Manjaco (q.v.) peoples, the Brames, also known as the Mancanhas, are hardly Islamized and are mainly animist. Their economy is based on slash and burn agriculture (q.v.) with limited hierarchical political organization. The 1950 census showed 16,300 Brames, while the 1960 estimate indicated that the population of Brames rose to 35,000; the 1979 census indicates 26,026 or 3.3 percent of the total population.

BRAZIL. *See* CABRAL, PEDRO ALVARES; COMPANHIA GERAL DE GRÃO PARA E MARANHÃO; POMBAL, MARQUIS DE; SLAVERY.

BUBA. Capital of the southern region of Guinala (q.v.), situated at the extreme end of Rio Grande de Buba. The name Buba is apparently a corruption of Buguba, a name found in early written [Portuguese] documents in connection with a kingdom, a river, and a port. From the seventeenth century onwards, the form Biguba became more widely used. But while the kingdom of Buguba/Biguba referred to a territory owned by the Beafadas (q.v.) (whose ruler was a subject of the Mandinka Mansa of Kaabu [q.v.]), and the Rio Grande de Buguba/Biguba is the actual Rio Grande de Buba, the old settlement and port of Buguba/Biguba is not the same place as the modern town and port of Buba. The former, a major entrepot during the heydays of the transatlantic slave trade, was situated some distance downstream, near the confluence of the rivers Jassonca and Uaja; the latter, the most important commercial center in the territory from the early 1840's to the late 1870's, was a center of rivalry and conflict between Fulas, Beafadas, and Portuguese during the last quarter of the nineteenth century.

Portuguese sailors reached the upper limits of the Rio Grande de Buba in the second half of the fifteenth century. With the onset of the transatlantic slave trade, the region became an important 'slaving district.' At the port of Buguba was found, during the second half of the sixteenth century, a significant nucleus of *lançados* (q.v.), who lived in a nearby fortified village and dedicated themselves to their most lucrative trade. From here, thousands of captives were annually shipped to the slave markets and plantations of the Americas. There was also a sizeable trade in gold, wax, ivory, and kola nuts. The port was an integral part of the intricate Beafada trade network which for centuries linked the coast to the interior and the territory's littoral region to that of Senegal and the Gambia in the north and Guinea-Conakry in the south. With the gradual transition to 'legitimate commerce,' Buguba became supplanted by Buba.

An important stop for the caravans from Futa Jallon (q.v.), Buba had, by the mid-nineteenth century, become the heartbeat of not only the Rio Grande region but the whole territory. Indeed, from the early decades of the nineteenth century, the hub of agricultural and commercial activities in the country centered in the Rio Grande region, where numerous *pontas* (q.v.) were established by European and Cape Verdean traders and trading companies. The *pontas* were engaged mainly in the cultivation and exploitation of the principal cash crop, *mancarra*; some covered large tracts of land and employed over 400 laborers—mostly Manjacos (q.v.) from the northern region of Cacheu (q.v.).

Buba's economic importance, evidenced by a great abundance of traders, foreign commercial houses, and a bustling trade in *mancarra*, gold, wax, ivory, cotton textiles, and kola nuts, prompted the Portuguese Governor-General of the Cape Verde islands to suggest in 1878 that it should be the capital of the "district of Guinea." Around this time, some 300,000 bushels of *mancarra* were being exported annually from the port of Buba, destined mainly to France, since the French trading companies of Bordeaux and Marseilles monopolized the trade. The foreign traders, including the Portuguese and

Cape Verdeans, were subjected to the payment of levies to the local rulers in the region.

With the administrative independence of the territory from Cape Verde in 1879, the Rio Grande region became a major preoccupation of the new Portuguese authorities in Bolama (q.v.), who were anxious to resolve the political crisis in the Forrea (q.v.) (an extensive country in the southwestern corner of Guinea-Bissau) which had exploded into bloody civil wars among the Fulas (q.v.) and between these and groups like the Beafadas.

Forrea, which was originally the land of the Beafadas and Nalus (q.v.), included Buba and the Rio Grande region. However, from the second half of the nineteenth century, with a large influx of Fulas from the neighboring regions (who, in a matter of two decades, wrestled political power from their hosts), the territory became a Fula-dominated state in the late 1860's, under the protection of the powerful Futa Jallon Confederation. But as the overwhelmed Beafadas and Nalus continued to challenge and resist the new rulers, the united front formed by various Fula factions (particularly the important Fulbe-ribe/Fulbe-djiabe unity which was crucial for the establishment of Fula dominance in Forrea) collapsed, and a civil war broke out. Buba's great importance as a trading center and Portugal's desire to establish sovereignty in her newly proclaimed "province" of *Guiné Portuguesa* would make Portuguese intervention inevitable.

With the outbreak of the internecine wars in the late 1870's, the agricultural output of the *pontas* declined dramatically, and the caravans from Futa Jallon became severely disrupted. As the bloody conflict raged, an increasing number of people sought refuge with the Portuguese garrison at Buba, where about 200 mostly Angolan soldiers were stationed. The Portuguese intervened directly by giving support particularly to the Fulbe-djiabe and launching military operations against the Fulbe-ribe, who retaliated by attacking the Buba and Geba garrisons and military detachments, as well as the *pontas* of the Rio Grande. After a decade of bloody conflict, virtually all the *pontas*, which numbered about 112 at the pinnacle of the *mancarra* trade, were abandoned by laborers and proprietors, a phenomenon which was paralleled by a large exodus of the local inhabitants. This meant a serious paralysis of Buba's trade, particularly the exportation of *mancarra* which, in 1880 had dropped to 150,000 bushels, and five years later it stood at 8,000 bushels.

By the time the Forrea conflicts were resolved and *Pax Lusitana* established during the early years of the twentieth century, the poles of attraction for agricultural and commercial activities had moved to the northern and eastern regions of the territory, with Bissau and Bafata (qq.v.) the most important trading centers. Buba, like Bolama (q.v.), languished into decadence. In 1910, of the ten commercial houses in the region, only one was located there. The number of ocean-going vessels which visisted the port during that year was merely seven.

The discovery of large deposits of bauxite (q.v.) around Boe, in the region of Gabu, estimated at about 200 million tons, holds hope for the economic revival of Buba. If the needed transport infrastructure, which includes a new port at Buba, could be realized, the town's chances for survival would be greatly enhanced.

BULL, BENJAMIN PINTO. Historian and university professor in Dakar who was President of the *União dos Naturais da Guiné Portuguesa* (UNGP, q.v.), which sought independence from Portugal (q.v.) without revolution. He held talks in Lisbon in July 1963 to achieve this end. B. Pinto Bull's brother is Jaime Pinto Bull (q.v.) who was the UNGP Vice President.

BULL, JAIME PINTO. One of the few Africans from Guinea-Bissau who served as a Deputy in the Portuguese National Legislative Assembly (NLA) in Lisbon in 1964. J. P. Bull was also the Inspector of Administration and Secretary General of the colonial administration in Guinea-Bissau. He served as the Vice President of the *União dos Naturais da Guiné Portuguesa* (UNGP, q.v.) and later as President of the *Frente de Luta Pela Independência Nacional da Guiné-Bissau* (FLING, q.v.) after 1966. In 1969 J.P. Bull was re-elected as the only African representative of Guinea in the NLA in Lisbon. He was killed in a helicopter crash in July 1970 while on a tour of the territory. He was the brother of Benjamin Pinto Bull (q.v.).

C

CABRAL, AMILCAR LOPES 'ABEL DJASSI' (12 September 1924–20 January 1973).Cabral was born in Bafatá in Guinea-Bissau of a Cape Verdean father, Juvenal Cabral. Since his father was educated, Amilcar was sent to the Liceu Gil Eanes in São Vicente, Cape Verde for his secondary education. At the age of twenty-one he entered the University of Lisbon, Institute of Agronomy from which he graduated with honors in 1950. In the early 1950's he was associated with the Lisbon Casa dos Estudantes do Império, CEI (q.v.), where he met with revolutionary intellectuals from other African colonies. While in Lisbon he met and married his Portuguese wife, Anna Maria, who herself was a dedicated revolutionary. This marriage ended in divorce, and he married Maria Helena Rodrigues of Cape Verdean ancestry. With his education complete, Cabral entered the colonial agricultural service in 1950, where he applied soil science, demography, and hydraulics engineering. During the period 1952 to 1954 Cabral traveled extensively in Guinea to conduct its first agricultural census and to gain an intimate and detailed knowledge of the land and people, a great asset in organizing the *Partido Africano do Independência de Guiné e Cabo Verde*, PAIGC (q.v.), the nationalist revolutionary party.

Cabral's first effort in mobilizing a nationalist movement in Guinea was the 'Recreation Association' in 1954 which led to the short-lived *Movimento para Independência Nacional da Guiné Portuguesa*, MING (q.v.), also founded by Cabral in the same year. In the mid 1950's Cabral met with his revolutionary friends from the CEI, and they formed the *Movimento Anti-Colonialista*, MAC (q.v.). Finally, on 19 September 1956, Cabral, his brother Luís, Aristides Pereira, Rafael Barbosa (qq.v.), and two others met secretly in Bissau (q.v.) to form the PAIGC. Cabral could not remain in Bissau at the time, as he had to return to Angola where he was at work with a private sugar company. In December 1956 Cabral, Agostinho Neto, and other Angolans met secretly to form the *Movimento Popular de Libertação da Angola* (MPLA). The clandestine organizing continued and sought to mobilize the workers of Bissau. On 3 August 1959, a dockworkers' strike at Pijiguiti (q.v.) in Bissau was met with savage colonial repression while Cabral was at work in Angola.

Following this event, Cabral returned to Bissau to discuss a change in tactics and to prepare for a protracted armed struggle to win independence for Guinea-Bissau and the Cape Verde Islands. In 1960 Cabral secretly left Bissau to continue organizing and to form the *Frente Revolucionária Africana para a Independência Nacional das Colónias Portuguesas*, FRAIN (q.v.) in Tunis; this was soon replaced by the *Conferência de Organizações Nacionalists das Colónias Portuguesas*, CONCP (q.v.), in April 1961. These organizations sought to unify the struggles in the different Portuguese colonies in Africa. After 1963 the PAIGC launched its war which had control of two thirds of the countryside by the end of the next ten years.

During that period of time (1963–1973), Cabral served as Secretary General of the PAIGC, directed the liberation struggle, and wrote a number of brilliant works on African liberation and culture, African and Guinean history, and class formation, for which he received worldwide acclaim. (There is a special section in the bibliography which cites the major works by and about A. Cabral).

In 1973 the PAIGC was able to declare itself the government of an independent Guinea-Bissau. Such actions severely demoralized a Lisbon regime which was already financially and politically exhausted from the endless wars in Africa. The April 1974 overthrow of the regime in Lisbon brought an end to decades of Fascism in Portugal and to the Portuguese colonial presence in Africa and elsewhere. In an abortive anti-PAIGC plot Cabral was assassinated in Conakry on 20 January 1973: he did not personally live to see all of his objectives fulfilled only a few months later. Achievements of such a scale for a man of such modest beginnings earned Cabral many international awards and honors.

He received the Nasser Award, the Joliot-Curie Medal, and honorary doctorates at Lincoln University (USA) and from the Soviet Academy of Science. Today Cabral is widely recognized as a major African revolutionary theoretician in both analysis and practice. He was survived by numerous half-brothers and half-sisters; most notable was Luís Cabral, who became the first President of Guinea-Bissau. A. Cabral was survived by his wife and three children. His wife continues to work in the Ministry of Health and Social Welfare. In recent years she has worked in educational and social fields while residing in Cape Verde. 12 September, Cabral's birthday, has been celebrated as a national holiday in Guinea-Bissau.

CABRAL, JUVENAL. (1889–?) Father of Amilcar and Luís Cabral (qq.v.) and author of *Memórias e Reflexões* (1947). J. Cabral studied at the Seminary of Viseu in Portugal and had a deep understanding of the cultural aspects of Portuguese colonial rule, which caused him great personal frustration. Such a context played an important role in the formation of the revolutionary nationalist ideology of his two sons.

CABRAL, LUÍS DE ALMEIDA. (1931–). One of the six original founders of the *Partido Africano da Independência de Guiné e*

Cabo Verde, PAIGC (q.v.), in 1956 in Bissau (q.v.). Cabral's training was as an accountant for *Companhia União Fabril*, CUF (q.v.). He left for Guinea-Conakry soon after the PAIGC was formed, since the Portuguese secret police were seeking his arrest. In 1961 Cabral became the founding Secretary General of the pro-PAIGC trade union group, the *União Nacional dos Trabalhadores da Guiné*, UNTG (q.v.). By 1963 Cabral was in charge of the strategic Quitafine frontier zone which was militarily active at that time. In 1965 he became a member of the PAIGC War Council. Following reorganization of the PAIGC in 1970, he became a member of the Permanent Commission of the *Comité Executivo da Luta*, CEL (q.v.), with the responsibility for national reconstruction in the liberated zones.

Independence of Guinea-Bissau followed his brother's assassination, and Luís Cabral became the first President of that new nation as well as the Deputy Secretary of the PAIGC. In November 1980 he was overthrown by 'Nino' Vieira and was jailed there until his negotiated release from a death sentence and initial exile to Cuba, and then to the Cape Verde Islands, and finally to Lisbon where he now lives. Recent efforts by Guinea-Bissau and Cape Verde have restored diplomatic relations, but Cabral's overthrow fractured unity between the Republics and the original goals of the PAIGC. Despite the democratization in Guinea-Bissau, L. Cabral is not allowed to return.

CABRAL, PEDRO ALVARES. Portuguese sea captain whose fleet reached the Cape Verde Islands on 22 March 1500. Rather than travel along the West African coast, he went far to the southwest and accidentally discovered Brazil (q.v.) in April 1500.

CABRAL, VASCO. (1924?–). Cabral was born in Guinea-Bissau but was one of the very few Africans to study in Lisbon University in 1950. In 1954 he was arrested for his political views and was held in prison for almost six years, including two years in solitary confinement. Upon his release in 1959 he completed his degree in Economics and met with Amilcar Cabral (q.v.), who was also in Lisbon at that time. V. Cabral fled from Portugal (q.v.), in July 1962 with A. Neto of the MPLA and soon joined the *Partido Africano da Independência de Guiné e Cabo Verde*, PAIGC (q.v.), to serve on its central committee and on the War Council. Cabral also served on the

Executive Council of the Struggle, CEL (q.v.) with his specialty in party ideology. He served as Minister of Economic Coordination and Planning from 1974 to 1982, devoting himself to fulltime party work since that time as well as serving as Economic Planning Advisor to President Vieira (q.v.) since 1984. Although he was injured during the 1980 coup in Bissau, he later escaped to the Swedish Embassy, and today he is the Second Vice President.

CACHEU (Fifteenth to Sixteenth Centuries). The settlement of Cacheu (12° 10' N, 16° 10'W) in Guinea-Bissau is located on the south bank of the river Cacheu, some twenty kilometers from the river's mouth. A point somewhere north of Cacheu was reached by Nuño Tristão, the first Portuguese regional explorer, in 1446. In the early sixteenth century, slaving became the notable activity at Cacheu, where there was trade in salt and horses from Cape Verde for slaves captured and sold by *lançados* (q.v.) along the coast and from the interior tributary kingdoms of Mali (q.v.).

Cacheu witnessed one of the earliest European attempts to undermine and usurp the power, authority, and sovereignty of the local West African rulers. Hosting the largest gathering of *lançados* during the second half of the sixteenth century, it was indeed the place where the foundations of Portuguese colonial rule were laid, following the dramtic confrontation between the *hospedeiros* (hosts) and the *hospedes* (guests) regarding the terms of the residential accord.

The presence of a significant number of *lançados* in the locality which became known as Cacheu was due to the hostility which they encountered and the chronic difficulties to trade caused by the widespread rebellions against the local ruler, Mansa Tamba, in Casanga (q.v.) territory on the north bank of the river Cacheu. Here, near the settlement of Sarar, they had constructed a village of their own, which they called São Filipe. But given the fact that their host, Mansa Tamba, long regarded as a 'friend of the whites,' was no longer able to guarantee them security of life and property, they felt themselves obliged to cross the river and, having reached agreement on the terms of residence with the local ruler, settled close to the port which became known as Cacheu, in the territory of Cacanda which formed part of the extensive land of the 'Buramos' or the Cobiana, Mancanha, Pepel, and Manjaco (qq.v.) ethnic groups.

As word spread about the relative peace and freedom, the

hospitality of the local inhabitants, and the lucrative trade in slaves, wax, and ivory, the influx of *lançados* into Cacheu increased significantly. Soon, the first Christian community in the territory of today's Guinea-Bissau arose. Under the jurisdiction of the Diocese of *Guiné do Cabo Verde*, created in 1533 and headquarted in Ribeira Grande, São Tiago, a visiting priest would, particularly during the period of Lent, often make confessions and say mass to some "seven to eight hundred persons, between black and white" (Alvares de Almada, 1594 [1964], 72).

But it was not all harmony and heavenly peace. With the increasing number of 'white guests,' conflicts also arose. Of these, the most serious from the point of view of the Cacheu ruling classes was the attempt by the 'whites' to undermine traditional power and privileges.

Such an attempt was first made in 1588, when Manuel Lopes Cardoso, the Cape Verdean representative of the Portuguese Crown, was appointed as the *feitor* (q.v.) for the Cacheu river trade. Cardoso convinced King Chapala, the ruler of Cacanda, that a fort was vital for the effective defense of the trading settlement against English and French 'pirates' and hostile 'interlopers'. The King needed little convincing. In the 1560's, a flotilla commanded by the English slave trader John Hawkins (q.v.) had carried out piratical acts on the Cacheu river, followed by a massive overland attack against the inhabitants of Cacanda. During the 1580's, French 'pirates' were very active along the coast of *Guiné do Cabo Verde*. However, when the required fortifications were completed, the African potentate was again convinced by Lopes Cardoso that it was absolutely necessary to build houses around the fort for the artillerymen. As soon as the houses were ready for occupation, the *lançados* moved from their lodgings with the local population to the newly fortified site.

Viewing this move as a concerted effort on the part of the *hospedes* to change the terms of the residential arrangement, the enraged ruler prepared his soldiers for an attack on the new settlement. Forewarned by two *grumete* (q.v.) women, who visited the fortified village during the night, the 'whites' loaded their cannons and waited. The battle in 1590 lasted three days, during which the angry 'Buramos' apparently suffered heavy losses. As a result of the victory of the *lançados*, the fortified settlement came to be called *Nossa Senhora do Vencimento* (Our Lady of Victory).

CACHEU (Seventeenth Century). With the construction of the stronghold and the successful battle against the local inhabitants, the stage was set. In spite of her annexation by Spain (1580–1640), Portugal moved quickly to capitalize on a situation created by the hiterto much-despised Lisbon-branded 'outlaw traders.' A special Crown agreement with Jewish (q.v.) *lançado* merchants in 1601 gave them permission to settle and trade in the Cacheu Rios area and to establish a local *capitão e ouvidor* (captain and overseer) who was subordinate to the Governor of Cape Verde.

On 29 December 1614, the Governor of Cape Verde, Nicolau de Castilho, appointed the first 'Factor and Receiver of the Royal Exchequer on the River São Domingos [today's river Cacheu] and the ports of Guinea.' The Factor was also the *capitão* of the port of Cacheu. According to the *Regimento* (written instructions) of João Tavares de Sousa, the new representative of the Portuguese Crown, duties were to be collected from all ships entering and leaving the port of Cacheu. Furthermore, not only was this official responsible for the maintenance of law and order among Portuguese/Cape Verdean residents, but he was also to ensure that the *gentios* ('heathens') of the district come into knowledge of 'Our Holy Faith.' A year later, three other *Regimentos* followed, all issued to Baltasar Pereira de Castello-Branco by the King of Portugal himself, Filipe II, investing de Castello-Branco with the grandiose title of 'Captain, Magistrate and Factor of the Settlements of Cacheu, Rio Grande, São Domingos, and others in Guinea.'

With intensification of the slave trade in the seventeenth century, the Dutch temporarily seized Cacheu in 1624. Then in 1630 Cacheu was fully returned to Portuguese control, as it began to be developed as the captaincy and economic nucleus for the province of Guinea. More *regimentos* were issued and factors dispatched to strengthen Cacheu. Security remained a problem. Cacheu was vulnerable to attacks by Africans, Luso-African *lançados*, and various European powers. Thus, under the 16 July 1641 nomination of the new Captain-Major of Cacheu, Gonçalo Gambôa de Ayala, fortifications were strengthened. Gambôa de Ayala left Lisbon for Cacheu on board the Portuguese warship *Santa Anna Maria*, with sixty men, fifty muskets, fifty arquebuses, 100 pikes, three artillery pieces, four carpenters, four masons, and a significant quantity of lime, bricks, and rooftiles (Baretto 1938, 98). The Captain-Major failed in his double objective of intimidating the ruling classes of Cacanda into submission and building a fort in

Cacheu. Although cleverly out-maneuvered with the construction of the fortified village and militarily defeated, the local populace nevertheless continued to resist all Portuguese entrenchment efforts such that, by 1670, the much emphasized need to fortify Cacheu was still not realized.

In 1669, the Cape Verdean slave trader and writer Francisco de Lemos Coelho observed that the *casa forte* (stronghold) was strong only in name. It was only a thatched-roofed mud building with a large terrace, surrounded by mangrove fencing and similar to other buildings in the 'white' area of Cacheu known as *villa fria* (cold town), except that on the side facing the river, there was a platform on which was mounted a few pieces of artillery, but "without one piece which could fire" (Coelho 1669 [1953], 34). Consequently, French, English, and Dutch 'pirates' freely called at the port, while the so-called *gentios* habitually harassed the occupants of the 'fort.'

On 26 September 1670, in a remarkable outburst of candor, a dejected *Conselho Ultramarino* (Overseas Council, a body which advised the Portuguese Crown) felt compelled to inform the king that the *Praça* of Cacheu had been kept "miraculously," notwithstanding the King's grand title of 'Lord of Guiné.' In fact, Portugal had nothing more there than a "small piece of land" maintained at a cost; the Portuguese flag was only allowed to fly over the settlement because "a tribute or fee" was paid to "a Negro King" (quoted in Silva Teixeira 1889/1950, 103).

Meanwhile, the new port settlement of Cacheu grew and expanded. Around the beginning of the seventeenth century, some 1,500 people were reckoned to have lived there; of these, some 500 were said to be 'white' (meaning not only Europeans, but also Luso-Africans, especially from Cape Verde). As the decades passed, Cacheu became a bustling but segregated town. Divided into two residential quarters, *villa fria* and *villa quente*, the 'whites' lived in the former while the *grumetes* (q.v.) and *gentios* lived in the latter. The two neighborhoods were separated from each other by a main road which ran along the river in an east-west direction, with the cooler part (*villa fria*) by the waterfront and the hot part (*villa quente*) away from the cool breeze blowing in from the river. In the 'white' quarter, the buildings (including the church of *Nossa Senhora do Vencimento*) were, in general, made of bricks and rooftiles. In the *bairro popular* (common people's area), they were all (including the chapel of *Santo António*) made of mud walls and thatch roofs. The hospice which was constructed in

1660 by the Portuguese Franciscans, Frs. Paulo de Lordelo and Sebastião de São Vicente, served as the first missionary base in the territory, from which proselytization and evangelization missions to the interior were launched. The zealous Fr. Paulo de Lordelo died in the Banyun (q.v.) country, near Cacheu, in 1664, apparently poisoned by the *gentios*.

The Portuguese preoccupation with their ineffective occupation and control of Cacheu led to the idea of creating a monopolistic trading company based on the model of the Royal African Company of England and the *Compagnie du Senegal* of France. In the 1660's the Cape Verdean-based slaving company *Cacheu Rios e Comércio da Guiné* had a slave trade monopoly from Senegal to Sierra Leone, including the rivers of Guinea. On 18 May 1676 this company was reorganized as the *Companhia do Cacheu, Rios e Comércio da Guiné*, but its main slaving activities were still based at Cacheu, which continued to dominate the slave trade in Senegambia. Not surprisingly, it undertook to build a proper fort at Cacheu within three years; to recruit and maintain, at its own expense, a force of fifty soldiers from Portugal (q.v.), before its six-year contract expired; and to recapture and monopolize the regional trade. Furthermore, the *Companhia* was granted the power to nominate the Portuguese Crown's chief representative in the area, the Captain-Major of Cacheu, António de Barros Bezerra (q.v.).

For reasons of a troubled and ineffective adminstration, Bezerra was replaced in 1682 by José Gonçalves de Oliveira, who quickly found himself embroiled in a similar and bitter conflict with the local rulers and traders, especially when he refused permission for French and English merchant ships to conduct business at Cacheu. Predictably, when the local rulers put their warriors on a war footing, the local traders not only supported the move but organized a campaign against the overzealous Captain-Major de Oliveira. In 1684, he was arrested and held captive for fourteen months by the *grupo de sediciosos* (seditious group), led by the wealthy and dynamic Afro-Portuguese trader Bibiana Vaz, who was reported to be one of the most powerful and influential women in *Guiné do Cabo Verde*. It was Bibiana Vaz's house in Farim (q.v.) where José Gonçalves de Oliveira was held prisoner until his escape.

The hostility of local rulers and traders notwithstanding, the Portuguese continued to believe in the monopoly system as a means to entrench themselves in the region. On 3 January 1690, the *Companhia do Cacheu e Cabo Verde* was launched with a six-year contract which gave it a regional trade monopoly, including that of the Cape Verde islands. Its principal objective was the supply of 4,000 African captives annually to the Spanish Indies. It was also responsible for paying the salary of the Governor of Cape Verde and maintaining twelve of his guards. However, like its precursor, this second Portuguese company also met with great hostility and stiff resistance from the local rulers, traders, and, of course, from the African captives. Like its predecessor, it failed in its objective to monopolize local trade and entrench the Portuguese. Thus, by the close of the seventeenth century the *Companhia do Cacheu e Cabo Verde* had ended its relative prosperity and ceased its slave trade to Spanish America.

CACHEU (Eighteenth Century). Frustrated, the Portuguese thought it wise to shift the center of gravity of their activities in the region to the island of Bissau (q.v.). Although the Captaincy of Bissau was established in 1696 and the fort of *Nossa Senhora de Conceição* was built by the end of the century, it was abundantly clear to the Portuguese, that their entrenchment efforts during the early 1700's, were a dismal failure. Indeed, on 5 December 1707, the Portuguese monarch João V ordered the extinction of the Captaincy of Bissau and the demolition of its fort. For the time being the Portuguese focus was shifted back to Cacheu.

At the beginning of the eighteenth century, the Portuguese garrison at Cacheu had about thirty undisciplined soldiers, mostly ex-slaves from Cape Verde and ex-*degredados* (q.v.) from Portugal, to man its dilapidated walls. The settlement was a place made further unsafe by the presence of dangerous Portuguese/Cape Verdean ruffians and cutthroats who killed their own kind at the slightest provocation and frightened the women off the streets of the *praça*. On the other hand, the Captain-Major reported in 1707 that the *gentios* remained 'insolent,' while the local rulers, who in the past were quite satisfied with 'a pipe of wine' as the *daxa* (duty tax) charged for each ship that dropped anchor at Cacheu, were now demanding payment in cash ("more than $100,000 reis"), besides the "constant extortions to the residents and traders of the settlement" (H. P. Barreto 1843, 142). With the expansion of slavery (q.v.) much further south along the West African coast, there was even some reduction in the importance of the slave trade at Cacheu. If this were not enough, the early eighteenth century saw repeated locust plagues in the region.

The *Praça Principal* (Cacheu) was central to the administration of Portuguese 'possessions' in the region (such as the *Praça* of Bissau and the *Presidios* of Geba, Farim, and Ziguinchor (qq.v.). Despite its top position, Cacheu retained a feeble existence. By the mid-eighteenth century the garrison town was reported to be 'totally exhausted'; there were no munitions, and the artillery was useless; the barefooted soldiers, who had no dormitories, were without arms; the 'fort' and its walls were all in ruins so too was the church; and there was not even a decent flag to be hoisted.

In fact, as Captain-Major Francisco Roque Sottomayor emphasized in his report of 1752, the place was rendered ungovernable by the relentless 'disobedience' of the *gentios*. A state of chaos and danger prevailed everywhere. A number of 'whites,' including a priest, had been kidnapped, to be released only through the payment of a ransom. Six soldiers had been assassinated as they gathered rocks to repair the ruined church. And since such 'abuses' by the *gentios* occurred so often and with impunity, the Captain-Major lamented that Portugal had not made "conquests" in "this limited part of Guinea" as she had apparently done in Brazil and Angola (Duarte 1951, 975).

The decline of Cacheu would be emphasized and re-emphasized in almost every official report. During the last quarter of the eighteenth century, the *praça* languished into even greater deterioration as Portugal virtually ceased to commit scarce resources for any further effort to establish its presence there. Yet from time to time, a zealous Captain-Major (who invariably was also a trader) would try to enforce Portugal's numerous restrictions, particularly those concerned with trade. Predictably, this would provoke tremendous hostility from both the local rulers and local traders. It is not surprising that the Portuguese in Cacheu (as well as in Cape Verde) could do little to stop the French and English from settling on Bolama (q.v.) in 1792.

CACHEU (Nineteenth Century) The poor state of Cacheu also underscored the feeble Portuguese protests against the French who hoisted their flag at the mouth of the Casamance (q.v.) in 1828 and occupied Karabane Island in 1836 for their trading purposes. Likewise, nothing much could be done throughout most of the first half of the nineteenth century to slow the often reported 'decadence' of Cacheu and the regional *praças* and *presídios*, nor could they check the 'insults' and 'abuse' of the *gentios*. These 'lamentable aspects' continued to be the principal preoccupation of the few overly enthusiastic representatives of the Portuguese Crown in Cacheu. Of these, none was perhaps more concerned, and ultimately more disillusioned, than the famous Honório Pereira Barreto (q.v.).

Another Portuguese official concerned and alarmed by the 'arrogance' of the *gentios* of Cacheu was José Joaquim Lopes de Lima, Secretary-General of the *Prefeitura de Cabo Verde e Costa da Guiné*, who, after visiting the *praça*, issued a warning to his fellow countrymen about the urgent need to be "continually on one's guard" since the "sad and sullen" natives always went about armed and, apparently, "without great provocation," often "[killing] one of our own and [fleeing] to the bush" (Lopes de Lima 1844, 124). Indeed, in 1833 a judge was assassinated "just ten paces" from the limits of the *praça*.

Relations between the Portuguese and the indigenous people of and around Cacheu continued to deteriorate. On the one hand, they had to contend with the increasingly intransigent positions of the local rulers, who remained fiercely independent and steadfastly held on to their rights to levy duties on ships dropping anchor at the port of Cacheu and to demand *daxas* from the resident foreigners. On the other, the *grumetes* were also increasingly uncooperative and rebellious, taking refuge in the *mato* (bush) following clashes with the *praça* authorities. The assassination of the Governor of Guinea in 1871 exemplified, in the eyes of the Portuguese, their 'treacherous' nature.

Apparently provoked by the killing of a *grumete* by a soldier from the Cacheu garrison, the assassin of Governor Alvaro Teles Caldeira fled to nearby Cacanda, where he was granted asylum by its ruler, who promptly refused to hand him over to the Portuguese authorities when requested to do so. The Cacanda ruler's act of defiance was supported by the neighboring potentates of Churo and Bianga, as well as the 'king of kings' in Basserel, capital of the Manjaco kingdom.

In a revengeful mood, the Portuguese in Cacheu organized a punitive campaign composed of over 200 well-armed soldiers and auxiliaries supported by two gunboats, which attacked Cacanda on 8 March 1887. After five hours of bloody fighting, the Manjaco/Pepel defenders retreated to the thick, surrounding forest, while the Portuguese-led force completely destroyed the settlement.

The massive demonstration of force by the Portuguese sufficiently intimidated some of the local rulers into signing peace treaties and relinquishing some important prerogatives. It was indeed a significant victory for the Portuguese, since they were able for the first time to get the rulers of Cacanda and Mata to give up their long-exercised right to demand and receive duties on all foreign merchant vessels entering the port of Cacheu. In return, they were paid monthly stipends by the Portuguese.

Exhilarated by this victory, the Portuguese seriously turned their attention to the question of the 'pacification' of the whole Cacheu region. But this new confidence was to dissipate abruptly when, determined to 'teach a lesson' to the Felupes (q.v.) who attacked the *presídio* of Bolor (q.v.) by surprise in September 1878, a punitive force of fifty-five regular soldiers, fifty *grumete* volunteers, and a number of auxiliaries set out to 'pacify' Bolor and neighboring districts. On 29 December 1878 as part of the expeditionary force was embarking, it was greeted by a rain of poison-tipped arrows, which left two officers and over fifty soldiers and auxiliaries dead. The so-called 'Disaster of Bolor' left the Portuguese resentful and revengeful but unable, for decades, to muster sufficient force to avenge the massacre and 'pacify' the region.

Meanwhile, apparently as a consequence of the 'Disaster of Bolor,' Portugal decided to pay more attention to the 'affairs of Guinea,' which came to entail the administrative independence of the territory from Cape Verde on 18 March 1879 and the proclamation of the province of *Guiné Portuguesa*, whose capital became not Cacheu, long considered as the *praça principal*, but Bolama (q.v.), internationally recognized as a Portuguese 'possession' by the 1870 arbitration verdict of American President Ulysses S. Grant. Further Portuguese efforts at 'pacification' of the Cacheu area were again sharply resisted by the Pepel people from 1891 to 1894. With the center of gravity of Portuguese activities shifting to Bolama, Cacheu plunged into even greater decline. By the end of the nineteenth century, most of the foreign traders and trading firms had moved out.

CACHEU (Twentieth Century). Resistence by the Pepels in the Cacheu region was noted by the Portuguese in 1904. By 1911 the exodus of traders from Cacheu town was such that there were only ten foreign establishments: four German, two Italian, and four Portuguese. The final 'pacification' of the region was launched in 1914, and the capital of the new administrative region termed *Costa de Baixo* was located at the increasingly important town of Canchungo (renamed Teixeira Pinto [q.v.] in honor of the *conquistador* of the region). Such were the circumstances of still further decay. For most of the colonial period, it remained a sleepy, although historic, town with very little economic or commercial activitity.

In the post-independence period not much has been done to revitalize the regional economy and arrest the decline of Cacheu. However, the realization of an International Colloquium on the 400th anniversary of the founding of Cacheu in November 1988 left the town with some improved infrastructure, including a new hotel, a conference hall, restaurant, technical school, paved roads, and street lights. The somewhat revived town is today the capital of both the *Região de Cacheu* and the *Província do Norte*. With the discovery of large deposits of phosphate in the region during the 1980's, there is optimism about its chances of growth and proposerity in the future. It has also served as a meeting place in efforts to resolve the MFDC (q.v.) conflict in the Casamance.

CACHEU RIOS E COMÉRCIO DA GUINÉ. *See* CACHEU.

CADAMOSTA (CA DA MOSTA; CADAMOSTO), ALVISE. Venetian navigator in Portuguese service who sailed in the Senegambian (q.v.) area between 1454 and 1456 in a ninety-ton vessel. In 1455 Cadamosta and Usodimare, a Genoan, separately reached the estuary of the River Gambia. In 1456 the two navigators sailed on a joint two-ship mission two miles up the Gambia River where the ships were strongly attacked by the local population and their ships' crews mutinied. The early reports by Cadamosta gave some information about the function of Mandinka (q.v.) (Dyula) trading systems and the contemporary structure of the empire of Mali (q.v.).

On the same voyage, they reported active trade of merchandise and slaves at Arguim Island in Mauretania. Three or four armed caravels attacked coastal fishing villages in the Gulf of Arguim to capture slaves for the return voyage. Still in 1456 Cadamosta and Usodimare reached the Rio Geba (Grande) and the Bijagós Islands (qq.v.).

CADERNETA. Labor passbook system started in the 1920's in conjunction with the *contratado* (q.v.) labor system. Similar to the South African system of passbooks of African labor registration.

CAETANO, MARCELLO. Prime Minister of Portugal (q.v.) from September 1968, following the stroke of Prime Minister Salazar, until April 25, 1974, when he was overthrown by the

Armed Forces Movement (MFA). Caetano was a professor of Public Law and the main author of the 1933 Constitution which institutionalized Portugese fascism and inaugurated the *Estado Novo*. He was the Minister of Colonies from 1944 to 1949 and was also instrumental in the 1951 revisions of the Portuguese constitution, which maintained Portugal's colonies in Africa. As head of Portugal during the key years of the nationalist wars in Guinea-Bissau, Mozambique, and Angola, Caetano presided over Portugal's historically doomed, though unyielding, efforts to retain direct imperial ('overseas') control of its African and Asian holdings, which led to massive discontent within the MFA in Portugal and the final overthrow of Portuguese Fascism.

CANARY CURRENT. South-flowing ocean current off the Atlantic coast of Morocco enabling early Portuguese sailors to pass easily down the coast in the epoch of great maritime exploration. Without tacking vessels that could sail close to the wind, the Canary Current sometimes made the return slow and difficult.

CANCHUNGO (12° 04'N; 16° 02'W). Town in northwestern Guinea-Bissau, formerly named Teixeira Pinto (q.v.) during the colonial era for the colonial militarist who was infamous in Guinea for his brutal 'pacification' program which brought twentieth century Portuguese colonialism. After independence Guineans changed the name to Canchungo.

CÃO, DIOGO. Born in the mid-fifteenth century, he was a Portuguese navigator who, in 1482, was the first to explore the west coast of Central Africa, just south of the equator. He reached the Kongo kingdom in 1483. Christopher Columbus (q.v.) sailed along the Guinea Coast between 1482 and 1484, possibly meeting Cão. Both Cão and Columbus sought to go around the Muslim world in the Middle East and secure an alternative route to India. Cão was thus the forerunner to the voyages of Bartolomeu Dias and Vasco Da Gama (qq.v.).

CAPITAÇÃO. Head tax; a key source of state revenue during the colonial era. This was applied specifically to the inhabitants of the Bijagós Islands.

CARAVELA. The *caravela* was the dominant fifteenth-century Portuguese and Spanish ship which had two or three masts and a lateen-rigged sail which allowed for improved tacking. The Portuguese conducted a significant amount of their West African exploration of that period with this type of vessel and the use of the astrolable for navigation. One of the ships of Christopher Columbus (q.v.) was a *caravela*. One of the islands in the Bijagós (q.v.) archipelago is called Caravela, no doubt with reference to this type of ship.

CASA DOS ESTUDANTES DO IMPÉRIO (CEI). This semi-official African student center in Lisbon was a center for African *assimilados* and intellectuals, including figures such as Marcelino dos Santos of Mozambique, Amilcar Cabral (q.v.) of Guinea, and Mario de Andrade of Angola. From the CEI, revolutionary thinkers formed the *Movimento Anti-Colonialista*, MAC (q.v.), in 1957. In 1965 the CEI was finally closed by the Salazar (q.v.) government which termed it subversive.

CASABLANCA GROUP. African organization formed in January 1961, which sought to unify the socialist-oriented states such as Egypt, Guinea-Conakry, Mali, Algeria, and Ghana in opposition to the moderate 'Brazzaville group' which was formed in December 1960. The Casablanca group was officially disbanded in 1963 upon the formation of the Organization of African Unity (OAU). As a result of the emergence of the 'Casablanca group,' the Conference of Nationalist Organizations in the Portuguese Colonies, CONCP (q.v.), was formed in April 1961.This represented a major African effort to unify the three leading nationalist movements fighting in the Portuguese colonies.

CASAMANCE. Region and river in southern Senegal forming a portion of the general area known as Senegambia. Its name is derived from Casa Mansa ('the king[s] of the Casas'), who had long traded with Portuguese *lançados* (q.v.). Today one of the main ethnic groups in the Casamance is still the Casangas (q.v.). Formerly the Casamance had been the home of the Banyuns (q.v.), but they were raided heavily for slaves by Fula (q.v.) from Futa Toro and Mali (qq.v.) from the fifteenth to nineteenth centuries. After the Empire of Mali collapsed, the Casamance became tributary to Mandinka Kaabu (qq.v.). However, as Kaabu weakened, especially in the late eighteenth and nineteenth centuries, the Casamance regained a measure of its autonomy. In the 1860's and 1870's under Alfa Molo (q.v.), the local Fula revolted against the Mandinka rulers of the Upper Casamance to link up with Fuladu.

The main trade and administrative center of Casamance is at Ziguinchor (q.v.), which was a portion of Portuguese Guinea until the late nineteenth century. Following the Berlin Congress (q.v.) in 1886, Portugal (q.v.) agreed to give up its claims to the Casamance Basin and Ziguinchor. On the southern frontier of Guinea-Bissau the French had garrisoned troops in Boke (Guinea-Conakry) as early as 1866, but especially under Faidhérbe (q.v.) the French maintained claims on Cacine in southern Guinea-Bissau until the 1880's. Other minor changes were made in the 1890's and early 1900's to settle the frontiers of France and Portugal, the two colonial powers of the immediate area. In the 1920's and 1930's French colonial traders continued to be very numerous in the Casamance region.

During the nationalist war the PAIGC had important offices and military bases in the southern Senegalese parts of the Casamance just across the border from Guinea-Bissau. Today, the Casamance harbors a large number of exiles from Guinea-Bissau, most of whom emigrated for economic reasons. Many hundreds of Guinean peasants temporarily migrate to the Casamance for trading purposes, and Crioulo is widely spoken in dozens of Casamance villages. Recently the *Mouvement des Forces Démocratiques de la Casamance*, MFDC (q.v.), is waging a small-scale armed struggle for greater autonomy from the Dakar administration.

CASANGAS. The Casangas are a main group of the inhabitants of the Casamance (q.v.) region. In the 1580's the Casanga King Mansa Tamba was considered a close ally to the *lançado* (q.v.) traders from Cacheu (q.v.). The King was celebrated for his sumptuous accomodations and many luxuries by Donelha in 1625. No doubt these were generated from his slave raids against the neigboring peoples, especially the Banyuns, Brames, and Pepels (qq.v.), whom he sold to the *lançados* for export. The unquestionable and demonstrably ruthless authority of Mansa Tamba resulted in a domain which was considered especially secure for white *lançados* and *tangomãos* (q.v.), who likewise treated him well when he sold ten to fifteen slaves for a good Cape Verdean horse. Normally the number of slaves might be only half of that. The stories of Mansa Tamba's swift justice under a very flimsy entrapment pretext, or *chai* which often resulted in sentences of death or slavery, were well known to the *lançados* for decades.

CENTRO DE INSTRUÇÃO POLITICO MILITAR (CIPM). In order to develop ideological unity with the cadres of the Partido Africano da Independência de Guiné e Cabo Verde [PAIGC] (q.v.) cadres, Amilcar Cabral (q.v.) founded the CIPM in about 1961 in the earliest period of the operation of an exile base in Conakry. A number of the leading figures such as João 'Nino' Vieira, Francisco Mendes (qq.v.), Domingo Ramos, Constantino Teixeira, and others attended this seminal party school. One of the functions was to link ideological and military training in the formation of 'bi-grupos,' the basic guerrilla army unit. The CIPM also trained those returning from abroad and offered basic education. In the early 1970's, 200–300 students in groups of twenty-five would be trained through a series of formal, informal, and role playing exercises during a program of several months. The curriculum included national and world history, a PAIGC code of behavior, lessons on the party program and organization, military and political tactics, decolonization, and foreign relations, as well as developing a strong sense of national unity and purpose. Stress was laid on the political rather than military dimensions of the struggle.

CHAMPALIMAUD. One of the major financial and industrial conglomerates of Portugal (q.v.) with ties to the Banco Nacional do Ultramar, BNU, and extensive colonial interests. Champalimaud virtually controls the Portuguese steel industry although it is, in turn, dominated by West German finance capital. Champalimaud operated a variety of firms in Guinea-Bissau. Today it is replaced by the Banco Nacional da Guiné (q.v.).

CLASS STRUCTURE. For a small, largely rural nation, the class structure of Guinea-Bissau is rather complex in its diversity but remains overwhelmingly geared toward agricultural production. Guinea-Bissau reflects the dominance of 'peasant' agriculture, and a cultural heritage of African values with peripheral participation in the 'Great Tradition' of Portugal. In Guinea the systems of plantation agriculture, share-cropping, and absentee landlords were very limited, in contrast to Cape Verde. The farming classes in Guinea may be divided into the coastal, largely stateless, rice farmers and the interior, more centralized peanut growers and cattle herders of the northeast. The acephalous peoples may be exemplified by the Balantas (q.v.) who have village level authority and are primarily animist in religious outlook. The most prominent centrally-governed people are the Fulas, who have local and regional leaders who traditionally commanded the respect of large numbers of their people, especially while the colonial authorities supported the local Islamic religious hierarchy of chiefs, local nobility, and traditional religious leaders.

The working class proper is quite small and generates rather little surplus value; it is centered around the few light industries which process agricultural (q.v.), animal, and fish products, the small lumber and dairy industry, and some relatively well-organized workers in the transport and port services. Service sector positions of drivers, repairmen, mechanics, street vendors, secretarial and clerical workers, and domestic servants are to be found. Some traditional artisans such as weavers, blacksmiths, leatherworkers, and musicians are also active.

During wartime the urban areas under Portuguese control also saw a sizeable minority of 'lumpen' or declassée strata of criminals and prostitutes, although in the period since independence the government has sought to curb such elements with innovative social programs. During the colonial times and during the war the military of Guinea-Bissau was very largely derived from Portuguese conscripts, but today the Guinean armed forces are made up of volunteers, many of whom fought during the war of independence.

There has also been a small group from the mercantile strata, including various shopkeepers, hotel operators, bankers, and those from the road and water transport industries. Industrial capitalists in Guinea were extremely few indeed. A large portion of the mercantile group was made up of Portuguese and some Lebanese merchants. Since independence a number of the larger firms have come under State control.

High ranking civil servants, government officials and functionaries are also associated with the upper classes. The colonial class structure in Guinea-Bissau followed rather sharp racial and rural-urban differences. Aside from the military, almost all Portuguese were found in the larger towns, with most found in Bissau (q.v.) itself. Likewise the top class positions were monopolized by Europeans or some Cape Verdeans including high government officials and bureaucrats, traders and businessmen, managers, and representatives of foreign firms. Social mobility or innovations in class formation were very limited under colonialism. The majority African population was generally excluded from these occupations and was overwhelmingly rural in location and agricultural in occupation.

At various points in the history of Guinea-Bissau, the Dyulas (q.v.), a Mandinka-derived itinerant trading group controlled the trade to the interior, with Afro-Portuguese *lançados* (q.v.) working along the coast. Similarly, there are traces of the traditional feudal theocratic class structure of Kaabu (q.v.) and of the subsequent Fula (q.v.), who are present today.

The departure of the Portuguese colonial authorities meant that top positions in Guinean society were vacated, and this resulted in a sharp struggle for power between the PAIGC cadres and a relatively weak petit bourgeoisie. Since independence, the leadership has consciously sought to attack the remnants of the traditional and colonial class structure. The cephalous quasi-feudal traditional authorities have lost considerable power, and most of the foreign monopolies, financial interests, and commercial sectors have either been nationalized or brought under strict control. The new leadership has formed a new state bureaucracy, and large-scale private ownership has been limited or placed in the State sector. This socialist program had also resulted in notable urban unemployment and a difficulty in attracting new foreign investments.

During Portuguese colonial rule the process of local class formation was very much repressed and abbreviated except for those traditional hierarchies which could be brought into the colonial administration.Thus, with the rather sudden exit of the Portuguese, the PAIGC initially moved into positions of power to block the formation of a local bourgeoisie based on private ownership of the means of production. However, since independence, the privileges of salary and status associated with government positions have allowed for the precipient formation of a state bourgeoisie, even though their material advantages are quite modest in comparison with their counterparts elsewhere in Africa.

COBIANAS. *See* BANYUNS.

COCOLIS (KOKOLIS). This small Senegambian (q.v.) group is related to the Bijagós (q.v.) peoples. The Cocolis are located near the Nalus (q.v.) peoples along coastal stretches at the mouth of the Geba River (q.v.).

COLI TENGUELLA. *See* TENGUELLA, COLI.

COLUMBUS, CHRISTOPHER. Credited with being the first European navigator to reach the New World. Between 1482 and 1484 Columbus visited the Guinea coast, which prompted a 1484 audience with King João II of Portugal (q.v.) to gain financing for further voyages. João II turned down his request, although Columbus visited him again in 1493 after his epic voyage across the Atlantic. Some reports indicate that Columbus stopped in the Cape Verde archipelago before making his crossing in 1498.

COMISSÃO PERMANENTE. *See* PERMANENT SECRETARIAT.

COMPANHIA DO CACHEU E CABO VERDE. *See* CACHEU.

COMPANHIA GERAL DO GRÃO PARA E MARANHÃO. This Portuguese-Brazilian slave company was formed in 1753 to supply the labor needs of the two northern, coastal Brazilian states of Pará and Maranhão. Initially there was a twenty (perhaps twenty-five) year lease on the slave trade in Guinea-Bissau, with indications that it continued well into the nineteenth century. This company revived a dying slave trade in Guinea. The Portuguese Marquis of Pombal (q.v.) was instrumental in arranging the charter of this company. *See* SLAVERY.

COMPANHIA LUSITANA DO ALUMINIO DA GUINE E ANGOLA. This Dutch firm was founded on 16 August 1957 to discover and process bauxites in Guinea-Bissau and Angola. The Portuguese government and Billiton Maatschappig N.V. of the Netherlands, with an initial investment of $172,000 USD, agreed to prospecting in the Boé area for an estimated 200,000 tons of bauxite related to the same field of aluminum bearing ore in neighboring Guinea-Conakry. Regular productive exploitation has not yet been achieved.

COMPANHIA UNIÃO FABRIL (CUF). CUF was one of the very largest Portuguese conglomerates, with large investments in Africa and with approximately ten percent of Portugal's (q.v.) total corporate capital. CUF is a multi-national concern involved in textiles, agriculture, petro-chemicals, steel, and shipbuilding. It has its own merchant ships and tens of thousands of employees. CUF is primarily owned by the powerful Mello family which, in turn, has links to the *Banco Nacional do Ultramar* and the Champalimaud (q.v.) conglomerate which share CUF's dominance of the Portuguese, and formerly the colonial, economy. CUF has important ties to American and French capital as well.

In Guinea-Bissau, the major CUF affiliate was Casa Gouveia, exporting palm and peanut oil, which also had very significant investments in shipping, insurance, light industry, and import-export concerns which were central to Guinea's colonial economy. CUF was actually only one of seven foreign firms in Guinea-Bissau until 1928 and was the only Portuguese firm in the colony at that time. As of that year, with Salazar's (q.v.) 'New State' having been proclaimed, Portugal asserted its economic (q.v.) interests in its African territories more forcefully, ousting the non-Portuguese firms and thereby allowing CUF to monopolize trade in Guinea for the remainder of the colonial period. Furthermore, Portugal bought into CUF, so that part of the profits went directly to the Guinean colonial state. The fact that peasants could only sell to CUF companies partially monetarized their economy, providing them with cash with which to pay colonial taxes, yet it also resulted in depressed rural living standards.

CONFERÊNCIA DAS ORGANIZAÇÕES NACIONALISTAS DAS COLÔNIAS PORTUGUESAS (CONCP). Founded in April 1961 in Casablanca (q.v.), Morocco with a Permanent Secretariat at Rabat under Marcelino dos Santos, who was to become a central leader of FRELIMO in Mozambique. The CONCP replaced the former umbrella organization Frente Revolutionária Africana para a Independência Nacional das Colônias Portuguesas, FRAIN. The Second CONCP Conference was held in Dar es Salaam, Tanzania in October 1965. In addition to other liberation movements and organizations, the PAIGC sent a five-person delegation consisting of A. Cabral, V. Cabral, A. Duarte, J. Araujo (qq.v.), and V. Saude Maria, as well as representatives from the trade union and women's groups.

CONHAQUES (CONHAGUIS). These small, isolated clusters of Senegambian (q.v.) people manifest considerable Mandinka acculturation, as they were separated from the main coastal Senegambian groups during Mandinka (q.v.) expansion. They are now found in the hilly areas in the extreme southeast of Guinea-Bissau and some small pockets in the Medina Boé area.

CONSELHO DE GUERRA (WAR COUNCIL). See PERMA-NENT SECRETARIAT; COMITÉ EXECUTÍVO DA LUTA; CONSELHO SUPERIOR DA LUTA.

COMITÉ EXECUTÍVO DA LUTA (CEL). Executive Committee of the Struggle. The 1964 Party Congress of the Partido Africano da Independência de Guiné e Cabo Verde (PAIGC),(q.v.) twenty-member (fifteen regular, five alternate) Political Bureau was replaced and enlarged by the CEL in 1970. During the close of the nationalist war (1970–73), the Council was central to the regulation of political and military affairs. This was especially the case as the CEL contained the seven-member Conselho de Guerra (War Council) and the powerful PAIGC three-member Permanent Secretariat (Commission). From 1970 to 1981, the CEL was elected during the annual meetings of the Conselho Superior da Luta, CSL (q.v.), and it functioned between CSL meetings, acting as the PAIGC's Political Bureau. It met at least every four months, or more often if needed; members of the CEL made up about one third of the CSL. Both councils were abolished in 1981 and replaced with a Politburo and a Central Committee.

CONSELHO SUPERIOR DA LUTA (CSL). The High Council of the Struggle functioned within the Partido Africano da Independência de Guiné e Cabo Verde, PAIGC (q.v.), as an organ roughly equivalent to a Central Committee; that is, it was the highest body except for the irregular meetings of the People's National Assembly, ANP (q.v.). Within the CSL were the CEL (see above), the War Council, and the Permanent Commission (qq.v.). The CSL has met annually since its first session in August 1971, when it replaced the PAIGC Central Committee (sixty-five members) that emerged from the Second Party Congress. In 1964 the Central Committee had seven departments but these were reduced to five by 1967. In 1970 the Central Committee was initially enlarged to seventy members and was newly named the CSL with about one third of its members also being on the CEL. At the time of the 1973 Second Party Congress the CSL increased its membership from eighty-one to eighty-five. The membership was raised to ninety at the 1977 meeting of the Peoples National Assembly. During the CSL meetings, members of the CEL were elected to serve between the yearly CSL meetings.

CONTRATADO. A contract laborer who agrees to sell his labor power for a proscribed period of time to a specific employer, used extensively in Guinea for palm oil production in the Bijagós (q.v.). In Cape Verde the *contratado* system served to reduce the population on the poor, desiccated islands and to generate remittances to be sent back to the islands. Often the *contratado* system was used for public works.

CORUBAL, RIO, CORUBAL RIVER. This major river of Guinea-Bissau has its headwaters in the vicinity of Labé in the Futa Jallon (q.v.) plateau of Guinea-Conakry. Before it reaches Guinea-Bissau it is known as the Koliba River, until it enters the eastern frontier of Guinea-Bissau south of Buruntuma curving back south through the Gabu (q.v.) and Boé areas before swinging northward again to empty into the upper portion of the Geba (q.v.) estuary. The Corubal River (q.v.) is about 280 miles in length, and it provided a convenient route for the export of slaves to the coast.

CRIOULO. Crioulo is the Cape Verdean-Guinean dialect based essentially on a Portuguese lexicon with varied African phonetic borrowing. There are loan words from both language stocks. Sometimes Crioulo refers to the Cape Verdean people and their culture. The language is spoken widely in Guinea-Bissau and was the linguistic result of the pentration of the *lançado* (q.v.) traders who also had mixed cultural and linguistic heritages. *See* HISTORICAL DICTIONARY OF CAPE VERDE.

D

DA GAMA, DUARTE LOBO. Da Gama was the first Governor of Cape Verde, appointed in 1587. This appointment ended the Captaincy system which had prevailed in Cape Verde from 1460.

DA GAMA, VASCO. Da Gama was the first Portuguese soldier-navigator to round the Cape of Good Hope and travel up the east coast of Africa to India. He initiated the Portuguese trade monopoly of the region. With relatively advanced navigational equipment, Da Gama sailed directly from the bulge in West Africa to the South African Cape on his trip to the region during the years 1502–1504. On his first trip, 1497 to 1499, Da Gama rounded the Cape with three ships. In 1498 he encountered Muslims at Quilemane on the east coast, then sailed to Malindi and on to Calicut and Malabar, India. On the 1502 trip he subdued Kilwa at gunpoint, opening the era of early sixteenth-century rivalry between the Portuguese and Muslims for East African coastal trade.

DA LUZ, SILVINO (1939–). While in Portugal (q.v.) studying medicine at the University of Coimbra, Da Luz was drafted as a Lieutenant in the Portuguese army and was sent to Angola to help suppress the uprisings which had begun in 1961. He gained practical military experience there but also witnessed the savagery of colonial 'pacification,' in which tens of thousands were killed. He deserted and escaped to Zaire and Nigeria, where he narrowly missed capture. He made his way through Ghana and finally to Conakry in 1963 to make contact with the headquarters of the *Partido Africano da Independência de Guiné e Cabo Verde*, (q.v.) there. He received additional military training in Algeria and was then sent to Dakar for more 'medical' studies while working in the PAIGC underground. Later he received military training in Cuba. He became known as a successful and clever Commander of *Forças Armadas Revolucionárias do Povo*, (q.v.) during the armed struggle, and he served as the Cape Verdean Minister of Defense and of Foreign Affairs as well as being a Member of the Cape Verdean National Council. Just before independence he is credited with, or blamed for, organizing the takeover of Radio Barlavento on 9 Dec 1974. This radio station had remained in the hands of anti-PAICV/pro-colonial forces. After the electoral defeat of the PAICV in 1991, he began working for a shipping company in Mindelo, São Vicente.

DEGREDADOS. Exiled Portuguese criminals, often charged with political crimes, who settled on the Guinea coast or in the Cape Verde islands. Some were confined there for a period of punishment or exile, while other *degredados* formed a permanent settler population and were sometimes considered as *lançados* (q.v.).

DEMBA, BAKARI. *See* ALFA MOLO.

DEMOGRAPHY. The demographic data for Guinea-Bissau are relatively limited. Under the best of conditions, unknown numbers of people avoided tax collectors, census-takers, and agents of the colonial government who sought military or labor conscription. Disruption during war years caused large scale emigration and population movement. As a consequence, all of the data offered must be considered as approximations.

A census in 1926 put the population of Guinea-Bissau at 343,000. The 1950 census was one of the better demographic studies taken in this nation and showed a total population of 510,777, of which 502,457 (98.3%) were 'uncivilized natives' or basically the rural agricultural population. '*Mestiços*' were numbered at 4,568 (0.8% of the population). These were often of Cape Verdean origin and were involved in small-scale commerce and some local government administration. The same census reported 2,263 Europeans (0.4%), a mere 1,478 '*assimilados*' (q.v.) (0.2%), and eleven Indians. In the following years the population statistics show greater variation for the same period and cannot be considered precise, but one may assume that the socioeconomic and ethnic composition of the population stayed relatively similar until 1974.

Estimates of the population have ranged as high as 800,000, but this figure seems unlikely. Most statistics did not include the 25–30,000 Portuguese soldiers stationed in Guinea-Bissau during the war years, and it was only in 1976 that some 70,000 refugees in Senegal and Guinea-Conakry began to return to their homes in Guinea-Bissau. The main demographic effects of the war were population relocation to secure areas over the borders and substantial rural to urban migration. Combatant deaths in the irregular war were perhaps more than 1,000 per year but were not of major demographic significance. By the mid–1960's the population had probably reached about 530,000. The 1979 census shows a total population of 777,214, with a national population density of approximately twenty-one inhabitants per square kilometer; this is up from eighteen per square kilometer about ten years ago. A 1982 estimate gives the population figure as 594,000, so it is difficult to determine which figure may be closer to demographic reality. The respective percentages of the largest ethnic groups are: Balantas, 27.2%; Fulas, 22.9%; Mandinkas, 12.2%; Manjacos, 10.6%; (qq.v.) and Pepels, 10.0%.

The most recent census in 1991 offers a comprehensive survey of Guinean demography.

The infant death rate in Guinea-Bissau is put at 149 per 1,000, although other sources give the rate of 80 per 1000. In either case the rate is substantially higher than for comparable European or North American rates. For the period between 1970 and 1975 the overall crude birth rate is 25.1 per 1,000 resulting in a rate of natural increase of 1.5% per year, which is generally low for Third World nations. Health conditions are generally poor in Guinea-Bissau, but life expectancy has risen

I. Distribution According to Age Groups and Sex

Age Group	Total	%	Men	%	Women	%
All Ages	979,213	100.0	472,022	48.2	507,157	51.8
1 to 9	336,671	34.4	170,033	17.3	166,638	17.0
10 to 19	213,053	21.8	106,574	10.9	106,479	10.9
20 to 29	142,949	14.6	61,794	6.3	81,155	8.3
30 to 49	171,401	17.5	76,890	7.9	94,511	9.6
50 to 64	65,818	6.7	30,635	3.1	35,183	3.6
65 +	49,321	5.0	26,096	2.7	23,225	2.4

Notes: 1.) The total population of 979,213 represents an increase of 211,474 people, or 27.5%, over the last (1979) population census of 767,739. 2.) The annual average growth rate during the period 1979–1991 was 2.3%. 3.) More than 56% of the population, approximately 550,000, were born after independence in 1973.

II. Distribution According to Ethnic Groups

Ethnic Group	Total	%	Male	%	Female	%
All Groups	979,213	100.0	472,022	48.2	507,157	51.8
Fula	248,813	25.4	123,032	12.6	125,781	12.8
Balanta	232,450	23.7	110,292	11.3	112,158	12.4
Mandinka	134,210	13.7	65,260	6.7	68,950	7.0
Manjaco	90, 598	9.3	41,923	4.3	48,675	5.0
Pepel	88,155	9.0	41,868	4.2	46,287	4.8
Mancanha	34,588	3.5	16, 163	1.6	18,245	1.9
Beafada	31,436	3.2	15,055	1 .5	16,381	1.7
Others	118,963	12.2	58,429	6.0	60,534	6.2

III. Distribution According to Religion (Percentage)

Religion	Total	Male	Female
Muslims	46.0	45.0	47.0
Traditional	36.0	37.0	35.0
Catholics	13.0	13.0	13.0
Protestants	2.0	2.0	2.0
Others	3.0	3.0	3.0

to about forty-one years on the average, with men living somewhat less on average and women (q.v.) living somewhat longer.

The most densely populated areas of Guinea-Bissau are in the east along a Bafatá-Gabu (qq.v.) axis and in the vicinity of Cacheu (q.v.). The capital city of Bissau (q.v.) has the largest urban population, with 14.6% of the nation up from 8% a decade ago. Nevertheless, the country remains overwhelmingly rural despite increasing rates of urbanization. The least populated *concelhos* (districts) are to be found in Bolama (q.v.) and in the Bijagós Islands.

DENIANKE, (DENANKE). The Deniake dynasty was founded by Coli Tenguella (q.v.) in about 1490 in Futa Toro (q.v.) (Tekrur) and lasted until about 1775 when ended by Fula (q.v.) jihads.

DE NOLI, ANTÓNIO. De Noli was a Genoese navigator in Portuguese service. In 1457 at Argium, de Noli and Gonçalo Ferreira traded with Diogo Gomes (q.v.) for slaves and horses. De Noli and Gomes are considered to have been the first Portuguese navigators to have set foot in the Cape Verde islands. In the early 1460's de Noli was in charge of one of the Captaincies on São Tiago Island from which trade on the Guinea coast could be regulated.

DGS. *See* PIDE.

DIALONKES, (DJALONKES, JALONCAS, JALLONKES). This small group appears to be of Senegambian (q.v.) stock but with very pronounced Mandinka (q.v.) acculturation, so that it is sometimes placed in the latter category. They are partly Islamized as a result of the eighteenth century Fula (q.v.) migrations from Futa Jallon (q.v.) and are now located east of Duas Fontes (Bangacia). The Dialonkes are the neighbors of the Quissincas, another Mandinka group.

DIAS, BARTOLOMEU. Portuguese navigator who rounded the Cape of Good Hope, South Africa in 1488 and returned along the Guinea coast to Portugal in December of that year.

DIAS, DINIZ. Portuguese navigator who 'discovered' the mouth of the Senegal River and the Cap Vert of Senegal in 1444 and 1445.

DIOLAS (DJOLAS, JOLAS). This group of Senegambian cultural stock is related to the Senegalese Serer (q.v.) and is thought to have split from them in about the fourteenth century with the creation of the Sine and Saloum (q.v.) kingdoms of that period. These animistic rice cultivators are found between the Casamance and Cacheu (qq.v.) rivers in the northwest and coastal portions of Guinea-Bissau; they have absorbed some of the Banyun and Felupe (qq.v.) populations living in the region. The term Diolas must be distinguished from the Mandinka-derived Dyulas (qq.v.). The Diolas were frequent targets of Mandinka slave raiders, who sold their captives to the *lançados* (q.v.) and other Portuguese traders.

DIREÇÃO GERAL DE SEGURANÇA (DGS). *See* PIDE.

DONATÁRIOS. The system of local rule in Cape Verde and some other colonial holdings in which a *capitão* was given a royal grant to administration with a high degree of local authority. The local Captain was appointed under Crown authority and was subject to inspection, review, and appeal by Lisbon. Although the donatario system was not practiced in Guinea-Bissau, it was normal to farm the *donatário* lands with slaves from the mainland.

DROUGHT. The Sahelian drought in Africa is a continuation of centuries of dessication of the Sahara and the Cape Verde archipelago. The drought in Cape Verde is accompanied by a major demographic (q.v.) transformation of the population of the islands. On the one hand, resultant famines have commonly cut the population by ten to forty percent.

Statistics have been kept from 1747 to 1970 which show fifty-eight years of famine and over 250,000 related deaths in some dozen drought periods. The drought cycles have also caused massive loss in crops and livestock. The drought of 1832 was associated with a severe famine in which ten percent of the population died. From 1854 to 1856 it is estimated that about twenty-five percent of the population perished, with the number of islanders falling from over 120,000 to less than 100,000. Famine and drought are also recorded for 1902 and 1903, in the 1940's, and in the late 1970's.

On the African mainland, especially in such countries as Senegal, Mali, and Chad, the situation has been parallel to that in the Cape Verde islands. Tens of thousands of people have died or have been improperly nourished, while hundreds of thousands of heads of livestock (q.v.) have perished. Those traditional people dependent upon pastoral economies have been shattered and forced to change their mode of production, sometimes irreversibly. The unpredictable role for agriculture (q.v.) has forced massive migration from the regions most severely affected in order to seek cash employment elsewhere.

A large factor in the drought and dessicated conditions has been a serious lack of proper land management and water conservation. In Guinea-Bissau the environment in the southern regions is forested and rainfall remains adequate, but in the northeast areas with Fula concentrations the effects of the drought were felt, with less than average rainfall and low production of animals and agricultural commodities. The land extensive slash-and-burn crop rotation system has offered some protection from the drought, at least in comparison to the far more severe effects in the Cape Verde islands and in regions further north in the Sahel proper.

DUARTE, ABÍLIO AUGUSTO MONTEIRO (1931–). Duarte is considered one of the 'old guard' of the *Partido Africano da Independência de Guiné e Cabo Verde*, PAIGC (q.v.), having played a critical organizational and recruiting role in the early years. In 1958 he was the main member of the PAIGC underground in the islands. He is the son of a Catholic priest and studied at the *liceu* in Mindelo, São Vicente while serving as a recruiter and party organizer (especially among the strategic dock workers). His recruits include: Luís Fonseca, Silvino da Luz, Joaquim Pedro da Silva, Ignácio Soares, and Manuel dos Santos.

He fled the islands in November 1960 to avoid arrest by a few days and reached Paris before going on to Algeria for military training. He served the PAIGC in many ways, including many foreign missions. He was a key member of the Cape Verdean National Council. While serving as the President of the Assembléia Nacional Popular (1975–1991), he declared Cape Verde independent on 5 July 1975 and signed the important Agrarian Reform Law in April 1982.

DUARTE, DULCE ALMADA. A sociologist by training and a liberationist by practice, Duarte was a very early member and supporter of the Partido Africano da Independência de Guiné e Cabo Verde, PAIGC (q.v.). In June 1962 she addressed the United Nations (q.v.) Committee on Decolonization, then meeting in Rabat, about the Portuguese resistance to de-colonized Guinea. She is the wife of Abílio Duarte (q.v.).

DYULAS (DIULAS, JULAS). This economically important ethnic group of Mandinka (q.v.) derivation must be distinguished from the Senegambian Diolas (q.v). The Dyulas are mainly from the Soninke (q.v.) branch with some Fula (q.v.) admixture. Functioning as a specialized class of itinerant traders, the Dyulas linked the Portuguese economic concerns along the coast with those people of the interior, especially in the early sixteenth century, until the arrival of the colonial era. During the decline of Mali (q.v.), the influence of the Dyulas appeared in a series of petty chiefdoms on the shores of the Gambia and Cacheu (q.v.) rivers and at the Dyula commercial center at Kankan. The Dyulas stimulated local production of gold, kola nuts, and the exchange of slaves for imported products such as salt, textiles, and firearms during the pre-colonial times. These items were traded throughout Guinea-Bissau and in much of the Upper Niger River. The Dyulas often worked in close association with Mali and various Mandinka sub-kingdoms. Most Dyulas were Muslims, but they did not carry out conversions or jihads. The penetration of the interior by the Portuguese broke into Dyula commerce, which helped cause the Dyula revolts from 1835 to the 1880's in the Upper Niger and in Guinea-Conakry, during which times they tried to reestablish their commerical authority in the business of slavery (q.v.). Dyula trading networks functioned clandestinely within the economy (q.v.) of the colonial period and have expanded markedly since independence.

E

EANNES, CONSALO. As a representative of the Portuguese Crown, Eannes was sent to visit the Prince of Tekrur (q.v.) and the Lord of Timbuktu of Mali (q.v.) in the last quarter of the fifteenth century in order to establish commercial and political relations.

EANNES, GIL. Sailing for Prince Henry (q.v.) in 1434 and 1435, Eannes made two trips in a cumbersome fifty-ton square-sailed *barca*. More efficient *caravelas* (q.v.) were operational after 1441. After returning to Lisbon in 1435, he later set sail with Afonso Gonçalves Baldaio and went south of the Tropic of

Cancer. These voyages were the first recorded in that region since the time of the Phoenicians (q.v.) in the seventh and fifth centuries BC. In subsequent expeditions, Eannes made three consecutive trips in 1444, 1445, and 1446 using the more advanced *caravel*-type of ship.

ECONOMIC COMMUNITY OF WEST AFRICAN STATES (ECOWAS). *See* ECONOMICS: REGIONAL.

ECONOMICS: COLONIAL POLICIES. Soon after the 'pacification' of *Guiné Portuguesa*, great efforts were made to secure the territory's economy as a special reserve for Portuguese exploitation. The consolidation efforts entailed the maintenance of a tight grip on the colonial economy, which meant subordinating it to that of Portugal. To secure this, the external trade of the territory had to be 'nationalized'; that is to say, Portuguese firms had to monopolize the trade. And in addition to *nationalização* (nationalization), a policy of *fiscalização* (control) of internal trade also had to be rigorously implemented.

The colonial economy was essentially a peasant economy, despite attempts to create a plantation economy during the early years. Commodity production (especially groundnuts) for export was achieved without any fundamental dislocation of indigenous institutions; there were, in other words, no major technological innovations involved. This also meant that there was no significant land alienation or ruthless displacement of peasants. In particular, Guineans were saved from the brutal enforcement of harsh labor codes as was done in Angola, Mozambique, São Tomé, Príncipe, and other colonies in Africa with plantation economies and/or a significant number of European settlers.

According to the 1953 Agricultural Census conducted by Amilcar Cabral (q.v.) in his capacity as an agronomist in the Portuguese colonial service, food crop production dominated economic activity. While cash production occupied 23.17% of cultivated land, that of food crops took up 76.29% (Cabral 1956, 31). Total output of groundnuts, the main cash crop, was calculated at 3,975 tons, while that of rice, the principle staple crop, was estimated at 100,277 tons.

Official promotion and encouragement of rice production, which met with a favorable response from especially Balanta (q.v.) migrants in the southern regions of Catio and Cacine, was motivated by the crop's export value rather than concern for the demands of domestic food supply. Indeed, up until the disruption of agricultural activities by the armed liberation struggle, rice produced in the south of the country was exported, "not to Cacheu and other deficit areas" (Galli and Jones 1987, 43) but mainly to Portugal, Cape Verde, Senegal, Gambia, and Guinea-Conakry.

The *nacionalização* efforts earnestly pursued after 'pacification' were such that by the end of the Second World War Portuguese firms had almost completely dominated the import-export trade, monopolized for a long time by French and German merchants. This was achieved mainly through such coercive policies as forced cultivation and forced delivery of cash crops to official trading centers; a policy which, predictably, met with significant resistance from the cultivators who, faced with disadvantageous producer prices and the poor range and quality of goods available, as compared to those in Senegal and The Gambia, registered their dissatisfaction by (among other strategies) withdrawal to subsistence agriculture, migration (permanently or seasonally), and engagement in clandestine cross-border trading.

The colonial state's lack of commitment to agricultural development, evident from its almost total neglect of vital infrastructure includes a poor road network, inadequate transport system, no agricultural credit or extension service, and rudimentary health and education facilities. These were all important disincentives for increasing peasant production. By 1965, the agricultural economy was still characterized by the "non existence of a basic institutional structure oriented towards development" (Picardo Horta 1965, 484). When, during the late 1960's and early 1970's, Governor António de Spínola (q.v.) felt himself obliged to implement a policy of *Guiné Melhor* (Better Guinea), which resulted in some improvement in the territory's economic and social infrastructure, it was indeed a case of too little too late.

The poor performance of Portuguese colonialism in *Guiné Portuguesa* is also reflected in the low level of industrial development. At the start of the armed liberation struggle in 1963, industrial activities, limited to rice husking, the extraction of groundnut and palm oils, and the production of soap, timber, and bricks, accounted for a meager 1.3% of GDP. According to the 1950 Census, less than two percent of the active population were employed by such enterprises. The output of these ventures were primarily destined for export or local consumption by the small *civilizado* population. By the end of the colonial period, the few new industries included a brewery and a shirt factory.

A salient feature of the territory's economic ties with Portugal, particularly during the post–1945 period, was a widening gap between imports and exports. Increasingly, the colony imported more from its metropole than it exported, thereby progressively worsening the balance of payments situation. Apart from the years 1949, 1953, and 1954, this period showed a steadily deteriorating balance of payments deficit which worsened sharply after 1959. Valued in 1965 at 313.5 million *escudos*, it more than doubled five years later to 702.6 million *escudos* (Picardo Horta 1965, 34).

The economic subordination of the territory and its use, through highly protective tariffs, as a dumping ground for Portugal's non-competitive non-capital goods manufactures assured that economic development remained rudimentary. Obsessed with balanced budgets and financially self-sufficient colonies, the *Estado Novo* kept investment for economic and social development at a minimum.

On the defensive both internationally and locally during the last days of colonial rule, Portugal felt herself obliged to launch the *Guiné Melhor* program which, by the time of independence, resulted in slightly expanding the economic and social infrastructure of the territory. At the end of the colonial period there were more paved roads (550 km.), health (q.v.) facilities (an extra military hospital, an increase of seven maternity clinics and twenty rural sanitary posts, a mental health unit, and a poly-clinic) and educational (q.v.) establishments (220 additional primary schools) with increased pupil enrollment (an extra 24,700 pupils in primary schools and 1,600 student in the only secondary school, the *Liceu Honório Pereira Barreto*).

Yet, as one critical observer noted, the fact remained that the departing colonialists "left Guiné with a woefully inadequate economic base" (Galli November 1990, 21). The meager investment in infrastructure, particularly transport and communication, was oriented towards forging strong links with the 'mother country,' not towards integration within the territory or with neighboring countries in the region. The major roads connected the main trade and administrative centers to Bissau, the capital and primary port. The poor network of secondary roads were "impassable during the rainy season and ill-maintained during the dry season" (ibid.). A telephone call from Bissau (q.v.) to Banjul, or Bissau to Dakar, required connection with an operator in London or Paris, then Lisbon, and finally a line to the required African city.

ECONOMICS: POST COLONIAL. When, on 24 September 1973, the PAIGC (q.v.) unilaterally declared the Portuguese colony of *Guiné Portuguesa* an independent sovereign state, to be known as *Republica da Guiné-Bissau*, anti-colonial and anti-imperialist forces worldwide celebrated. Hopes were raised that this small West African country, whose inhabitants number about a million people, who had made so many sacrifices in order to liberate themselves from oppressive Portuguese colonial domination, would establish 'genuine' political and economic independence.

The PAIGC Program, and numerous policy statements had stressed political and economic independence, unity within and between Guinea-Bissau and Cape Verde, and a radical economic and social development premised on the needs of the majority of the inhabitants, (that is, over eighty percent of the population living in the rural areas) throughout the period of the armed liberation struggle (1963–1974).

More than two decades after that historic event, it is evident that the radical liberation movement has failed to realize its commitment to transform Guinean society. The failure has important implications for, among other things, the country's commitment to Pan African unity and regional integration through ECOWAS (q.v.). Clearly, the colonial heritage of Guinea-Bissau has had a major impact on her efforts at national economic development and integration as projected by PAIGC ideology and practice.

In Guinea-Bissau, unlike the situation in Angola or Mozambique, the victorious liberation movement entered the country's capital without facing any serious challenge for power from any rival nationalist organization. Unlike the triumphant liberators in those two countries (MPLA and FRELIMO respectively), the PAIGC never defined itself, or the state it inherited, as a Marxist-Leninist entity. Rather, it viewed itself simply as a 'liberation movement in power,' in a country it characterized as 'a democratic, anti-colonial and anti-imperialist state.' It was to this state that the task of implementing the PAIGC's radical economic, social, and cultural agenda was entrusted.

During the armed liberation struggle, the PAIGC responded to Amilcar Cabral's call to "destroy the economy of the enemy and build our own, to destroy the negative influences of the culture of the enemy and develop our own," and to "destroy the physical ills which colonialism has brought us in order to build a stronger and more capable new being" (Cabral 1980,

239). The party embarked on a bold experiment in the liberated areas which created the village committees, the people's court, the people's stores, the health clinics, and the schools.

With the coming of independence, the task of 'nationalizing' the new structures created during the war apparently became a major preoccupation of the new PAIGC government. At the same time, with the arrival of the liberators in the capital and the takeover of state power, particularly the adoption almost *in extenso*, of the colonial state bureaucracy, the effective control of the populations of the urban centers, which had been held by the Portuguese throughout the war, also became a major preoccupation.

The problems confronting the liberators were real and pressing. The colonial economy laid in ruins. Its transformation or revival required substantial investment. The inherited colonial bureaucracy meant continuity with the past. Its relatively privileged functionaries, steeped in the colonial tradition and resentful of the sudden disappearance of their privileges, had an aspiration to a metropolitan lifestyle which local resources could not support. Although held suspect by the new rulers, the disabling scarcity of skilled manpower meant not only dependence on their expertise but that material inducements had to be made for their unwilling or reluctant collaboration in the supposed 'Socialist experiment.'

The priority to consolidate and reinforce state power and maintain stability at all cost, reflected in the increased tendency towards bureaucratic centralization and the obsession with 'security,' had the consequence of insulating the leadership from the populace. The retreat from PAIGC's radical program and the adoption of policies deemed 'realistic' were conditioned by the colonial legacy, among other factors. The evidence of such retreat is clearest with regards post-colonial economic policies.

ECONOMICS: POST-COLONIAL DEVELOPMENT STRATEGIES. At independence the people of Guinea-Bissau inherited a seriously underdeveloped and distorted economy, a war-ravaged economy characterized by a low level of agricultural activity, a retarded industrial sector, high rates of unemployment and under-employment, a declining GDP, and *inter alia*, a negative balance of trade.

By 1970, the trade deficit, which was valued at 195.5 million *escudos* a decade earlier, had more than tripled to 702.6 million *escudos*. Four years later at the time of independence, it had swollen to a billion *escudos*. Whereas in 1961 the territory's exports covered eighty-five percent of imports, at independence only eight percent of imports could be paid for by exports. The post-independence period has never had any trade surpluses, and the export/import ratio (the proportion of imports paid for by exports) has never exceeded thirty-five percent. This has meant greater dependence on foreign aid and loans. The economic development strategy pursued by the PAIGC government made little attempt to break with Guinea-Bissau's past: the post-colonial state actually continued many of the policies of the colonial administration.

In its drive to consolidate sovereignty over the economy, it not only tried to monopolize external trade but also attempted to control internal trading activities, much as the colonial state had done. Little effort was made to improve the inherited physical infrastructure and marketing conditions or to stimulate and expand production and trade. Consequently, there were widespread shortages of basic necessities, and rural producers increasingly turned to informal markets and the smuggling of goods across the borders, just like they had done during colonial times.

Rural-urban disparities increased, in spite of the PAIGC's stated aim of reducing them. In 1979, for example, 54.8% of State investment funds was allocated to the capital, which contained 14.1% of the country's population. On the other hand, the three largest regions of the country, Oio, Cacheu, and Bafatá (qq.v.), with 17.8%, 17.2%, and 15.1% respectively of the national population, received 10.2%, 5.4%, and 9.0% of total state investment. In 1970, 67 of the 105 industrial units in the country were located in Bissau. According to the *Junta de Investigação Ultramarina* (1972, 117), in 1979, 1,466 (eighty percent) of the 1,833 "industrial workers" nationwide were employed in and around the capital (CECEP: 1980a, 84).

Today, most of the post-independence industrial units are located in the Bissau area and serve mainly Bissau. They are an oxy-acetylene factory, a prefabrication plant, several machine and vehicle repair shops, an automobile assembly plant (now closed), a tin barrel plant, a foam mattress factory, several bakeries and distilleries, a factory converting powdered milk into liquid milk, a pottery, a ceramics factory, a timber processing plant, and a highly controversial agro-industrial complex near Bissau (Cumere) whose construction was stopped by the Vieira government following the coup of 14 November 1980 after it had absorbed some $28 million of public funds.

Since 1980, the Vieira (q.v.) government has significantly reduced State investment in industrial development and halted a number of projects. It has also made some attempts to concentrate a higher proportion of very scarce resources on agriculture (q.v.). In 1981, for example, State spending on industrial projects was reduced from $12.3 million to $1.5 million (Chabal 1986, 92). At the same time, a number of rural development projects and programs were established, the major ones being: the Cotton and Groundnuts Projects in Bafatá financed by European aid; the Geba Valley Rice Project financed by FAO and USAID; the Zone I (Cacheu, Biombo, and Oio regions) Integrated Rural Development Program, financed by the Swedish International Development Authority (SIDA) to promote rice production and crop diversification; and the Integrated Development Program of Tombali Region, financed by the World Council of Churches and OXFAM also aimed to promote rice production. With a credit facility and an extension service attached to each of them, these projects were complemented by two Seed Multiplication Centers in Contuboel (Bafatá Region) and Caboxanque (Tombali Region).

Since 1983, with the adoption of a stabilization program, the economy has been undergoing some 'structural adjustment' on the advice and supervision of the World Bank/International Monetary Fund (IMF) and the country's major creditors. A Structural Adjustment Program (SAP) package was also adopted in 1986, again advised and supervised by the World Bank/IMF-led creditors, aimed at 'adjusting' the ecomony further by the implementation of a series of measures including the reduction of State expenditure and the size of the bureaucracy; the reduction and eventual removal of subsidies on essential items like food and fuel; the ending of State monopolies and their privatization; liberalization of foreign and domestic trade; and administrative reform.

The state continues to rely on foreign aid and loans for food provisioning, the funding of development projects, and the payment of salaries (and the regalias) of government officials and bureaucrats. The growing indebtedness undermines efforts at national and regional economic integration by encouraging maintenance of the colonial mode of production. Fundamentally, it reinforces dependency.

For example, in 1989 debt service payments amounted to 79.2% of exports of goods and non-factor services and 7.3% of GNP, while total debt represented 298.4% of the national product. On the other hand, the deficit on the current account stood at $38.6 million, or 24.2% of GDP. The country's international reserves, calculated at $14.7 million the previous year, fell to zero. In spite of massive injections of foreign aid, Guinea-Bissau is no closer to extricating herself from underdevelopment and dependency. The continuities with the past dependence on Portugal in particular and Europe in general have not been altered radically.

Although there was a tendency to move away from the colonial pattern of international trade and positive steps made towards developing intra-African trade during the early post-independence period, the trend has now been reversed. As during colonial times, Portugal continues to be Guinea-Bissau's most important trading partner.

ECONOMICS: REGIONAL, ECOWAS (ECONOMIC COMMUNITY OF WEST AFRICAN STATES). ECOWAS is a regional union which has sought to assist in achieving West African integration. It works on a variety of levels from trade and commerce, to health, education, communication, and military affairs. Because of the intended unity between Guinea and Cape Verde, there was a high level of optimism that these two countries would have exemplary foreign relations (q.v.) as ECOWAS member nations. However, the failed attempt at unification between Guinea-Bissau and Cape Verde highlights some of the many problems inherent in interstate integration.

The varied structures and experiences inherited from colonial economics (q.v.) constitute an illustration of the wider regional problems. This is compounded by the interests of the ruling parties which are presented as "the interests of the nation." The failed experiment may be instructive about the ongoing efforts at economic integration between impoverished, underdeveloped, debt-burdened, and dependent nations in contemporary Africa.

Cognizant of the country's underdeveloped, distorted and externally-oriented economy, an economy with built-in biases favoring export crop production, dependent on and subservient to the vagaries of international commodity markets, Guinea-Bissau became a founder-member of ECOWAS with the signing of the Treaty of Lagos on 28 May 1975. To date, of the twenty-eight protocols and conventions adopted by the Community, the country has ratified twenty-six; the remaining two, the 1991 Abuja protocol on the creation of a Community Court and the 1992 Dakar convention regarding mutual assistance in penal matters, are all very sensitive judicial questions which Guinean legal experts are still studying. Furthermore, in 1990 she paid all her outstanding membership dues.

However, it is implementation of acts and decisions, rather than ratification and payment of subscriptions, that indicates a country's commitment to an organization. Non-implementation of ECOWAS protocols by member states is at the heart of the little progress made thus far, which reflects a lack of political will, which itself is conditioned by, among other things, the heavy weight of colonial legacies and considerations of 'national interests.'

The colonial legacy in Guinea-Bissau, as in the other states of West Africa, constitutes a formidable obstacle to national and interstate integration efforts. Continuities with the past continue unabated, and the country, like others in the region, is as ever caught in a vicious cycle of underdevelopment. With her radical development strategy virtually abandoned, she is now moving closer and closer to Portugal (q.v.), with numerous bilateral accords in the economic, political, cultural, and, ironically, military fields. The deepening crisis is reflected in the growing disparity between the rate of resource inflows and outflows. Growing indebtedness has meant growing dependency. In 1990, total debt, calculated at $592.8 million, represented 321.3% of GNP, the highest ratio in West African.

Indeed, the debt burden is a serious problem not only for Guinea-Bissau, but for all the other member states of ECOWAS. Among other things, it undermines their commitment to the integration effort. The fundamental challenge of ECOWAS, therefore, is the willingness, or ability, of the ruling classes of the member states to restructure their inherited colonial economies to meet the basic needs of the majority of their increasingly marginalized and impoverished citizens.

ECONOMICS: STRUCTURAL ADJUSTMENTS, 1986–1993. The eleven years of armed struggle meant the destruction of dams and dikes crucial for rice production; the disruption of normal production, particularly in the agricultural sector where over eight-five percent of the economically active population was, and still is, employed; and a large rural exodus (estimated by United Nations [q.v.] High Commission for Refugees at 150,000 or twenty percent of the total population).

Early post-independence economic development strategies emphasized industrial development, processing of primary products, and import substitution of some essential consumer goods, which turned out to be a failure. During the first decade of independent statehood (1973–1983), tight control over internal and external trade, failure to improve the poor inherited physical infrastructure and marketing conditions, stimulate, and expand production and trading activities led to chronic shortages of basic necessities, growth of parallel markets, smuggling of goods across the borders, and emigration to neighboring countries.

In March 1983, an economic stablization/recovery program aimed at restructuring the economy and addressing the appalling economic situation was adopted by the Guinean government, with financial support from the World Bank and the country's major creditors such as Sweden, Holland, Kuwait, Saudia Arabia, the United States, the European Economic Community (EEC), the UN, and the African Development Bank. The new strategy was aimed at expanding agricultural production and export, reducing the importation of basic food items like rice, correcting internal and external price distortions, and improving the efficiency of the public sector. Although still controlled, the prices of agricultural products were raised in a move to stimulate production. Taxes were also raised.

With delayed implementation of the necessary institutional reforms, as well as the resultant inadequate fiscal control, the anticipated economic recovery did not happen. Between 1983 and 1986, budget deficits and the balance of payments steadily grew worse. Increased domestic borrowing contributed to the growth of the money supply, which in turn contributed to growing inflation. Increased foreign borrowing to cover budget deficits led to growing external debt and debt servicing obligations. Whereas in 1980 the total external debt was US $134.1 million, in 1985 it more than doubled to US $307.8 million; while in 1980 debt servicing charges amounted to US $4.6 million, five years later it stood at US $9.0 million.

An outcome of the failure of the economic stablization/recovery program was the structural adjustment program introduced in 1987. This was advised and financially supported by the World Bank/International Monetary Fund (WB/IMF)-led creditors. It aimed at further restructuring the economy through such measures as the dramatic reduction of state expenditures and the size of the bureaucracy; the reduction and eventual removal of the subsidies on essential items like food and fuel; the dismantling and privatizing of state monopolies; stimulation of the expansion of agricultural production and export; liberalization of internal and external trade; and institutional/administrative reforms. Controlling inflation and stablizing prices, in order to achieve some macroeconomic stablity by the end of 1989, was a major preoccupation of the two-year program. The strategies adopted included devaluations, tax increases on persons and consumer goods, price hikes for utilities such as water, electricity, gas, transport, and telephone, and for the first time, charges for health care services.

Between 1987 and 1989, the Guinean economy grew, in real terms, at very significant rates: 5.6% in 1987; 6.9% in 1988; and 9.6% in 1989. The volume of both exports and imports increased significantly. The local currency, the *peso*, was devalued substantially to bring it closer to the parallel 'black' market rate. Numerous import restrictions were relaxed, and the state monopoly on the import of grains was abolished. Consequently, the most conspicuous and welcomed change in the economy became the availability of a variety of consumer goods in shops and markets, particularly in the urban areas. The liberalization measures had significantly stimulated commerce and trade, ending the chronic shortages of, and long lines for, basic necessities like rice, bread, cooking oil, and sugar. Some of the the other major objectives of the structural adjustment program still remained to be achieved, however.

The volume of exports had significantly increased (mainly cashew nuts and groundnuts) from about 16,000 tons in 1986 to 29,650 tons in 1989; fishery products from about 500 tons in 1986 to about 560 tons in 1989; and forestry products from about 3,800 tons in 1986 to about 24,600 tons in 1989. However, the value of cashew nuts, which account for two-thirds of total exports, was eroded by falling world market prices. Exports continued to be destined to a few international markets: cashew nuts (sixty-six percent of total exports) mainly to India; the rest mainly to western Europe, Africa and the United States, each taking only one percent of the export trade. The balance of trade grew progressively worse: it was US$ 29.3 million in 1987; US$ 42.9 million in 1988; and $54.7 million in 1989. Moreover, the volume and composition of imports remained highly biased toward consumption goods, with rice, the staple crop which is also locally produced in large quantitites, making up more than fifty percent of the food import bill, while personal and passenger vehicles account for more than fifty percent of the import of transport equipment.

On the other hand, inflation, a major preoccupation of the adjustment program, was still out of control, at a yearly average

The Trade Deficit, 1987–1991 (US $millions)

Year	Export	Import	Deficit	Exp/Imp Ratio
1987	15.4	44.7	29.3	34
1988	15.9	58.9	43.0	27
1989	14.2	68.9	54.7	21
1990	19.2	68.0	48.8	33
1991	20.4	67.4	47.0	30

Source: BCGB, Boletim Estatistico, 1993

of ninety-seven percent in 1987, sixty percent in 1988, and eighty percent in 1989. This was a result of an exaggerated expansion of credit and uncontrolled public expenditures. At the same time, the country plunged into greater indebtedness. In 1989, the total foreign debt increased to US$ 498.4 million, from US$ 336.0 million three years earlier, representing 298.4% of the national product. Debt servicing payments that year amounted to 79.2% of the export of goods and non-factor services and 7.3% of the GNP. The country's international reserves, calculated at US$ 14.7 million dollars in 1988, fell to zero.

At the end of the three-year program, the over US$ 100 million of foreign aid loans and grants which poured into the country did not give much stimulation to the productive sectors of the economy. In particular, loans for agricultural development mainly benefitted the privileged class of merchants, senior civil servants, high-ranking military and police officers, and top politicians, who, as a result of the liberalization of the economy, were also the principal beneficiaries of the phenome-

The Debt Burden, 1985–1990 (US $ millions)

Year	GNP	Total Debt	Debt Service	TD/GNP (%)	DS/GNP (%)
1985	155.9	307.8	9.0	197.4	5.8
1986	124.6	336.0	6.0	269.4	4.8
1987	160.1	437.5	10.2	273.2	6.8
1988	151.0	455.0	7.2	301.3	4.8
1989	167.0	498.4	12.2	298.4	7.3
1990	184.5	592.8	8.7	321.3	4.8

Source: World Bank, World Debt Tables, 1991

nal increase in land concessions (*pontas*, q.v.). Much of the money borrowed by these *ponteiros* did not go towards the development of the *pontas*; instead it was used to finance import/export businesses, purchase passenger and personal vehicles, and construct houses.

In spite of the limited success of the first structural adjustment program, the Guinean government reached agreement with the World Bank and the country's major donors to launch the second adjustment program, to cover the period 1989–91. Soon it too ran into difficulties in implementation, and poor performance led to dissatisfaction by the WB/IMF and delays in releasing the second and third *tranches*, or installments, of the Structural Adjustment Credit (SAC) arrangement. The former had been scheduled for the first quarter of 1990 but was not released until January 1991. The latter was expected in March 1991 but was not paid until June 1993. Forced to adopt more severe austerity measures, the government was able to reduce the budget deficit and bring down the rate of inflation from eighty percent in 1989 to around thirty-three percent in 1990. In 1991 there was an expansion of uncontrolled credit facilitated by the establishment of the *Banco de Crédito Nacional* (BCN) in April 1990. This accounted, in part, for the rise of inflation to fifty-seven percent in 1990 and 1991, when the respective targets were respectively twenty-five percent and twenty percent. By 1992 the rate had again soared to seventy percent.

The overall economic impact of the two adjustment programs had not been great, especially with regard to the rural areas where the overwhelming majority of the population resides. In spite of the availability of funds, small farmers did not have, and still remain without, access to agricultural credit. Producer prices have not risen enough to have significant impact on living standards. Largely at the expense of small family farms, the proliferation of large land concessions, or *pontas*, has favored the largely absentee owners who monopolize whatever funds are available. This has also meant conflicts relating to family-held land, as well as land which is owned communally or has sacred usages for spiritual shrines or burials.

Although all land is declared to be state land, customary law is also recognized regarding possession and use of land surrounding the *tabancas* (q.v.). A feature of the land concessions boom is precisely a consequence of the violation of customary law when 'unused' or 'unoccupied' communal lands are awarded to the *pontas*. It is estimated that of the 1,653 concessions made between 1974 and 1990, over eighty percent were granted since the economic liberalization of 1986.

Attempts to restructure the Guinean economy have cost the country dearly in the social sector. The already inadequate health (q.v.) care provisions have seriously deteriorated, with chronic shortages of qualified personnel and vital medications. In most cases, hospitals and health centers do not even measure up to the most minimum standard of hygiene. Malaria remains the main cause of death for the population as a whole. The poor health situation is compounded by the country's sanitation problems, limited access to drinking water, and reductions in social services. The educational system is also deteriorating. Decaying infrastructure, poor training, and badly paid and highly unmotivated teachers leave the majority of children wishing to be anywhere but school. Many schools do not open for quite some time after the official beginning of the academic year because of teacher shortages.

Problems with attempts to restructure the Guinean economy are reflected in the fact that, to date, no agreement has been reached for launching the third structural adjustment program, in spite of the government's almost complete withdrawal and the extensive privatization program in progress thus far. Such entities as the Port of Bissau, the telephone network, *Armazéns do Povo* (People's Stores, q.v.), *Hotel 24 de Setembro*, the bus company *Silô Diata*, the shipping line *Guiné-Mar*, and the national airline *TAGB*, are partially or wholly privatized. For the first time, there are two private banks in the country. The *Banco International da Guiné-Bissau* (BIGB), a Luso-Guinean joint venture, was started in March 1990; the Guinean government holds twenty-six percent of the shares, Guinean investors twenty-five percent, and the remaining forty-nine percent belongs to Portuguese financial institutions (including the *Banco Pinto Sotto-Mayor*, 17%; *Crédito Predial Português*, 17.5%; *Geofinança*, 14%); and *Totta & Açores.*

ECONOMICS: TRADE, DEVELOPMENT. The vast majority of trading in Guinea-Bissau occurs through barter and cash-purchased exchanges carried out between individual peasant producers or at village, regional, and urban markets. This barter and cash trade is of food surpluses, fish caught locally by village fishermen, small-scale livestock (q.v.) (chicken, pigs, goats, sheep), as well as large livestock (cattle), collected wild fruits (bananas, coconuts, cashews), collected firewood, and artisanal products. These artisanal products are fabricated within villages and include soap, pots, calabashes, baskets, palm oil, peanut oil, cashew wine, cloths, and clothes made by weavers and tailors, iron farm tools wrought by blacksmiths, and salt extracted from brackish riverine paddies. While weaving, tailoring, blacksmithing, and large-scale herding are carried out by men, the remainder of the artisanal activities are undertaken by women (q.v.), and it is the women who also do most of the barter and cash trading.

While cash was introduced into the rural economy during the colonial era, mainly through the coercing of peasants to pay colonial taxes and through the attraction of some imported goods in the urban areas, trade remained dominated by barter exchanges. Some fifty to seventy percent of rural exchange is still carried out through barter trading, but the economic crisis that emerged during and after the independence struggle did force rural people to rely more heavily on monetary exchanges. This has not only stimulated greater efforts at cash crop and surplus food production, artisan production, fishing, livestock raising, and fruit and firewood gathering but has also generated an enormous amount of seasonal migration, such as young men travelling to Senegal and Guinea-Conakry during the agricultural (q.v.) off-season to labor for wages or to sell products grown or fabricated in Guinea-Bissau.

To a large extent, the continuing predominance of barter and local cash trading reflects the failure of the state to construct a viable official marketing structure in the post-colonial period. After independence, the government set up two State-owned retail/wholesale companies, *Socomin* and a network of *Armazéns do Povo* (People's Stores, q.v.), together totaling 216 official trading centers. There was much optimism, as the *Armazéns do Povo* had expanded successfully during the anti-colonial struggle, providing peasants with foreign supplied goods (such as sugar and lamps) in return for cash crops. However, large-scale difficulties emerged during the independence era, including a lack of trained and competent managers, the inability to distribute basic grains to needy sectors of the population during periods of food shortage, and a lack of foreign exchange with which to purchase goods that could have stimulated peasants to bring their cash crops to these State stores. As a result, not only did the traditional local trading continue to predominate, but a long distance unofficial trade network, carried out by *Dyula* (q.v.) and Senegalese merchants, has emerged. This trade is based on foreign currency, such as the French West African franc, and it has expanded through the late 1970's and early 1980's.

In addition to these problems, the few industrial enterprises that had been constructed operated far from productive capacity and generated substantial investment losses. Macroeconomic statistics indicate the depth of the difficulties: between 1975 and 1979, the external debt tripled; the external debt in 1983 was $200 million, as exports barely covered one-fourth of imports; the 1982 balance of payments showed a $32 million deficit. The country remains highly dependent on overseas aid, with a predicted $110 million a year of such aid necessary to keep the economy afloat from 1983 to 1986. In recognition of all these difficulties, radical reforms were carried out in 1984 with the specific goals of revitalizing officially sanctioned trade and boosting the level of marketed agricultural surplus. Large-scale industrial projects were discontinued or radically reduced in scale, and the State trading companies, especially the *Armazéns do Povo*, were privatised in order to encourage the flow of consumer goods to the countryside. Producer prices were raised seventy-six percent for rice, seventy-two for groundnuts, eighty-four percent for cashew nuts, and ninety-two percent for palm kernels; export earnings for all these crops increased as a result of these price rises. These reforms, combined with a 50 percent devaluation of the Guinean *peso* and price rises for basic food, were viewed positively by the WB/IMF, which made loans in 1984 totaling US $26 million. It is expected that budgetary and external deficits will be reduced.

Between 1980 and 1984, production of groundnuts rose from 20,000 to 30,000 tons, although only 17,600 and 19,000 tons, respectively for 1980 and 1984, were sold to the official market, with 6,800 and 10,000 tons being exported. In 1980, 8,800 tons of palm kernels were marketed, and 6,000 tons were exported, with the figure rising in 1984 to 11,000 tons marketed, and 10,600 tons exported. In the same four-year period, the amount of cashew nuts marketed rose from 1,000 to 7,000 tons, with 900 tons exported in 1980 and 6,000 tons in 1984.

The most significant exports are cashew nuts, followed by groundnuts, palm kernels, and palm oil, together comprising $6.1 million in exports; shellfish and fish, totaling $5.5 million in exports; industrial products, with $1.7 million of exports; and timber, with $0.7 million. While the exported agricultural commodities are the same as under colonial rule, the development of fish exports is a post-colonial development: they grew from $0.3 million in 1976 to $5.5 million in 1982. Regarding imports, food, especially rice, and beverages constitute the largest single item, followed by industrial and commercial supplies, petroleum, and capital goods. While this represents a shift from most of the colonial period, when the country exported rice and peanuts and textiles, it is the logical consequence of the agricultural destruction which occurred during the anti-colonial struggle and forced Guinea to begin relying on food imports as early as the mid–1960's.

Portugal monopolized ninety percent of trade during the colonial era, but since independence Guinea-Bissau has accumulated an extraordinary diversity of trading and development partners. Portugal remains the largest single importer, providing forty-three percent of Guinea-Bissau's imports in 1982, followed by France with nine percent, Sweden with seven percent, the U.S. with six percent, the Netherlands and the USSR with five percent each, and Burma with two percent. Portugal is also Guinea-Bissau's principal purchaser of exports, buying thirty-four percent. Spain buys most of Guinea-Bissau's caught fish, followed by Senegal and China. Guinea-Bissau receives international aid from the World Bank, the European Union, the IMF, and OPEC, and enjoys bilateral development funding from Abu Dhabi, Saudi Arabia, Kuwait, Canada, Norway, Sweden, Denmark, France, West Germany, Britain, Italy, Spain, Greece, Luxembourg, Belgium, Austria, the United States, Brazil, Chile, China, India, Pakistan, Burma, Thailand, Japan, South Korea, the former Soviet Union, East Germany, Hungary, and Yugoslavia. As a result of this diversity, Guinea-Bissau is able to avoid economic dependency on any one political bloc or superpower and to uphold an international political stance of genuine nonalignment. *See* GUINEA-BISSAU: FOREIGN RELATIONS.

EDUCATION. Metropolitan Portugal (q.v.) was notable in Europe for a particularly low level of public education. For example, in 1960 in Portugal only 9.8 percent of the population was enrolled in primary school, while the comparable statistic for Holland was 13.0 percent, the USSR, 14.2 percent, and the United States, 18.4 percent. As expected, in Portugal's African colonies the situation was far worse. Only 3.8 percent of the population of Guinea-Bissau was enrolled in primary school in these late years of colonialism. Such low rates were typical of the European colonies in Africa, but following independence this proportion has changed markedly.

The main function of the colony of Portuguese Guinea was for primary production and some labor recruitment; formal mass education was deemed unnecessary or even counter-productive to these goals. Judging from a 98 percent illiteracy rate in 1950, a heyday of colonialism, one may easily see the educational policy of Portugal in Guinea-Bissau. Even mission education, which sometimes played an important role in other African countries, was virtually negligible in Guinea-Bissau. Even as late as 1972 the educational budget for Guinea-Bissau was an absurd forty-two cents per student per year.

The available educational statistics are also unclear, as they do not indicate whether students were simply enrolled, actively attended, or actually completed a given level of education. Just prior to independence, the 1973 Provincial Report on Educational Services of Guinea-Bissau offered the following data which should be considered as maxima for the various categories.

To the credit of Portugal, it is notable that in the one decade just before they departed from Guinea-Bissau they not only quadrupled the number of primary students but also improved the student teacher ratio from 73:1 in 1962 to a far better 48:1 in 1973. The level of adult literacy in the 1970's was twenty-five percent for men but only thirteen percent for women (q.v.). This inequality by sex is also expressed at the primary

Education in Guinea-Bissau

	Primary		Secondary	
Dates	Students	Teachers	Students	Teachers
1962–63	11,827	162	987	46
1963–64	11,877	164	874	44
1964–65	12,210	163	1,095	45
1965–66	22,489	192	1,293	42
1966–67	24,099	204	1,039	43
1967–68	24,603	244	1,152	40
1968–69	25,213	315	1,773	111
1969–70	25,854	363	1,919	147
1970–71	32,051	601	2,765	110
1971–72	40,843	803	3,188	158
1972–73	47,626	974	4,033	171
1986	77,004	3,121		
1988–89	82,442	3,695	5,131	597
1996–97	95,055	(projected)	6,045	(projected)

Sources: Repatição Provincial do Servicos de Educação, Provincia da Guiné, February 1973; UNESCO, Statistical Yearbook, 1986; Ministério de Educação Nacional da Guiné-Bissau, 1988–89.

level, with almost twice the number of boys as girls enrolled in school.

In 1960, the Portuguese policy had resulted in only fourteen university graduates in the entire country, while between 1964 and 1973 the ruling PAIGC party itself arranged to send some 422 students overseas for advanced education, and by 1973 there were some thirty-five PAIGC-supported university graduates.

During the nationalist war the PAIGC also constructed its own educational system in the liberated areas. This effort to achieve mass primary education did not surpass the Portuguese in numbers, given the great adversity of air attacks by Portuguese fighter-bombers and security problems for the young students. However, because of this context it was a remarkable achievement. Enrollment fluctuated as periods of Portuguese counterinsurgency required that the simple school buildings were moved to new locations, new air attack trenches dug, and supplies carried from place to place.

The leading PAIGC facility was the Pilot School in Guinea-Conakry,which usually had about 120 students (about 80 boys, and 40 girls). This secondary school was very disciplined and was often a source of direct recruitment into the PAIGC through the operation of the Pioneers of the Party youth organization which operated within the PAIGC educational system. A kindergarten for absent PAIGC Party officials and war orphans was also located in Conakry. Each of the three regions inside liberated Guinea-Bissau also had a boarding school as well as the more than 200 primary day schools under the forest canopy. The data on PAIGC schools during the war for primary students (ages seven to fifteen) follow.

Since independence, the PAIGC claims to have achieved a twenty-three percent decline in illiteracy to about seventy-five percent, as the educational facilities have been able to operate openly under peaceful conditions. Needless to say, the educational task still has a very long way to go. The statistics for the early 1980's suggest that there is still forward progress with 89,720 students enrolled in primary school, 6,236 in secondary schools, 135 students in technical and higher-level courses, and 1,130 students receiving secondary, university, or specialized training in such areas as medicine, vocations, and administration in a variety of foreign countries. By 1986 continued improvement was registered in both primary and secondary enrollment as well as the numbers of teachers and schools. The level of illiteracy had fallen to 68.6 percent.

PAIGC Primary Schools in Liberated Zones

Year	Students	Teachers	Schools
1965	13,361	191	127
1966	14,380	220	159
1967	9,384	284	158
1968	8,130	243	134
1969	8,559	248	149
1970	8,574	251	157
1971	14,531	258	164
1972	20,000	251	200
1975	60,000	—	400

Source: PAIGC Document

Aside from these institutions, personnel, and students in formal education, there are now mass circulation newspapers, radio programs, community organizations, and adult literacy programs which play an important role in the goal of upgrading and constructing expanded educational services.

ELECTIONS. At first multi-party elections in Guinea-Bissau were excluded by the one-party state, however, in the democratic reforms in the early 1990's the legal provisions were changed to allow this possibility. Elections were promised and postponed in 1993 and 1994, and it appeared that they would not be held before the completion of this book. At last, on 3 July 1994 the elections were held. The elections provided a plurality for the ruling party but they did not provide the required majority margins. This necessitated a run-off election, between the two leading candidates, João 'Nino' Vieira of the *Partido Africano da Independência de Guiné e Cabo Verde*, PAIGC (q.v.), and Kumba Yala of the *Partido da Renovação Social*, PRS (q.v.). The results of the Legislative and Presidential elections follow.

The very surprising result of this part of the election was the much underestimated young candidate of the PRS, Kumba Yala. The demography (q.v.) of Guinea-Bissau shows that more that fifty-six percent of the population was born after independence in 1973. Bissau itself has a population heavily composed of youth. Election laws required a run-off election if the greatest percentage of votes cast for President did not exceed fifty percent. Thus, the incumbent President Vieira was required to face Kumba Yala in a second run-off election scheduled for 7 August 1994.

I. Results of the Legislative Elections, 3 July 1994

Party	Votes	Percentage	Deputies
PAIGC	143,982	37.92	62
RGB/MB	57,566	16.17	18
UM	17,797	10.34	6
PRS	29,957	8.42	12
PCD	15,411	4.33	0
PUSD	8,286	2.33	0
FLING	7,475	2.10	1
FGC-SD	494	0.14	0

Notes: Of the 400,000 registered voters, there was an 88.91% turnout. The full names of the parties are found in the list of abbreviations and in the dictionary entries, with the exception of UM which is a coalition of six parties led by Bubacar Djaló, who is the President of Liga Guineense de Protecção Ecológia, LIPE (q.v.). The UM coalition consists of the Frente Democrática, the Frente Democrática Social, LIPE, the Movimento para a Unidade e Democracia, the Partido Democrático para Progresso, and the Partido para Renovação e Desenvolvimento.

II. Results of the Presidential Elections, 3 July 1994

Candidate	Party	Votes	Percentage
Nino Vieira	PAIGC	142,577	46.20
Kumba Yala	PRS	67,518	21.88
Domingos Fernandes	RGB/MB	53,825	17.44
Carlos Gomes	PCD	15,645	5.07
François Mendy	FLING	8,655	2.80
Bubacar Djaló	UM	8,506	2.76
Victor S. Maria	PUSD	6,388	2.07
Antonieta R. Gomes	FCG-SD	5,509	1.79

Notes: See above notes and main entries for further party reference. Carlos Gomes (PCD) was an independent candidate supported only by PCD whose leader, Victor Mandinga, was not eligible to run for President under the current election laws, which require that both parents of the candidate be Guineans born in the country. The overall turnout was 89.3% of the eligible voters.

ETHNIC/SOCIAL GROUPS OF GUINEA. *See* APPENDIX H and I; BAGAS; BAIOTES; BALANTAS; BAMBARAS; BANYUNS; BEAFADAS, BIJAGÓS; BRAMES; COCOLIS; CONHAQUES; DIALONKES; DIOLAS; DYULAS; FELUPES; FULAS; FUTA TORO; FUTA JALLON; JEWS; LANDUMAS; MANDINKAS; MANJACOS; NALUS; SENEGAMBIANS; SERER; SONINKES; SUSUS; TANDAS; TIMENES.

III. Results of the Second Round Presidential Elections.

Region	Vieira	Yala
Tombali	9,337	12,093
Quinara	8,450	6,003
Oio	19,400	31,588
Biombo	14,145	4,699
Bolama/Bijagós	9,866	877
Bafata	24,788	16,715
Gabu	24,105	14,130
Cacheu	13,572	20,160
Bissau	36,267	41,253
Total	159,930	147,518
Percentage	(52.02%)	(47.98%)

Notes: These results have been much contested by the coalition built among supporters of Kumba Yala. They claim that they have won instead. Yala hardly campaigned in the Bolama area. Supporters of the PAIGC have been celebrating with great enthusiasm, including congratulations from the heads of State of Senegal, France, Cape Verde, and Portugal.

EXPLORERS AND TRAVELLERS. *See* AFRICANUS, L.; AZAMBUJA, D.; AZURARA, G.; CADAMOSTA, A.; CÃO, D.; COLUMBUS, C; DA GAMA, V.; DE NOLI, A.; DIAS, B.; DIAS, D.; EANNES, C.; EANNES, G.; GOMES, D.; GOMES, F.; GONÇALVES, A.; HENRY; MALFANTE; A.; TRISTÃO, N.

EXXON EXPLORATION OF GUINEA. *See* MINERALS.

F

FAIDHÉRBE, LOUIS LÉON CÉSAR. Appointed as the French Governor of Senegal in 1854. He had been a poor student at the famed Ecolé Polytechnique and then entered the French Army Corps of Engineers. His first service was in Algeria, which he found exciting and adventuresome. His arrival in West Africa coincided with the expansion of French imperialism, so he was able to gain unimagined prominence. His first service in Senegal began in 1852 as a military engineer, and he impressed the contemporary Governor Protet with his knowledge as an amateur ethnologist. Protet, the Governor of Senegal, quickly promoted Faidherbe as his replacement. After achieving his top appointment he developed expansive plans for military conquest and extensive trade to the Upper Niger. This was part of his strategic objective to undercut the trans-Saharan trade and divert this trade toward French controlled ports along the West African coast. A parallel goal was to offer energetic competition with the British who had similar objectives. The British continued with their probes from Sierra Leone and Gambia to take over the island of Bolama (q.v.), the future capital of Guinea-Bissau.

The Portuguese were caught in the middle between these two spheres of influence, with the French pushing hard into the Casamance (q.v.), still under weak Portuguese control at Ziguinchor, and against Guinea-Bissau's southern border with today's Guinea-Conakry, driving in from the coast. Faidhérbe was especially successful in making a strong base for the French in coastal Senegal, but initially the interior region such as the Almamate of Futa Toro (q.v.) was allowed autonomy but was later to be contested by the Islamic revival of Al-Imami Umar Tall (q.v.).

At first the French conceded to pay taxes to the Imam of Futa Toro, but they were not pleased when he put up a stiff resistance, especially at Medina in 1857 on the upper reaches of the Senegal River in Futa Toro where the French wanted access to the gold mines of Bambuk. From 1858 to 1860 the region was intensely contested between these two separate spheres of influence. The first appointment of Faidhérbe as Governor ended in 1861.

With the region destabilized, tens of thousands of Fula (q.v.) were dispersed or fled into eastern Guinea-Bissau, the upper Gambia, and to Futa Jallon (q.v.). In 1863, General Faidhérbe was brought back as Governor to launch a military campaign in Senegal in which he was 'credited' with the 'pacification' of the colony. His second term ended in 1865. Initially he used an efficient policy of indirect colonial rule which sought to create local-level French colonial administrators from traditional elites. Later this gave way to their more direct assimilation policy. One may consult F. T. McNamara, 1989, *France in Black Africa*, (Washington: National Defense University Press) or David Robinson, 1975, *Chiefs and Clerics* (Oxford: Clarendon Press) for additional contextual information.

FARIM. The modern town of Farim, situated on the north bank of the River Farim/Cacheu (q.v.), some 135 kilometers upriver from the port of Cacheu (q.v.), was for centuries an important port and caravan stop. It was apparently founded in 1641 by the Captain-Major of Cacheu, *Gonçalo Gambôa de Ayala*, who encouraged the significant *lançado* inhabitants of Geba (q.v.) on the river of the same name to abandon that settlement and move to a site which was relatively less vulnerable to African influence and domination. No doubt this move was with a view to control the activities of these 'illegal' traders. It was named Farim, because it was in the territory of a Mandinka (q.v.) *farim*, who was a provincial ruler of a constituent state of the Kaabu (q.v.) Empire. Originally the *farim* (*farma*, pl.) owed allegiance to the Mansa (Emperor) of Mali (q.v.), but when Mali collapsed to attacks from Songhai the *farma* gained a great deal of local autonomy as regional slave raiders who worked in conjunction with the *Dyulas* (q.v.) and the *lançados* (q.v.), who traded in slaves, kola nuts, wax, ivory, and gold from the Bure and Bambuk gold fields on the Upper Niger River. The settlement was referred to by the local Mandinka/ Soninke (q.v.) inhabitants as *Tubabodaga* ('village of the whites'). It was indeed a principal port for the Cacheu-based traders, who would ascend the river in sailing vessels of various sizes to obtain captives secured by Kaabu's never-ending wars (fomented mainly for that purpose).

On 10 November 1696, a *regimento* (written instructions guiding the actions of Portuguese officials) was issued creating the *presídio* (garrison) of Farim. This was apparently prompted by the anticipated revolt of the inhabitants of nearby Canico who three months earlier had threatened to expel the *tubabos* ('whites') of Tubabodaga. Ostensibly, the 'whites' had dared to apprehend, tie up, and hold captive the ruler of Canico, allegedly because of some altercation he had with a *morador cristão* (Christian dweller). Convinced that the enraged subjects of the ruler would attack, the residents made a desperate appeal for help to the Captain-Major of Cacheu, Santos Vidigal Castanho, who responded promptly with a well-armed force of some 172 men. Although this show of force did not result in a clash of arms, it nevertheless sufficiently intimidated the local rulers to make a number of critical concessions which seriously compromised their sovereignty and independence and resulted in the establishment of the *presídio* and a permanent Portuguese military presence. To the stockaded settlement were added three protective walls and a few pieces of artillery transferred from Cacheu. Known as the *Baluarte de São Sebastião* (Bulwark of St. Sebastian), this fortification was subordinated to the *Fortaleza* (Fortress) of Cacheu.

However, Farim's subordination to Cacheu was short-lived.

By the end of the seventeenth century it was experiencing the familiar 'decadence' of the Portuguese establishments in the region, and its inhabitants were subjected to the much reported 'insults' and 'abuses' of the *gentios*. In 1733, for example, the Captain-Major of Cacheu, Manuel António Roiz de Silveira, reported that the three defensive walls were all dilapidated, the artillery was dismounted and useless, and the stockade had several openings; as a consequence, the 'garrison' was unable to defend or take any punitive action against the *gentios*. A century later in 1835, the energetic Honório Pereira Barreto (q.v.), as *provedor* (purveyor) of Cacheu, alarmed at the state of 'decadence' of the *presídio*, reached an agreement with the local rulers to fortify the settlement (at his own expense) with six pieces of artillery. But this obviously did not mean the establishment of Portuguese sovereignty, for the Portuguese and other foreigners continued to pay *daxa* (duty tax) to the local rulers.

Indeed, in 1895 when the Portuguese, in a desperate attempt to establish Pax Lusitana, insisted on the payment of an unprecedented head tax by the Mandinkas, Soninkes, and Balantas (qq.v.) in the immediate surroundings of Farim, a rebellion flared up. Determined to 'punish' the 'rebels,' the Portuguese organized columns in Bolama, Bissau, and Geba (qq.v.) to boost the tiny garrison at Farim, which had been reinforced with a contingent of Angolan soldiers since 1892. On 29 March 1897, the large army of some 9,200 men, armed with Snyder rifles and Krupp machine-guns and bolstered by two Portuguese gunboats, had bloody encounters with an estimated force of about 12,000 'rebels' in the territory of Oio, on the left bank of the river Cacheu/Farim. As the battles intensified and the casualties inflicted on the invading column mounted, a large number of African auxiliaries abandoned the expedition. Before long, the Portuguese were left with about 200 men, most of them regular soldiers. After about eight hours of battle, some of these soldiers also decided to abandon what seemed a hopeless situation. When the firing finally stopped, the Portuguese casualty count listed two officers, three sergeants, one corporal, and thirteen soldiers dead, besides numerous fatalities among the auxiliaries. The commander of the expedition, Lieutenant Jaimé Augusto Graça Falcão, was himself seriously wounded and left to find his own way back to the garrison at Farim. A legend was thus born.

The so-called 'Disaster of Oio' sapped the morale of the Portuguese and left them evermore frustrated with the burdensome task of 'pacifying' *Guiné Portuguesa*. Five years later, on 18 March 1902, another punitive 'pacification' campaign was launched against the Oincas which, notwithstanding wanton destruction of life and property, still did not establish Pax Lusitana in the region. Eleven years would elapse before the bitter and revengeful Portuguese could break the legend of invincibility of the inhabitants of Oio through the use of ruthless mercenaries led by the Senegalese fugitive Abdul Injai (q.v.). For the central role played by this notorious figure in the 'pacification' of the territory as a whole, he was rewarded the Chieftancy of Oio, whose inhabitants lived under a reign of terror until 1919 when, ostensibly unable to tolerate the 'abuses,' of the 'terror of Guinea,' the Portuguese launched a successful campaign against him, which resulted in his surrender and subsequent exile to Cape Verde, where he died some years later.

Meanwhile, Farim grew and expanded. Urbanization started in earnest following the 'pacification' of the region in 1913. That year, the overzealous *residente* of the region, Caetano José Barbosa, easily mobilized sufficient forced labor to ensure the construction and repair of a number of public buildings, roads, and other colonial state development projects. In 1918, the settlement acquired the status of a *vila* (town). With the establishment of a number of European and Levantine traders and trading houses, economic and commerical activities expanded enormously. Already during the first decade of the twentieth century, there were some twenty-four trading firms belonging to Italians, Germans, Belgians, French, and Portuguese, with the French *franc* the most common currency. Farim became a first class *centro comercial* by 1925, and Lebanese and Syrians came to dominate commercial transactions in the town, especially with the abrupt departure of the Germans and Italians at the outbreak of World War II. *Mancarra* (peanuts) and timber were the principal export commodities. The town's growing importance as a commercial and administrative center was reflected by the substantial concentration of *civilizados* there, which by 1950 was estimated at 789, second only to Bolama (q.v.), the old capital.

Like other important towns in the territory, the protracted armed liberation struggle had devastating effects on Farim, with the disruption of economic activities, the paralysis of trade, and the displacement of a significant proportion of residents. Recovery and revival has yet to be achieved.

FARIM-CACHEU, RIOS (Farim and Cacheu Rivers). With head-waters to the north on Contuboel on the Geba River (q.v.), the Farim River flows almost directly west until it reaches the town of Farim. At this point it begins to widen and proceed westward until it becomes known as the Cacheu (q.v.) River since it is in the vicinity of the town of that name. As with the other rivers penetrating the coastal swamps, the Farim and Cacheu rivers were important corridors for the export of slaves and for commerce with the interior through *lançados* and Dyula (qq.v.) traders. The combined length of these rivers is about one hundred and sixty miles, although ships of 2,000 tons are only able to navigate about sixty-two miles to the interior.

FEITOR, FEITORIA. Portuguese royal trade monopolies and private mercantile concerns were usually represented by a *feitor* or local business agent, sometimes with very consider-able powers. A *feitor* occupied a *feitoria* or sometimes-fortified trading outpost. The official or royal backing of the *feitor* can be contrasted with the informal and private traders known as *lançados* (q.v.), although both might be found in the vicinity of a *feitoria*.

FELUPE. A minor Senegambian (q.v.) group most closely re-lated to the Diolas and Baiotes (qq.v.). They have a limited hierarchical structure, but there are some reports of a small tributary kingdom of Mali (q.v.) among the Felupes in the fifteenth century. However, this may have just been imposed by Mali (q.v.) itself. Felupes were often victims of the slave raiders.

The Felupes are famed rice cultivators using flood irrigation techniques of the *bolanhas* (q.v.). They are mainly located in the northwest corner of Guinea-Bissau, especially south of the Casamance (q.v.), but north of the Cacheu River (q.v.), reach-ing the ocean coast in that region. During the period of aggres-sive Portuguese colonization, military reports show acts of resistance by the Felupes from 1878 to 1890, in 1901, 1903 and finally 1915 when they were repressed in the campaigns of Teixeira Pinto (q.v.).

FERNANDES, GIL VINCENTE VAZ. (10 May 1937–). Born in Bolama (q.v.), Guinea-Bissau, Fernandes attended high school in Bissau (q.v.). Because of his early affiliation with the *Partido Africano da Independência de Guiné e Cabo Verde*, (PAIGC, q.v.) he fled to Senegal in September 1960. With plans to study in Poland, he was recruited to attend the University of New Hampshire from which he earned a B.A. degree in Political Science in 1965. Later he received an M.A. from American University in Washington, D.C. Fernandes is a pioneer of the PAIGC on the international scene. From 1970 to 1972 he was the party representative in Cairo and from 1973 to 1974 in Scandinavia. At the time of independence he was a roving ambassador of the Foreign Affairs Commission. He has played a significant role in representing the party at the United Nations (q.v.). He was the first Ambassador of the Republic of Guinea-Bissau to the United States. *See* GUINEA-BISSAU: AMERICAN RELATIONS; GUINEA-BISSAU: FOREIGN RELATIONS.

FERNANDES, VALENTIM. Fernandes was a fifteenth century Portuguese sailor who explored the Senegambian (q.v.) region along with such others as Cadamosta and Tristão (qq.v.). Fernandes's reports added to regional knowledge of the coast and interior kingdoms. His description of the gold trade of Mali (q.v.) helped to stimulate Portuguese interest in the region.

FERREIRA, ANTÓNIO BATICA (Dec. 25, 1939–). Ferreira is one of the few published Guinean poets of African origin. He is the son of a village head in the Canchungo area. He spent seven years in Dakar then lived and studied in Lisbon and Paris and went on to study medicine in Switzerland. His poetry has been published in Portuguese, French, Senegalese, and German journals. Most notable are his poems in *Poetry and Fiction*, published by the Society of the Portuguese Language in 1972. His poems "Infancia" and "Pais Natal" are perhaps his best known. *See* LITERATURE.

FODÉ KABA. *See* ALFA MOLO; MUSA MOLO.

FONIO. This native cereal grain is important in West African agriculture (q.v.) as a basic member of the Sudanic food complex. The scientific name is *Digitaria exilis*; in Portuguese it is known as *fundo*. It is a hardy plant needing little rain or cultivation and has been a basic foodstuff in the Empire of Mali (q.v.) and surrounding secondary kingdoms.

FORÇAS ARMADAS REVOLUCIONARIAS DO POVO (FARP). This was the regular armed forces of the *Partido Africano da Independência de Guiné e Cabo Verde* (PAIGC) during the war. FARP was formed in 1964 in order to wage a more aggressive war against Portuguese colonialism. The function of civilian defense was then handled by the PAIGC local militia units known as the *Forças Armadas Locais* (FAL). The present armed forces of Guinea-Bissau are derived from FARP but are now separate from those in Cape Verde following the 1980 coup d'état in Guinea. The total armed forces of Guinea Bissau number about 6,250 with a ratio of 1:131 in the military versus the general population.

FORCED EMIGRATION. *See* SÃO TOMÉ.

FOREIGN AFFAIRS. *See* CONFERÊNCIA DE ORGANI-ZAÇÕES NACIONALISTAS DAS COLÔNIAS PORTU-GUESAS; GUINEA-BISSAU: AMERICAN (USA) RELA-TIONS, CAPE VERDE RELATIONS, FOREIGN RELATIONS; MOUVEMENT DES FORCES DEMOCRAT-IQUES DE LA CASAMANCE; PARTIDO AFRICANO DA INDEPENDÊNCIA DE CABO VERDE.

FORREA. Forrea is a former territory of the Beafadas and Nalus (qq.v.), located in the southwestern corner of Guinea-Bissau, delimited in the north by the river Corubal (q.v.), in the west by the Rio Sahol (formerly the Rio Matto Grande, a tributary of the Rio Grande), in the south by the Cacine region, and in the east by a small stretch of land beyond the border with Guinea-Conakry. Divided into fifteen Chieftaincies, the Beafa-das, who were the dominant group, controlled eleven, includ-ing Buba, Bolola (qq.v.), Buifada, Contabani, and Inchola; on the other hand, the Nalus, protégés of the Beafadas, were in charge of the remaining four—Combijan, Sanixa, Nalu, and Simbel. The rulers of these territories, which the Mandinkas (q.v.) called Forrea, that is to say, 'free land,' paid tribute to the Mandinka Mansa of Kaabu (q.v.), who did not exercise direct political control. The Beafada and Nalu inhabitants enjoyed a relatively peaceful co-existence for centuries, until the arrival of the Fulas (q.v.) in large numbers during the second half of the nineteenth century.

Fleeing from the extortions and excesses of the Mandinka ruling classes in the neighboring provinces of the Kaabu Em-pire, the Fulas set out, with their slaves and cattle, on a southward migration. In Forrea, the dominant Beafada lords of the land allowed them to settle, provided each family was willing to pay an annual tax of one young bull and sixty bands of *panos* (q.v.). The trickling flow of immigrants soon developed into a great influx as word spread about the relative freedom, the fertility of the soil, and the abundance of pasture. Less than twenty years later, with the help of their slaves and Fula warriors from the Futa Jallon (q.v.) Confederation, the newcomers managed to dispossess their hosts of their land and drive a large number of them out of the territory.

In 1868, the Fula state of Forrea was established, with the Almami (supreme political and religious leader) of the Futa Jallon Confederation recognized as 'protector and principal lord,' thus ending Mandinka suzerainty. However, shortly after the establishment of Fula dominance in Forrea, a bloody civil war broke out among the Fulas and between these and other groups like the Beafadas and Mandinkas. This protracted conflict, which raged furiously from about 1878 to 1890, gave the Portuguese a much-needed pretext to intervene directly in order to bolster their weak position in the region. Open conflict with the rulers of Forrea was rendered inevitable by the increasing number of refugees and rebels seeking the safety of the Portuguese garrison at Buba. The Portuguese authorities constantly refused to meet the demands of the rulers of Forrea to release these asylum seekers. As well, the rebels' use of Buba as a base for launching attacks on Forrea to destroy the properties of their former masters and to steal their cattle all made a Fula-Portuguese conflict inevitable.

Angry with this state of affairs, the Fula (Fulbe-ribe) rulers of Forrea decided to hit at the Portuguese themselves by attacking their garrison at Geba and raiding a number of *pontas* (q.v.) along the Rio Grande. The Portuguese responded with punitive 'pacification' campaigns consisting of large columns of African auxiliaries, Fulbe-djiabe, Mandinkas, and Beafadas with deeply ingrained enmities towards the Fulbe-ribe. The outcome of these campaigns, which increased significantly with the arrival of the bellicose Governor Pedro Inacio Gouveia in 1882, was the signing of a number of 'peace, friendship and obedience' treaties with powerful Fulbe-ribe warlords like Mamadú Paté (q.v.), the ruler of the Chieftancy of Bolola, and Bacar Quidali, the principal ruler of Forrea. These were to become the greatest allies of the aspiring Portuguese colonialists during the protracted 'pacification' wars.

The civil and expansionist wars in Forrea also resulted in the serious disruption of economic activities and the depopulation of the region. The thriving pre-war economy, evidenced by the existance of some 112 *pontas* on the fertile banks of the Rio

Grande and a bustling trade in mancarra, gold, ivory, wax, kola nuts, and *panos* centered around Buba, stagnated to a level from which it has never recovered. Today, Forrea is one of the least developed regions of Guinea-Bissau.

FRENTE DE LIBERTAÇÃO DA GUINÉ (FLG). In 1961 the FLG was created with the merger of the *Movimento de Libertação da Guiné*, (MLG), of François Mendy and the *Rassemblement Démocratique Africaine de la Guinée*, RDAG, (q.v.). By 1962 the FLG had combined its forces with the moderate *Frente de Luta Pela Independência Nacional da Guiné-Bissau*, FLING, (q.v.).

FRENTE DE LIBERTAÇÃO DA GUINÉ PORTUGUESA E CABO VERDE (FLGC). The FLGC emerged in 1960 under the leadership of Henri Labéry, the founder of the *União Popular da Guiné*, UPG (q.v.), in 1957. Essentially the FLGC replaced the *Mouvement de Libération de la Guinée "Portugaise" et des Îles du Cap Vert*, MLGCV (q.v.), of Dakar and its three constituent organizations. The FLGC included the *Movimento de Libertação da Guiné Portuguesa*, MLGP (q.v.), and the *Mouvement de Liberation des Îles du Cap Vert*, MLICV (q.v.), so as to broaden the base of support to provide more effective opposition to the growing *Partido Africano da Independência de Guiné e Cabo Verde*, PAIGC (q.v.), founded four years earlier. While the FLGC united new groups, it lasted only one additional year until it was replaced by *Front Uni de Libération*, FUL (q.v.), following factional divisions within the FLGC. FUL and some former FLGC members led to the formation of *Frente de Luta Pela Independência Nacional da Guiné-Bissau*, FLING (q.v.), in 1962.

FRENTE DE LUTA PELA INDEPENDÊNCIA NACIONAL DA GUINE-BISSAU (FLING). FLING was founded on 3 August 1962 in Dakar, Senegal, as a coalition of seven political parties which were generally hostile to Cape Verdeans in Guinea-Bissau. Having distant memories of the role of Cape Verdean merchants in the slave trade and recent and unhappy memories of Cape Verdeans serving as colonial functionaries in dominant positions, FLING was opposed to any potential for their continued role in a position of superiority. Thus FLING had a strong opposition to unity with Cape Verde as a political objective, and as such, FLING was a serious rival of the *Partido Africano da Independência de Guiné e Cabo Verde*,

PAIGC (q.v.), during the period of anti-colonial nationalism. The principal differences lay in the moderate program, ethnic allegiances, and exclusion of Cape Verdean alliances with FLING versus the social reforms, anti-tribal program, and the projected unity of Guinea-Bissau and Cape Verde for the PAIGC. FLING emerged in a July-August 1962 meeting which unified seven ethnically-based groups such as the *Movimento de Libertação da Guiné*, MLG (q.v.), and the *Rassemblement Démocratique Africaine de la Guinée*, RDAG (q.v.), under the leadership of Henri Labéry. In 1966, Jaime Pinto Bull (q.v.) became the President of FLING and the main operation continued from a Dakar office.

As the successes of the PAIGC mounted, FLING continued to rival PAIGC thereby creating an opportunity for the Portuguese to fuel these divisions. Even within the PAIGC, the Portuguese sought to create distrust among the rank and file African majority in the movement, which was dominated by Cape Verdean leadership. These tensions were maintained even up to the assassination of Amilcar Cabral (q.v.) in 1973. FLING undertook some military activities shortly after being founded but not after 1963. Between 1963 and 1967 the Organization of African Unity (OAU) sought to merge FLING and the PAIGC with active encouragement by Senegal's moderate President Senghor. After 1967, Senghor reluctantly accepted the supremacy of the PAIGC, although Senegal's support for FLING continued quietly from 1967 to 1970. It was long assumed that the Portuguese Polícia Internacional e de Defesa do Estado (PIDE) and the American CIA favored FLING to divide the supporters of the PAIGC. The most militant members of FLING were the former MLG members, while most of the other member groups held reformist, rather than revolutionary, goals.

In 1970 FLING was reorganized with Domingos Joseph Da Silva as the new Secretary General of FLING-UNIFIÉ. In 1973 the leadership passed again to Mario Jones Fernandes. FLING was charged with creating disturbances in Bissau, Bolama, and Bafatá (qq.v.) in May 1974, and FLING members were arrested by the Guinea-Bissau government in April 1976. In the intense rivalry between FLING and the PAIGC there may even be cases of one party charging 'innocent' people of being a member of the opposing group simply to discredit them within their own organization. Throughout the 1980's there has been no reported activity of FLING in either Guinea-Bissau or Senegal. However, under the policy of multi-party opposition,

FLING has reappeared under the leadership of François Kankola Mendy as as legalized party on 24 May 1992. Its motto is, 'Work, Discipline and Social Justice.'

FRENTE DEMOCRATICA (FD). This party was founded on 18 April 1991 and was legalized on 18 November 1991. The motto of the FD is 'Justice, Peace, Truth and Fraternity.' Its leader is Aristides Celso de Menezes Fernandes, who is a former member of the *Partido Africano da Independência de Guiné e Cabo Verde* (PAIGC). He served as Secretary of State for International Cooperation (1988–1990) and as Secretary of State for Planning (1990–1991).

FRENTE DEMOCRATICA SOCIAL (FDS). The FDS was founded 20 March 1990 and legalized 26 December 1991. Its motto is 'Liberty, Work and Justice.' Its leader is Rafael Paula Barbosa (q.v.), one of the founding members and first President of the *Partido Africano da Independência de Guiné e Cabo Verde*, PAIGC (q.v.), who was arrested and imprisoned by the colonial authorities (1962–1969) for subversive activities. It is believed that the Portuguese sought to turn Barbosa against the PAIGC while he was confined. In any case, divisions with Amilcar Cabral (q.v.) caused him to become *persona non grata* with the PAIGC and his role as a founder was obscured.

In 1974 he was arrested and charged with high treason and involvement in the assassination of Amilcar Cabral. He was sentenced to death, but this was commuted; he was still condemned to fifteen years hard labor. He was released briefly in 1980 in the wake of the coup of 'Nino' Vieira (q.v.) but returned to prison until his release in 1990, having spent a total of twenty-three years in prison.

FRENTE REVOLUCIONÁRIA AFRICANA PARA A INDEPENDÊNCIA NACIONAL DAS COLÔNIAS PORTUGUESAS (FRAIN). This umbrella organization was formed in Tunis, Tunisia in 1960 to link the *Partido Africano da Independência de Guiné e Cabo Verde*, PAIGC (q.v.), and the MPLA of Angola in their common programs against Portuguese colonialism. The first leader of FRAIN was Mario de Andrade of the MPLA. Just as FRAIN replaced the *Movimento Anti-Colonialista*, MAC (q.v.), it was replaced in 1961 by the *Conferência de Organizações Nacionalistas das Colônias Portuguesas*, CONCP (q.v.), which continued the same function but included FRELIMO of Mozambique as well.

FRONT UNI DE LIBÉRATION (de Guinée et du Cap Vert) FUL. In July 1961 Amilcar Cabral (q.v.) again sought to unify the *Partido Africano da Independência de Guiné e Cabo Verde*, PAIGC (q.v.) with Henri Labéry's *Frente de Libertação da Guiné Portuguesea e Cabo Verde*, FLGC (q.v.) and some other groups. This attempt to make a united front failed because of the hesitating support of the FLGC and the refusal of the *Movimento de Libertação da Guiné*, MLG (q.v.) to participate because of its concern about the role and future of Cape Verde. The effort to create FUL was the last attempt to create a united front for national independence. Once FUL became moribund, Cabral returned to organize the PAIGC in Conakry in 1962. The other leaders agreed to form the *Frente de Luta Pela Independência Nacional da Guiné-Bissau*, FLING (q.v.), which subsequently proved to be the only substantial rival to the PAIGC during the years of armed struggle.

FULA, (FULBE, FULANI, PEUL, FELLANI, FUL, FOU-LAH, FELLATA). The Fula are known by a variety of names, depending upon local usage. They are members of the West Atlantic sub-branch of the Niger-Congo (q.v.) language stock, but their history is quite different from the other Senegambians (q.v.). The Fulani language (Fulbe) is much closer to that of the Serer (q.v.) of Senegal from which they may have origi-nated. Some scholars, however, have attributed Fula origins to the Nile valley in prehistoric times, with westward migration across the Sahel or southern Sahara. Fula-like people are shown in Saharan rock paintings drawn during periods when the Sahara region was much wetter. This effort at reconstruct-ing Fula cultural history is still considered speculative. The Fulas may be subdivided into two main categories, the seden-tary and more fully Islamized Fula versus those who still practice a degree of pastoral nomadism and have syncretic belief systems which mix Islam and animism.

The sedentary Fula are rather strongly hierarchical in socio-political organization and were influential in the spread of Islam through much of the sub-Saharan region. In the southward migration to and through Guinea-Bissau some Fula adopted local cultural patterns and became known as the *Fulas pretos* who are much less cephalous than the Fulas of Futa Jallon or Futa Toro (qq.v.). Essentially, *Fulas pretos* is a Portuguese term for 'black' (dark-skinned) Fulas who were the ex-slaves of the Fulas Foros who were themselves the true Fulas. *Fulas pretos* were originally from other local ethnic groups who became 'Fulanized'; likewise most regional Fula have adopted some Mandinka cultural patterns when the Mindinka were the dominant group during the times of Mali and Kaabu (qq.v.).

Where the Fulas did not establish their own local rule they often served as herdsmen for the various kingdoms in the western Sudan. The more immediate origins of the Fula are now clearly traced to Tekrur (q.v.) and Futa Toro in the Senegal River valley. The Fula are related to the Berber, Tukulor, Wolof, and Serer peoples. The 1950 census of Guinea-Bissau put the Fula population at 108,400 or 21.5 percent of the total population. In 1960 the Fula population was estimated at 100,000. Clearly this is a major ethnic group of Guinea-Bissau; because of their numbers there are a variety of local names, but these are often overlapping and ambiguous rather than indicative of more substantial differences.

In any case, first there are the most numerous *Fulas pretos* concentrated in a wide area between Gabu and Bafatá (qq.v.) and in scattered groups in the southeast of Guinea-Bissau. The large numbers and wide distribution of this major Fula grouping attest to the centuries of admixture with local Mandinka people long before the conquest of Kansala (with the help of the *Futa-Jalonkas*). The second Fula grouping is known as the *Futa-jalonkas* (*Foutajalonkes*) including the *Futa-fulas* of the north-central Gabú-Pitche area. Fulas in the Quebo area of Guinea-Bissau are sometimes known as *Quebuncas,* who generally originated from Labé province in Futa Jallon. It was these Fula who brought about an end to the Mandinka kingdom of Kaabu. The *Futa-jalonkas* also incorporate the Boéncas, just to the north of Gabu, and the *Futa-fulas* in the extreme southeast near Madina Boé and adjacent to the former Labé province from which they originated. The third group of Fulas is considered to have had its origins in Futa Toro in Senegal. They are known by several local names, such as *Torancas, Futancas, Tocurures, Fula-forros,* or *Vassolancas* depending again upon local usage. Members of this group are found in the northeast and especially in scattered groups in the southeastern regions which they share with the *Futa-fulas* (*pretos* or *forros*).

Some non-Islamic pastoral Fula may have spread into remote eastern parts of Guinea-Bissau as early as the twelfth or thirteenth centuries. More significant numbers of cattle-herding Fula arrived in Guinea-Bissau in the fifteenth century from Futa Toro. From the fifteenth to eighteenth centuries the Fula population was in formation, although there was continued peaceful settlement of other Fula peoples who arrived and mixed with the Mandinkas. Another wave of Fula migrants came from Massina after the Fula and Mande peoples became allied in their joint efforts to destroy Songhai (q.v.) in 1591. These migrants paved the way for the open Fula conquest of Futa Jallon during the later period of the formation of revivalist theocratic states based on local Islamic brotherhoods. Such migrants were especially involved in the group of sedentary town Fula. This epoch was filled with religious and military campaigns against the Wolof and Serer of Senegal, against the local peoples of Futa Jallon, and against the various secondary states of Mali (q.v.) including Kaabu in Guinea-Bissau.

Still another wave of migration took place when the Fulas and others left Futa Toro between 1650 and 1700 to settle in Futa Jallon and eastern Guinea-Bissau amongst some Mandinka populations. In general, Fula have been either cattle-owners or pastoralists, while Mandinkas were more committed to agricultural pursuits.

The policy of Fula settlement in Guinea-Bissau was endorsed by the fifteenth and sixteenth century Fula leader, Coli Tenguella (q.v.). Fula migrations were stepped up in the eighteenth century although the Fulas of Guinea-Bissau were still subordinate to Kaabu at that time. Until then, the Fula were essentially stateless pastoralists, although they were the most extensive and numerous of such groups in West Africa. By the nineteenth century Fulas were expanding everywhere in Sahelian West Africa as noted in the Senegambian travels of the Scot, Mungo Park in 1805. Elsewhere, there were important *jihads* led by Usman dan Fodio in northern Nigeria from 1804 to 1820 and the Fulani arrived as far east as Cameroon in about 1900. In the Casamance (q.v.) region in 1843 Fula from Futa Toro allied with the small Mandinka kingdom of Pakao to wage a *jihad* against local non-Muslim groups. This area was still part of Portuguese Guinea at the time.

Probably one of the contributing causes to the *jihads* was also the French commercial intervention which sometimes favored the non-Muslim kingdoms and undermined Muslim economic domination of the region. The Fula from the northeast in Futa Toro, led by the Silla family, continued to press for conquest and control against both the French and local non-Muslims.

From the mid-eighteenth century until 1867, the Fulas from the southeast in Futa Jallon (especially from Labé province) frequently attacked Kaabu until it finally collapsed. This long-term Fula offensive against Kaabu may have received some

Portuguese support, or at least little opposition, since the on-going presence of Kaabu was a barrier to the consolidation of Portuguese penetration and control of the interior. Following the fall of Kaabu in 1867 the entire eastern portion of Guinea-Bissau was administered from Labé province. This develop-ment excluded the remaining fragment of Mandinka rule at Braço, but Fula influence reached as close to the coast as areas south of Buba (q.v.). However, with the power at Kaabu removed, the Portuguese colonial authorities began to carry out military expeditions from 1880 to 1882 and in 1900 against the Fula and finally brought them under control by means of the Fula's increasingly hierarchical political system which they had developed for the administration of their conquered terri-tory. Later, under Portuguese colonial rule, the now central-ized Fula society proved to be well suited to a form of indirect colonial rule which reinforced a Chief structure by paying them and giving them social privileges within colonial society. *See* ALFA MOLO; MUSA MOLO.

FULADU. *See* ALFA MOLO.

FUNANA. Funana is a musical and dance genre originating with the *badius* (q.v.) of Cape Verde. The Cape Verdean musical influence in Guinea, through cassette tapes and the radio is great, so funana has been re-exported back to the African mainland. In the second edition of this book, Peter Manuel has precisely defined this form as typically including a vocalist who "improvises verses in a fast quadratic rhythm, while playing a simple chordal ostinato on the the concertina-like *gaita*. An-other musician provides rhythmic accompaniment on the *fer-rinho*, a strip of metal which is scraped like a rasp with a small peg. Others present may sing loose choral responses to the lead vocalist's lines. The harmonic pattern usually consists of a simple alternation between two adjacent chords. Funana accompanies informal couple dancing, which may be erotic and often resembles Caribbean dances like the merengue."

Like *batuko*, and *finaçon*, funana has seen a popular revival since independence and now appears on a number of records, and tapes and in the performances of modern dance bands. Perhaps the best example of this was in the musical work of Carlos 'Cachass' Martins, who was born on the east coast of São Tiago in 1951 and became the 'King of Funana.' As a pioneer in the funana revival he is credited with forming the first funana band which liberated the African musical traditions in Cape Verde from colonial cultural oppression. It is said that he 'brought funana to the plateau,' meaning that his style was so popular and widespread that even the high society living in the plateau area of Praia could not help but recognize it. Most of today's funana bands pay great respect to the road opened by 'Cachass.'

FUTA JALLON (FOUTA DJALLON, DJALONKES, JA-LONKE, DIALONKE, JAALO). This plateau area of the interior of Guinea-Conkary, rising to 4,500 feet, is the highlands for the Niger, Senegal, and Gambia Rivers. It has served as the homeland for a portion of the Fula people of Guinea-Bissau and is a major source for the regional spread of Islam. Fula (q.v.) peoples arrived in Guinea-Bissau by the fifteenth century at least particularly as an effect of the movements of Coli Tenguella (I) (q.v.), but the greatest period of Fula migration took place between 1654 and 1700.

The Fula were disorganized and nomadic and at first lived peacefully with Mandinka (q.v.) and Dialonkes peoples but paid tribute to the Mandinka state of Kaabu (q.v.). In 1725 the first Fula *jihad* (holy war) against the Dialonke of Futa Jallon took place but was indecisive at this time. By the mid-eighteenth century Kaabu was increasingly under attack by the Labé branch of the Fulas from Futa Jallon. This period of intense and complex local conflicts was also related to the heavy demand for slaves and the widespread introduction of firearms. Whichever group was the victor in any given battle found a ready market for its prisoners of war as slaves at such places as Cacheu, Bissau, or on the Casamance (qq.v.) or Gambia Rivers.

Late in the eighteenth century the Fula peoples had conquered the Dialonke branch of Mali (q.v.) in Futa Jallon. As a result of this, a constitution for this theocratic military state was drawn up by nine Fula leaders. The influence of this state in Futa Jallon was widely felt as, for example, in the formation of Labé province adjacent to Guinea-Bissau. By 1788 the Fula ruling aristocracy had been stabilized and former residents of the region, like the Susu (q.v.), had been pushed toward the coast in Guinea-Conakry and into southern Guinea-Bissau where they assimilated coastal cultural patterns. Islamization of many neighboring peoples grew considerably in extent if not in depth. At the close of the eighteenth century a holy war had been declared against the non-believers in Kaabu, and while the Mandinka state lasted another seventy years it underwent rather steady weakening. In one case, from 1836 to 1837 the Mandinka state of Braço in Guinea-Bissau attempted resistance and defeated Almami Bubakar of Labé, but this represented only a short-lived pause in the deterioration of Kaabu.

Throughout the first quarter of the nineteenth century the Fula *jihads* intensified, and the power of Kaabu continued to decline. No fewer than a dozen military missions were carried out against Kaabu from Labé. The holy war was justified by the fact that the Mandinka were mainly animists, even though some had converted to Islam as early as the time of Coli Tenguella. Ironically, even the Fula founder of Labé, Kalidou, was not a Muslim himself, although he was not opposed to Islam. One of the most prominent nineteenth century *jihad* leaders was Al-Haj Al-Mami Umaru Tall, a Fula from Futa Toro (q.v.) who had joined a Tijaniya religious brotherhood during his pilgrimage to Mecca. Upon his return he revitalized the holy war movement in Futa Jallon, prepared his disciples, and entered into a full-scale slave trade to acquire firearms on the Atlantic coast. In 1848 Al-Haj Umaru declared his *hijira* or holy emigration from Futa Jallon to Dinguiray, a small kingdom near Futa Toro. On the way north he passed through Guinea-Bissau and killed the King of Kaabu, Yangi Sayon, in 1849. Kaabu was also suffering internal weakness from various revolts of indigenous Fula peoples, such as the 1850 upheaval which led to the creation of the small Fula state of Forrea (q.v.) on the Corubal River (q.v.). In 1862 Al-Haj Umaru initiated his major *jihad*, first against Futa Toro where he met defeat, but his army still grew in size and later went on to capture Segou and Masina.

In 1865 Al-Haj Umaru made preparations for the final conquest of Kansala, the capital town of Kaabu. In direct association with Alfa Yaya Maudo of Labé and Musa Molo of Jimara (q.v.), a siege by Al-Haj Umaru was laid against Kansala from 1866 to 1867 when the King, Mansa Dianke Walli, finally capitulated and conceded the collapse of Kaabu. This shift in power brought about relocation of many of the peoples of Guinea-Bissau. On the one hand, it represented the start of still another wave of assimilation by Fula migrants from Futa Jallon. On the other hand, the fall of Kansala also stimulated Mandinka migrations to the Gambia area where their town of Braço remained unconquered, even though some Fulas in Braço drove Mandinka peoples out of the lower Casamance (q.v.) and lower Gambia regions. In addition, Beafadas and Nalus who had been living under the control of Kaabu were driven further west to the coastal river lowlands where they resettled, with some Portuguese aid, at the forts at Geba and Buba (qq.v.).

With the end of the military campaign, Kaabu was placed under the authority of Alfa Yaya, the Fula leader of Labé. When Al-Haj Umaru went back to Futa Toro, he was engaged in battle with the French under General Louis Faidhérbe (q.v.) who blocked his advance into the middle sections of the Senegal River valley. In 1878 Faidhérbe completed his task and gave Al-Haj Umaru his final defeat. At the height of his conquests (1862–78), Al-Haj Umaru briefly controlled an area about as large as the former Empire of Mali (q.v.). In the wake of the Berlin Congress (q.v.), the French placed the Al-Mamy of Futa Jallon under direct French authority in 1888.

FUTA TORO. Geographically adjacent to the Senegal River valley is the plateau region of Senegal known as Futa Toro, which is also the name usually given to the Fula (q.v.) state built upon Tekrur (q.v.), itself known from ancient times. By the eleventh century the Islamic state of Tekrur was founded by War Jabi. Futa Toro was ruled by peoples from the mergers of Berber, Tukulor, and Soninke (q.v.) ethnic stocks who controlled local Wolof and Serer (q.v.) populations.

During the eleventh century some Serer left Futa Toro to resist the Islamization of Tekrur. These Serer moved to the Sine and Saloum (q.v.) areas of Senegal where they set up their own small but powerful states. Between the thirteenth and fifteenth centuries Sine and Saloum assimilated local Mandinka (q.v.) and Serer culture and society, which was highly stratified with Mandinka warriors in the dominant positions. The Mandinka penetration of the upper reaches of the Gambia was limited to that area, because it was at the frontiers of control from Futa Toro. Some Wolof also left Futa Toro in the mid-fourteenth century in opposition to the Tekrur rulers, thus starting some small Wolof states in Senegal.

From Futa Toro, the Islamic Fula peoples spread widely in the twelfth and thirteenth centuries as the most important pastoralists and disseminators of Islam in West Africa. As Mali (q.v.) grew in power and influence in the thirteenth and fourteenth centuries under Sundiata and his followers, the Fula ruling class of Futa Toro was composed mainly of Fula refugees from the kingdom of Kaniaga which had already fallen to the Malian Keita dynasty. Under the rule of Mansa Kankan Musa (1312–1337?) of Mali the Wolof and Tekrur areas were maintained as tributary states, thus extending the rule of Mali virtually to the Atlantic coast.

When Mali declined in the fifteenth century, both Tekrur and Wolof states re-emerged. The best known Fula leader of this period was Coli Tenguella (q.v.), who established the new Denianke dynasty of Futa Toro in about 1490 when he attacked the western flanks of Mali. The Denianke dynasty of Futa Toro lasted until the 1770's. During the period of this dynasty the Portuguese made some of their first contacts with the peoples in the interior of Africa. King João II sent missions to Mali in 1494, and under the reign of João III another mission was undertaken in 1534. Portuguese trade in the African interior between the fifteenth and sixteenth centuries was largely conducted on the Senegal River for slaves, gold, and ivory from Mali and Futa Toro and on the river systems on the Gambia and the Geba (q.v.), which gave some access to the Futa Jallon plateau region to which some Fula from Futa Toro had already migrated.

Throughout the fifteenth century, Fula from Futa Toro drifted eastward and southward to Guinea-Bissau where they settled peacefully with the existing Mandinka speakers and other Senegambians (q.v.). Between 1654 and 1694(?) the greatest wave of Fula and Dialonke migration left Futa Toro. In 1750 the theocratic state in Futa Toro launched a *jihad* against the animist Dialonke located, in small part, in Guinea-Bissau and against various Senegambians inhabiting Futa Jallon.

This *jihad* resulted in a cultural admixture known as Futa-Jalonke. A second major wave of Fula migration and *jihad* left from Futa Toro in about 1770. Between 1770 and 1818 two additional *jihads* were initiated in Futa Toro. With this pattern clearly established, it was Al-Haj Umaru (q.v.), originally from Futa Toro, who began his own series of *jihads* against Futa Toro and brought an end to the Denianke dynasty. Despite his final defeat by the French general Faidhérbe (q.v.), Al-Haj Umar and his army briefly held an area about the equivalent of former Mali, reaching as far east as Jenne. During these migrations and holy wars, the Fula people crossed over eastern Guinea-Bissau and added to the already existing regions of Fula population concentration.

G

GABÚ. Gabú is the designation of an administrative division and its headquarters. Gabú is a corruption of the name of the once powerful Mandinka kingdom of Kaabu (qq.v.), whose former capital, Kansala, was situated near the modern city of Gabú. Thus, the term Kaabu refers to this area from the mid thirteenth century to 1867; Gabú refers to the region after 1867.

Predominantly inhabited by the Fulbe-speaking Fulas (q.v.), the whole region was originally the homeland of the dwindling Beafada (q.v.) ethnic group, a people displaced by the invading Mandinkas who incorporated the territory into the Empire of Mali (q.v.). Later Kaabu was established as an empire in its own right. With the destruction of Kaabu by the Fulas at the decisive battle at Kansala in 1867, the territory became a protectorate of the Confederation of Futa Jallon (q.v.) in modern Guinea-Conakry in their *jihad* against the 'infidels' of Kaabu. Shortly after their liberation from Mandinka dominance, the Fulas of Gabú united with those of Forrea (q.v.), another Fula polity in southwestern Guinea-Bissau, but this was shortlived.

The civil wars which erupted in both Forrea and Gabú, apparently between *Fulbe-ribe* ('freeborn Fulas') and *Fulbe-djiabe* (former Fula slaves), raged furiously from about 1878 to 1890. These conflicts were fully exploited by the Portuguese, who, having defined the borders of their colony of Guiné Portuguesa in 1886, were desperate to demonstrate Pax Lusitania. By the end of the second decade of the twentieth century, Gabú and other Fula mini-kingdoms in the territory were well integrated into the colony and its administration. Traditional Fula chiefs and nobles became important elements of local rule under colonialism.

Indeed, in 1919, the *circunscrição* of Gabú was created, with its headquarters at Oco, a short distance from the settlement of Gabú-Sára. Five years later, the headquarters moved to this settlement, which was renamed Vila Lamego and renamed again in 1927 as Vila Gabú-Sára. With the arrival of Lebanese and Syrian merchants, commercial activities increased enormously, and the town grew rapidly. In 1948, the name reverted to Nova Lamego, which it remained until after independence, when it changed once again, to Gabú. An important administrative and commercial center through the remaining colonial period, it was also a heavily fortified garrison town during the armed liberation struggle (1963–1974).

Today, with the country's economy liberalized, Gabú is a bustling and growing town, with numerous economic and commercial activities dominated by dynamic Fula traders and entrepreneurs. It is currently overtaking Bafatá (q.v.) as the second most important city in Guinea-Bissau, attracting a number of people from neighboring regions and countries such as Guinea-Conakry, Senegal, and Gambia. *See also* KAABU.

GALVÃO, HENRIQUES. After the defeat of the Portuguese Republicans and the establishment of the Fascist 'New State' there was a persistent effort to restore democracy in Portugal (q.v.). One of the more famous cases is that of Portuguese Captain Henriques Galvão who led an anti-Fascist revolt in 1945. His hope was that in the wake of the Second World War the Fascist movement with which Salazar (q.v.) was sympathetic had been discredited and could be overthrown. At the same period the Portuguese had created their internal security organ, Polícia Internacional e de Defesa do Estado, PIDE (q.v.), to provide intelligence and suppress such opposition which was put down.

Not to be discouraged, Galvão was able to address a secret meeting of the Portuguese National Assembly in 1947, where he sought to expose the oppressive labor conditions in the African colonies. Essentially the Portuguese response was seen in the opening of the PIDE prison in 1949 in Tarrafal (q.v.), Cape Verde to confine its dissidents. Quieted down by such repression, Galvão was not heard from until 1961 when he hijacked a Portuguese ocean liner to dramatize the continuing colonial oppression of Portugal.

GEBA. The town of Geba is situated on the Geba River (q.v.) some twelve kilometers west of the city of Bafatá. Before the 1641 withdrawal of the numerous *lançado* (q.v.) residents to Farim (q.v.) Geba was the second Portuguese settlement in Guinea-Bissau after Cacheu (q.v.). But even with the exodus of the *lançados*, the remaining *filhos de terra* (mixed descendants of the *lançados*) and the *grumetes* (q.v.) numbered "more than 200 christian souls" according to a visiting Portuguese missionary (Lemos Coelho 1669, 49).

Around this time, the settlement had, beside the church of *Nossa Senhora da Graça*, a chapel dedicated to *Santo António*, but no resident clergy. Occasionally a visiting priest would appear from Cacheu, Bissau (q.v.), or Cape Verde to say mass and baptize new converts to Catholicism. The 'Christian' population continued to grow over the centuries, in spite of the scarcity of priests and the fact that the settlement was surrounded mainly by Muslim and animist Mandinkas, Fulas, and Beafadas (qq.v.). In 1886, for example, whereas Bissau was reckoned to have about 877 'Christians,' the number in Geba was estimated to be 1,502 (*Anuário da Guiné Portuguesa* 1948, 519). These *Cristões* or *grumetes* of Geba have remained a self-conscious subgroup of the Crioulos of Guinea-Bissau.

It is not clear when the *presidio* of Geba was created, but from the onset, it was subordinated to the *praça* of Bissau, which first came into being in 1696 with the establishment of a Captaincy there. In this Portuguese 'possession,' the descendants of the *lançados* and the *grumetes* were normally put in charge of safeguarding and promoting Portugal's interests, with the highest ranking official given the title of *Capitão-Cabo* (Captain-Corporal). Representing a feeble Portuguese military presence, the *Capitão-Cabo* was accountable to the *Capitão-Mor* (Captain-Major) of Bissau. However, the mainly 'Christian' population, which was supposed to be loyal to Portugal, was throughout the centuries usually described as being 'very rebellious.'

An important caravan stop as well as a port, Geba was, throughout the seventeenth, eighteenth, and first half of the nineteenth centuries, a principal trading center, with an abundance of slaves, kola, ivory, and wax. The settlement stagnated and declined as the slave trade concluded.

With the Portuguese proclamation of the ill-defined 'province' of Guiné Portuguesa in 1879, as a result of the 'independence' of the *praças* and *presídios* of Guinea from Cape Verde, Geba began to regain some importance. It was here that the ambitious Portuguese, eager to firmly establish their authority, hoped to penetrate further into the interior of the territory. In July 1880, the Portuguese warship *Guiné*, carrying the first governor of the new 'province,' Lieutenant-Colonel Agostinho Coelho, dropped anchor at the port. The first steamship to appear there, it attracted a large crowd and an occasion for the governor to display the ship's fire-power. After several cannons were fired, much to the fright of the spectators and obviously calculated to intimidate the local ruling classes, a message was left with the Mandinka ruler of the region that the Portuguese sought his friendship. Following his favorable response, three pieces of artillery were immediately sent to Geba upon the governor's return to Bolama, to strengthen the small garrison there.

As an entity within the kingdom of Kaabu (q.v.), the settlement of Geba had been undergoing a process of disintegration since the 1840's. In this context it had experienced many demonstrations of force as the Beafadas, Mandinkas, and Fulas fought each other for territorial gains. In 1869, the vast *Fulbe-djiabe* (otherwise called *Fula-pretos*, or 'black Fulas') kingdom of Fuladu was founded by the great warlord Alfa Molo (q.v.) in a zone straddling large areas of the Gambia, Casamance (q.v.), and Guinea-Bissau. His capital was established at Indornal in the territory of Firdu, which lay mainly in the Casamance region of southern Senegal. Making up the several provinces of Fuladu were territories in Guinea-Bissau like Kolla, Sankolla, Ganadu (or Kanadu), and Gabu (q.v.). Located in Ganadu, Geba was an important trading center which provided enormous tax revenues for the kingdom's rulers. With the death of Alfa Molo in 1881, his brother Bakari Demba (or Dembel) ascended to the throne. Before long however, Alfa Molo's restless favorite son, Musa Molo (q.v.), became the all-powerful and most feared ruler of Fuladu.

During the 1880's, Fuladu underwent great upheavals caused by internal power struggles, a fierce *jihad*, and a rule characterized by a cruel ruthlessness that alienated the overwhelming majority of the masses. In Geba, the Portuguese often watched impotently as Musa Molo and his army terrorized the inhabitants, demanding the payment of taxes and other kinds of levies. They could do little but court his friendship.

However, to their good fortune Nbuku, the ruler of Ganadu, had become one of Musa Molo's most disenchanted and disaffected provincial chiefs by 1886. Predictably, when the Portuguese made overtures to him to ally with them against Musa Molo, the warrior-king, he promptly accepted. Immediately, he got busy mobilizing other discontented neighboring rulers. As a result, the commandant of the Geba garrison, Lieutenant Francisco António Marques Grealdes, was able to launch a campaign aimed at forcing Musa Molo to leave the neighboring states to this *presídio* and become nothing more than a 'simple chief.'

This took place toward the end of September 1886, when, with a force of eighty Portuguese soldiers, 4,300 Fulas and Mandinkas, 170 Beafadas, 120 *grumetes* and two pieces of artillery, Nbuku and Marques Geraldes attacked the well-fortified *tabanca* of Fancá, in the Fuladu province of Sankolla (in the modern Guinea-Bissau region of Gabú). The battle lasted three hours, after which Musa Molo and his warriors abandoned their positions and fled north to Casamance, leaving behind a number of dead and wounded. The incorporation of Fuladu's rebellious provinces situated in Portugal's newly proclaimed 'province' of *Guiné Portuguesa* was now only a matter of time.

Geba thus became the most important Portuguese military garrison in the hinterland, reinforced with soldiers from Cape Verde and Angola. With Geba's inhabitants and neighboring groups readily available as dispensable frontline troops, the town played a crucial role in Portugal's numerous and often frustrated 'pacification' campaigns until about 1913. Then, with the use of brutal African mercenaries led by the Senegalese fugitive, Abdul Injai (q.v.) (or Abdoul Ndiaye), the defiant peoples of the mainland began to be effectively and finally conquered.

In 1906, an administrative reform made Geba the headquarters of one of the six residences into which the 'province' was divided. A year later the headquarters of the new residency of Geba was transferred to nearby Bafatá (q.v.), and the gradual decline in importance of that historic settlement continued until today, where it is in a state of abandoned decay.

GEBA, RIO DE (Geba River). The Geba River has its headwaters in northernmost Guinea-Conakry but then curves through regions of the upper Casamance (q.v.) area of Senegal before turning back toward the southwest and into Guinea-Bissau through the northeast. At the town of Bafatá (q.v.) the Geba is joined by the small Colufe River flowing from the town at Gabú (q.v.). The river remains relatively narrow, flowing by Geba town and Bambadinca, but at Xime it broadens very widely, joined by the Corubal (q.v.) to become ultimately a huge estuary with a mouth of about ten miles across near Bissau (q.v.). The Geba was an important route to the interior for commerce and slavery (q.v.) and gave an axis around which the Kaabu state was formed. The Geba is about 340 miles in total length, but it is only navigable for ships up to 2,000 tons for about 93 miles.

GOMES, DIOGO. Portuguese navigator and pilot. In 1455, along with the Venetian Cadamosta (q.v.), Gomes established commercial relations with the Wolof people at the mouth of the Senegal River and with the Mandinka (q.v.) states on the Gambia, thereby strengthening early Portuguese relations with Mali (q.v.) itself. In 1457 Gomes reportedly arrived at Arguim with four horses, one horse usually purchasing between ten and fifteen slaves. Gomes found Gonçalo Ferreira and the Genoese António De Noli (q.v.) already trading at Arguim at that time. By exercising the royal Portuguese trade monopoly, Gomes gave De Noli and Ferreira seven slaves per horse, but received fourteen to fifteen slaves per horse from the African traders. Gomes is credited with being one of the discoverers of the Cape Verde Islands. This occurred when he was blown off course returning from a coastal exploration in 1460. He landed at what is now São Tiago and also visited Fogo. Since he landed on São Tiago on 1 May he named it in honor of that Saint's Day. Later he reported on Boa Vista, Maio, and Sal islands as he sailed northward. In 1461 Gomes sailed to coastal Liberia and Sierra Leone.

GOMES, FERNÃO. Gomes was a Lisbon merchant. In 1468 Gomes received a lease for Guinea trade for five years from King Alfonso V (1438–1481) for the price of 200 *milreis* a year on the condition that he explore 100 leagues of West African coastline to the east of Sierra Leone. This lease excluded land opposite the Cape Verde Islands. Gomes was also required to sell ivory to King Alfonso V at a fixed price. Between 1469 and 1475 Gomes carried out his explorations and is credited with the discovery of the Gold Coast (Ghana) during this period.In 1477 Gomes reached the Bight of Biafra. In 1482 a Portuguese fort was constructed at Al-Mina as a result of Gomes's travels and reports. The Crown granted Gomes a trading monopoly along the Guinea coast, but the operation was based in the Cape Verde Islands, which had only been settled a few years earlier.

GONÇALVES, ANTÃO. With Nuño Tristão (q.v.), Gonçalves was the first to capture Moorish slaves at Cape Blanco and thus began the age of slavery (q.v.) in 1441. Although the Africans were initially seized for information and ransom, Gonçalves returned to Portugal (q.v.) with this cargo of slaves and gold dust, to stimulate further exploration. Gonçalves made at least five voyages in 1441, 1443, 1444, 1445, and in 1447 to the upper Guinea coast in West Africa.

GORÉE. While Gorée Island is not part of Guinea-Bissau today, it was part of the larger Portuguese presence in the Upper Guinea coast in the fifteenth century when first reached and settled by Diniz Dias (q.v.) while exploring the coast in 1444 and 1445. Given its strategic and defensive position, in sight of but removed from the coast, it has long been critical in Euro-African trade, especially for slaves and other African products such as animal hides, woods, dyes, ivory, wax, and ship supplies. Gorée was usually governed by the *lançados* (q.v.), and the *signoras* (women merchants) of the great 'slave houses' who entertained prospective slave buyers with famed opulence and sexual indulgence.

Slaves were held in the ground level cellars until a sufficient number was accumulated. They would then be presented in a locked courtyard to the buyers who would select their human cargo. On the upper floors one would negotiate the prices to be paid to the *signoras* for their slaves while being diverted with the 'pleasures' of drink and flesh. These decadent ladies and men of commerce managed to persist even when flags changed from Portuguese to Dutch, French, and British over the seventeenth and eighteenth centuries. Traders still came from Bissau, Cacheu (qq.v), and elsewhere on the Guinea coast to buy and sell their goods and slaves. Today, one may still see one example of these 'houses' on Gorée Island.

GRIOT. Griot is the general French name for a caste of professional musicians, oral historians, and poets in the West African Sahel. Especially in Senegambia, they are known for their music (q.v.) as arbitrators and as keepers of lineages. In Mandinka societies, they are called *jali*. They are part of an ancient hierarchical society consisting of two major components: free born people (*horo*) and slaves (*jongo*). The *horo* were further broken down into the categories of *sula* (ordinary people) and *nyamalo*, the group to which the *jali* belong. The *nyamalo* are people who are believed to have a special connection to the spiritual world because of their ability to manipulate leather, gold, iron, or the spoken or sung word. Formerly the *sula* acted as patrons for the *nyamalo*.

Although slavery (q.v.) has disappeared and blacksmiths, goldsmiths, and leatherworkers work for themselves now, the *jali* serve as verbal artists and are still sponsored, to a large extent, by wealthy *sula* families. The *jali* have a low social status but are respected for their skills in singing praise songs, recounting long lineages and oral histories, and entertaining. These musicians generally accompany themselves on the *kora* (an instrument of the harp family), *balafon* (q.v.) (a wooden xylophone), or on the *kontingo* (a plucked lute). The women (q.v.) in *jali* families sing and play a tubular iron bell called *neo*, *karinya*, or *karanyango*. (S. Hurley-Glowa).

GROUNDNUTS. *See* AGRICULTURE.

GRUMETES, GRUMETTAS. Grumetes were 'detribalized' Africans or Crioulo sailors or members of private slave-raiding armies of the *lançados* (q.v.). They functioned as mercenaries, but at times of regional insecurity they played key roles in mutinies, uprisings, and giving strength and protection to slave raiders and traders. The *grumetes* gave the armed strength for the *tangomãos* (q.v.) to negotiate for slaves and other trade items and to protect these goods at the trading posts and *feitorias*, such as Cacheu and Bissau (qq.v.). Some reports suggest that *grumetes* were Christianized former slaves.

GRUPO DE ACÇÃO DEMOCRATICA DE CABO VERDE E DA GUINÉ (GADCVG).The Democratic Action Group of Cape Verde and Guinea-Bissau emerged in the period after the fall of the Caetano (q.v.) government in Lisbon, Portugal (q.v.). The GADCVG essentially represented the position of the Partido Africano da Independência de Guiné e Cabo Verde, PAIGC (q.v.), regarding the unity of Guinea-Bissau and Cape Verde. The GADCVG rapidly became a mass organization which blocked the organizing efforts of the União Democrática de Cabo Verde, UDCV (q.v.), and the União das Populações das Ilhas de Cabo Verde, UPICV (q.v.), particularly in mid-November 1974 when it organized a twenty-four-hour general strike to back the PAIGC demand that it alone would be in the negotiations with Portugal regarding independence in 1975.

GUERRA, SOFIA POMBA. Guerra was a Portuguese pharmacist working in Bissau in the early period of the Partido Africano da Independência de Guiné e Cabo Verde, PAIGC (q.v.). In her semi-exile from Portugal as a supporter of the Portuguese Communist Party she had access to Marxist literature which was passed on to the PAIGC members, such as Osvaldo Vieira. B. Davidson notes in his *Fortunate Isles* that in this way she became significant in the ideological understanding and analysis which helped to create the PAIGC political program and strategy.

GUILEDGE. Throughout the war of national liberation, the Portuguese used a wide variety of military security measures including collective punishments, terror, arrest and imprisonment, pass controls, and forced resettlement camps or *aldeamentos* (q.v.). In the border regions they used a series of forts from which war parties would seek to control the Partido Africano da Independência de Guiné e Cabo Verde, PAIGC (q.v.), incursions and supply missions from Senegal and Guinea-Conakry. The fort at Guiledge was one of several such forts in this counterinsurgency strategy. It was located only a few kilometers from the central-southern border of Guinea-Bissau. It was encircled with barbed wire, flood lights, motion detectors, and sensitive mine fields and had very controlled access. The center of the base was about 500 meters square with mortar positions at each corner. Soldiers were quartered in subterranean bunkers. A small airfield, ammunition supplies, tanks and armored vehicles, military transport, and field howitzers added to its defensive and offensive capacity.

After the assassination of Amilcar Cabral (q.v.) in January 1973, the PAIGC and its armed forces wanted to recover from this shock and rebuild the military initiative. For the spring months of 1973 the PAIGC forces repeatedly attacked Guiledge. This offensive finally led to Operation Amilcar Cabral, which laid a full-scale seige to the base with 60mm mortars and 80mm canons. The introduction of surface-to-air, hand-held Soviet *Estrella* missiles eliminated the Portuguese air support and reconnaisance for Guiledge and in desperation the Portuguese commander sought relief by forest road, which fell under PAIGC ambush. Meanwhile PAIGC engineering units had placed eighteen anti-tank mines which were able to destroy fleeing trucks and kill twenty-six soldiers along the escape route. The Major of Guiledge then called for a full-scale evacuation of Guiledge and retreat to Gadamael on 25 May.

The PAIGC victory was not only symbolic of its military strength, but it also broke a large hole through the Portuguese southern defenses. Not surprisingly, it was only months later that independence was declared in September 1973 and fully achieved the following year. It should also be noted that many of the young Portuguese army officers who overthrew the Portuguese dictatorship in April 1975 had seen military service in Guinea-Bissau. In short, the battle for Guiledge can be considered the last major battle of the war which gained the final initiative leading to complete independence.

GUINALA (QUINARA). The name of one of the most important kingdoms making up the once extensive territory of the Beafadas (q.v.), located between the south bank of the river Geba (q.v.) and the north bank of the Rio Grande de Buba (q.v.) in the modern coastal region of Quinara, a name which itself is a corruption of Guinala. Centuries before the onset of the colonial period, Guinala was also an important port and trading center on what was then Rio Guinala or Rio Buduco, and today Rio Barca, a tributary of the Rio Grande de Buba. It was a vital link in the complex trade networks which existed in the region long before the arrival of the Europeans.

A short distance north of the port of Guinala was Bruco or Buduco, seat of the King of Guinala, a subject of the Mandinka Mansa of Kaabu (qq.v.), who during the sixteenth and seventeenth centuries had also exercised some important politico-religious influence over the Pepel (q.v.) ruler of Bissau (q.v.). It was the custom for the latter's ascension to the throne of Bissau to be confirmed by the former, and the subjects of the two kingdoms performed joint religious rites and ceremonies.

Succession to the throne at Bruco was apparently not confined to the nobility (unlike the situation in other Beafada kingdoms like Buguba/Biguba and Balola/Bolola); members of artisan categories like blacksmiths and leatherworkers were also eligible to be chosen as ruler. The likely candidate had to be an old man, and the process appeared to be a simple enough affair, entailing the abduction of the most elderly man sighted by a group of nobles and high-ranking state officials and his thorough whipping before enthronement, ostensibly to sensitize him to the meaning of physical punishment so that he could dispense justice fairly and mercifully. He would reign for a limited time, at the end of which, if he were still alive, he would be killed to make room for another King to be crowned.

According to traditions recounted to early Portuguese travelers (André Alvares de Almada during the 1560's and 1570's; and André Donelha during the early 1580's), it was at Bruco, towards the end of the fifteenth century, where a terrifying Fula (q.v.) army of invasion, originating from Senegambia and comprising of calvary, infantry, herds of cows, and swarms of bees, was soundly defeated. This formidible force is said to have left a trail of death and destruction as it marched south, overcoming such physical obstacles as wide rivers and fast currents, and overwhelming the resistances of such peoples as the Wolofs, Mandinkas, Casangas, Banhuns, Manjacos (qq.v.), and Pepels, among others, with deadly cavalry charges, skillful archery and the releasing of swarms of terrible bees. When this conquering army arrived in the Kingdom of Guinala, it was challenged by King Famena, who mobilized various Beafada potentates and their soldiers, and in a pitched battle dealt a devastating blow to the intrusive invaders.

During the second half of the sixteenth century, a significant number of lançados (q.v.) were found at the port of Guinala, where they constructed a wooden fort armed with a cannon. This fortified settlement was named Porto da Cruz, or Porto da

Santa Cruz, an allusion to the towering wooden cross which was erected there a few years earlier. A church was also built. The fort was erected as defense against the incursions of the French, who had previously attacked Portuguese ships there. This Portuguese entrenchment effort did not go unchallenged. Although there was no armed confrontation (as would later happen with the Pepels and Manjacos of Cacheu (q.v.), the strategies of passive resistance deployed by the Beafadas, which included the imposition of travel restrictions, the withdrawal of protection, and the introduction of price increases for local exports, were nevertheless effective enough to bring about the abandonment of the fortified village and the return to the status quo arrangments of *hospedeiro* (host) and *hospede* (guest).

Until about the end of the sixteenth century, the port of Guinala bustled as the principal center of the Portuguese slave trade in the region, evidenced by the presence of numerous vessels of various sizes which exported on average nearly 3,000 captives a year to the Americas. It was here, during the early 1500's, that the Portuguese navigator Duarte Pacheco Pereira noted that a horse of 'small value' would barter for six or seven captives. According to the Cape Verdean trader, André Alvares D'Almada, the kingdom of Guinala also had, at the end of that century, the largest weekly market in the region, situated at a place called Bijorei, were some 12,000 people from the neighboring territories would gather to buy and sell slaves, cattle, cotton cloth, country produce (including kola nuts), and gold.

The commercial importance of Guinala, as well as its geographic location on the navigable Rio Grande, rendered it vulnerable to external attacks from foreigners other than Europeans. At the beginning of the seventeenth century, the most dangerous threat facing the inhabitants of the kingdom, as well as those in the littoral areas, was posed by the Bijagós (q.v.) who, having overcome rivalry and conflict among themselves and responding to the increased European demand for slaves, would disembark from their famous *almadias* (ocean-going canoes) and furiously attack ill-defended communities, burning down houses, killing those who resisted, and taking captive those who surrrendered. It was in this manner that Porto da Cruz was attacked around 1610, burning the church and thereafter seriously disrupting commercial activities.

With the paralysis of trade at the port of Guinala and the stagnation of the once great market at Bijorei, the Portuguese and *lançados* abandoned Porto da Cruz in 1636 and moved to

Bolola (q.v.). Guinala's economic importance as the best 'slaving district' in the region gradually diminished with the slowing down and eventual ending of the slave trade during the second half of the nineteenth century.

GUINEA-BISSAU: AMERICAN (USA) RELATIONS. During the course of the liberation struggle, Amilcar Cabral (q.v.) made contacts with, and visits to, the United States. Cabral was not only heard at the United Nations (q.v.) in New York (the Fourth Committee of the UN General Assembly, 12 December 1962 and the UN Security Council, 1 February 1972), but he also delivered a famous lecture on national culture at Syracuse University (20 February 1970), appeared before the US House of Representatives Sub-Committee on African Affairs (26 February 1970), and was conferred an honorary doctorate degree by the prestigious African-American insitute of higher learning, Lincoln University (15 October 1972), which had been the alma mater of such African nationalist giants as Kwame Nkrumah (Ghana) and Nnamdi Azikiwe (Nigeria).

The historical links between what became modern Guinea-Bissau and what became the United States of America go back much further into the past, to the early sixteenth century with the arrival of European slave traders and their forced removal of Africans from their homes to be transported across the Atlantic to the Americas. For almost four centuries this sad link between Guinea and the Americas remained unbroken.

A number of settlements on the banks of Guinea's major rivers became the points of departure for hundreds of thousands of Guinea's sons and daughters condemned to a life of servitude. The entrepôt towns of Cacheu and Bissau (qq.v.), on the rivers Cacheu and Geba (qq.v.) respectively, were notorious slave trading centers. Every year, hundreds of Balantas, Mandinkas, Fulas, Manjacos, Beafadas, Felupes, Diolas (qq.v.), and Pepels among others, were violently uprooted and kidnapped from their homelands, often with active involvement of African states such as Kaabu and Fuladu (qq.v.). A significant number ended up in the plantations of sugar cane, tobacco, and cotton in the circum-Caribbean region, including the southern American states. One authority notes that over the four hundred years of slavery (q.v.) in the region, "the Upper Guinea coast was involved in all the phases of the slave trade. It supplied Europe, the mines of Central and South America, and the plantations of the Caribbean and North America" (Rodney 1970, 95).

The Portuguese monopolized this commerce in human beings for over a century. However, by the late sixteenth century Spanish, English, and Dutch slavers began to erode the monopoly. During this period, for example, the English Royal African Company, operating from bases in Gambia and Sierra Leone, shipped slaves of Guinean origin. An average of 10,000 were shipped annually to the English colonies in North America and the West Indies. The mid-seventeenth century was probably the most prolific period for Bissau slaving. During the first five months of 1748, for instance, the English took 1,000 slaves from Bissau, and by 1775 Portuguese officials reported that English slave ships collected about 5,000 slaves annually.

North American involvement in the slave trade in Guinea can be clearly dated back to the early seventeenth century. New England merchants, particularly those from Rhode Island, acquired slave-produced tobacco, cotton, and cane molasses from the southern states and the Caribbean. From the molasses treacle, Rhode Islanders distilled rum, which was heavily exported to trade for more slaves on the West African coast and endlessly repeat the trans-Atlantic 'Triangular trade.' One distinguished American historian of the region and period notes that "New England's own triangular trade with Africa and the West Indies was considered vital to its own economic growth and prosperity, for some of the profits were used to redress the colonies' chronic imblance of trade with Britain" (Brooks 1970, 16). During the American war of independence, Rhode Island slaves were sold to the state to be used as soldiers, who fought in several significant battles which led to their relatively earlier emancipation in 1787.

But contacts between the peoples of the territory and North America did not end with the abolition of the slave trade in the nineteenth century. Indeed, with the establishment of 'legitimate commerce,' merchants from the United States, especially from New York and Massachusetts, continued their commercial links, exchanging 'Yankee rum' and tobacco, as well as European goods, for hides, wax, ivory, and gum copal. The importance of this trade was evidenced by the fact that when, in 1844, the Pepels in Bissau threatened revolt, the American warship *Preble* was dispatched from Cape Verde to protect US commercial interests in that town. The commerce expanded considerably during the 1850's and early 1860's making the American traders second only to the French in order of importance.

United States interest in the area was not only economic.

During the 1820's and 1830's, American colonization societies manifested great interest in Bolama (q.v.) as a prospective site for the settlement of emancipated slaves. It is interesting to note that the resettling of freed African Americans in Africa was seen by such white American advocates as a way to develop American commerce with Africa (Brooks 1973, 13). Recommending Bolama as a suitable site, Samuel Hodges, the first American Consul in Cape Verde, noted that ". . . the soil is fertile, and the Island [of Bolama] more healthy than any other spot from Senegal to the Equator, and we firmly believe it to be more healthy than the State of Virginia generally" (cited in Brooks 1973, 15).

It should be mentioned that the French and the British had, decades earlier, been interested in Bolama as a site for white settlement, with the latter actually occupying and settling 275 colonists on the island in 1792. This attempt was short-lived due mainly to gross miscalculation on the part of the project promoters about the response of the local African rulers, especially those from Canhabaque in the Bijagós (q.v.), who violently opposed this plan to take over their lands. Thus, the projected American settlement of African-Americans on Bolama was never realized because of this local opposition and inability to raise adequate finances and because Bolama was the focus of a long-term dispute between English and Portugal over 'ownership.'

Diplomatically, the United States was involved in Guinea-Bissau because of trading interests, and it established its first Vice-Consulate in Bissau in 1849; this was under the jurisdiction of the regional Consulate in Praia in Cape Verde. In addition, the Anglo-Portuguese dispute over Bolama was finally sent to American President U. S. Grant for final arbitration on 21 April 1870, when he ruled in Portugal's favor. This act was commemorated in Bolama by erecting a statue of Grant on the central *praça*. Nine years later, when the territory was separated from the administration of the Cape Verde Islands, the Portuguese hastily fixed the capital of their newly proclaimed colony of *Guiné Portuguesa* at Bolama.

The last quarter of the nineteenth and first quarter of the twentieth centuries witnessed desperate and repeated efforts by the Portuguese to 'pacify' this territory. By the late 1930's this had been largely achieved, and local commerce was revived after years of warfare. American interest was expressed in the region in 1933 when the famed air explorers Anne and Charles Lindburgh landed in Gambia and Cape Verde to help scout out the possibilities for commercial air routes. In 1940 Pan American Airways opened an office in Bolama and regularly began to use the island's excellent bay as a stop over for its famous 'clipper' seaplanes. Unfortunately this air service was not long lasting, because the intensification of World War II brought the transfer of the capital from Bolama to Bissau in 1941 and the closure of many Bolama firms and enterprises. Pan American soon closed its office as well. In 1958, the oil giant Esso (Exxon) obtained exclusive oil prospecting rights from the Portuguese in the territory, but as the war of national liberation had already been initiated this never realized substantive results.

Economic, diplomatic, and cultural relations and exchanges with the United States developed dramatically following Guinea's independence in 1973. In particular the United States has become Guinea's fourth largest provider of imports since the 1980's. By 1984, bilateral American development aid totaled over $4 million USD. This did not include a USAID program which allowed nearly 200 (Bissau) Guineans to attend universitites and training colleges in the United States since 1978. It can only be hoped that the centuries-old historical ties between Guinea-Bissau and the United States will always be maintained for the mutual benefit of the peoples of the two nations.

GUINEA-BISSAU: CAPE VERDE RELATIONS. Mobilization for the successful armed liberation struggle conducted by the Partido Africano da Independência de Guiné e Cabo Verde, PAIGC (q.v.), was predicated not just on the goal of "immediate and total independence" for the two Portuguese colonies of *Guiné-Portuguesa* and *Cabo Verde*, as the party's name implies, but also on their unification. Soon after the independence of these two countries, the idea of unity was strongly defended on historical, cultural, and ideological grounds: "shared experience" of Portuguese "colonial oppression"; "cultural and ethnic unity"; and the Pan-Africanist imperative of "the unity of our continent" (PAIGC 1978, 50).

The historical justification for Guinea-Bissau/Cape Verde unity used to be defended on the centuries-old links between the two countries; links which go back to the "discovery" of the apparently uninhabited archipelago of ten islands by Portuguese sailors in 1460 and their subsequent settlement with Portuguese adventurers, political exiles, *degredados* (q.v.), and African captives from the adjacent mainland—especially from the Cacheu and Bissau (qq.v.) regions, the principal Portuguese slave trading centers.

Situated about 455 kilometers off the Senegalese coast and some 900 kilometers northwest of Bissau, the archipelago was from the beginning used as a launching pad for Portuguese commercial, diplomatic, and military onslaughts on the much-prized mainland. With pretensions of sovereignty, *Guiné de Cabo Verde* ("Guinea of Cape Verde,") originally the area between Senegal and Sierra Leone but reduced over the centuries to a size roughly the same coastal area as that of present-day Guinea-Bissau, was administered from São Tiago until 1879.

Over the five centuries of Portuguese entrenchment efforts in Guinean territory, thousands of Cape Verdean lives were sacrificed for the 'honor and glory' of Portugal. After 'pacification,' Cape Verdeans made up more than seventy-five percent of the colonial functionaries in *Guiné-Portuguesa*.

It is precisely their role as administrators and *chefes de posto*, as instruments of Portuguese brutal domination which has left a deep-seated resentment towards Cape Verdeans. For the real victims of Portuguese colonial domination, the overwhelming majority of the population in the rural areas contemptuously referred to as *gentios*, the worst aspect of the Portuguese colonial presence is associated with the Cape Verdeans, the colonial officials who taxed them, forced them to work gratuitously on 'public projects,' and punished them summarily for the slightest infringement of the *indigenato* (native) code.

The predominance of Cape Verdeans in *Guiné Portuguesa* was a consequence of the relatively high rate of literacy in the archipelago, where all the inhabitants were arbitrarily classified as *civilizados* and enjoyed, at least theoretically, the same legal status as the metropolitan Portuguese. With a seventy-eight percent illiteracy rate in 1950, compared with ninety-nine percent in *Guiné Portuguesa*, ninety-nine percent in Mozambique, and ninety-seven percent in Angola, Cape Verde was indeed the main beneficiary of the Portuguese educational enterprise in Africa.

This relatively high rate of literacy provided the Portuguese colonialists with a reservoir of eager collaborators, the eagerness being conditioned by the prevalent poverty and limited job opportunities. Yet, in spite of the enthusiasm with which the Cape Verdean privileged classes embraced Portugal's great folly of a *missão civilizadora* in Africa, the fact remained that

Cape Verde was a colony and Cape Verdeans a colonized people with a history punctuated with brutal exploitation and callous abandonment to the mercies of droughts and famines.

The historical links between Guinea-Bissau and Cape Verde are indeed undeniable. These links were reinforced during the struggle for national liberation against a common colonizer, a bloody struggle fought in the forests of Guinea-Bissau in which Cape Verdeans made central and significant contributions. They have played important roles in both the colonial domination and national liberation of Guineans.

Nevertheless, for the majority of Guineans, the visibly "bad colonialists" were indeed the Cape Verdeans. The deep wounds caused by their negative involvement in *Guiné Portuguesa*, which the Portuguese colonialists fully exploited during the armed liberation struggle (resulting in the murder of Amilcar Cabral, who was a Guinean of Cape Verdean descent), were not yet healed at the time concerted efforts were being made to unify the two countries. The unhealed wounds were largely ignored by the Cape Verdean-dominated leadership of the PAIGC, which was insensitive to the fact that there was no grassroot support in Guinea-Bissau for unification between the so-called "sister republics." Moreover, the rather cavalier manners of state functionaries, a significant number of whom were Cape Verdean or of Cape Verdean descent, as well as the dogmatic position of the party in Guinea-Bissau regarding the unity issue (silencing dissidents with imprisonment and execution and blocking democratic opposition with a one-party state), further alienated many Guineans.

The cultural/ethnic argument for Guinea-Bissau/Cape Verde unity was often that the majority of the African population in the archipelago originated from what is the area today Guinea-Bissau and that the existence of a common language, *Crioulo*, which developed as a result of the centuries-old Luso-African encounter, binds the two peoples. This is amply correct.

While it is true that the majority of the population of Cape Verde is deeply founded in African cultures and races, the fact remains that the five centuries of effective Portuguese occupation, entailing systematic attempts to wipe out the diverse African cultural heritages in the name of "civilization," left Cape Verdeans with a colonial experience markedly different from that of Guineans, who only came under effective occupation during the early part of this century.

Indeed, for the educated and predominantly *mestiço* colonial elite, 'civilization' entailed internalization of most of the racist assumptions of the Portuguese. Considering themselves 'Portuguese,' 'civilized,' and naturally superior to the other Africans, this group mainly remained spiritually and psychologically amputated from Africa, and the question of Cape Verdean self-identity remains a thorny and sensitive issue even among the many diaspora communities of Cape Verdeans.

As colonial functionaries in *Guiné Portuguesa*, the relatively privileged Cape Verdeans alienated the majority of the population by their aloof and sometimes racist attitudes. There was indeed a significant social-economic and cultural distance separating them from the 'uncivilized' Guinean masses. In fact, it was not the case that the whole unity issue did not have mass support in either Guinea-Bissau or Cape Verde (where hostile opposition, particularly from members of the privileged classes who felt that they had neither cultural affinity nor racial kinship with Guineans, was tolerated by the leadership of the same party that brutally suppressed dissent in Guinea-Bissau), but there were conflicts of interest, represented as 'national interest,' between the ruling classes of the two countries right from the start.

According to one critical analyst of the Guinea-Bissau/Cape Verde unity question, as early as the Second Congress of the PAIGC in July 1973, before either country attained independence, "relations began to worsen" (Lopes 1987, 135). With the PAIGC itself split into two national bodies, policies of "national interest" soon began to be pursued, particularly by the Cape Verdean national leaders who defended their position more forcefully and with impunity.

On 5 July 1975, Cape Verde attained independence, and Aristides Pereira (q.v.), Secretary General of the PAIGC became the nation's first President. The single party now held power in two sovereign states. The adoption of the national anthem and flag of Guinea-Bissau pointed positively towards unification. However, apparently eager to please the Cape Verdean elites who were socially, culturally, and ideologically much more coherent than their Guinean counterpart, the PAIGC leadership in the archipelago weakened the ideal of unity in the years after independence. Prime Minister Pedro Pires (q.v.), however, saw the advantage of a reserve army in Guinea which could strengthen his position in the islands. The new Government was also under pressure from vociferous Cape Verdean emigrants, particularly in the United States, Portugal, and Holland. They inundated the PAIGC with strong protests against the proposed unification. The increasingly substantial remittances of emigrants, which grew from $7.95 million in 1974 to $20 million in 1979, at a time of severe drought, serious economic crisis, and uncertainty about viability and survival as an independent nation were in reality a factor to be considered.

It was precisely in the economic field that the Cape Verdean Government most strongly defended its "national interests." Although by 1977 customs duties were eliminated for domestically produced goods and a joint long-distance shipping line was established, the Cape Verdean authorities were still 'carefully' considering a fundamental requirement of economic integration, the establishment of a complementary economy: "In the context of Guiné/Cape Verde Unity, which must be achieved step by step . . . we shall carefully consider the conditions under which our countries can complement one another economically" (PAIGC 1978, 37).

At the same time, Cape Verde had an economic development strategy which aimed "for an economy independent of Guinea-Bissau," with plans for "the building of factories that were already projected in the Guinean program which was designed to meet both countries' needs" (Lopes 1987, 135).

As Appendix Tables G.III and G.IV clearly demonstrate, commercial exchanges between the two 'sister republics' formed an insignificant proportion of their total international trade. In 1980 this represented only six percent of Guinea-Bissau's exports to, and less than one percent of her imports from, Africa. Indeed, even before the rupture apparently caused by the November 1980 coup in Guinea-Bissau, Cape Verde had bilateral and multilateral cooperations quite different from those of her 'sister republic,' besides differences in foreign and diplomatic policies (for example, relations with South Africa and the question of granting diplomatic status to the Palestine Liberation Organization). This state of affairs was forcefully defended in 1980 in the Cape Verdean National Assembly, by Pedro Pires, the Prime Minister (before the coup d'état in Guinea-Bissau), in these terms: "One of the main concerns of the Cape Verdean Government is that its positions on international questions should always take into account the highest interests of the people of Cape Verde" (Quoted in Lopes 1987, 136).

Lack of harmonization and coordination also manifested itself in the differences between the new constitutions of the two 'sister republics.' A glaring incongruity which reinforced the sense of inequality felt by Guineans was the fact that in the archipelago Cape Verdean citizenship was required for holding public office, particularly that of Prime Minister and President of the Republic; in Guinea-Bissau, not only was this not a constitutional requirement, but Cape Verdeans continued to occupy important public offices, including that of President of the Republic. Furthermore, while Cape Verde's constitution banned the death penalty that of Guinea-Bissau maintained it.

It is not surprising, therefore, that the November 1980 coup was enthusiastically supported in Guinea-Bissau. It is worth noting that a welcome outcome of the *Movimento Reajustador,* Readjustment Movement, as the coup became known, has been the drastic decrease of political repression, arbitrary arrests and imprisonment, and flagrant human rights abuses.

As for the Pan Africanist argument for Guinea-Bissau/Cape Verde unity, it is clear that the spirit of Pan Africanism was not able to counteract what Lopes calls "the exaggerated nationalism of Cape Verdean leaders."

It is clear that the November 1980 coup by João Vieira in Guinea-Bissau was not the cause of the death of Amilcar Cabral's dream of unity; it merely hastened it. Also obvious is the fact that a strategy of unification which did not seriously attempt to reduce social/cultural distances, heal lingering wounds, and change ingrained prejudices was doomed to fail. At a very fundamental level, the necessary groundwork and the political will to realize the dream were missing. The speed with which the Cape Verdean leadership converted the PAIGC wing in their country into the PAICV, a mere two months after the November coup, raises serious questions about the commitment to Guinea-Bissau/Cape Verde unity.

GUINEA-BISSAU: FOREIGN RELATIONS 1983–1993. The year 1983 was designated by President Vieira (q.v.) as 'The Year of Action, Not Words.' In search of practical solutions to pressing economic and social problems, the former radical PAIGC ideology (q.v) was being increasingly abandoned, and the government became guided by 'realism' and 'pragmatism.' The characterization of the country and its foreign policy as 'anti-colonialist and anti-imperialist' was de-emphasized. It was during this year that an economic stablization/recovery program was adopted. This program was supported by such formerly 'reactionary' and 'conservative' international organizations and nations such as the World Bank, the United States, Kuwait, and Saudi Arabia. The adoption of the 'realistic' policies led not only to structural adjustment and economic reform, but also to a radical review of Guinea-Bissau's foreign relations, which culminated in the ending of diplomatic ties with its long-time ally, the People's Republic of China. China had been the first country to give military training to the liberation fighters, including its national hero and President João "Niño" Vieira, who established diplomatic ties with Taiwan.

Forged during the years of the national liberation struggle, Guinea-Bissau's foreign policy during the first decade of independence (1973–1983) reflected the pragmatic approach and skillful diplomacy of the legendary Amilcar Cabral (q.v.), leader of the liberation movement and ruling party the *Partido Africano da Independência de Guiné e Cabo Verde*, PAIGC (q.v.). Although espousing an essentially socialist ideology, Cabral and the PAIGC managed from the outset to avoid being the victims of the 'cold war' which raged at the time. Stressing the needs and objectives of the armed struggle, the PAIGC sought material support from all ideological blocs. Ties established with countries of the then-Socialist bloc were largely inherited with the new independent nation. Originally this was because of the willingness and readiness of those countries (especially the People's Republic of China, the Soviet Union, and Cuba) to provide material support at a critical time. In contrast, the relatively weak or even hostile attitude of the United States and other members of the North American Treaty Organization, NATO (q.v.), to the national liberation struggle stemmed from Portugal's membership in the NATO alliance.

With independence, adherence to the non-alignment principle of non-membership of ideological camps allowed the new nation to establish diplomatic, economic, and cultural relations with a wide array of countries. The result was an enormous outpouring of much needed financial support and technical assistance. Nevertheless, during the first decade of independence Guinea-Bissau's foreign policy leaned more toward the Socialist camp. The country was a vocal 'anti-colonial and anti-imperialist' country in international forums like the United Nations, (q.v.) and the Organization of African Unity, OAU (q.v.). In her 'radical' posture, she consistently and openly condemned *apartheid* in South Africa and South African aggression against neighboring nations such as Angola and Mozambique. Guinea-Bissau also supported and granted diplomatic status to the Palestine Liberation Organization and recognized Polisario's unilateral declaration of independence for the Western Sahara, among other manifestations of political and ideological solidarity. However, this stance began to be radically modified as the underlying economic crisis deepened in Guinea.

Until the World Bank supported the Economic Stabilization Program in 1983, the Guinean economy was characterized by central planning, low levels of agricultural and industrial activities, poor and rapidly deteriorating physical infrastructure, State monopoly of internal and external trade, widespread corruption and smuggling, shortages of basic necessities, and growing parallel markets. To address the chronic situation, which was generating serious social and political problems, the Guinean government decided to restructure the economy (q.v.), which meant the abandonment of its Socialist tendencies and the forging of closer links with capitalist countries like the United States (q.v.), France, the United Kingdom, and especially Portugal (q.v), the former colonial power.

Indeed, a prelude to the launching of the Economic Stabilization Program was a three-day visit to the country by Portuguese President General António Ramalho Eanes in December 1982, an event with great pomp and ceremony. It should be noted that during the early post-independence period, there still remained some lingering hostility and distrust in spite of the establishment of full diplomatic relatiions between the two countries as well as Portugal's generous offer to bear the cost of providing university education and technical training for a large number of young Guineans.

President Eanes's visit resulted in the signing of a number of bilateral accords which committed Portugal to providing technical assistance in the area of economic planning and supporting Guinea-Bissau's proposals and projects submitted to such international organizations as the World Bank and the International Monetary Fund. In fact, in December 1983 Lisbon hosted a round table of Guinean officials, economic experts, and representatives of financial institutions and donor countries on the issue of aid for economic reforms. Thus started a period of closer cooperation between the two countries, a cooperation which embraces economic, social, cultural, and military affairs that has been fortified over the years by regular contacts and official visits (at Presidential and Prime Ministerial levels) that have invariably been reciprocated. It is worth noting that in September 1989 the Portuguese national television network, *Radio Televisão Portuguesa* (RTP) set up, and has since been running, Guinea-Bissau's national television station, *Televisão Experimental da Guiné-Bissau* (TVE-GB).

Also in 1983, Guinea-Bissau's new 'realistic' approach to international relations, geared toward securing vital development aid, led to the establishment of diplomatic relations with the United Kingdom and recognition of South Korea, which offered the Guinean government a Presidential Cadillac limousine, five Mercedes Benz sedans, and twenty-two other vehicles, as well as forty mechanized ploughs (*Nô Pintcha*, 31/12/83). Considering the strong links with North Korea, which date back to the war years, the establishment of diplomatic ties with South Korea was indeed a turn-about of great significance.

During his speech at the Non-Aligned Summit held in New Delhi, India in March 1983, President Vieira stressed his government's preoccupation with solving his country's "arduous problems of development" (*Nô Pintcha*, 12/3/83). On his way home from India, he paid a short visit to Saudi Arabia, a member of the Non-Aligned movement and was warmly received by King Fahad. Two months later, the King's special envoy, the Saudi Ambassador to Senegal, Abdulla Altobaishi, visited Bissau, and shortly afterward diplomatic relations were established. To Guinea-Bissau's large Muslim community (about thirty percent of the population; especially among Mandinkas and Fulas [qq.v.]), Saudi Arabia has become an important source of much needed development funds.

By the end of December 1983, Bissau (q.v.) was twinned with Lisbon; diplomatic relations were renewed with Cape Verde (having been severed in November 1980); membership was attained in the regional organization for the development of the Gambia river basin; the Fourth Summit of the five Luso-phone nations was held in Bissau; and there were official presidential visits from Moussa Traoré of Mali, João Baptista Figueiredo of Brazil, and Abdou Diouf of Senegal.

Although Senegal and Brazil had been viewed with suspicion by the liberation fighters during the war years, relations have become very warm and friendly since independence. While Senegal's President Leopold Senghor had consistently limited the PAIGC's military bases during the armed struggle, notwithstanding the conflict in the Casamance (q.v.) as well as maritime disputes, the relations between Guinea-Bissau and Senegal are generally friendly and close. Likewise, relations with Brazil have moved from the time when Brazil's right-wing military dictatorship had strong relations with colonial Portugal to today's diplomatic warmth and expanded ties in trade, cultural exchange, and educational assistance to Guinea-Bissau.

By the mid–1980's, Guinea-Bissau's leanings away from the Socialist bloc were much in evidence. She was increasingly critical of the Soviet occupation of Afghanistan and of the bloody regime of the Khmer Rouge in Cambodia. The decision to implement structural adjustment programs and open up the economy meant greater reliance on, and the forging of closer links with, the traditional western capitalist nations, including the Scandinavian states. Sweden, since the early years of the armed struggle, had been a supporter and was an important source of aid. Also included on this new list were the 'Newly Industrializing Countries' (NICs) of Asia, of which the relations with Taiwan were the most dramatic and controversial.

From 8 to 12 October 1990, in an undisguised search for scarce financial resources to pay for his country's numerous development projects, President Vieira paid a four-day visit to Taiwan (Republic of China), whose legitimacy had long been contested by the giant Peoples Republic of China (Beijing). This was further complicated by the fact that Vieira was a graduate of China's Nanking Military School and that numerous projects in Guinea-Bissau were being funded by Beijing, including a large hospital in Canchungo, fishing and farming projects, a rice project in Bafatá, and the large multi-purpose sports stadium in Bissau.

President Vieira's visit to Taiwan was preceded four months earlier by the visit of a high-level economic delegation led by the then Minister of the Economy and Finance Manuel 'Manecas' dos Santos, which so enraged Beijing that she immediately recalled all her diplomats and technical assistants in Guinea-Bissau. She terminated the courses of all Guinean students studying in China and promptly deported them.

Shortly after the Guinean President's visit to Taiwan, the two countries signed some twenty bilateral accords lasting five years and covering such vital areas as agriculture, fisheries, transport, and health. In particular, the Taiwanese were committed to finance a new terminal building at Bissau's Osvaldo Vieira International Airport, a number of public housing projects, the new National Assembly, and a highway linking the capital to the international aiport. The highway project had been started in the late 1970's but was viewed as overly 'ambitious' and was abandoned after 14 November 1980. The protocol also covers scholarships for Guinean students and central government budget support.

Refering to the People's Republic of China's unilateral move to sever all relations with Guinea-Bissau, President Vieira noted the 'divergences' between the two countries dating back to the period of the armed liberation struggle. Apparently because of the prevailing Sino-Soviet rivalry, the Chinese had wanted the PAIGC, which was also receiving substantial Soviet aid, to take the Chinese side in this dispute. The PAIGC refused, and according to President Vieira this led to the suspension of all Chinese aid to the liberation movement; it was only after independence that relations were re-established (*Nô Pintcha* 10/11/90).

Thus by the beginning of the 1990's, 'realism' and 'pragmatism' and the 'national interest,' rather than radical Socialist/ Pan Africanist ideology, had become the guiding principles of Guinean foreign policy. This transition was greatly facilitated by the easing of tension between the two major ideological blocs and the eventual ending of the cold war. Today, Guinea-Bissau, one of the poorest and least developed nations on the planet, is struggling more than ever to survive in the new international order despite 'structural adjustment,' growing indebtedness, and greater dependency. These realities have narrowed the range of choices to the adoption of 'realistic' options only. In his speech celebrating ten years of the 14 November 1980 coup which brought him to power, President Vieira stressed the need "to continue to develop a prudent and realistic policy" (*Nô Pintcha*, 17/11/90).

GUINEA-BISSAU: POLITICAL TRANSITION 1991. At an Extraordinary Meeting of the *Partido Africano da Independência de Guiné e Cabo Verde*, PAIGC (q.v.) in January 1991, President João 'Nino' Vieira (q.v.) announced the launching of a process of transition from a one-party state to a multi-party system of government. Specifically, he stipulated that legislative and presidential elections would be held by the end of 1992. The year 1991 was then officially designated 'The Year of Democratization.'

On 5 May 1991, the Constitution of the Republic of Guinea-Bissau was amended to allow for political pluralism and liberal democracy. In particular, the legislators abolished articles four and six which respectively defined the PAIGC as the 'driving force of society' and the 'supreme expression of the sovereign will of the people.' Now, article four permits the formation of political parties while article six separates state and 'legally recognized' religious institutions and stipulates that the former will 'respect' and 'protect' the latter. The revised Constitution also guarantees fundamental liberties such as freedom of thought, assembly, association, demonstration, and the press.

Since the approval of the new Constitution, Guinean lawmakers have worked furiously to enact laws aimed at facilitating the political liberalization process. On 26 August 1991, an amendment regarding the formation of political parties reduced the requirement of 2,000 signatures (with a minimum of 100 signatures from each of the country's nine regions) for legalization to only 1,000 signatures (and a minimum of 50 signatures from each region). In an Extraordinary Session of the ANP (q.v.) held between 25 September and 3 October 1991, a series of laws were passed. Among these were laws regarding freedom of the press, rights of journalists, the right of legal political parties to air time, the right of workers to form independent trade unions, and the right to strike. By the end of the year, three opposition political parties were formally recognized.

Moves toward the liberalization of the Guinean polity continued. A *Comissão Multipartidária da Transição* (CMT), (Multiparty Commission of Transition) was created in August 1992 and consisted of three members from each of the legal parties. The CMT is the forum for discussing all legislative aspects leading to the establishment of a multi-party system in the country. A law establishing a *Comissão Nacional das Eleições* (National Electoral Commission) was approved by the ANP on 24 January 1993 and was charged with coordinating and supervising the electoral process. It is composed of one representative from each legal political party, one representative from each of the Presidential candidates, a representative of the Ministries of the Interior and Territorial Administration, a representative from the Social Communication Council, and four independent persons. Regional Electoral Commissions were established later.

By the end of 1992, eleven legal political parties (including the ruling PAIGC) were in existence, but no elections, Legislative or Presidential, had been held. The elections postponed due to insufficient pre-electoral preparation as well as unresolved disagreements between the ruling party and the opposition (such as the question of whether to hold successive or simultaneous elections and when they should be held, and the right of Guineans abroad to vote), were rescheduled for 1993. No date had been established and, it seemed increasingly unlikely that they would be held then. The date for elections

Plate 1B. Fula Woman, 19th century

Plate 1A. Papel Chief and Assistants, 19th century

Plate 2B. *Homen Grande* and his Wife

Plate 2A. Guinean *Regulo* in Traditional Costume

Plate 3A. *Regulo* of Guinea-Bissau, with status hat

Plate 3B. Fula Prince of Propana

Plate 4B. Honório Barreto, Governor of Guinea

Plate 4A. Arnaldo Schultz, Governor of Guinea

Plate 5A. Amilcar Cabral at the United Nations. Photo courtesy of the United Nations.

Plate 5B. Luís Cabral in the Liberated Zones

Plate 6A. Aristides Pereira and João Vieira

Plate 6B. Author with bi-grupo, North Front 1973

Plate 7A. Estrella-2 Surface-to-Air Missile

Plate 7B. The fall of Guiledge in 1973

Plate 8A. Woman Leader during the liberation struggle

Plate 8B. Faces of the Future in northern Guinea

was shifted several times in 1994, but they were finally held in July. The postponements were due because of the overall level of electoral preparation was only in its primary stages in early 1994 (no electoral census had been conducted by the second half of 1993) and the fact that no provisions had been made in the 1993 budget for electoral costs.

Regarding these costs, a study by the Washington-based International Foundation for Electoral Systems (IFES) esti-mated in December 1991 that the amount for two successive (Presidential and Legislative) elections to be about US $ 8.0 million. It would appear that the Guinean government was relying almost entirely on external assistance, in cash or in kind, for financing this electoral process. The country has been facing serious economic problems and is heavily indebted. In 1990, the total debt was calculated by the World Bank at US $ 592.8 million, representing 321.3% of the GNP, the highest in West Africa. However, a number of countries, including Swe-den, France, the Netherlands, the United States, and Portugal have indicated their willingness to support the process through financial contributions and/or the provision of technical assis-tance.

Since the announcement of the transition to multi-partyism in 1991, the political *"abertura"* (openness) had ushered in an atmosphere of increasing toleration and great expectations in the country. There is open criticism of the government and lots of lively debates in the press, radio, and television. In addition to the official newspaper, *Nô Pintcha*, there is the independent weekly *Expresso Bissau*, besides the newspapers of the politi-cal parties, including *Baguera* (*Partido da Convergência Dem-ocrática*), *Corubal* (*Resistência da Guiné-Bissau/Movimento Bafata*), *O Democrata* (*Partido Democrático do Progresso*), *Ganga Real* (*Frente Democratica*), and *Libertação* (*Partido Africano da Independência da Guiné e Cabo Verde*), (see entries on the individual parties). Long deprived of such funda-mental rights such as freedom of speech and association, Guineans have enthusiastically embraced this *"abertura."* Since the thrust of the current debate on democracy in the country presents the cause of the lack of development as a result of the lack of democracy, the enthusiasm is under-standable.

It is also a fact that Guineans have never experienced an open and competitive multi-party system. Inexperience with the conduct and organization of such elections, inadequate and decaying infrastructure, and mistrust and suspicions among the leaders of the political parties remain factors which could undermine the process of political liberalization. In the final analysis, the whole process depends to a large extent on the soldiers in the barracks. The critical role of the military in either promoting or curbing the necessary environment should be taken into consideration.

Aside from those parties just noted, the other legal parties as of 31 July 1993 also included *Frente Democrática Social, Frente de Luta Pela Independência Nacional da Guiné, Movimento de Unidade para A Democracia, Partido da Renovação Social*, and *Partido Unido Social Democrata* (qq.v.).

Other political parties expecting legal recognition include: *Partido Socialista da Guiné-Bissau* (PSG) founded by Cirilo Augusto Rodrigues de Oliveira on 25 March 1991 in France; the *Forum Civico Guineense-Social Democracia* (FGC/SD) founded by Antonieta Rosa Gomes in Brazil (she is the only woman to found a party); and the *Liga Guineense de Protecção Ecológica* (LIPE), this 'green' party was founded on 20 July 1991 and is led by Bubacar Djaló.

GUINEA-CONAKRY. *See* FUTA JALLON; GUINEA-BISSAU: FOREIGN AFFAIRS.

H

HAWKINS, SIR JOHN (1532–1595). Like his father William Hawkins, John was a merchant adventurer from England, but the main items of commerce for John Hawkins were African slaves. In 1559 John moved from London to the port town of Plymouth where he married the daughter of Benjamin Gonson, Treasurer of the Navy, an office that John Hawkins was later to hold. Backed by English merchants, Hawkins left for Africa in 1562 in three small ships named *Salomon, Swallow*, and *Jonas*. This first adventure in English slaving was sufficiently profitable that it attracted the secret financial backing of Queen Elizabeth and several of her Privy Councillors. The second voyage took place in 1564 and met armed resistance by the Portuguese, forcefully broken by Hawkins, who seized several Portuguese ships. For these successes Hawkins was knighted by the Queen and given a royal emblem showing an African slave in chains. The rapid gain in popularity of sugar as a sweetener encouraged a third voyage in 1566 under a different captain and in 1567 with Hawkins again in charge. On his last trip Hawkins was attacked and defeated by Spanish ships, thus ending this first period of English slaving.

HEALTH. In 1972 the Portuguese health budget for Guinea-Bissau was ten million *escudos* (2.7 percent of the total budget). The processing industries took fifty-six percent of the budget, while transport used twenty-six percent of these revenues. These proportions suggest the limited concern for African health by the colonial government, and they demonstrate the financial base for the extremely low level of the health delivery system. In all, the Portuguese spent about $350,000 US or sixty-six cents per person for health in one of their last years as the colonial power, and the vast majority of health services were located in the capital city and were geared to the White and 'assimilated' sectors of the populace. To meet these needs in 1959 there was about one doctor for every 20,000 inhabitants. Although thousands never saw a doctor, there were some health gains in the closing years of colonialism as the following data indicate.

By 1964 the doctor-to-inhabitant ratio had improved to one doctor for every 15,400 people, and by 1989 this had improved to one doctor to every 7,742 inhabitants. By 1964 the per capita expenditure had risen to $1.45 US per person annually. Obviously the improvements were still hopelessly inadequate, and many of the increased services were simply involved with the treatment of war-related injuries as the anti-colonial war intensified.

During the course of the nationalist struggle the *Partido Africano da Independência de Guiné e Cabo Verde*, PAIGC (q.v.), began to develop its own health and military facilities to treat war casualties and to serve the increasing numbers of people in the expanding liberated zones of the country. In the midst of guerrilla warfare, the services were crude and decentralized but relatively effective given the combat environ-

Health Data for Guinea-Bissau

	1960	1961	1963	1966	1971	1990
Doctors	25	26	344	846	129	
Nurses/RNs	100	150	202	—	285	250
Hospitals	10	—	31	34	—	22
Beds	300	—	839	850	1,027	1,442

Sources: PAIGC Government; World Bank

ment. Each village committee had specific health assignments and close personal contacts, resulting in the fact that the number of sanitary posts (dressing stations) of the PAIGC exceeded those of the Portuguese by 1970. Throughout the war the PAIGC sent people overseas for nursing and medical training, while some foreign doctors, especially those from eastern Europe and Cuba, came to serve as doctors in the liberated regions. In addition to the village health committees, the PAIGC organized travelling health brigades.

By 1972 there were five PAIGC hospitals in the south, two in the north, and two in the east. These primitive facilities were concealed under the tree canopy and were sometimes moved several times a year for security reasons. Operations such as Caesarean sections, amputations, and appendectomies were performed using blood plasma, local anesthetics, and antibiotics to which there was an unusually good response. The main goal in these field hospitals was to get patients ambulatory, so they might be transported to the 123–bed PAIGC hospital at Boké, Guinea-Conakry or to the 50–bed facilities at Koundara or Ziguinchor (q.v.) in Senegal. In 1972, Boké processed 5,000 outpatients. By the same year the total number of doctors working with the PAIGC was forty-one, thereby approximating the number used by the Portuguese at that time.

In Guinea-Bissau there are numerous and very widespread debilitating tropical diseases such as malaria, biharzia, filariasis, diarrhea, and various gastrointestinal and respiratory disorders. Tuberculosis and nutritional deficiencies are also common problems. Even in the early 1980's, the average caloric intake is just seventy-four percent of the minimum daily requirement.

Since independence, the PAIGC has inherited the colonial facilities and has sought improvements in health services. In absolute terms these services are still very underdeveloped and much further growth is still required, since existing health services continue to suffer chronic shortages of medicines, hospital facilities, and medical personnel. The following World Bank statistics are appropriately revealing. Life expectancy at birth was only forty-one years in about 1980 but has risen to forty-four years by 1990. The infant death rate was extremely high at 149/1,000 (ca. 1980) but has fallen to 138/1,000 by 1990. While these modest gains are positive, the main hospital in Bissau (q.v.) is 'in a state of near ruins,' although there is some optimism about the Cacheu hospital being built in Canchungo. This hospital was first built with aid from China and was operational for years, but after Beijing-Bissau relations were broken, the Taiwanese assumed this responsibility.

According to the World Bank, future amelioration of the health conditions will not take place without major training of all health workers from doctors and nurses to administrators; large-scale renovation and new construction must soon be initiated. Health related services such as family planning, maternal health care, power and water supply, refrigeration, nutritional advice, AIDS information, and basic sanitation all need immediate attention as well.

HENRY. *See* PRINCE HENRY.

I

ILHAS DE BARLAVENTO. Northern, windward islands of Cape Verde including Santo Antão, São Vicente, Santa Luzia, São Nicolau, Sal, and Boa Vista.

ILHAS DE SOTAVENTO. Southern, leeward islands of Cape Verde including Maio, São Tiago, Fogo, Brava, and the islets of Grande, Luís Carneiro, and Sapado.

INDIGENA. *See* ASSIMILADO; REGIME DO INDI-GENATO.

INDIGO. Indigo (*Indigofera sp.*) and urzella (*Litmus roccella*) are both plant dyes originally from the Rio Nuño area on the Guinea-Conakry coast which have been exports from Cape Verde. They were planted to help revive stagnant agriculture (q.v.), but the commerce in these dyes was controlled by the British to the disadvantage of Cape Verdeans. While indigo and urzella were used to dye Cape Verdean textiles, especially the *panos* (q.v.), (cloths used in the slave trade), they never became significant cash crop exports; today this role is largely taken over by coffee production.

INFALI SONCO. Infali Sonco, a Beafada *regulo* (qq.v.), had been recognized by the Portuguese in their effort to establish rule over the *indigenas* in the wake of the Berlin Congress (q.v.) in 1884–85. In the 1890's there were uprisings led by Mamadú Paté (q.v.) attacking at Buba (q.v.), by Pepel and *grumete* (q.v.) revolts in such places as Bissau and Geba (q.v.), and Musa Molo (q.v.) attacking in Farim (q.v.). During a period of Portuguese counterattacks on the Balantas (q.v.) and Oio Mandinkas (q.v.) in 1898, Infali defected from the Portuguese and joined this resistance to colonial rule.

By 1906 Infali was still very effective in his opposition, as illustrated in his river and road blockade from Bissau to Bafatá (qq.v). Again, this was in association with other such resistance acts by Felupes, Balantas (qq.v.), and Pepels in other areas. Seeing that Infali was obstructing their claims of 'effective colonial rule' the Portuguese mounted a major offensive against him in central Guinea-Bissau in 1907. While they were not able to defeat him there, he was forced to retreat to Oio, while the people of the central Guinea towns were subjected to a pattern of atrocious destruction under Portuguese First Lieutenant Oliveira Musanty.

INJAI. *See* ABDUL INJAI.

ISNA, PANSAU NA. Isna was a famous national liberation war hero who made his name during the battle of Como Island, which first demonstrated the capability of the guerrillas of the *Partido Africano da Independência de Guiné e Cabo Verde*, PAIGC (q.v.). A Balanta (q.v.) born in the tiny island of N'Fanda in the southern coastal region of Tombali, Isna was a guerrillas fighter from the very beginning of the liberation war in 1963. He attacked Portuguese posts and patrols in the south before taking part in the battle for control of the strategic island of Como in 1964. Cut off and surrounded by a well-armed Portuguese force of some 3,000 soldiers, the guerrilla force commanded by Isna withstood the almost seventy-five day siege and bloody battle which cost heavily in lives on both sides. With the withdrawal of the colonial troops the island became the first territory to be liberated.

Two years later, Isna led attacks which dislodged the colonial forces from their fortified camps in Balana and Gandembel, leaving the PAIGC in effective control of the south. In 1969, the guerrilla Commander Isna was transferred to the northern front, where he led attacks against several Portuguese targets. He was killed in action in Nhacra, near Bissau (q.v.), that same year. Pansau Na Isna Avenue in Bissau commemorates his name.

J

JEWS OF THE UPPER GUINEA COAST, CAPE VERDE, AND PORTUGAL. Jewish history plays a role in Cape Verde and Guinea that is far greater than expected or recognized. On the one hand, the alliance of Jews and Moors was remembered and resented by the *Reconquista* and the Inquisition. On the other, the dispersed and converted Jews saw their own religious and cultural identity transformed in Cape Verde, Senegambia, and Guinea.

Anti-Semitism against Jews and Muslims has a regrettably long European history. The close association between Jews and Moors in commerce, administration, education, and science placed Jews in a significant and effective position which was later to engender both admiration and jealousy. The seven centuries of Moorish presence in Iberia and the Islamic hold on the Christian aspects of the Holy Land gave abundant time for such emotions to evolve.

In Africa, Jews had dispersed widely in the centuries both before and after the birth of Christ, and one may safely assume that they were present in Carthage and even in trans-Saharan trade. The Star of David is still a part of Berber iconography. In Tunisia, a synagogue which dates back to the third century BC still functions. Sizeable Jewish enclaves were widespread in Algeria and Morocco even up to 1967.

The complexity of this relationship may be seen in the expulsion of Moors (and some Jews) from Portugal (q.v) in 1249. But in contemporary Spain, King Pedro of Aragon used Jews as middlemen in commerce with the Arab nations in the Maghreb from 1284 to 1286. In 1290 King Edward I expelled all Jews from England. The Jews who remained in Iberia were particularly distinguished as cartographers, showing the Kingdom of Mali (q.v.) in a map of 1330. In 1375 the Jewish mapmaker Abraham Cresques provided correct details about the Moroccan coast which were to assist Prince Henry (q.v.) decades later. But it was in 1391 that Andalusian Jews were subject to vicious pogroms which began a long process of flight and exile.

In 1422, under the command of the Grand Master of the Order of Calatrava, Don Luís de Guzman of Castille directed that the noted Hebrew scholar Rabbi Moses Arrangel de Maqueda prepare a proper Spanish translation of the Bible from Hebrew. This Bible later became the possession of the Duke of Alba and its known as the Alba Bible. In 1473, the Spanish Jew Abraham Zacuto made pioneering advances in navigational tables, showing nautical declination in otherwise unknown waters. His Jewish student José Vizinho became a Spanish court astronomer.

Despite these distinctions and achievements, Iberian Jews faced steadily increasing discrimination, and by the late fifteenth century, they were sometimes known as *Marranos* (Moorish Jews) or *Judeus Segredos* (Secret Jews) who officially converted to Catholicism, but privately maintained some Jewish practices. It is interesting to note that a critical financier for the famed voyage of Christopher Columbus (q.v.), who is sometimes claimed to have Jewish roots, was the Valencian Luís de Santangel. De Santangel was a Jewish convert to Christianity and was the keeper of the Privy Purse for the Spanish Crown. Such important contributions were minimized or overlooked in the 1480's when Andalusian Jews were expelled, and in 1492 when large numbers of Jews and Moors were also expelled from Spanish Granada. After the Inquisition began and forced conversions took place, Jews became known as *Novos Cristãos* (New Christians). For centuries, many Sephardic Jews continued to speak *Ladino* (q.v.), a fifteenth century varient of Judeo-Spanish.

Some Jews were allowed to remain, upon payment of large ransoms and under severe restrictions. Jewish children were seized and baptised. As much as half of the Jewish population was compelled to accept forced conversion to Christianity or were sent to Cape Verde, Senegambia, or São Tomé and Al-Mina as galley rowers, slaves, and convicts. In addition to exile to Africa and the Middle East it is estimated that as many as 120,000 Sephardic Jews fled to Turkey, which still had as many as 250,000 Jews at the end of the nineteenth century.

The genocide and racism in Spain continued. In 1497 in Spain, 20,000 Jews were forcibly converted and baptised. Yet in 1502, Pedro Nunes, a Jew, was appointed as Royal Cosmographer for the Portuguese King. The 'Great Circle' navigation conceptualized by Nunes was considered essential for shortening long voyages. He died in Coimbra in 1578 with a royal pension. This supportive treatment was followed by savage anti-Jewish riots in Lisbon in 1504, in which 2,000 Jews were killed.

The merger of Spanish and Portuguese crowns from 1580 to 1640 only added to the pressure on Jews to seek exile or conversion and to fear expulsion to North Africa, Senegambia, or to the Atlantic Islands. Even those Portuguese Jews who reappeared as *Novos Cristãos* were not completely absorbed. Indeed, it was not until 1768 that Portugal officially abolished the distinction between 'Old' and 'New' (i.e., Jewish) Christians.

The excellent research of Jean Boulegue has brought to light many fascinating details of the Portuguese Jewish presence in Senegambia and Guinea. For example, in 1517 Portuguese King Manuel I made reference to a group of *lançados* (q.v.) on the Senegambian coast; most of these were Portuguese Jews who had been deported. The term *lançados*, derived from the Portuguese verb 'to throw out,' is related to their outcast or fugitive roles in Luso-African coastal commerce. In the fifteenth and sixteenth centuries the *lançados* presence on the coast was as far north as Gorée (q.v.) and the Senegalese towns of Portudal (the port of Ali), Joal, Kayor, Baol, and Beziguiche where the *lançados* traded with the chiefs of the Wolof, Sine, and Saloum (q.v.) kingdoms. In Portuguese Guinea they were found on the Cacheu and Geba (q.v.) Rivers and further south as well at the trading towns on the Nunez, Scarcies, and Rokelle Rivers.

The formation of the Inquisition in Portugal in 1536 had as one of its main tasks the supervision and repression of those *Novos Cristãos* just baptized. A tribunal in Coimbra, operating between 1567 and 1595 condemned some 958 *Marranos* to rowing as galley slaves.

Another phase in the complex love-hate relationship still between Iberians and Jews was seen in the Portuguese Crown's order in 1601 which allowed (or encouraged) the Jewish *lançados* to settle along the Senegambian and Upper Guinea coast to trade for ivory, hides, slaves, gold, gum, wax, and amber while based in Cape Verde. Within the islands Jews would receive these same items for later resale to those traders who preferred not to take the risks of coastal trade even if it meant higher costs in the islands. Jews were also active in the trade of hides, urzela, indigo, (q.v.) and coffee.

Restrictions for the *lançados* prohibited them from selling iron bars, firearms, and navigational instruments, yet the *lançados* were clearly critical in the economic network which linked the Crown trade monopolies to the coast. Spanish and English smuggler-traders were frequent violators of these Portuguese prohibitions.

Thus as early as the later fifteenth century and through the sixteenth and even seventeenth centuries a Jewish coastal presence was deeply established. This brought on an important synthesis dynamic which was responsible for playing a central role in the creation of Crioulo (q.v.) culture. These Jews, both in the Cape Verde Islands and on the coast, were at the heart of the Afro-Portuguese merger which became Crioulo culture.

The anti-Semitism of Spain and Portugal and the financial goals of the Portuguese Crown were constantly trying to restrict their success. The more successful, the more restrictions, but also the more deeply struck were the commerical and cultural roots of these people. The *lançados* were themselves undergoing a transformation because of their intermediary and collaborative relation with African cultures. This contradictory nature at once set them apart, while burying themselves into a multiracial and multi-cultural identity that they were synthesizing. In Cape Verde this was to become the essence of Crioulo culture. This process has its close parallels in East Africa with the commercial presence of Omani and Shirazi Muslims who were trading for ivory and slaves from the African interior. A trade language and an entire cultural group, now known as KiSwahili evolved in this context. In the Senegambian (q.v.) case, French and British expansion finally reduced the presence of the *lançados* and their military associates the *grumetes* (q.v.) to only Portuguese Guinea and to urban and coastal entrepots. Until the war of national liberation (1963–1974) in Guinea-Bissau Crioulo people, culture, and language was mainly still isolated in urban areas. During the war the use of Crioulo spread throughout the countryside.

Jews were already known in Joal as early as 1591, and a synagogue was noted there in 1641. In 1606, in Portudal also on the Senegalese coast, there were 100 Portuguese following the 'Laws of Moses.' Boulegue notes that in 1614 the Governor of Cape Verde recorded that the greatest number of *lançados* were Jews. In 1622, the Cape Verdean Governor, Dom Francisco de Mourra reported to the Portuguese King that the Guinea coast rivers were "full of Jews who were masters of the local regions and were quite independent of the Crown." No doubt such information relating to 'the Jewish danger' caused the Portuguese to 'punish' two wealthy members of the Jewish comunity around the synagogue in Rufisque, Senegal for economic excesses in 1629. When a branch of the Portuguese Inquisition was established in Cape Verde in 1672, one result was the seizure of Jewish-owned merchandise. As the seventeenth century evolved, the Portuguese were steadily displaced from Senegambia, but they retained their hold in Guinea at Cacheu, Bissau, Geba (qq.v.), and in the Cape Verde Islands. To this extent the role and number of the coastal *lançados* was reduced.

In the sixteenth and seventeenth centuries the term *ganagoga* was also used. Not only did this imply Jewish *lançados*, but in practice *ganagoga* also meant people who were able to speak many local African languages. Allied with this concept was the term *tangomão* (q.v.) which essentially overlapped with *lançado*. It seems most likely that *tangomão* is a corrupted form of *targuman*, which means 'translator' in Arabic. Muslims and Arabic-speakers were and are widespread in this area, especially the northern and interior regions where the *tangomãos* or *lançados* traded. The Jewish and Moorish alliance was already of very great historical depth.

This relationship was based upon several factors. On the one hand, the Portuguese Crown and its *feitors* (q.v.) and *capitãos* gained tremendous wealth from the slave trade and did little to oppose it. However, they were pleased to have a social pariah group like the *lançados* be responsible for the frontline operation of the trade. Meanwhile, the commercial skills and high level of literacy of this group of Jews put them in a strong position to have a critical role in the economy and society which otherwise shunned them. It should be made clear that primarily it was Portuguese royalty and their contractors who were involved in the slave trade; only some of these traders were Jewish. A reference to a *lançado* expedition to the goldfields of Bambuk in the period 1785 to 1788 refered to a Jewish *ganagoga* who married a daughter of the Imam of Futa Toro (q.v.).

By the late eighteenth century, a clearly defined *lançado* community in Senegambia was gone but not really departed. Virtually all *lançados* had African wives and consorts, and their subsequent generations played a central and substantial role in the culturo-linguistic melange which consitutes Cape Verdean Crioulo culture. This was formed in the context of the merging and blending of Iberian, Moorish, Jewish, and African peoples.

Following the 'Liberal Wars' in Portugal in the 1820's, some 'Miguelista' Jews fled to the mountains of Santo Antão. Several became leading traders and professionals, according to Meintel (1984). In the mid-nineteenth century the population of Cape Verdean Jews was increased by some small scale Jewish migration from Rabat, Morocco, especially for the trade in animal hides. During the early nineteenth century, Jews also came to settle in Santo Antão where there are still traces of their influx in the name of the village of Sinagoga, located on the north coast between Riberia Grande and Janela, and in the Jewish cemetary at the town of Ponta da Sol. Jewish cemetaries or graves are in Brava (at Cova da Judeu), Boa Vista, São Tiago (in Praia and Cidade Velha), Santo Antão (at Ponta da Sol and perhaps at Sinagoga), São Vincent (at Mindelo), Fogo, and perhaps in other islands as well. In the nineteenth- and twentieth-century Praia cemetery, for example, there are about eight grave markers with Hebrew inscriptions still extant. The Portuguese Crown slave trade monopolies used Crioulos, Cape Verdean Jews, and coastal *lançados* in the slave trade. The Atlantic slave trade has also been known as the *Triangle Trade,* as it described a vast triangular shape linking West Africa with the Caribbean and then to New England and Europe and thence back to Africa. As a result, in the Caribbean in Curação, Surinam, and Jamaica, there were Jewish populations similar to, and linked with, those in West Africa. The case of Jamaica parallels that of the *lançados,* since it was in its period of growth from the 1630's to 1670's. Eighteenth century Portuguese Jews in Jamaica include names such as: Alvarez, Cardoso, Corea, DaCosta, Gomes, Gonsalis, Gutteres, Lamego, Quisano, and Torres families.

Meanwhile in New England, virtually all Jews were of Portuguese origin and they lived mainly in Newport, Rhode Island. Before the American Revolution, about a fourth of all Jews in the colonies lived in Rhode Island. In the period between 1658 and 1677 there were at least fifteen Jewish families in this port town. By the eighteenth century the number of families had doubled. In 1763 when the Newport Touro synagogue was built there were some sixty Jewish families in town. By the mid-eighteenth century only about ten percent of the largest merchants of Newport were Jews, noting that the majority were Americans or English. Among these were Aaron Lopes and his father-in-law Jacob Rodriques Rivera who made huge sums in the slave trade, which certainly existed before they even arrived. Their shipping included an important American coastal commerce in diversified merchandise, but they financed an average of two slaving voyages each year and certainly drew their slaves from the Upper Guinea coast and Cape Verde (which was then the main source of slaves, especially for Portuguese-speakers). In 1788, slavery was abolished in Rhode Island, and by 1822 the last Jewish family of Portuguese origin had left Newport.

JOÃO II (ruled 1477, 1481–1495). João II was the King of Portugal (q.v.) during the later period of the age of maritime exploration launched by Prince Henry (q.v). He was the son of King Alfonso V. During his reign, settlers began arriving in the Cape

Verde Islands. Under João II, chartmaking began in Lisbon, including the work of Bartolomeu Columbus, brother of Christopher Columbus (q.v.). In 1484 João II turned down a request by Christopher Columbus to finance further voyages after the explorer had visited the Guinea Coast between 1482 and 1484. Columbus visited João II again in 1493 after his historic voyage to 'India' (the New World).

JUVENTUDE AFRICANA AMILCAR CABRAL (JAAC). *See* PIONEIROS DE PARTIDO

K

KAABU (GABÚ, KABU). Kaabu is the name of a once powerful Mandinka (q.v.) kingdom. The Kingdom of Kaabu is sometimes confused with the Gabú administrative division, which is a much smaller territory. For this book, Kaabu refers to the territory from the mid-thirteenth century until 1867; while Gabú refers to the territory from 1867 into the modern era.

Its original capital at Kansala was situated near the modern city of Gabú. In its earliest times, Kaabu was a tributary kingdom of the Mandinka Empire of Mali (q.v.). It was founded in the mid-thirteenth century by Tiramakhan (q.v.) Traore, a General under the famous Malian King Sundiata. It was at this time that Traore brought his soldiers to regions around northeastern Guinea-Bissau and the middle Gambia and Casamance (q.v.) rivers to lay the foundations of Kaabu, then a secondary kingdom of Mali. Subsequently, local Mandinkas were appointed to serve as regular administrators. The first King, *Mansa*, of Kaabu, Mansa Sama (q.v.) Coli (Kelemankoto Baa Saane) was said to have been the son or grandson of Traore. Some historical accounts consider that Kaabu formally began with Mansa Sama Coli rather than with his ancestor. Early in the history of Kaabu there were three royal Provinces: Pachana (Pathiana) on the headwaters of the Geba, Jimara (Djimara) in Senegal south of the headwaters of the Gambia River, and Sama on the Casamance. The capital town of all of Kaabu was at Kansala in northeastern Guinea-Bissau, near the city of Gabú, just south of today's border with Senegal. Mali used the well-situated Kaabu to secure the trade in salt, gold, and slaves on the coastal river estuaries. The Mandinka-derived Dyulas (q.v.) were important links in this early trade with the Portuguese. Kaabu's influence extended from the Gambia to the Corubal River (q.v.); that is, most of the upper Casamance and virtually all of eastern Guinea-Bissau.

During the period of subordinance to Mali each provincial *Farim* (q.v.) (*Faren*) or governor had considerable local authority and was accorded his own administrative council, symbolic war drums, and personal army. On the other hand, the rule of the *Mansa* was considered sacred and even followed the matrilineal line of succession rather than the patrilineal descent followed by the *Farims* and ordinary people. The Mansa of Kaabu was selected from the eldest of the leaders of the royal provinces. The selection was done on a rotation basis along matrilineal lines from eligible members of the ruling Sane and Mane families. Each provincial capital town was fortified and had a regular guard. Some of these armed forces could be supplied to the *Mansa* in time of war. The degree of centralized control of the Empire of Mali slipped away in the late fifteenth and early sixteenth centuries as it increasingly fell to the attacks of Songhai (q.v.). At this time Kaabu gained full autonomy and was able to expand and maintain its own kingdom until 1867. Between the mid-sixteenth century and the eighteenth century, Kaabu was still ruled from Kansala, but it also included some twenty or thirty royal trading towns and several additional royal Provinces, e.g., Manna, Payinko, Paquessi, Kusara, Badora, Tumanna, and Koliba.

Not only had Mali lost its control of Kaabu, but it happened at a time when the Portuguese slave traders became an important factor on the coast. Kaabu became the most important and strongest of the regional slave trading states, and under its direct stimulation the small but strong Serer (q.v.) states of Sine and Saloum (q.v.) came under the authority of Kaabu's Guelowar (Gelwar) dynasty. Saloum was just north of the River Gambia, and Sine was to the northwest of Saloum in Senegal. However, the effort to have direct Mandinka rule of Sine and Saloum from Kaabu did not last out the sixteenth century, and the Guelowar dynasty was assimilated by the Serer who became small, independent, centralized, Senegalese states.

Also coming under the control of Kaabu were two Provinces of Oio and Braço, but these two maintained a greater degree of local autonomy than the other Provinces. Oio was south of the headwaters of the Cacheu River (q.v.) and Braço to the north of the headwaters. Just beyond Braço's control further north lived the Casangas (q.v.) with their capital at Brikama. The Casangas are related to the Banyun (q.v.) of Guinea-Bissau and formed their own secondary Mandinka kingdom on the south bank of the Casamance River. The Casanga king was called Cassa Mansa in the Mandinka tradition, and it is from this that the term Cassamance is derived. These various Mandinka kingdoms were all under the general Malian authority at Niani until its fall in 1546.

Despite the breakaway of Sine and Saloum, Kaabu maintained its power in the seventeenth and eighteenth centuries through various military operations which produced many slaves for the export trade. It is estimated that perhaps as many as half of all African slaves in the late sixteenth and early seventeenth centuries were generated from Kaabu's wars. While at its strength, Kaabu kept the Fula (q.v.) pastoralists and farmers as a subordinate, subject population. At times there was comparative harmony between the ruling Mandinkas and the Fulas; other periods, however, were marked by struggle, conflict, insult, and oppression by the Mandinka ruling classes of Kaabu.

These precarious socio-political relations engendered a long pattern of Fula revolts. At the end of the eighteenth century Kaabu was increasingly the victim of Fula (q.v.) attacks from Futa Jallon (q.v.), sometimes in local alliances with the Fula of Guinea-Bissau. Into the nineteenth century, the Fula pressed their attacks, and at least one *Farim* of the royal Province of Paquessi was converted to Islam, while the Fula *jihad* leader, Al-Haj Umaru (q.v.) killed Farim Yangi Sayon in 1849. The following year local Fulas in Guinea-Bissau broke away to form their own small states. In the mid-nineteenth century King Siibo ruled Kaabu, but he died with no clear successor. The Kaabu throne was contested by Saama, Tumanna, and Waali groups, with *Mansa* Janke (Djanke) Waali finally prevailing.

In 1867, Mansa Walli, then at Kansala (the capital), capitulated to the Fulas under a purported force of 12,000 soldiers led by Alfa Molo (q.v.), who was backed by the Fula *marabout* of Timbo, Abdul Khudus. After three days of siege, Janke Waali realized the futility of his resistance and blew up his powder magazine with many family members inside. Alfa Molo and his son Musa Molo (q.v.) absorbed Kaabu within the new Fula state, which served as a protectorate of the theocratic state of Futa Jallon in neighboring Guinea-Conakry. Now under Fula control the former kingdom of Kaabu was organized in the following provinces [their respective chiefs are in parentheses]: Tumana, and Chanha (Alfa Bacar Guidali), Boe (Mama Gibairu), Paxana (Coba Balde), Paxixe (Mansa Iiri

Cunto Ba), Mana (Samba Gide Balo), Propana (Issa Djau), Sama (Mama Samba Tchemara), Gada-Contimbo (Amadi Gai), Cam-Cumba (Bacar Cam Tchicame), Binafa (Mamadú Samba Balde), Pai-Ai (Mamadú Sadjo Djau), and Basse (Bodjo Ligue).

Around this time the Portuguese, eager to control or influence the events in the interior, came to refer to the territory as Gabú (q.v.). Civil wars erupted in Forrea and Fuladu, apparently between Fulbe-ribe (free-born Fulas) and Fulbe-djiabe (former Fula slaves), and raged furiously from about 1878 to 1890. Thus, the six centuries of the Kaabu empire had come to an end, although some small Mandinka states lingered on into the nineteenth century.

Taking advantage of this condition of internal disorganization and Mandinka-Fula rivalries, the Portuguese initiated a series of protracted military campaigns between 1891 and 1910 and concentrated attacks on the Oincas (Oio Mandinkas and Balantas) in 1897, 1902, and from 1912 to 1915. With such aggression, first from the Fula and then by the Portuguese, the Mandinkas were stripped of their former glory and power.

KANI, INOCENCIO. Kani was a naval commander and ex-member of the Executive Committee of the *Partido Africano da Independência de Guiné e Cabo Verde*, PAIGC (q.v.). He was expelled for 'misconduct and abuse of power' and was later the assassin of Amilcar Cabral (q.v.), the famous leader of the PAIGC liberation movement, on 20 January 1973 in Conakry. Although his personal motives have still to be clearly established, it is strongly believed that he was working in collaboration with the Portuguese Secret Police, which was exploiting the serious Guinean/Cape Verdean divisions in the PAIGC in particular and in the country in general as a strategy to halt the progress of the liberation war. Kani's co-conspirators were disgruntled and disgraced PAIGC militants and recruited Portuguese agents. Some of these had been imprisoned by the colonial authorities for nationalist agitation, such as Mamadú Turé and former PAIGC chairman Rafael Barbosa, and they may have been determined to replace the Cape Verdean-dominated leadership of the PAIGC and reach a separate independence for Guinea-Bissau from Portugal.

Cabral was shot by Kani when he refused to have his hands tied at the PAIGC Conakry office. As Kani and his men sped off with Aristides Pereira (q.v.), Vasco Cabral (q.v.), and a number of high-ranking party officials to awaiting vessels in international waters, they were intercepted by vessels of the

Guinea-Conakry Navy, which arrested the conspirators and rescued the captives. The subsequent trial in Conakry followed soon afterwards and involved some 450 alleged conspirators. Forty-three people were found guilty of direct participation in the assassination plot, and fifty-one were found guilty of complicity or suspected complicity (Chabal 1983, 133). Among them, at least ten were executed as ringleaders including Inocencio Kani, Mamadú Turé, Aristides Barbosa, Inacio Soares da Gama, Luís Teixeira, Emilio Costa, Mamadú Injai, João Tomas, and Bassir Turé (Ignatiev 1975, 185).

KANSALA (CANSALA). *See* KAABU; FULA.

KATI, MAHMOUD. *See* ALFA MAHMOUD KATI.

KUSSUNDE. Kussunde is a traditional Balanta (q.v.) festivity that is realized when agricultural (q.v.) harvests have been especially plentiful. The entire village population participates in ceremonial activities related to this festivity. Special dances and songs, leading up to a religious ceremony, are performed repeatedly from October or November to February or March, when the rice (q.v.) is harvested and the festival begins. The festival itself involves singing, drumming, and acrobatic dancing, an enormous meal in which a variety of dishes are served, and a ceremonial planting of seeds. The point of the ceremony is to gain the favor of certain spirits, re-legitimizing the villagers' acceptance by deceased ancestors and securing the optimum conditions for continued agricultural success. Depressed crop outputs, migrations, and bombings of rice fields by the Portuguese did not allow *kussunde* to be carried out during the nationalist struggle, but the ceremony was recommenced after independence, varying in intensity and duration from year to year depending on the output of each year's harvests. *See also* MUSIC.

L

LABÉRY, HENRI. Founder of the União Popular da Guiné, UPG, in 1957 which led to his direct involvement of the founding of the Frente de Libertação da Guiné, FLGC (q.v.), in 1960. Some elements of the FLGC appeared in 1961 as Front Uni de Libération, FUL (q.v.). In 1962 Labery emerged as the head of *Frente de Luta Pela Independência Nacional da Guiné-*

Bissau, FLING (q.v.). Labéry is of Cape Verdean extraction and was an early associate of Amilcar Cabral (q.v.). He went to schools in Lisbon but lived mainly in Guinea-Bissau. Labéry's program was less clear on ideological matters and was essentially concerned with only the independence of Guinea.

LADINOS. This ethnic group constituted a portion of early migrants to the Cape Verde Islands. They may be remnants of some of the (Sephardic) Jews (q.v.) from the Iberian peninsula who, at one time, spoke a Spanish form of Hebrew. Exiles, out-groups such as the *lançados* (q.v.), and political prisoners were often sent, or escaped, to Portuguese possessions in Africa and its offshore archipelagos, as well as Turkey where some elements of the Ladino language are still known.

LANÇADOS. The *lançados* were settlers, often of Portuguese Jewish (q.v.) origin. They often had African wives from the local ethnic groups. As such, the *lançados* served as intermediaries or middlemen for the Portuguese or Cape Verdeans; literally, outcast. *Lançados* also included fugitives or *degredados* (q.v.). They, and especially their descendants, were famed as enterprising half-caste traders living in or near African coastal communities where they maintained semi-autonomous economic control. They were often economic rivals of the Portuguese Crown monopolies, yet they were central in the economies of such towns as Cacheu and Bissau (qq.v.). Although their numbers were small, their economic and cultural role was central in the formation of the Crioulo (q.v.) language and culture which emerged on the coast and in the Cape Verde islands in the sixteenth century as a regional *lingua franca* trade language (q.v.).

LANDUMAS, LANDOMAS. This is a very small Senegambian (q.v.) grouplet inhabiting the area along the southern border area and around the southern town of Catio. Like other coastal Senegambians they were essentially overrun by the Susus (q.v.) in their own retreat from the Fula (q.v.) *jihads* of Futa Jallon (q.v.). It is not clear if they were found in deeper interior regions at an earlier time, and then pushed to the coast or if the coastal regions are their former native home. They speak a language related to the Bagas, Cocolis, or Nalus (qq.v.).

LANGUAGES. According to the 1979 national census, 54.4 percent of the total population speak only one of the approximately fifteen languages of Guinea-Bissau, while 45.6 percent are bi- or multi-lingual. Of the latter group, thirty percent speak two languages, twelve percent are conversant in three languages, and three percent speak four or more languages.

This polyglot complexity of languages is tempered by the fact that almost half of the populace (forty-four percent) speak Crioulo (q.v.), which serves as the *lingua franca* of the country. Crioulo is based on a combined Portuguese morphology and African phonetic system with loan words from both sides. Although it was used mainly by the urban population for most of the colonial period, the language developed on a larger basis during the nationalist struggle in order to facilitate communication among the various ethnic groups, and it has continued to expand since independence. Crioulo is today the major language of discourse among both the general population and the elite in urban areas. Its usage in the rural areas varies from eighteen percent in Gabú (q.v.) (where Fula predominates), to seventy-nine percent in Bolama (q.v.) on the coast. Thus while Portuguese is the official national language and official documents are usually composed in Portuguese, it is Crioulo that is usually spoken within government ministries and by party members. Crioulo is the *de facto* dominant language in Bissau (q.v.), and most educated Guineans grew up speaking Crioulo before they learned Portuguese.

Regarding the other principal languages, Balanta (q.v.) is the second most widely spoken language (spoken by 24.5 percent of Guineans), followed by Fula (20.3 percent), Portuguese (11.1 percent), Mandinka (10.1 percent), Manjaco (8.1 percent), and Pepel (7.2 percent). These figures reflect the relative size of the respective ethnic groups, although it is also the case that many Guineans of one ethnic group have learned the language of others. Portuguese is spoken almost exclusively by educated Guineans located in and near the capital of Bissau and, to a lesser degree, in Bafatá, Bolama, Gabú, and other smaller semi-urban centers. This reflects the fact that the Portuguese colonial population resided mostly in or near the center of these urban areas and that the national educational system has not yet effectively disseminated Portuguese into the countryside.

LEBANESE. All along the West African coast and in the Cape Verde Islands, families or small communities of Lebanese and Syrians are found. They were almost entirely Christian, rather than Muslim Lebanese. Typically they arrived in the late nineteenth or early twentieth centuries to work as a shopkeepers or in small-scale commerce where they could sell the products of the large Portuguese monopolies. In the context of racism and colonial values, the Lebanese were often favored over African merchants, who were given few opportunities in modern commerce. A few were engaged in agricultural production for bulk farm produce, others were found in real estate, labor contracting, and transport. Although they commonly found their spouses within their own ethnic communities, there are numerous cases of Lebanese with African wives, and thus they followed a socio-cultural pattern somewhat similar to the *lançados* (q.v.). Noting that the Phoenicians (q.v.) (ancestral Lebanese) were among the very first exogenous population along the coast, the Lebanese of Africa have a very long history indeed.

LEGISLATIVE ASSEMBLY (COLONIAL PERIOD). The 130–member Legislative Assembly of Portugal provided for two representatives from Cape Verde and one from Guinea-Bissau. In the two colonies there were separate Legislative Assemblies replacing the former legislative councils. In Guinea-Bissau the Assembly consisted of seventeen members: five elected, three traditional chiefs, three administrative representatives, two commercial representatives, two from workers' organizations, and two representing 'cultural and moral' concerns. In Cape Verde there were twenty-one members of the Assembly expanded from the eighteen-member Council. The composition included: eleven elected by vote, four administrative appointments, two commercial representatives, two workers representatives, and two representing 'cultural and moral' concerns. Both Guinea and Cape Verde were 'Overseas Provinces' of Portugal after 1971 with subdivisions of *concelhos* (q.v.) (municipalities) and civil parishes (administrative posts). In Guinea-Bissau a provision was made to have traditional ethnic group leaders meet in an annual People's Congress, which had no real power.

LIGA GUINEÉNSE. This was the first modern African voluntary association in Guinea-Bissau. This proto-nationalist formation emerged in 1910 under the leadership of Oliveira Dugu. The Portuguese government forced it to disband in 1915.

LIMA, ARISTIDES RAIMUNDO (31 December 1955–). Lima was born in the town of Sal Rei on Boa Vista, Cape Verde where he later worked as a teacher of Portuguese and French just before and after independence. In 1976 he became a journalist for the Cape Verdean newspaper *Voz di Povo* until pursuing a law degree from the University of Leipzig, from which he graduated in 1983. Lima worked in the Ministry of Justice from 1985 to 1986 in the section concerned with the support and dynamization of district tribunals. Concurrently Lima was a member of the third legislature of the Cape Verdean Assembléia National Popular (ANP) (q.v.) from 1985 to 1990 while also serving, from 1986 to 1989, as an Adviser to the President on constitutional and legal affairs and as a Teacher of Constitutional Law at the Amilcar Cabral Institute.

Within the *Partido Africano da Independência de Cabo Verde*, PAICV (q.v.) Lima was the Director of State Institutions, where he played a critical role in the transition to democracy starting with the liberalizations of 1988, the major PAICV reforms leading to revisions of the national constitution, formation of the electoral Code of Conduct, and electoral procedures throughout 1990 which provided for the formal abolition of one-party rule to the transition to the multi-party system with the Movimento para Democracia (MpD) and the União das Populações das Ilhas do Cabo Verde, UPICV (qq.v). Lima's book, *Reforma Política em Cabo Verde (Do Paternalismo a Modernização do Estado)* (1992) sets out the details of this transition.

After the 1991 elections and the defeat of the PAICV, Lima worked from 1991 to 1992 in the Cabinet for Studies and Legislation of the Ministry of Justice, dealing with public administration and labor issues while teaching Public Law in Praia. It was widely expected in 1991 and 1992 that the party leadership of former Prime Minister Pedro Pires (q.v.) would have to change, and in the 1993 PAICV Party Congress it was determined that Pires would move into a behind-the-scenes position with Lima brought forward as the party's new Secretary General. Thus, Lima continues to be the leader of the minority opposition party (PAICV) in the ANP during its fourth legislative period from 1991 to 1996, but he is strengthened by also being the PAICV Secretary General. In this capacity, he intends to address the issues of minority representation and oversight as well as seeking to curb the strength of the MpD, especially in areas of economic policy.

Lima is the author of numerous legal publications in German, English, and Portuguese, which make him both a sophisticated observer of and active participant in the Cape Verdean legal system and a significant number of national and international conferences focusing on legal issues. His bid to be elected Prime Minister in 1995 failed by a margin similar to Pedro Pires in 1991, although he retains his seat in the Legislative Assembly.

LITERATURE. The literature and folklore of Guinea-Bissau have three main sources. Cape Verdean and *Crioulo* (q.v.) culture, Portuguese culture, and a diversity of African sources. The deep Cape Verdean ties to Guinea-Bissau have resulted in the development of *Crioulo* as the *lingua franca* of Guinea-Bissau. Crioulo, particularly in Cape Verde, has rich traditions in literature, poetry, and music in such forms as the *mornas* and *coladeras* and has incorporated African elements especially in the populations of *badius,* as seen in the *batuko* and *funana*. These, in turn, resonate back in Guinea-Bissau in many ways, but especially with those many Guineans of Cape Verdean extraction born or residing in Guinea such as the following writers: Fausto Duarte, Terencio Anahory, João Alves das Neves, and Jorge Miranda Alfama.

European Portuguese residing in Guinea-Bissau were relatively few in number, but those who wrote usually used paternalistic or romanticized images of Africans as derived from a colonial psychology. An example of this may be found in the work of Fernanda de Castro.

Finally, the vast majority of Guineans belong to the Mandinka, Senegambian, and Fula (qq.v.) ethnic groups which have great traditions in oral literature and narratives and in some cases written records that were kept in Arabic or in a European language. Portuguese ethnographers of Guinea have compiled and translated some of the traditional African sources of literature. The most important example of modern literature by a Guinean of African origin is found in the poetry by António Batican Ferreira (q.v.), Helder Proença, and Abdulai Sila.

LIVESTOCK. In both Guinea-Bissau and Cape Verde, the Portuguese paid only marginal attention to systematic livestock raising. The post-colonial governments have also not made a significant attempt to develop animal husbandry for commercial purposes, although Guinea-Bissau has exported a small number of animal hides. Livestock raising is practiced extensively throughout the countryside in Guinea-Bissau for the purposes of domestic consumption and village market trading.

National livestock totals in the early 1980's show approximately 220,000 cattle, 125,000 pigs, 140,000 goats, 60,000 sheep, 420,000 chickens, and 12,000 ducks. These figures have been typical for at least the last twenty years, although higher numbers of cattle have been known. While cattle may be found on at least a small scale virtually everywhere in the country, most of the large-scale herding, is monopolized by Fula (q.v.) groups in the north and east and some of the Beafada and Mandinka (qq.v.) peoples. Among all groups, men are largely responsible for tending the cattle, but women (q.v.) usually raise the other livestock.

M

MAC. *See* MOVIMENTO ANTI-COLONIALISTA.

MALFANTE, ANTÓNIO. Genoese merchant who visited Timbuktu in 1447 in pursuit of early Portuguese efforts to contact the Empire of Mali (q.v.) and established commercial and diplomatic relations. While he crossed the Sahara, Portuguese sailors such as Cadamosto and Tristão were beginning their voyages along the Upper Guinea coast.

MALI. Following the collapse of the Empire of Ghana, the Empire of Mali entered its formative phase in the late eleventh century. Mali's early capital was at Kangaba on the Upper Niger River. Its economy was based on trade, especially of slaves, and subsistence agriculture of the Sudanic crops. The gold traded in Mali was mainly from the Bure and Bambuk goldfields south of Niani and out of Mali's military control and Islamic influence. Likewise the source of ivory was mainly south of the Sahel, but trade in ivory, gold, and slaves was what built the Sudanic states. The most important group of Mandinka (q.v.) traders upon whom Mali depended were the Soninke-derived Dyulas (qq.v.) (sometimes known as Wangarawa) who were instrumental in the Islamization of Mali. Islamic conversion of the Malian ruling class and large numbers of the farming people took place between the eleventh and thirteenth centuries. Perhaps the first member of the Malian ruling class to be converted was Barmandana Keita in 1050. Mali was very hierarchical in socio-political structure which included nobility, soldiers, traders, artisan castes, and slaves.

Mali is formally dated from 1230, when Sundiata (Sundjata)

and his general Maridiata defeated the Susu (q.v.) leader Suma-guru at the battle of Kirina, thus ending the Susu resurgence and beginning a Susu dispersal of refugees toward the coast. Sundiata was the son of Nare Famaghan, of the Keita dynasty of Mali (at Kangaba). Earlier Famaghan had been defeated by Sumagura in the effort to re-establish the Empire of Ghana. Sundiata ruled Mali from 1230 to 1255 and made Islam the state religion. It was probably during the reign of Sundiata that large number of Mandinka people entered Gambia, the Casamance (q.v.), and eastern Guinea, especially under his military leader Tirmakhan Traore.

Sundiata's son, Mansa Uli (1255–1270) extended the rule of Mali to the trade center at Gao. Under Mansa Sakura (d. 1300) Tekrur (q.v.) was conquered in 1285. According to the Arab historian Umari, Mansa Musa related to the Governor of Cairo that seafaring Malians had actually ventured to the New World before 1312. Under the rule of Mansa Muhammad (son of Qu) 200 ships with men and 200 with gold, water, and supplies were sent. One of the ships returned to be followed by another 1,000 with men and 1,000 with supplies. These reports have not been fully substantiated but remain a fascinating area for future research.

It was during the reign of Mansa Kankan Musa (1312–1337) that Mali reached its greatest influence. From 1324 to 1325 for example, Mansa Musa is reported to have made a flamboyant pilgrimage to Mecca via Egypt with an entourage of thousands of followers carrying gold gifts of astonishing abundance. In the year of his return his soldiers occupied Dar Tichitt, Walata, and other key trading centers. The following year Gao, the capital city of Songhai, and Timbuktu also came under the armies of Mansa Musa. By 1375 Mali was noted on European maps, even though Europeans had still not travelled along the West African coast.

From the thirteenth to the seventeenth century a score of small Senegambian kingdoms were formed as tributary states to Mali. One of the larger and most influential of these was Kaabu in Guinea-Bissau. Kaabu (q.v.) was located in an area between the upper Corubal and upper Cacheu Rivers (qq.v.) to the Gambia River, then all the way to the Atlantic coast through Wolof, Serer (q.v.), and Tukulor areas northward up the coast until just north of the mouth of the Senegal River. At this time Mali controlled Futa Jallon (q.v.) through the Dia-lonke tributary chiefs, and a lesser degree of control was exerted in subduing rebellions in Tekrur.

Through the late fourteenth and early fifteenth centuries Mali thrived, as the Empire supplied as much as 1/16th of the entire world supply of gold. Arab travellers and early historians visited Mali from 1352 to 1353 and brought back reports about its glories to northern Africa and Europe. However, by the fifteenth century the fortunes of Mali had gradually begun to decline. Tekrur and the Wolof provinces rebelled and regained their independence in the early fifteenth century, and by 1433, Timbuktu had seceded.

The Portuguese were on the scene in the late fifteenth century and noted the state of hostility between Mali and its neighbors, but the Portuguese, who only wanted African products and slaves, were not concerned with the outcome and gave no aid to Mali. In 1473 Jenne was lost to the Empire, and this prompted Mansa Mahmoud I of Mali to send a message to King João II of Portugal (q.v.) requesting military aid against Fula (q.v.) and Songhai enemies. The Portuguese still did not respond, so by the sixteenth century Mali's power had eroded even further, although it is interesting to note that it was still producing more gold than the New World gold mines of the time. In 1534 another request for aid was directed to Portugal's King João III, and ambassadors from Mali actually travelled to Portugal.

Desiring slaves and war captives and not wanting to back a loser, Portugal again declined to provide any aid to Mali. This trend reached its climax in 1546 when Songhai invaders sacked Niani, the Malian capital, thereby bringing to an end this major West African empire. When the Empire of Songhai finally replaced Mali, the former secondary kingdoms became their own masters as the control of Songhai did not reach Guinea-Bissau. The period of Kaabu's autonomy coincided with the height of the Senegambian (q.v.) slave trade, so Kaabu's many wars produced a great supply of slaves, especially from the small-scale coastal people who were trapped between the coastal forces of *grumetes* and *lançados*, and the interior force of Kaabu.

MAMADU. *See* PATÉ, MAMADU.

MANDINKA (MANDING, MANDINGA, MANDINGO, MAL-INKE, MANDE). The Mandinka and related peoples of Guinea-Bissau are representatives of the Nuclear Mande language family of the Niger-Congo linguistic stock. Mande is a principal language of Africa and is spoken in one form or another in about nine West African countries, with as many as ten million speakers. As with many West African languages, it is tonal with no uniformly accepted written form. The Mandinka began to arrive in their present distribution in the mid thirteenth century with the expansion of the Empire of Mali (q.v.) to which they are all related to various degrees. Even though Mali fell in 1546, the Mandinka kingdom of Kaabu (q.v.) in Guinea-Bissau continued on until 1867. Before the consolidation and expansion of Kaabu, many Senegambians (q.v) such as the Manjacos, and Brames (qq.v.) and Pepels were found in eastern Guinea-Bissau. These three groups assimilated a moderately hierarchical system of political administration from the intrusive Malians. Some of these Senegambians were driven west toward the coast, where they are mainly found today.

Other Senegambians such as the Balantes, Banyuns, and Beafadas (qq.v.) were either driven west toward the coast or were simply stranded as pockets within expanding Kaabu. Various Fula (q.v.) peoples became interspersed in Kaabu as cattle herders until the time when the Fulas themselves destroyed Kaabu in 1867 and formed their own states.

When the Portuguese arrived they called the language of the Mande peoples 'Mandunca' from which the term Mandinka is derived. Throughout the centuries of slavery (q.v.), the Mandinkas of Kaabu had important trade centers at Farim (q.v.) on the Cacheu River headwaters; at Cacheu (qq.v.) at the River's mouth; at Ziguinchor (q.v.) on the Casamance (q.v.) ; and at Geba (q.v.) on the Geba River. These posts permitted contact with Europeans (e.g., Portuguese, French, and English) and access to firearms in exchange for war captives/slaves. The local Fula herdsmen provided livestock while the Mandinka farmers grew the basic staples of the Sudanic food complex. In the mid-nineteenth century the Fulas (particularly from Futa Jallon [q.v.]) expanded and brought an end to Mandinka dominance. By the end of the century, after the Berlin Congress (q.v.), Portuguese incursions to the interior were laying the groundwork for the colonial wars against the Mandinka in the early twentieth century. In 1900 the Mandinka formally submitted to Portuguese rule, but the Oio branch showed continued resistance to Portuguese 'pacification' in the campaigns of 1897, 1902, and 1913. From 1913 to 1915 Portuguese Captain Teixeira Pinto (q.v.), known for his brutality and widespread destruction, was able to use Mandinka auxiliaries equipped with modern arms in 'pacification' programs elsewhere in Guinea-Bissau.

Today the Mandinka people are still concentrated around Oio and Gabú in the north and central areas, but there are various clusters throughout the eastern and interior regions. The Mandinka represent about fourteen percent of the total population of Guinea-Bissau.

MANJACO (MANDYAKO). Ethnic group of the Senegambian (q.v.) cultural stock, Atlantic subfamily of the Niger-Congo or Nigritic language (q.v.) group. The Manjacos show some very slight Islamization and some hierarchical organization which they may have acquired through contact with the Mandinkas (q.v.). The Manjacos are related to the Brame/Mancanha (q.v.) and Pepel peoples. Their economy is based on shifting agriculture and rice cultivation. They are mainly concentrated in the area south of the Cacheu River (q.v.) and north of the Mansoa (q.v.) River. The Manjacos provided stiff resistance as early as 1588 against the Portuguese presence at Cacheu; in the period from 1878 to 1890 they were among the first to try to halt the Portuguese penetration of the interior. They also fought between 1913 and 1915 against the pacification campaigns of Teixeira Pinto (q.v.). The 1950 population identified 71,700 Manjacos (14.2 percent of the population); in 1960 their population was put at an estimated 80,000.

MANSA MUSA. *See* MALI.

MANSOA, RIO (Mansoa River). The fourth longest river of Guinea-Bissau, the Mansoa courses about 120 miles from the coast and is navigable at least two-thirds of the way. Its route is roughly parallel to that of the Farim-Cacheu River (q.v.), which flows roughly parallel and to the north of the Mansoa. The headwaters of the Mansoa are found to the east of Mansaba in the Farim (q.v.) *concelho*. The Mansoa was used as a corridor through the coastal swamps for trade to the interior.

MENDES, FRANCISCO ('CHICO TE,' 1939–1978). Prime Minister of Guinea-Bissau, Mendes did not complete his formal education, because he joined the *Partido Africano da Independência de Guiné e Cabo Verde*, PAIGC (q.v.), in 1960 at the age of twenty-one. He was born in southern Guinea-Bissau in the village of Enxude. From 1960 to 1962 Mendes was the Political Commissioner at the PAIGC training program in Conakry. From 1962 to 1963 he was assigned to underground organizational work in the eastern town of Bafatá (q.v.), and from 1963 to 1964 he served as the Political Commissioner in the North Front. He received military training from the Nanking Military Academy. During the war, Chico Te was one of the most courageous, even audacious, front line combatants.

At the time of the first PAIGC Congress in 1964 Mendes became a member of the Political Bureau, and in 1965 he was appointed to the War Council in the capacity of Political Commissioner. From 1970 to 1971 his War Council responsibility was military logistics. In 1972 Mendes was appointed to the Comité Executivo da Luta, CEL (q.v.), and following the independence of Guinea-Bissau he became the Prime Minister of the Permanent Secretariat of the nation.

He and Luís Cabral (q.v.) were close supporters of policy which linked Cape Verde with Guinea-Bissau. He often noted that Cape Verdeans were risking their lives in the liberation of the mainland and that was proof of their sacrifice. After independence he rewarded those who had lived in the liberated zones by a three-year suspension of taxes. He stressed that the struggle was, first of all, for the peasants. Programs of water supply, rural electrification, and veterans' services were other main areas of his work in building the new nation. Mendes was killed in an automobile accident in Bafatá in July 1978.

MENDES, SIMÕES ANTÓNIO. Mendes was born in Canchungo (q.v.) in 1930. He was a Portuguese-trained nurse who was jailed by the infamous Portuguese secret police, PIDE (q.v.), for his nationalist activities in 1961. Upon his release, he was posted to the Safim sanitary post near Bissau (q.v.) from which he escaped to the PAIGC (q.v.) base in Morés in the northern front when his re-arrest by PIDE seemed imminent.

At Morés, with João da Costa (who became the Mininster of Health during the regime of Luís Cabral, q.v.) as his assistant, Simões Mendes dedicated his life to caring for the wounded liberation fighters as well as the inhabitants of the region who became victims of the destructive bombing raids of the Portuguese airforce, until he himself became the victim of one of those deadly bombs, toward the end of February 1966. After independence, the central hospital in Bissau was renamed after him.

MESTIÇOS. *Mestiços* are people of a mixed "racial" heritage and were often incorporated into middle-level administrative and economic strata in the Portuguese colonial system. *Cri-*

oulos of Cape Verde are sometimes considered to be *mestiços*, and those Cape Verdeans in Guinea-Bissau are likewise in an ambiguous position, since they may have connections to the slave and colonial systems but were born and raised in Guinea. Such complex relations result in a certain continuing tension between those Guineans of African heritage and those of *mestiço* or Crioulo origin, such as was also the case with the *lançados*, and *tangomãos* (qq.v.)

MILLET. *See* AGRICULTURE

MINDELO. *See* SÃO VICENTE.

MINERALS. In March 1958, the Portuguese gave the American oil company ESSO (now Exxon, q.v.), exclusive oil prospecting rights in Guinea-Bissau at an annual cost of $250,000 U.S. An additional $14 to $60 were paid for each square kilometer where prospecting actually took place. Beyond this, there was a 12.5% tax on production and a 50 percent tax on profits. In 1966 and in 1973 the contract between the Portuguese colonial government and Esso Exploration was renewed and expanded to include other minerals. The revenue generated by the terms of this contract gave the Portuguese badly needed financial support during the period of nationalist insurgency.

In 1980, the World Bank financed a loan of $6.8 million for a 3,900 mile seismic survey along Guinea-Bissau's coast, which was carried out by Digicon (USA) in 1981. In 1983, ten data packages were purchased by a consortium of Western oil companies for $400,000 a piece, and a second series of offshore seismic studies was carried out by Digicon with an additional $13.1 million IDA loan. The State-run oil company, Petrominas, signed its first exploration agreement with foreign oil companies (from Canada, England, and West Germany) in 1984.

Petrominas also regulates mining and prospecting in Guinea-Bissau. Total bauxite deposits are now said to be 200 million tons (42 to 48 percent alumnia); phosphate deposits were discovered in Cacheu (q.v.) and Oio Provinces in 1981, and gold has also be found. However, the enormous investments in ports, railroad, and other transport linkages that would be required for the mining and processing of these minerals have thus far been found to be far too expensive to merit constructing. As a consequence, these mineral resources remain virtually untapped.

MONTEIRO, ANTÓNIO MASCARENHAS GOMES (1943–). Monteiro studied Law at the Universities of Lisbon and Coimbra. He joined the *Partido Africano da Independência de Guiné e Cabo Verde*, PAIGC (q.v.), in 1969 but broke with it over policy in 1971. He continued his study of Law at the Catholic University of Louvain in Belgium and become a researcher at the International Center for Public Law there.

He was appointed as Judge of the Cape Verde Supreme Court in July 1977 by the Popular National Assembly. He served in the Supreme Court until 1990. He was an independent Presidential candidate in the elections of January 1991 against Aristides Pereira of the PAICV and won. This victory was repeated in the 1996 Cape Verde elections in which he ran unopposed. His work continues to focus on democracy and human rights.

MORANÇA. Extended family grouping within villages in Guinea-Bissau, especially among the Balantes (q.v.).

MOUVEMENT DE LIBÉRATION DES ÎLES DU CAP VERT (MLICV). The MLICV was formed in 1960 and immediately joined the *Frente de Libertação da Guiné Portuguesa e Cabo Verde*, FLGC (q.v.), in the same year. Its role was very minor and represented little more than a paper organization. THE MLICV was based in Dakar and was led by Mello e Castro. At times the MLICV called for the liberation of the Cape Verde Islands by armed struggle, but this tactic and goal was only enunciated, not practiced, by the MLICV in the islands.

MOUVEMENT DE LIBÉRATION DE LA GUINÉE "PORTUGAISE" ET DES ÎLES DU CAP VERT (MLGCV). This united front organization was based in Dakar and was constituted primarily of the *União Popular de Guiné* UPG, of Henri Labéry (q.v.). The other two member organizations, the *União Democrática da Guiné* UDG (q.v.) and the *União Democrática de Cabo Verde*, UDCV (q.v.) were of far less significance. The MLGCV joined with the UPA (*União das Populações de Angola*) in 1962 to form a front called the *Frente Africana Contra O Colonialismo Português* FACCP. While little is known of the MLGCV, it is established that the UPA was receiving funds from the American CIA at the time and that the FACCP was set up to rival the more militant FRAIN (founded two years earlier). The MLGCV was a temporary affiliate of the *Partido Africano da Independência de Guiné e*

Cabo Verde (PAIGC) (q.v.) in 1960, and some reports suggest that Amilcar Cabral (q.v.) sought to establish unity with the MLGCV in 1958 but soon realized it would be impossible to find a common program.

MOUVEMENT DES FORCES DÉMOCRATIQUES DE LA CASAMANCE (MFDC). The MFDC was founded in 1974 by Emile Badiane, a Diola (q.v.), and Ibou Diallo to address issues of regional underdevelopment in the Casamance (q.v.) region of southern Senegal adjoining Guinea-Bissau. In the 1980's its efforts were intensified to achieve regional autonomy or secession for the Casamance. By the late 1980's and early 1990's this struggle became more violent, even resulting in a two-day war between Guinea-Bissau and Senegal. Ziguinchor (q.v.), the capital city of the Casamance, had been a part of Portuguese Guinea through the nineteenth century. The MFDC appears to be heavily composed of Diola peoples who are found throughout the Casamance and in the southern neighbor of Guinea-Bissau which is sometimes blamed for giving them support. On 31 May 1991 a cease-fire lowered the level of armed conflict between the MFDC and the Senegalese military, but tensions and strife persisted through 1991 and early 1992.

A substantial new effort was made by religious and political leaders to resolve the conflict with the accords reached between the moderate MFDC leader Sidy Badji and the then Senegalese Minister of Defense Madoiun Fall on 17 April 1992 in Cacheu, (q.v.) Guinea-Bissau. Even though the leadership of the conflicting groups has agreed to an end of hostilities, the destablized region has resulted in acts of small scale banditry and reprisals which are not easily controlled. In this context, the summer of 1992 saw renewed cease-fire violations and clashes between Diola and Mandinka (q.v.) people with frequent reports of assaults and deaths.

In early July 1992 at least 400 refugees arrived in Kartong in neighboring Gambia to the north. These refugees were Diola, Mandinka, Fula (q.v.), and Karoninka from the villages of Kafunting, Abenneh, Kabadior, Katak, and Jannah. Reprisals by the MFDC against those who did not show support apparently provoked this exodus. With ethnic distrust deepened, both sides complained of robberies, assaults, and destruction of livestock and property. In mid July the customs post at Kandiadiou in Bignona was attacked, with two officials injured. By August 1992 new fighting had broken out between Diola and Mandinka groups, especially in the town of Madina Daffeh near to Brikama in the Casamance. In this case, the attacks left eight dead, ten beaten or wounded, and hundreds more fleeing to refuge in Gambia.

During this period, the Dakar government was active in trying to have amnesty, cease-fire, and peace negotiations so that plans for national elections in 1993 could go forward. The atmosphere for the Senegalese Presidential elections on 21 February 1993, and the Legislative elections in May 1993, was substantially disrupted and tense because of the MFDC. The atmosphere was already disturbed in early September 1992, as a result of bloody clashes at Kaguitte and Cap Skirring near Ziguinchor. Because the northern Badji forces within the MFDC could not control the more radical southern MFDC elements, the Senegalese government claimed that the MFDC was violating the Cacheu accords. Thus the Senegalese military redeployed government troops in the Casamance. Dakar sources claimed fifty MFDC members killed and sixty wounded, while the government troops had two dead and nine wounded. On 17 January 1993 the regional Casamance airport was subject to a rocket attack just two weeks before the visit of President Abdou Diouf. On the day before the elections, twenty members of Diouf's ruling party hit a landmine fifteen miles at Niadiou south of Ziguinchor and were killed. Only a few weeks earlier seven Red Cross workers had died in a similar incident. On election day another six were killed and ten wounded in a bus ambush. Voters in the area between Ziguichor and Guinea-Bissau feared further reprisals, and the United Nations (q.v.) estimated that at least 17,000 have fled the region for security in refugee camps inside northern Guinea-Bissau and another 6,000 had sought safety in neighboring Gambia. This followed the assassination of Imam Kutubo Manafang, a Muslim leader who spoke out against the rising violence. Pursuing a military policy at present, the Senegalese government forces launched a search and destroy program in March 1993 in which eighty MFDC militants were killed and their bodies as well as gris-gris amulets were exhibited at the Ziguinchor hospital as a deterent to others.

Although Guinea-Bissau did not formally side with the MFDC, its own tensions with Senegal or various frontier issues, as well as ethnic links to groups within the MFDC and overlooking access to weapons, made Guinea-Bissau's role quite significant. Similarly, with the growing initiatives toward democracy and political liberalism in Bissau, it was reasonable to support the Casamance peace initiative. This step was achieved with important intervention by a group of six Catholic priests in Ziguinchor. The discussions were facilitated by Robert Sagna, who served as Mayor of Ziguinchor and Senegal's Minister of State for Agriculture. Among the priests, the role of Fr. Augustin Diamacoune Senghor stands out. Fr. Senghor had formerly been sentenced to prison for his past support of the MFDC, and after his release he lived in Cacheu and Bissau. With the informal backing of the Bissau government Fr. Senghor left Guinea-Bissau to return to Ziguinchor on 19 March 1993 and engage in serious negotiations. The close ties between Fr. Senghor and Leopold Sagna, another MFDC leader, gives reason to hope that these accords may prove fruitful and lasting. A subsequent cease-fire between the MFDC majority and Senegalese authorities was negotiated and accords signed on 8 July 1993 in Ziguinchor. While accepting the territorial integrity of Senegal as demanded by Senegalese President Diouf and Madieng Khary Dieng, Senegalese Minister of Defense, the agreements have addressed a wide range of issues and have resulted in the liberation of 257 MFDC supporters held in Senegalese prisons.

MOVIMENTO ANTI-COLONIALISTA (MAC). The MAC was formed in Lisbon in 1957 by revolutionary intellectuals from Portuguese African colonies. Thus, the MAC was the precursor of *Frente Revolutionária Africana para a Independência Nacional das Colônias Portuguesas*, FRAIN (q.v.), which started in 1960 and the *Conferência de Organizações Nacionalistas da Colônias Portuguesas*, CONCP (q.v.), which began in 1961. The unity nurtured in the MAC persisted in the programs of the other nationalist movements in Lusophone Africa until recent years.

MOVIMENTO DE LIBERTAÇÃO DA GUINÉ (MLG). The MLG was headed by François Mendy Kankoila who based much of the organization on the Manjaco ethnic group partly residing in Senegal. In July 1961, while Amilcar Cabral (q.v.) was trying to develop the Front Uni de Libération, FUL (q.v.), Mendy launched attacks at Suzanna and at a Varela hotel. These isolated acts confirm that the MLG was the most militant member group of the *Frente de Luta Pela Independência Nacional da Guiné-Bissau*, FLING (q.v.). Mendy was anxious about any loss of autonomy within FLING, to which he gave only hesitating support, just as he had to the *Frente de Libertação da Guiné Portuguesea e Cabo Verde*, FLGC (q.v.) which preceded FLING. Neither the MLG nor FLING had programs relating to the independence of the Cape Verde Islands. The MLG joined the RDAG in 1961 to form the FLG, which joined FLING in 1962. As a result of the military efforts of the MLG in 1961, the Portuguese staged a swift counterattack which resulted in the breaking of diplomatic relations between Senegal and Portugal. Despite this event, the government of Senegal was lukewarm at best to the *Partido Africano da Independência de Guiné e Cabo Verde*, PAIGC (q.v.), at that time and preferred to support the MLG and, more broadly, the FLING which had some base of support with Senegalese Manjacos (q.v.) and was anti-PAIGC. The MLG also sought to divide Cape Verdean supporters from the PAIGC, and it is alleged that it bribed PAIGC members to stimulate desertion. The MLG was dissolved in 1964.

MOVIMENTO DE LIBERTAÇÃO DA GUINÉ PORTUGUESA (MLGP). The MLGP was one of the three component groups which merged in 1960 to form the *Frente de Libertação da Guiné*, FLG (q.v.) later leading to the *Frente de Luta Pela Independência Nacional da Guiné-Bissau*, FLING (q.v.).

MOVIMENTO DE UNIDADE PARA A DEMOCRACIA (MUDe). The MUDe is another new party founded in the period of Democratization in the early 1990's. It was founded in Lisbon, Portugal by Filinto Vaz Martins, a former member of the *Partido Africano da Independência de Guiné e Cabo Verde*, PAIGC (q.v.), who served as the Commissioner of State for Industry, Energy, and Natural Resources in the Government of Luis Cabral (q.v.), as well as Minister of Education (1980–1981).

MOVIMENTO PARA DEMOCRACIA (MpD). The Movement for Democracy can be understood with a view of its founder Carlos Veiga (q.v.) and his contemporary political context. Veiga had pursued a professional legal career under colonialism, but after independence he returned to Cape Verde to work in public legal service. These rapidly evolved to his position as the Attorney General of the Republic under the *Partido Africano da Independência de Guiné e Cabo Verde*, PAIGC (q.v.), government by 1978. At this time, the constitution only allowed for a single party state. In 1980, just before the PAIGC changed names to the *Partido Africano da Independência de Cabo Verde*, PAICV (q.v.), Veiga began to have disagreements with governmental polices relating to the lack of democracy and centralized control of the party, as well as limits placed on free enterprise. As a result he resigned to continue his private legal practice but was still involved in counseling public legal projects. In particular, it was his experience with the Special Commission on Constitutional and Judicial Issues of the Cape Verdean Assembléia Nacional Popular (q.v.) from 1985 to 1990 that kept him involved but without direct responsibility to the PAICV.

Playing upon fears of increased centralization of the PAICV in the ANP and upon some harsh measures taken against opponents and dissidents, a group within the PAICV began to formulate a political program allowing for broader discussion and participation. The PAICV leadership assumed it to be small and isolated. To increase this perceived isolation, the PAICV Prime Minister, Pedro Pires (q.v.), allowed the MpD to be formed and to compete in elections provided by a revision of the one-party Constitution.

Meanwhile, as a close observer of Cape Verdean politics, Veiga became the leading member of the MpD, which he had started to organize in early 1990. In November 1990 the MpD nominated him as their party candidate for Prime Minister in the forthcoming elections promised by the PAICV Democratization effort. Surprising the PAICV leaders, the national ANP elections in January 1991 ousted the PAICV which had ruled since independence in 1975. In the elections the MpD won sixty-nine percent of the popular vote which earned it fifty-six seats in the ANP, while the PAICV won only twenty-three seats. Veiga has served as the Prime Minister of the Republic since February 1991. The elections also gave the Independent candidate for President, António Mascarenhas Monteiro (q.v.), an even greater popular vote, and he replaced the former PAICV President Aristides Pereira (q.v.). Thus, Cape Verde has joined a number of other African states in their drive toward political pluralism.

Various factors has been proposed to account for this victory, including the strong role of the Catholic Church which felt restrained by some PAICV policies such as liberal access to abortion. The lack of armed conflict in the islands during the war of liberation meant that only the PAIGC/PAICV leadership had experienced this important frontline struggle, while other Cape Verdeans had positions opposed to the PAICV. The 1975 elections failed to include parties other than the PAIGC/PAICV so that the intervening years saw their complete control of power erode some degree of mass participation. Anti-state agitation was followed by measures including the suspension of habeas corpus and brutality; these widened the gap. To its credit, the PAICV demonstrated its commitment to the plural, democratic process by its willingness to step aside after the elections. This transition was accomplished without bloodshed or subsequent recriminations.

The collapse of the Socialist system in eastern Europe also weakened the PAICV government. Aside from the international and regional context in which the Veiga government is situated, it has a significance much greater than one would expect for a small, insular nation. This is due to Cape Verde's chair on the Security Council at the United Nations (q.v.) and because of the large Cape Verdean constituency in southeastern New England. Newly elected Prime Minister Veiga visited Massachusetts and Rhode Island from 30 September to 6 October 1992, where he first raised the new flag of Cape Verde.

The Veiga government has endorsed privatization of the economy and has reversed some of the nationalization and state control by the PAICV of a wide range of enterprises. Human rights, expansion of a mixed free market political economy, and an irreversible commitment to plural democracy and human rights are also stated as guiding principles. Given the widespread diaspora population, which contributes significantly to the Cape Verdean economy, the MpD also intends to have a more integrated and effective policy for emigrants. A new constitution, flag, and national emblem have already been approved. The MpD intends to rule by consensus and local level empowerment and involvement. Future political debates will be balanced by the existance of the PAICV opposition. Veiga has been the Prime Minister of Cape Verde from 1991 and he was re-elected for a second term by almost the same margin in the 1996 elections.

MOVIMENTO PARA INDEPENDÊNCIA NACIONAL DA GUINÉ PORTUGUESA (MING). MING was founded in 1954 but soon proved to be ineffective. However MING was the direct forerunner of the *Partido Africano da Independência de Guiné e Cabo Verde*, PAIGC (q.v.), which was founded in 1956. MING was organized by Amilcar Cabral (q.v.) and Henri Labéry (q.v.) and was formed clandestinely in Bissau (q.v.) by commercial workers and civil servants. Apparently there was no reference to the Cape Verde Islands in its initial program.

MUSA. *See* MANSA MUSA.

MUSA MOLO BALDÉ (? –1931). Musa Molo was the son of Alfa Molo (q.v.), and the last effective King of a Fula (q.v.) state in Guinea-Bissau. The son of Musa Molo, Cherno Bande (d. 1950's) acted as a Fula chief afterward but with no real power. When Alfa Molo died in 1881 he was to be succeeded by Musa Molo's uncle Bakari Demba, but by 1893, through continuous intrigues and conspiracies, Musa Molo had become the Chief of Fuladu, which included areas of former Kaabu (q.v.) which had been destroyed in 1867. By this time Fuladu had ceased its tributary relationship with Futa Jallon (q.v.). During his reign Musa Molo sought to consolidate and expand his rule to the northwest into the territory of the south bank of the Gambia, then controlled by Fodé Kaba (c.1818–1901), a Muslim soldier-cleric and local slave trader.

Alfa Molo had killed the father of Fodé Kaba, so the conflict was inherited by both sons. Fodé Kaba proved very intractable to French and British attempts to curb the slave trade. Often the efforts to expand 'legitimate' trade in the Gambia in the 1880's had been frustrated by Fodé Kaba, but they recognized that he was still valuable in local rule. In 1891 and 1893 they negotiated with him to establish some sort of fragile *détente*. This precarious relation with France, Britain, and Portugal, as well as the old rivalries with Musa Molo, all came to an end in March 1901 when a common attack was mounted against Fodé Kaba, in which he was killed. Musa Molo seized slaves and property and returned southeast to Fuladu.

Musa Molo saw this as part of his attempt to unify and expand Fula control to the north, while the French saw it only as an application of divide-and-rule in the Casamance (q.v.) and Gambia. In 1903, he fled into Gambia from a French counterattack at his base in the Upper Casamance at Hamdallahi. There the British indirect rule system awarded him a 500 pound stipend annually. Such experiences, as well as a revolt by his brother Dikori, caused Musa Molo to be suspicious; frequently he eliminated his contenders by assassination. As a result, his rule was generally considered ruthless. In 1919 he was exiled to Sierra Leone but returned to Gambia in 1923 where he died in 1931. After the death of Musa Molo the British appointed Cherno Bande as the head of the Fula. Bande's real function was to encourage local peanut production as an agent for the British United Africa Company.

MUSIC. In a country as ethnically diverse as Guinea-Bissau, it is not surprising to find scores of distinctive music cultures. Despite the introduction of the radio and recorded music during this century, folk music and dance traditions flourish, existing alongside new popular music from Guinea-Bissau, Luso-African countries, the French Antilles, and other areas. Because of a shared Creole language and colonial past, *Crioulo* music, including *mornas*, *coladeras*, and *funana* from Cape Verde are familiar and popular with urban dwellers in Guinea-Bissau. Names in popular music from Guinea-Bissau such as Tabanka Djaz (led by Mikas Cabral), Ramiro Naka, Kaba Mané, Sidonio Pais, and N'Kassa Cobra are not only familiar to Cape Verdean audiences but have earned an international following. Other recording artists who are very popular in Guinea-Bissau are Manecas Costa, Dulce Maria Neves, Maio Cooperante, Justino Delgado, Tino Trimo, Gentil Policarpo, and Pacheco de Gumbé, to name a few.

Music and dance, whether in traditional or contemporary form, are an integral part of daily life for most people of Guinea-Bissau. In traditional culture, there are special songs for almost every sphere of life including songs for use in rituals and rites of passage, songs for praise, work, and play, songs for begging and declarations of love, and songs for recounting oral history. In the areas of Guinea-Bissau where people are Muslim, there is a special caste of professional musicians called *griots* (q.v.) or *jali*, who provide music for many occasions. Although they have a low status in the social hierarchy, they are respected and feared for the power and influence of their songs. The *jali* are praise singers, oral historians, and keen observers (and sometimes critics) of society. *Jali* musicians usually accompany themselves with the *kora*, a harp-lute, the *balo* or *balafon* (q.v.), or the *kontingo*, a plucked lute. Women in *jali* families sing and keep rhythm on an iron tubular bell called *neo* or *karinya*.

Of course, not all music in Guinea-Bissau is made by professional musicians; nearly everyone sings and dances in various contexts, whether it be in a local nightclub or a community gathering in the countryside. In traditional societies, the population is divided into musical groups along lines of age and sex, and each group has its own repertoire. During communal performances in rural Guinea-Bissau, people are most likely to perform circle dances as part of a group of peers. Although there are numerous instruments used in Guinea-Bissau, the most prevalent means of producing music is with the human body, singing and hand-clapping having a part in most music performances. Rows of jinglers attached to dancer's bodies and musical instruments provide another important source of musical sound that is often overlooked. Call-and-response structure, an interchange between a song leader and a chorus, is the most common song form, and songs are usually accompanied by movement. As in much of Africa, music and dance are tightly interwoven traditions, one seldom occurring without the other. The traditional dance apparel in Guinea-Bissau can be considered among the world's most elaborate and beautiful. For some performances, dancers wear costumes made of dried grass, large horned masks, head dresses made from palm leaves, and streamers hanging from their arms. Dances which parody a steer or other horned animals are common. In the Bissagos Islands in particular, a typical dance ensemble might wear horned masks and arm and leg bands with green leaves stuck in them.

Some of the Guinea-Bissau island people have an unusual tradition that seems to break the rules set by the majority of African music cultures. In this particular island society, women take on many roles from domains usually exclusively reserved for men. For example, women play drums, something rarely seen in folk cultures worldwide. Sex role reversals are evident in other customs, too. In this society, young men are the ones who make themselves attractive by adorning themselves with jewelery, elaborate hairstyles, clothing, and make-up in the hopes of catching the eye of someone of the opposite sex. The youths present themselves in a line and the women pick their spouses from them. On the surface at least, it seems that this is a rare instance where courtship roles, music-making, and power over reproductive rights are controlled by women instead of men.

There is an enormous variety of instruments in Guinea-Bissau, especially in the coastal regions. One finds a variety of indigenous lutes, harps, drums, xylophones, side blown trumpets made from wood, animal horns, or gourds, bullroarers, mirlitons, whistles, iron bells, rattles, and flutes. Of these, several instruments stand out as being particularly widespread and important. There is a large slit drum, (sometimes called the *bombólon*) which is sometimes two meters in length. It is made from a hollowed-out tree trunk and is played with two heavy, wooden sticks. Because this drum can be heard for miles and is used as a signal to announce deaths or sound an alarm, it is sometimes referred to as the '*telegrafo indigena*,' ('native telegraph'). Besides the large slit drum, there are many types of wooden drums with skin heads in various shapes and sizes including an hourglass-shaped tension drum and a long thin drum sometimes called the *gilá* which is carried with a shoulder harness. Drums are frequently played with one stick and one open hand.

A wooden xylophone with gourd resonators is another commonly found instrument. Called the *balafon* (q.v.) (or *balafou, bálá, balafom*), it has between sixteen and twenty-four wooden slabs and is tuned to an equitional, heptatoic scale. It is played with two wooden mallets. It is played both as a solo and an ensemble instrument.

Variations on the fiddle are widespread. *Calande* is the *crioulo* name for a commonly-found one-stringed bowed or plucked lute. It is made of a calabash that is dried, cut in half, and covered with a skin. It has a neck and one gut string. Other names for this instrument are *molo, riti,* and *cimbôa.*

Oval shaped lutes with three, four, or five strings are found throughout West Africa. These lutes have wooden resonating boxes covered with animal skins and are about forty to forty-five centimeters long and ten centimenters wide. Instruments of this type have many names including *koonting, kurango, konting, kontino, kontigo, koni, viola, xalam, toncrum,* and *haddu.* These instruments usually have a rattling device on the neck that vibrates when the instrument is played, adding an additional timbre.

Instruments from the harp-lute family such as the *kora* exist in Guinea-Bissau, especially among the Mandinka, they are usually found in association with the *griots* (q.v.) throughout West Africa. Scholars believe that the *kora* originates from the Kansala region of Guinea-Bissau, or the capital of Kaabu (q.v.). These large harp-lutes usually have from eighteen to twenty-one strings strung between a large calabash resonating chamber and a long curving neck. Smaller harps with seven or eight strings called *simbing, simbingo* and *bolon* are also widespread. Popular recording artists use conventional Western instruments such as the guitar, drumset, keyboard, horn, and bass in their music. (S. Hurley-Glowa).

N

NALUS (NALOUS). The Nalus are a Senegambian (q.v.) rice-cultivating people whose political organization is that of small-scale chiefdoms which developed as a result of notable Mandinka and Susu (qq.v.) contact over the last six hundred years. As with such groups as the Bagas and the Landumas (qq.v.), the Nalus have been acculturated to the Susus who were themselves driven out of Futa Jallon (q.v.) by the Fula (q.v.) *jihads*. The Nalus are also closely related to the Bijagós people, who are much less influenced by the Susus. The Nalus are mainly concentrated in the Susu area near the town of Catio but also range down the northern coast of Guinea-Conakry.

NIGER-CONGO LANGUAGES. This large family of African languages is also known by the term *Nigritic* or *Congo-Kordofanian* languages; the classification is subject to various interpretations and organization of the various member language groups. In any case, the Niger-Congo languages include the West Atlantic and Senegambian (q.v.) stocks as well as the Mandinka (q.v.) languages which are spoken in Guinea-Bissau. Even the Fula (q.v.) languages which also have Berber derivation have a basic origin in the West Atlantic group of the Niger-Congo family. Since most of the Guinean people speak languages of the Niger-Congo language family, and since most slaves exported to Cape Verde came from this region, it may be said that the Niger-Congo languages have also made some linguistic contribution to Cape Verdean *Crioulo* (q.v.) language. Crioulo has borrowed words, rhythms, tones, and folklore from these languages, not to mention aspects of material culture such as *funco* house styles, *pano* (q.v.) textiles, *pilão* food mortars, and *ouri* (q.v.) gaming boards.

NORTH ATLANTIC TREATY ORGANIZATION (NATO). At the conclusion of World War II the United States proposed the creation of a military alliance of the capitalist nations of the North Atlantic. The pact came into effect on 18 March 1949, the same year in which Portugal (q.v.) joined. While areas to the south of the equator were officially out of NATO's jurisdiction, Portugal's membership permitted NATO to contribute very significant military and economic aid to Portugal under Salazar and Caetano (qq.v.), thus directly assisting the Portuguese with their counterinsurgency wars in their African colonies. Portugal carefully portrayed the African wars as part of a global anti-Communist campaign during an intense period of the Cold War. As such, all NATO members overlooked African aspirations for national independence, seeing the African nationalists as simply pawns of the Soviet Union or China.

Before 1958 Portugal spent between three and four percent of GNP on the military which was similar to other Western European nations. By 1964 Portugal's 'defense' requirements had reached eight percent of GNP. In 1965 more than half of the state revenues went to the military. Portugal was supported mainly through military loans and grants by West Germany and the United States and by purchases of Portuguese colonial products.

United States' aid to Portugal through NATO was measured in the hundreds of millions of dollars. Between 1949 and 1968 American military aid to Portugal officially reached $349 million, but this does not include other bilateral agreements which eased Portugal's own hard-pressed economy. In 1972 alone the United States arranged financial assistance to Portugal of well over $400 million. The vast portion of Portugal's NATO committed forces were actually in Africa and NATO equipment, especially heavy artillery, armored vehicles and aircraft, not to mention American-trained counterinsurgency specialists, all figured importantly in Portugal's wars in Africa from 1961 to 1974.

NOVA LAMEGO. Town in eastern Guinea-Bissau formerly known as Gabú (q.v.) before the advent of colonial rule and known by that name since independence. Nova Lamego was located in the Gabú *circunscrição* at 12° 17'N; 14° 13'W.

O

OIL PALM. This oil-bearing palm is a major contributor to fats in the diet of West Africans. In addition, palm oil is an important export commodity with various food and commercial purposes. To a large degree the decline of the slavery (q.v.) relates to the rise in the 'legitimate' trade in palm oil for industrial and cosmetic uses. The oil palm (*Elaeis guineensis*) is native to West Africa and is found especially in the tropics. In areas of less rainfall closer to the savanna regions, the oil palm is replaced by the shea-butter tree (*Butyrospermum parkii*) also known as *karite*. The oil-bearing fruits produce large amounts of oil for use as a foodstuff and body lotion.

ORGANIZATION OF AFRICAN UNITY (OAU). This first modern PanAfrican organization was formed on 25 May 1963 by the then independent African nations. The African Liberation

Committee of the OAU sought to coordinate political and military support for the liberation movements such as the *Partido Africano da Independência de Guiné e Cabo Verde*, PAIGC (q.v.). From 1963 to 1967 the OAU sought to unite the *Frente de Luta Pela Independência Nacional da Guiné-Bissau*, FLING (q.v.), with the PAIGC to build a broader and more moderate unity. After 1967 it gave recognition only to the PAIGC as the sole legitimate political expression of the people of Guinea-Bissau and Cape Verde. The Republic of Guinea-Bissau became the forty-second member nation of the OAU when it joined in November 1973. The Republic of Cape Verde joined the OAU on 18 July 1975.

OURI (AYO, MANKALA, MANKARA, OHWAREE, OMW-ESO, WARI). *Ouri* is one of the most ancient Middle East and African 'store-and-capture' games, present in pharaonic Egypt or the ancient Levant. This game is known by a wide variety of names, and it is now played extensively throughout Africa, the Middle East, the Caribbean, and among a few Afro-American populations. In Guinea, Cape Verde, and Cape Verdean diaspora enclaves *ouri* is played with great enthusiasm. A family's hand-carved wooden *ouri* board is considered a prized possession. In Africa the game of *ouri* is sometimes played using only pebbles with depressions in the sand serving as the 'board.'

Ouri may be considered an evolutionary forerunner of backgammon. However, *ouri* may be considered as more complex, since only strategy is involved, and there is no role for chance as no dice or throwing sticks are used to determine moves. The game is more complex than checkers but less complicated than chess. West African *ouri* is usually played on boards of two rows of six depressions, but other forms provide for four rows. Usually it is played with two players, but some forms of the game allow for three or four players. The object is to hoard your own seed, pebble, or button markers defensively, which usually number forty-eight or sixty to start. While in an offensive 'seeding' play, the objective is to seize the markers of your opponents from their game board 'territory' on the basis of 'hitting' your opponent with the final marker in your turn at seeding.

P

PADRÃO. A *padrão* is a stone column, standard, or cross erected as a Royal territorial marker on the African coast, especially by fifteenth century Portuguese navigators. This marked the extent of a voyage or a Royal claim by a specific Captain. Portuguese padrãos are found in Cape Verde, along the Lower Guinea coast, and as far as South Africa.

PAJADINCAS. In the fifteenth century, the Pajadincas were a small Senegambian (q.v.) group was distributed throughout Kaabu (q.v.) and along the headwaters of the Casamance (q.v.) and Gambia but not down to the coast. The widespread slave wars of Mandinka-based Kaabu, and its successor state Fuladu established by Musa Molo (q.v), had a very negative effect on the Pajadinca population, which was much reduced in number and extent. The small minority of modern Pajadincas are found in the border area of northeasternmost Guinea-Bissau.

PALMATÓRIA. This instrument of severe corporal punishment was used extensively by the Portuguese *regime do indigenato* (q.v.) in particular in Guinea, Angola, and Mozambique. Used brutally, the *palmatória* tore the skin and broke bones of hands and feet.

PANO. A unique form of untailored Guinean and Cape Verdean textile which has been produced for centuries. *Panos* are woven from cotton fiber grown in the islands and are made on a narrow loom of Mandinka (q.v.) or Wolof style. Six strips (about fifteen to seventeen centimeters each) are sown together to make a wider cloth, typically dark blue and white colors. This weaving technique is of Mande origin and reached Cape Verde through its trade with Africa. African weavers often use more than two colors, however.

The blue is from the urzella and indigo (qq.v.) dyes found regionally, while the white is natural cotton. *Panos* are worn exclusively by women as a shawl or waist sash as part of the traditional costume and for folk dancing. *Panos* are wadded in a tight ball and beaten by Cape Verdean women to accompany the *batuko* (q.v.) dance chants. African mothers typically use *panos* to carry their infants on their hips.

Both the dyes and the *panos* have long been important in the Guinean economy. Higher value would be ascribed to those *panos* with more intricate designs in the weaving and better skills in sewing the strips together. The Cape Verdean islands of Fogo (famed for the deep indigo *panos pretos*) and São Tiago (qq.v) had excellent reputations in the volume and quality of *panos* which were used in the Guinean trade.

Facing a relative scarcity of iron bars to exchange in the slave (q.v.) trade, the *panos* came to be a measure of value in the 16th century, when they were used widely in barter, as elsewhere in Africa, such as for the rafia cloths of the Congo. The local economy of *pano* production incorporated cotton growing, dyeing, spinning, and weaving, and there was a high price set for the sale of slaves who were skilled in weaving.

By 1680 two high quality *panos* were standardized in value as equal to one standardized iron bar. Gradually individual Cape Verdeans were becoming successfully and independently involved in the slave trade. However, the Decree of 23 January 1687 proclaimed that the sale of locally-made *panos* to foreigners was punishable by death; selling raw cotton could receive the same penalty. By 1721 the Portuguese still declared that the trade in *panos* was illegal, carrying severe penalties, in an effort to reassert the Crown monopoly and to keep Cape Verdeans from dealing in this trade.

PARK, MUNGO (1771–1805). This Scot was a pioneer among the European explorers of Senegambia (q.v.) and the Upper Niger. Between 1795 and 1796 he visited the kingdoms of Barra, Bondu, Bambara, Jinbala, Kaarta, Kajaaga, Kasson, Ludamar, Masina, Serawooli, and other small states in the Gambia River valley where he learned to speak Mandinka (q.v.) and described the Felupes, Fula (qq.v.), Jalofs, Moors, and even Moorish Jews. His journal also informed the public about the degree to which Islam had already penetrated the local society. Park noted everywhere the large numbers of slaves in service, being sold in the markets, and being driven in coffles. Park notes that slaves were mainly generated by widespread war, but also by famine, criminal penalty, and through famine conditions. At Tendacunda Park met an 'aged black female called Seniora Camilla, a person who had resided many years at the English factory,' who was presumably of *lançado* (q.v.) descent. After sailing from Gambia to Gorée (q.v.) on an American slave ship, the *Charlestown* (with the 130 slaves on board), he sailed on to Antigua on this very leaky ship which arrived thirty-five days later (with the death of twenty slaves). In a much larger second expedition in 1805 Park engaged a local Mandinka merchant, Isaaco, as his guide; presumably he was of Dyula (q.v.) descent but related to the Portuguese traders as a *tangomão* (q.v.). Park was killed in 1805 when his raft was attacked on the Upper Niger.

PARTIDO AFRICANO DA INDEPENDÊNCIA DE CABO VERDE (PAICV). This is the direct successor political party to the *Partido Africano da Independência de Guiné e Cabo Verde*, PAIGC (q.v.). The PAICV ruled in the Republic of Cape Verde until the elections of 1991. The PAICV was formed in January 1981, following the November 1980 Bissau coup which toppled Luís Cabral (q.v.), President of Guinea-Bissau. With this breach in party policy and decision making, the PAIGC in Cape Verde was renamed to symbolize its separate path, despite the years of effort to unify the two nations, peoples, and parties under the single nationalist banner. The major policies and leading figures of the PAICV stayed the same as the former PAIGC. The PAICV pursued a program of non-alignment in international relations, with friendly ties to the socialist nations and a large State-controlled public sector in Cape Verde.

From 1981 to 1991 the PAICV was constitutionally the *partido unico* (sole ruling party). Indeed, the lack of change in the PAICV ruling structure led to some notable defections such as Carlos Veiga (q.v) who went on to form a dissident opposition party. The old guard of the PAICV also used charges of 'Trotskyism' to justify internal party purges; some repressive measures were taken against the opposition groups such as the *União Cabo Verdeano Independente e Democratico*. To one degree or another, these policies and practices of the PAICV led to declining credibility and legitimacy. Seeking to recover from these problems, the PAICV accepted revisions in the Constitution which paved the way for two-party elections in the islands and inspired the Democratization movement in Bissau (q.v.).

This resulted in the defeat of the PAICV, which was replaced by the MpD as the new ruling party in 1991. PAICV Prime Minister and Secretary General Pedro Pires (q.v.) then became a member of the 'loyal opposition' when the new Prime Minister, Carlos Viega was installed in this position. Aristides Pereira (q.v.), the former President of Cape Verde under PAICV rule, has made some steps to distance himself from his defeated party. In addition, the PAICV Congress has elected Aristides Lima as the new Secretary General in September 1993, with Pedro Pires still playing an active role in party affairs. The new ruling party, the Movimento para Democracia, MpD, has taken a number of steps to delegitimize the PAIGC/PAICV by changing the national flag, which had been the former party banner, by large-scale privatization and liquidation of public firms, by defending political pluralism, and by reducing the prominence of some national figures closely associated with the PAIGC/ PAICV, such as Amilcar Cabral (q.v.). In the 1995 Cape Verde elections the PAICV was defeated again by viturally the same margin so it remains as the minority opposition party.

PARTIDO AFRICANA DA INDEPENDÊNCIA DE GUINÉ E CABO VERDE (PAIGC or PAI). The PAIGC was the victorious nationalist organization based in Guinea-Bissau and Cape Verde which was founded clandestinely in Bissau (q.v.) on 19 September 1956. The PAIGC was the organizational descendant of the *Movimento Para Independência Nacional da Guiné Portuguesa*, MING (q.v.), founded in 1954 by Henri Labéry and Amilcar Cabral (qq.v.). The main difference between the MING and the PAIGC arose over the inclusion of independence for the Cape Verde Islands. Also, there were more craftsmen and manual workers in the PAIGC than in the MING grouping. Labéry later went on to form the *Frente de Luta Pela Independência Nacional da Guiné-Bissau*, FLING (q.v.), a small, but persistent rival to the PAIGC, while Amilcar Cabral and his associates were the founders of the PAIGC. As the PAIGC began to grow it attracted some port and transport workers who later helped to organize the *União Nacional dos Trabalhadores da Guiné*, UNTG (q.v.), in 1961.

The independence of Guinea-Conkary in 1958 aided in stimulating an effort to hold a nationalist-oriented strike of the Pijiguiti (q.v.) dockworkers in Bissau on 3 August 1959. To counter this growing militancy, the Portuguese soldiers and armed settlers reacted with twenty minutes of gunfire, killing perhaps 50 and wounding about 100, subsequently resulting in the conviction of 21 persons for subversion. In September 1959 the PAIGC General Secretariat was moved to Conakry, and in the following year the Portuguese began a more serious effort at arrests and repression of the PAIGC. The PAIGC responded from December 1960 to September 1961 with an agitation program calling for a peaceful end to colonial rule by distributing some 14,000 tracts and writing two open letters to the Portuguese people as well as sending various documents to the United Nations (q.v.) with the same appeal. April 1961 saw the creation of the *Conferência de Organizações Nacionalistas das Colónias Portuguesas*, CONCP (q.v.), in Casablanca with the PAIGC playing a leading role in this organization which linked the struggle in Guinea and Cape Verde to those initiated in Angola and Mozambique. Toward the end of 1961 the PAIGC determined that a course of direct armed action would be the only realistic approach to bring national independence. In order to block this move the Portuguese secret police, *Polícia International e de Defesa do Estado*, PIDE (q.v.), arrested Rafael Barbosa (q.v.) in March 1962, the same month when the PAIGC had planned an attack on Praia in the Cape Verde Islands. In June and July the PAIGC may have initiated a few small scale acts of sabotage inside Guinea-Bissau. This escalation soon put Bissau under martial law with upwards of 2,000 suspected activists arrested and the Portuguese military strength reaching about 10,000 soldiers.

The years from 1959 to 1963 were carefully devoted to building a hierarchical structure of groups and sections united into thirteen zones and six regions so that all activities could be closely coordinated. In January 1963 the movement entered a new phase of protracted armed struggle when it launched a series of attacks in the southern regions of the country. By July 1963 the PAIGC had opened a second front of military activity in northern Guinea-Bissau. By November, Portugal (q.v.) made a feeble effort to conceal the colonial status of Guinea-Bissau, and a special decree from Lisbon was issued saying that Guinea-Bissau had become an 'overseas province,' hence an integral part of metropolitan Portugal. This was a case of too little, too late, and the PAIGC continued to consolidate its gains to such a degree that, from 13 to 17 February 1964, the first Party Congress was held in the liberated zones in the southern front at Cassaca. Some of the notable positions taken at this Congress were: 1) an enlargement of the Central Committee from thirty to sixty-five members; 2) the establishment of the following seven departments: armed forces, foreign affairs, cadre control, training and information, security, economy and finance, and mass organizations; and 3) the formation of the *Forças Armadas Revolutionárias* do Povo (FARP) (q.v.) as well as People's Stores and an expansion of medical and educational services.

In April 1964 the PAIGC engaged the Portuguese in an intensive military confrontation on the large southern coastal island of Como. This sixty-five-day offensive forced the Portuguese to withdraw 3,000 troops after losing hundreds. By 1965 approximately fifty percent of the countryside was under PAIGC control even though the Portuguese soldiers now numbered about 25,000. From 1965 to 1966 there was something of a military standoff until, in the later part of 1966, the PAIGC reintensified its efforts to gain the initiative, particularly in the newly opened eastern front which included parts of the former northern and southern regions. The December 1966 reorganization of the FARP helped to restore momentum to the struggle. The military headway accounted for political gains at the Organization of African Unity, OAU (q.v.), which now gave its full support to the PAIGC in 1967, thus abandoning efforts to reconcile the FLING with the PAIGC. Other accomplishments of the Party in that year included the start of the Party's *Radio Libertação* and the restructuring of the original seven departments of the Central Committee by reducing them to the following five: control, security, foreign relations, national reconstruction, and internal organization and orientation. In 1968 the main thrust was the consolidation of the political organization and strengthening of the infrastructure in the liberated zones. On 19 February 1968 the PAIGC military forces stunned the Portuguese occupation forces by attacking the Bissalanca International Airport at Bissau (q.v). By February 1969 the Portuguese were forced out of Medina Boé in the south, thus giving the FARP units of the PAIGC a much broader area of entry. Throughout 1969 and 1970 more notable military and political reverses befell the Portuguese despite their claims of 614 PAIGC dead in 1969 and 895 killed in 1970.

In Rome, Italy, on 1 July 1970, Amilcar Cabral and leaders of the FRELIMO from Mozambique and the MPLA from Angola were given an audience with the Pope. As residents of a strongly Catholic nation the Portuguese officials were enraged at this diplomatic victory for the liberation forces. In a futile and frustrated gesture, on 22 November 1970 a Portuguese raiding party from Bissau invaded the neighboring capital city of Conakry with the intention of overthrowing the government of President Sekou Touré and killing the leading members of the PAIGC who then had offices based in that city. The abortive invasion failed after bloody fighting but served to underscore the frantic efforts to halt the spread of PAIGC control and influence. The Portuguese made another effort in the early 1970's to halt the PAIGC with the introduction of General Spínola's (q.v.) 'Better Guinea' program which proclaimed certain minimal reforms. The PAIGC response in 1971 was even bolder attacks against the main towns of Farim, Bafatá, (qq.v.) and Bissau with rockets and light artillery. The Portuguese claim for PAIGC dead in 1971 reached 1,257, the highest such statistic for the war, and served to indicate the heightened intensity of the fighting. Revisions of the Portuguese Constitution in 1971 and the Overseas Organic Law of 1972 gave still more formal autonomy to the 'overseas provinces' of Guinea and Cape Verde, but the pace set by the PAIGC was now beyond the control of the Lisbon authorities.

New anti-aircraft guns and small but effective surface-to-air (SAM) missiles from the Soviet Union permitted the PAIGC to open competition for the airspace over Guinea-Bissau, which had formerly been the exclusive domain of Portuguese helicopter gunships and deadly napalm and white phosphorus dropped by fighter-bombers. As a rule, the PAIGC was beginning to bring down two or three enemy aircraft each month by this time. In April 1972 a unique mission of the United Nations actually visited the liberated zones, and the 848th sessions of the UN Decolonization Committee recognized the PAIGC as the only effective movement operating inside Guinea-Bissau. The observations and recognition of the Special Mission were endorsed by the twenty-seventh session of the United Nations General Assembly later in the same year. This was a major diplomatic triumph for the PAIGC's long effort to isolate and discredit Portuguese colonial rule. In August 1972 another first occurred with provisions for elections in the liberated zones for 273 regional commissioners and 99 representatives to the PAIGC's *Assembléia Nacional Popular* (ANP) (q.v.) to be held in late 1973.

In an address in the United States, Amilcar Cabral announced that soon the PAIGC would declare that the national independence of Guinea-Bissau had been achieved, but, on 20 January 1973, this towering African nationalist and revolutionary philosopher was assassinated in Conakry in an intricate plot to take over the PAIGC and protect certain strategic interests of the Portuguese. The conspiracy had been well organized using PAIGC disssident elements, FLING partisans, and logistic and intelligence support from the Portuguese. While the loss was sharply felt, the organization that Amilcar Cabral had carefully built went on to greater achievements. In May 1973 'Operation Amilcar Cabral' resulted in the seizure of Guiledge (q.v.), a large fortified base near the southern frontier. This was possible, in part, because of the introduction of the new anti-aircraft weapons, but especially because of the collective resolve of the PAIGC military organization to redress the loss of Secretary General Cabral.

From 18 to 22 July 1973 the PAIGC held its second Party Congress at Boé, which elected Aristides Pereira (q.v.) as the new Secretary General, made certain revisions in the proposed Constitution, enlarged the *Conselho Superior da Luta* (CSL) (q.v.) from eighty-one to eighty-five members, and created a

Permanent Secretariat (q.v.) of the Executive Committee. This new formation was headed by Pereira, with the Deputy Secretary General being Luís Cabral (q.v.); the two other members were Francisco Mendes and João Vieira (qq.v.). The July Congress put the last official touches to the preparations for the 23 to 24 September 1973 historic first meeting of the ANP, which formally proclaimed the Declaration of State, adopted the Constitution, and elected the executives of the State including Luís Cabral as the President of the fifteen-member Council of State, eight State Commissioners (Ministers), and eight Sub-Commissioners of State (Deputy Ministers). Immediately scores of nations around the world recognized the new Republic, and by early October 1973 diplomatic recognition had been extended by sixty-one nations even though Portuguese troops still occupied the major towns.

Elsewhere in Africa, especially in Mozambique, the liberation movements were showing comparable gains, and it was increasingly clear that the end was near for Portuguese colonialism. On 25 April 1974 the Portugese Armed Forces Movement (MFA) overthrew the colonial, Fascist regime of Prime Minister Caetano and made General Spinola (qq.v.), recently returned from Guinea-Bissau, the new President of Portugal. The leader of the Portuguese Socialist Party, Mario Soares, met with Aristides Pereira on 15 May 1974, and negotiations for Portugal's recognition of Guinea-Bissau's independence and Portugal's withdrawal were underway. By 27 July Portugal officially stated that it was prepared to grant independence and, in accords reached at meetings held in Algiers in August, the final details were determined. On 4 September the first representatives of the *Comité Executívo da Luta*, CEL (q.v.), entered Bissau, and on 10 September Portugal gave de jure recognition to the new Republic of Guinea-Bissau. Luís Cabral and Aristides Pereira officially entered Bissau on 19 October 1974.

Meanwhile, in Cape Verde matters were more complicated, as the PAIGC had had a different history in the islands and had not engaged in any meaningful armed struggle but had concentrated on clandestine political organizing. A number of rival Cape Verdean groups emerged, and a climate of uneasiness prevailed through late September and into October until it was made clear in discussions, negotiations, demonstrations, and a general strike that the PAIGC was to be the sovereign political party in the islands. On 18 December 1974 a transitional government had been formed from members of the

PAIGC and of the MFA. In early 1975 relations between Portugal and Guinea-Bissau became strained over financial matters, and the PAIGC nationalized the Portuguese *Banco Nacional Ultramarino*.

In this context of instability it was rumored that the FLING movement made an attempted coup d'état on March 21. In any case, the apparatus of the new state became more fully engaged with the 28 April to 6 May *Assembléia Nacional Popular* held for the first time in Bissau, the first meeting of the ANP since the Declaration of State in the southern forests a year earlier. On 30 June 1975 there was an election for representatives to the Cape Verdean ANP and, with this act, the islands became the independent Republic of Cape Verde on 5 July 1975. However, since the PAIGC program called for unity between the sister republics there were already many agreements which united the two lands in commerce, transport, education, and communication. Most importantly, the PAIGC was the ruling party in both countries, although there were two separate national assemblies.

Notable events in 1976 as a result of PAIGC policy included the creation of the Guinean *peso* to replace the Portuguese *escudo* on 28 February and the Second Session of the *Assembléia Nacional Popular* from 22 April to 3 May, as well as visits to Bissau from President Samora Machel of Mozambique and President Agostino Neto of Angola. The PAIGC held its Third Party Congress from 15 to 20 November 1977. After some delays and about a year of meticulous and widespread preparation, the central themes of this major event were unity between Guinea-Bissau and Cape Verde, economic development, and political consolidation. The former Permanent Secretariat of four members was enlarged to eight, the CSL was increased to ninety members, and the new CEL was expanded from twenty-four to twenty-six members. The four new members of the Permanent Secretariat were Pedro Pires (q.v.), Umaro Djalo, Constantino Teixeira, and Abílio Duarte (q.v.). The new thrust of the PAIGC was to form a vanguard political party which would organize, dynamize, and mobilize the peoples of Guinea-Bissau and Cape Verde.

Since the November 1980 coup d'état of João Vieira the two Republics have become separated, and the PAIGC is no longer considered the ruling party of the Cape Verde Islands. It was replaced by the PAICV (q.v.) in 1981, and in 1991 the PAICV was voted out of office. The high level of political integration proposed to link the two lands in the post-independence period was not achieved despite the contemporary sense of euphoria for independence in both lands. Meanwhile, in Guinea-Bissau the PAIGC remained the sole legal party or political entity until the constitutional revision of May 1991. Under the new law governing the existance of legal political parties, the PAIGC did not have to satisfy the requirements for official recognition. Its official motto continues to be 'Unity, Struggle, and Progress,' and its leader remains João Vieira. In 1994 elections the PAIGC at first earned less than the fifty percent required to form a government and a second run-off was held.

PAIGC IDEOLOGY. Founded in 1956 as a national liberation movement, with the most immediate goal of political independence from Portuguese colonial domination, the *Partido Africano da Independência da Guiné e Cabo Verde*, PAIGC (q.v.), espoused a radical ideology very much influenced by contemporary Marxist perspectives. This influence was perhaps inevitable, since the party's celebrated leader, Amilcar Cabral (q.v.), whose various writings form the core of PAIGC ideology, used the method of Historical Materialism to analyze social transformation in Guinea-Bissau.

The fundamental principles of PAIGC ideology are Socialist in character, in spite of the fact that the word 'Socialism' never appeared in the original party program and was hardly used in authoritative policy statements. The movement was committed not just to the goal of 'immediate and total independence,' but also to the 'elimination of the exploitation of man by man'; the 'elimination of all relationships of a colonialist and imperialist nature'; and, *inter alia*, the 'attainment of economic independence' (Cabral 1969, 137).

Besides such typical Socialist formulations, the commitment to socialism was also evident from the party's adoption of the Marxist-Leninist doctrine of 'democratic centralism,' as well as its concept of 'revolutionary democracy.' As articulated by Amilcar Cabral, the former meant that decisions made in 'representative' institutions must be arrived at democratically, "... on the basis of respect for the opinions and interests of the majority ... after a full and free discussion" (Cabral 1980, 249). The latter required "that the responsible workers and leaders should live among the people, before the people, behind the people," that the party "deliver power" to the people, who should "have the certainty that power is in fact theirs" (ibid, 97).

The PAIGC economic development strategy stressed that

since agriculture is the basis of the economy (q.v.) of Guinea-Bissau, it would be given top priority, because national development and industrialization would depend on it. According to Cabral, the emphasis on agriculture meant more than cultivation: "it means realizing what people can do, can actually do. That's a question of village democracy, of village schools, of village clinics, of village cooperation" (quoted in Davidson 1969, 137). The strategy implied a planned economy and increasing state intervention.

As to the form of administration independent Guinea-Bissau should have, there was virtually no program, although Amilcar Cabral did point out the need to build "a type of administration which will be completely new in personnel and structure when compared with the apparatus of colonial times" (ibid, 136). He also expressed the necessity "to decentralize as much as may be possible," which was one reason why he thought that Bissau should not continue to be the administrative capital of the country after independence. He asked: "Why should we saddle ourselves with the paraphernalia of a presidential palace, a concentration of ministries, the clear sign of an emergent elite which can soon become a privileged group" (ibid, 137).

On the issue of Pan African unity and interstate cooperation, besides the specific question of Guinea-Bissau/Cape Verde union, the party's major program also included a commitment to "fight for the unity of all African peoples, considered as a whole or by continental regions," as well as their "right to political, economic, social and cultural progress (PAIGC Program, in Rudebeck 1974, 254).

Amilcar Cabral himself believed that there are "no real conflicts between the peoples of Africa;" instead, there are "only conflicts between their elites" (quoted in Davidson 1969, 139). When the African peoples "take power into their own hands", he pointed out, "there will remain no great obstacles to effective African Solidarity" (ibid).

The liberation movement attached great importance to education (q.v.), which was considered intimately related to the overall plan for the transformation of Guinean society. Predicated on the belief that "man is the most powerful force of nature," the role of education was seen to be the liberation of man from "submissiveness before nature and natural forces" (ibid, 243), as well as the "total elimination of the complexes created by colonialism, and of the consequences of colonialist culture and exploitation" (Cabral 1969, 139).

According to PAIGC ideology, education should be meaningful and liberating, and not only concerned with the basic skills of reading, writing, and arithmetic. It should develop critical consciousness to enable the individual to perceive social, political and economic contradictions in society and encourage "active, creative and critical participation in the work of national reconstruction" (PAIGC 1978, 44).

PARTIDO DA CONVERGÊNCIA DEMOCRÁTICA (PCD). This new party was founded on 2 August 1991, apparently the outcome of four months of critical reflection on the situation of the country by a group of young professionals, businessmen, and intellectuals. They refer to themselves as the *Grupo de Reflexão para a Convergência Democrática*. The PCD was legalized on 27 December 1991 under the motto, 'Liberty, Democracy and Development.' Its leader is Vitor Luís Mandinga, a former member of the *Partido Africano da Independência de Guiné e Cabo Verde*.

PARTIDO DA RENOVAÇÃO SOCIAL (PRS). The PRS was founded on 14 January 1992 as a result of a split in the *Frente Democrática Social* (FDS) which led to to the expulsion of the dissident founder-members. This party was legalized on 9 October 1992 under the motto, 'Liberty, Transparency and Justice.' The PRS leader Kumba Yala (Iala) had even more than expected electoral popularity among the youth in the largely young population of Guinea-Bissau and was able to face the PAIGC's President 'Nino' in a run-off election.

PARTIDO DEMOCRATICO DO PROGRESSO (PDP). This new political party was founded by Amine Michel Saad. It was legalized on 7 August 1992 under the motto, 'Liberty, Development, and Solidarity.'

PARTIDO PARA RENOVAÇÃO E DESENVOLVIMENTO (PRD). This party was founded as an offshoot of the 'Group of 121,' which was a group of 121 dissident members of the PAIGC who were signatories to a letter addressed to the Secretary General of the Party, João 'Nino' Vieira, on 30 June 1991. This letter urged change and reform for effective participation in the emerging multiparty system. Subsequently, they were forced to leave. The PRD was legalized on 9 October 1992, under the slogan of 'Democracy, Development, and Social Justice.' This movement is parallel to events in Cape Verde which gave rise to the MpD, which defeated the PAICV in open elections in 1992. The leader of the PRD is João da Costa, a noted veteran of the armed liberation struggle, former member of the PAIGC, and Minister of Health (1974–1980) in the Government of Luís Cabral.

PARTIDO UNIDO SOCIAL DEMOCRATA (PUSD). The PUSD was founded on 30 May 1991 and was legalized 6 June 1992. Its leader is Vitor Saude Maria, who served as the Minister of Foreign Affairs (1974–1980) in the Government of Luís Cabral (q.v.) and was briefly the Prime Minister after the coup d'état of 14 November 1980. In 1984 he was accused of plotting to overthrow the Government of João 'Nino' Vieira (q.v.). He was expelled from the *Partido Africano da Independência de Guiné e Cabo Verde*, PAIGC (q.v.), and for a period he was kept under house arrest. The motto of the PUSD is 'Peace, Justice and Progress.'

PATÉ, MAMADÚ. Although the Portuguese gave some tacit support to the Fula (q.v.) in their effort to topple the Mandinka (q.v.) state of Kaabu (q.v.) in 1867, this was only in their general strategy of "divide and rule." As a consequence, by 1879 the Portuguese were facing serious clashes with the Fula throughout eastern Guinea-Bissau. Mamadú Paté was a *regulo* of Bololo, (q.v.) a subordinate chieftaincy of the ruler Bacar Quidali of Forrea, (q.v.) both of whom put up a fierce resistance against the Portuguese penetration of the interior. The Portuguese sought to conquer Bololo in 1883.

In 1886 Paté killed his superior Bacar Quidali and thereby extended his domain to include Forrea. This was done in conjunction with widespread regional campaign initiated by the Fulas of Futa Jallon and under the local leadership of Musa Molo (q.v.), the ruler of Fuladu. In the 1890s Paté engaged Portuguese forces at Buba, near the coast, while Musa Molo engaged them at Farim (q.v.). As late as 1898 Mamadú Paté was still subjecting the Portuguese to military defeats.

PEANUTS: See AGRICULTURE.

PEOPLES NATIONAL ASSEMBLY. See ASSEMBLÉIA NACIONAL POPULAR; LEGISLATIVE ASSEMBLY.

PEOPLES' STORES. See ARMAZENS DO POVO.

PEPELS, PEPEIS. See BISSAU.

PEREIRA, ARISTIDES MARIA (1924–). A founder of the *Partido Africano da Independência de Guiné e Cabo Verde*,

PAIGC (q.v.), Pereira was the son of a priest in Boa Vista in the Cape Verde Islands where he attended the *liceu* (q.v.) before receiving specialized training as a radio-telegraph technician. He worked as the Chief of Telecommunications at the Bissau (q.v.) central post office, and it is said by the colonial security service that he played a vital role in the interception of intelligence about the activities of the PAIGC. Pereira was one of the organizers of the Pijiguiti (q.v.) strike in 1959, but in 1960 he left Bissau for security reasons to join Amilcar Cabral (q.v.) in Conakry. Pereira was a member of the Political Bureau of the Central Committee who organized in Bissau and other urban areas. In 1964 Pereira was the joint Secretary General of the PAIGC and a member of the *Conselho de Guerra* (q.v.) after 1965. Following organizational restructuring in 1970, Pereira became a member of the Permanent Commission of the CEL with Amilcar and Luís Cabral (q.v.). In this position his chief responsibilities were security and control and foreign affairs.

Before the death of Amilcar Cabral, Pereira was the Deputy Secretary General of the Party, but after Cabral's passing, Pereira became the top political officer of the PAIGC. Subsequent to the independence of Cape Verde on 5 July 1975, Pereira also became the President of the Republic of Cape Verde. In this position he maintained his commitment to social democracy and non-alignment and has often been a mediator among the non-aligned nations. After the electoral defeat PAICV (q.v.) in 1992 Pereira was replaced by President Anto-´nio Monteiro (q.v.). Pereira did not enter the presidential contest in 1996. He went into semi-retirement but continued to play a role as senior statesman in African affairs.

PEREIRA, CARMEN (1937–). Born in Guinea-Bissau (q.v.), the daughter of a lawyer, she joined the *Partido Africano da Independência de Guiné e Cabo Verde*, PAIGC (q.v.), in 1962. She and her husband Umaru Djallo were both party activists. He fled to avoid arrest, but initially she stayed in Bissau (q.v.) to work as a dressmaker as a cover for her underground role. In 1964 she also left Guinea-Bissau to engage in full-time party assignments. In 1965 Pereira headed a nurses training delegation to the Soviet Union. As the liberation war progressed she became the Political Commissioner for the entire South Front. She was the only woman (q.v.) in the twenty-four-member *Comité Executívo da Luta* (CEL) (q.v.) of the PAIGC, and she was the head of the Women's Commission which operated in both Guinea and Cape Verde from 1975 to 1981. Pereira was the Second Vice-President of the *Assembléia Nacional Popular* (q.v.) in Guinea, and she was one of the fifteen members of the Council of State.

PEREIRA, DUARTE PACHECO. Pereira was a frequent fifteenth- and sixteenth-century visitor to Cape Verde and the African coast. He may have been at the site of Al-Mina as early as 1475, when he reported on a Flemish ship with a Spanish captain which took on a cargo of gold. A few years later this Portuguese pilot, explorer, and cosmographer accompanied Azambuja (q.v.) in the founding of Al-Mina in 1482. He was at Al-Mina when Cão (q.v.) sailed south from that fort. His glowing accounts of the great profits to be made from the sale of Portuguese goods and the return cargo of gold were an important factor in the decision of Portugal (q.v.) to build at that site.

As the commander of a supply ship in the 1480's and 1490's he made numerous trips to Africa. Once Pereira was rescued by Barthólomeu Dias (q.v.) on his return from the Cape of Good Hope. Pereira later sailed to India. Between 1505 and 1508 he wrote *Esmeraldo de Sita Orbis*, a book of sea routes, in which he described the West African coast. He also gave details about coastal trade in gold, ivory, and slaves at Arguim at a time when Lisbon eagerly backed slavery (q.v.). For his long experience Pereira, of *fidalgo* social rank, was appointed Governor of Al-Mina from 1519 to 1521. However, when the flow of gold slowed from its former high of 240,000 cruzados per year, he was recalled to Lisbon for reassignment.

PEREIRA, FRANCISCA. Pereira is a veteran of the liberation war and presently serves as the Minister of Social Affairs and Women's Promotion in the Guinea-Bissau government. She was born in the old capital of Bolama (q.v.) and joined the *Partido Africano da Independência de Guiné e Cabo Verde*, PAIGC (q.v.), as a teenager in 1960. She worked in the PAIGC Secretariat in Conakry before being sent to the USSR to train as a nurse in 1965. Two years later, she was the Deputy Director of the PAIGC pilot school in Conakry.

Shortly afterwards, she was moved to the liberated areas of the south to take charge of health and sanitary matters. In 1970, she was transferred to the north, where she also took care of health issues and worked as a nurse in the PAIGC hospital at Ziguinchor (q.v.). Between 1970 and 1974, she represented the women's wing of the PAIGC in various international conferences. Since independence, she has held several important posts, including that of Mayor of Bolama, President of the Democratic Union of Women (of Guinea-Bissau), and Minister for Women's Promotion.

PERMANENT SECRETARIAT/COMMISSION. Within the *Comité Executivo da Luta* and the *Conselho de Guerra* (qq.v.) was found the Permanent Secretariat of the *Partido Africano da Independência de Guiné e Cabo Verde*, PAIGC (q.v.). Until 1973 the Permanent Secretariat was composed of Amilcar Cabral (q.v.), the PAIGC Secretary General in charge of political and military affairs, Aristides Pereira (q.v.), Vice Secretary General and *Responsable* for economy and security, and Luís Cabral (q.v.), *Responsable* for national reconstruction, health, and education. After the 1973 death of Amilcar Cabral and the Second Party Congress, the Secretariat changed its name to the Permanent Commission and was expanded to include João Bernardo Vieira and Francisco Mendes (qq.v.) as Secretaries of the Commission. The Commission handled the day-to-day decisions of the government, and during the war all members were also members of the seven-man *Conselho de Guerra* (q.v.). After independence the Commission was expanded again to eight members.

PETROFINA and SOCIEDADE ANONIMA DE REFINAÇÃO DE PETROLEOS (SACOR). These two oil companies have been the main suppliers of petrochemical products in Guinea-Bissau (q.v.) and Cape Verde. Both Petrofina and SACOR were long affiliated with the Portuguese Banco Nacional Ultramarino (BNU) and were thus linked to the huge Portuguese monopoly, the Companhia União Fabril, CUF (q.v.), through political alliances and interlocking directorates.

PHOENICIANS. Phoenicians were masters of the eastern Mediterranean Sea as early as the time of the Old Kingdom in Egypt in the third millenium BC. In the first millenium BC their voyages extended throughout the Mediterranean and by the nineth or eighth centuries BC they had knowledge of the Red Sea as well as the coastal Atlantic as far north as France and as far south as Morocco. It is reported by Herodotus that during the reign of Pharoah Necho II (610–594 BC) a three-year exploration of the entire African coast took place with stops long enough to plant food for the next leg which kept Africa on their right for the whole voyage.

According to Pomonius Melo's, *De Situ Orbis*, in 445 BC the Phoenician captain Hanno sailed from Cadiz southward along the African coast until he reached the Red Sea on a five-year voyage. He passed the Fortunate (Canary) Islands and then some small islands which he called Hesperias because of their westerly location a few days' sail off the coast. It is reasonable to assume that these were, in fact, the Cape Verde Islands, since they are the first islands reached after sailing south from the Canaries. On one voyage he reported seeing a large volcano off the west African coast, which one might consider to be the volcano at Fogo (q.v.). This smoke plume might be seen at great distance, and the fire of Fogo was noted as a useful navigational beacon in Cape Verdean waters by Christopher Columbus (q.v.).

There was speculation that the obscure stone inscriptions (q.v.) found in the Cape Verde Islands are Phonecian, but it seems more reasonable on several grounds to assume that they are fifteenth century Portuguese writings instead. Indisputable proof of the Phoenicians as the first to visit the Cape Verde Islands is not established, but one may consider this as a possibility on the basis of these ancient accounts.

PIJIGUITI. Site of the dockyards in Bissau (q.v.) at the broad estuary of the Geba River (q.v.). Pijiguiti was also the site of a famed dock workers' strike. According to the *Partido Africano da Independência de Guiné e Cabo Verde*, PAIGC (q.v.), the strike was organized to express labor grievances and proto-nationalist sentiments. On August 3, 1959, the colonial government responded with gun fire, reportedly killing 50 and wounding more than 100. The 'Pijiguiti Massacre,' as it came to be known, was a turning point for the PAIGC, which determined that a course of armed struggle would be the only way to achieve independence. In recent years the claims about the number of casualties and the degree of PAIGC involvement have been questioned.

PINTO, MAJOR JOÃO TEIXEIRA (1876–1917). Pinto is best known for a series of four brutal 'pacification' campaigns carried out in Guinea-Bissau between 1913 and 1915, during which he used field action, sea coverage, foreign mercenaries, collaboration with Fula and Mandinka chiefs, and modern arms to destroy villages of the Bijagos, Balantas, Felupes, Manjacos, (qq.v.) Oincas and Pepels. His military force was commanded by six European officers and about 400 Africans, especially Fulas and Mandinkas (qq.v.) who had long made war on the coastal peoples. Before the campaigns, Pinto traveled in the Oio River area disguised as a French trader to spy on some Mandinka groups. He was aided in this intelligence work and the campaigns themselves by the Senegalese chief and adventurer Abdul Injai (q.v.). At the conclusion of the campaigns the town of Canchungo was named Teixeira Pinto, but the former name was restored after independence in 1974. In 1915 a public outcry in Lisbon against the excesses of Pinto forced an inquiry into his brutal administration. In World War I, Pinto was stationed in Mozambique, where he was killed in combat.

PIONEIROS DE PARTIDO (PP). The PP was also known as the Pioneiros Abel Djassi (the nom de guerre of Amilcar Cabral, q.v.). The Pioneers of the Party was a youth organ of the *Partido Africano da Independência de Guiné e Cabo Verde*, PAIGC (q.v.), during the period of armed struggle and afterward. It sought to educate children under the leadership of the Party. The PP acted as the political branch of the education (q.v.) policy in the liberated areas and at the Pilot School, especially after 1972. Children from ten to fifteen were eligible to join and participate under the slogan of 'Study, Work, Struggle.' While the PP was relatively small in the beginning, it was very active at PAIGC partial boarding schools (*semi-internatos*) and carefully cultivated youth leadership qualities within Guinea and contacts at international youth forums and festivals. The journal of the PP, called *Blufo*, was published more or less quarterly and featured educational, cultural, and political articles and puzzles.

Since 12 September 1974 the main work of youth organizing was channelled through the Juventude Africana Amilcar Cabral (JAAC), which had chapters in most schools and neighborhoods. The JAAC concentrated its efforts on national reconstruction projects such as drug eradication, literacy campaigns, and general youth improvement. It was particularly targeted for work among urban youth who had not been integrated into the structures of the liberated zones during the war.

PIRES, GENERAL PEDRO VERONA RODRIGUES (1934–). Pires was born on Fogo island in Cape Verde in an isolated village within the volcanic crater making up the bulk of the island. After school in Cape Verde he went on to Lisbon where he studied Engineering and met other nationalists from Africa. By 1959 he was already involved with the underground movement in Lisbon for the liberation of Portugal's (q.v.) African colonies. Being subject to military draft in the Portuguese colonial army, he deserted and fled to Ghana with the hope of meeting Amilcar Cabral (q.v.).

After joining the *Partido Africano da Independência de Guiné e Cabo Verde*, PAIGC (q.v.), he received additional military training in Algeria and in 1966 was sent to Cuba to be a member of a thirty-man team to prepare for a two-pronged invasion of the Cape Verde Islands. This plan was never implemented. He served as the *Responsable* for Health and Education (qq.v.) in the Southern Front and was a Commander for this region. Pires was a leading member of the *Comité Executívo da Luta*, CEL and a member of the *Conselho de Guerra* (qq.v).

In 1974 Pires led the PAIGC delegation in London and Algiers which resulted in Portugal's recognition of the independence of Guinea-Bissau—liberty that had been declared since 24 September 1973. He was also the principal negotiator for the independence of Cape Verde on 5 July 1975. With the independence of Cape Verde, its first *Assembléia Nacional Popular* (q.v.) elected him the nation's first Prime Minister. His foreign policy was one of non-alignment, anti-imperialist, anti-apartheid, and regional peace and stability. Domestically he developed a program of ecological conservation and fiscal accountability, especially to donor nations. In Cape Verde his policies of national reconstruction and development were widely regarded as effective. Pires was the Chairman of the Cape Verdean National Committee of the *Partido Africano da Independência de Cabo Verde*, PAICV (q.v.).

He was also able to convince American Congressmen that Cape Verde would not be used as a Soviet base, thereby gaining critical American economic aid and political support. Some people give great credit to these pioneering achievements, while others, now in the Movimento para Democracia, MpD (q.v.), criticize his administration as too centralized and inherently undemocratic as a result of the one-party state and the military means which brought the PAIGC to power.

After the 1980 coup d'état in Bissau, Pires continued as the leader of the newly founded PAICV. Through the 1980's Pires and the PAICV accumulated enemies who opposed him for being too close to the Soviet Union and for advancing extensive nationalization and land reform. As a result of such criticism, the PAICV took steps to isolate the opponents within the party by expulsion, and some of those outside the party were arrested. Due to these measures, the PAICV created more opponents, ultimately leading to pressure for pluralistic Democracy rather than a one-party state.

In January 1991 Pires and the PAICV lost the first multiparty elections in Cape Verdean history to the new ruling party, the MpD. The peaceful transition of power was heralded around Africa and the world as a model to follow. Pires is now a member of the 'loyal opposition.' In July 1992 Pires attended the Democratic Party convention in the United States. His formal leadership as Secretary General of the PAICV ended with the appointment of Aristides Lima (q.v.) to that post, but Pires is likely to play an important behind-the-scenes role. He currently holds as seat as a PAICV representative of Fogo in the National Assembly.

POLICIA INTERNACIONAL PARA DEFESA DO ESTADO (PIDE). PIDE was the secret police organization of Portugal (q.v.) in its fascist period. As early as 1957 the PIDE arrived in Guinea-Bissau to assist in intelligence, counterinsurgency operations, and especially widespread arrests of suspected nationalists. In 1961 an additional organ, the *Polícia de Segurança Pública* (PSP), was introduced to curb the anti-Fascist and anti-colonial movements in Portugal and in the African colonies. In 1971 a contingent of 105 PIDE agents arrived in Cape Verde to infiltrate and break up underground operatives of the *Partido Africano da Independência de Guiné e Cabo Verde*, PAIGC (q.v.). By the early 1970's the PIDE had received such notoriety that it changed its name to the *Direção Geral de Segurança* (DGS).

POLITICAL TRANSITION. *See* GUINEA-BISSAU: POLITICAL TRANSITION.

POMBAL, MARQUIS DE. The Marquis de Pombal was the title given to Sebastião José de Carvalho e Melo who served as the Prime Minister for King José I (1750–77) of Portugal (q.v.). The Marquis was of lower level aristocratic birth and had served as a diplomat in the late 1730s. His administration can be characterized as relatively enlightened economic development coupled with increasing State despotism. The Pombal Laws of 1751–53 brought greater centralization of State powers, especially the repressive powers of the police. Under the

Pombal administration there was also strong opposition to the liberal perspectives of the Jesuits.

His administration included expanded foreign trade, more autonomy from English trade, and import replacement from a budding Portuguese industry. He founded a number of state-backed monopoly trading companies, most of which were failures. Of those *companhias* which were successful one could include a company which traded Douro Wine and one for the commerce in Pernambuco-Paraiba. In 1755 he created the *Companhia do Grão Pará e Maranhão* (q.v.) for the development of these two states in Brazil. Relative to Cape Verde, the Companhia called for expanded slave trade to the Guinea coast to meet labor needs through substantial imports of slaves. This company persisted until 1778.

An assassination attempt against King José in 1758 resulted in the 1759 expulsion of the Jesuits, whom he accused of involvement and who had allegedly opposed him. In 1760 the Marquis instituted a 'reform' of the kingdom's police. In 1761 he founded the Royal Treasury and formally abolished slavery (q.v.) in Portugal. Contributing to wider literacy and publishing, he launched the Royal Printing Press in 1768, but this was coupled with vigilant political censorship. In Cape Verde in 1769 he arranged for the permanent transfer of power to Praia from Ribeira Grande, and he introduced his 'Law of Good Reason' which, in the name of Enlightenment, gave more restrictions to the feudalists. His reforms in education and the university system and the creation of a more secular state were likewise significant. His attacks against the Jesuits were renewed in 1773 when their order was formally dissolved.

Thus, the liberal economic policies were matched with a carefully controlled enlightenment, increasingly centralized and repressive police and state structures, intensified African slavery, a decline of the feudal relations which had prevailed, and the beginning of a more powerful state bureaucracy. The Marquis de Pombal represented a major turning point in Portugal's history, and he set it on the path leading directly to the present.

PONTAS. Large land holding concessions in Guinea-Bissau are often termed *pontas*. Especially after the 'structural adjustment program' the number of *pontas* has increased phenomenally. Historically they have played a large role in the Guinean economy (q.v.), especially in the cultivation and export of the main cash crop, peanuts (known locally as *mancarra*).

POPULATIONS. *See* DEMOGRAPHY.

PORTUGAL. In 1143 Portugal broke away from Spain which was largely under Moorish control and established its own King under Dom Henriques. From 1384 to 1910 the House of Aviz (Knights of Calatrava) was the royal ruling lineage. Between 1420 and 1470 Portugal was absolute master of the seas and, under the influence of João II, Prince Henry's (qq.v.) significant navigational achievements and exploration of Africa took place. The coast of Guinea was reached in the 1440's and the Cape Verde Islands in the 1460's. In West Africa, Portugal's dominance declined rather quickly to the French, English, and Dutch through the following centuries, but Portugal continued to be a major supplier of slaves (q.v.) to the New World, especially to Brazil up to the late nineteenth century. From 1580 to 1640 Portugal was ruled under the Spanish Crown. The repression known under the Spanish Inquisition resulted in some additional migration to the Cape Verde Islands by *degredados* and Jews (qq.v.) from Portugal.

In 1656 private Cape Verdean tax collection was eliminated, and a direct officer of the Portuguese Crown was appointed to strengthen Portugal's hold on the islands and the African coast. Throughout the seventeenth and eighteenth centuries Guinea-Bissau and Cape Verde continued to supply slaves to the New World through the services of Luso-African traders (*lançados* [q.v.]) on the coast. In 1836 Portugal officially ended the slave trade, but it continued for several more decades. In 1870 Britain yielded its claims on Bolama (q.v.) to Portugal and, following the 1884–85 Berlin Congress (q.v.), Portugal and France agreed on the southern and northern borders of Guinea-Bissau. At the close of the nineteenth century Portugal was virtually bankrupt, and the monarchy sought dictatorial powers to make certain reforms. Following the assassination of the King and Crown Prince in 1908 and a popular revolt in 1910, the monarchy was abolished and the House of Bragança was banished. The Republican government prevailed from 1911 until 28 May 1926, when a military putsch overthrew the democratic republic and installed the Fascist *Estado Novo* government. A case of resistance to the Fascist government is recorded in Guinea-Bissau in 1931 with a month-long revolt of deported politicians.

From 1886 to the 1930's the Portuguese conducted military expeditions of 'pacification' against most of the coastal peoples of Guinea-Bissau. The Colonial Act of 1933 brought Portugal's relations with Africa into the Portuguese Constitution, and they were maintained until the 1974 revolution. In 1963 the nationalist movement in Guinea, led by the *Partido Africano da Independência de Guiné e Cabo Verde*, PAIGC (q.v.), began a protracted armed struggle which paralleled those in Angola and Mozambique.

As a result of these wars and economic and political contradictions inside Portugal, the Armed Forces Movement (MFA) overthrew the dictatorship on 25 April 1974 and thereby brought an end to Portuguese fascism. Amidst considerable political instability in Portugal itself, the question of colonialism had to be resolved. During the second half of 1974, conservatives were still hopeful that Cape Verde could be persuaded to keep a special relationship with the colonial power, but independence was to be complete. Indeed, the change of power in Lisbon was a consequence of the wars in Africa, and thus it led directly to recognition of the independence of Guinea-Bissau on 24 September 1974 and of Cape Verde on 5 July 1975. However, both countries have maintained close and vital economic ties with Portugal since independence. Portugal is Guinea-Bissau's primary trading partner (56.6 percent of imports and 45.3 percent of exports in 1990). *See* AFONSO, D.; AZAMBUJA, D.; AZURARA, G.; BARRETO, H.; CADAMOSTA, CAETANO, M.; CÃO, D.; COLUMBUS, C.; DAGAMA, V.; DE NOLI, A. and B.; EANNES, G.; ECONOMICS; FEITOR; GOMES, D. and F.; NATO; PIDE; PINTO, T.; POMBAL; RESISTENCE; SALAZAR, A.; SINTRA, P.; SPINOLA, A.; TARRAFAL; TRISTÃO, N. ZURARA, G.

PRINCE HENRY (1394–1460). Prince Henry, 'The Navigator,' was the son of King João I (1358–1433) and Philippa, daughter of the Englishman, John of Gaunt. Henry was responsible for organizing about one third of the early Portuguese exploration of the West African coast during the great age of Portuguese maritime innovation in the first half of the fifteenth century. Henry led the military expedition against Ceuta, Morocco in 1415 for the Royal Portuguese House of Avis. Stimulated by reports of the mysterious Christian, Prester John, and lured by the knowledge of gold mines feeding trans-Saharan trade, Prince Henry sent ships along the coast of Morocco looking for an easier route to the interior of Africa. Since Moors were still ruling some portions of Spanish Iberia and all of north Africa, they had controlled the trade to the east and had blocked Portuguese and European penetration of Africa. In

1434 ships of Prince Henry reached Cape Bojador (Saharan Arab Democratic Republic/Morocco), the furthest point reached by Portugal until that time due to the limitation of prevailing winds, navigational skills, and equipment. In 1436 Prince Henry led an unsuccessful military effort against Tangiers. In 1441 a ship captained by Antão Gonçalves (q.v.), sailing for Prince Henry, returned to Portugal with the first documented African slaves (Moors from an area probably along southern coastal Morocco). Prince Henry usually received twenty percent of slave cargos.

In 1453, Gomes Eanes de Azurara (q.v.), a well-known chronicler for Prince Henry, wrote his *Cronica de Guiné* which described some of the aspects of this early exploration and slave trading. In 1456 the Genoan captain Usodimare and the Venetian captain Cadamosta (q.v.) both sailed under Prince Henry's flag when they reached the Geba River (q.v.) in today's Guinea-Bissau. During the period 1419–1460 there were at least thirty-five voyages under the Portuguese flag. Of these, eight were initiated directly by Prince Henry, and two were co-sponsored by him, although at his death in 1460 he had never actually participated in an exploration mission, as it was not considered appropriate for a man of his status. *See* EXPLORERS AND TRAVELLERS.

R

RAMOS, DOMINGOS (JAO CA). Ramos was a hero of the liberation war (1963–1974) who died on 10 November 1966, aged thirty-one years, apparently from wounds resulting from a fierce assault on the Portuguese fortified camp at Madina do Boé on the eastern front. Born in Bissau (q.v.), he worked briefly as a hospital auxiliary before being compelled to join the colonial army. In 1957, he clandestinely joined the *Partido Africano da Independência de Guiné e Cabo Verde*, PAIGC, (q.v.), and in the aftermath of the Pijiguiti (q.v.) massacre of 3 August 1959, he left the colonial army to become an active nationalist agitator.

As a PAIGC militant, he was sent to the Xitole area (in the south) in 1961 to mobilize the population. In the *tabanca* (q.v.) of Satacuta, he managed to get the inhabitants to refuse to pay their taxes to the colonial authorities, an act which was promptly met with Portuguese brute force. Then, with a price on his head, Ramos escaped to Conakry, from which he was sent to Ghana for military training. Further military training took him, together with other PAIGC militants like Francisco Mendes (q.v.), Constantino Teixeira, João 'Nino' Vieira, and Osvaldo Vieira (qq.v.), to the Nanking Military Academy in the People's Republic of China in 1964, returning at the end of that year to be nominated as the commander of the eastern front.

He formed the first organized guerrilla fighting unit of the liberation struggle in December 1964. With some 600 men under his direct command, he carried out several attacks against Portuguese targets before the assault on the Madina do Boé fort which cost him his life. Charismatic and much respected by his men and peers, especially Amilcar Cabral (q.v.), Domingos Ramos was also a member of the political bureau of the PAIGC. His memory is commemorated in Guinea-Bissau by a fifty *pesos* banknote, a boarding school in Boé, an agricultural cooperative and *inter alia*, an avenue in Bissau. In Cape Verde, a *liceu* in Praia, São Tiago (q.v.) is named for him, as well as having his image on a coin.

RASSEMBLEMENT DÉMOCRATIQUE AFRICAIN DE LA GUINÉE (RDAG). This Mandinka-oriented, Senegalese-based organization led to the formation of the *Frente de Libertação*, FLG (q.v.), when it merged with the *Movimento de Libertação da Guiné*, MLG (q.v.), in 1961. In 1962 the FLG joined with *Frente de Luta Pela Independência Nacional da Guiné-Bissau*, FLING (q.v).

REGIME DO INDIGENATO. Although armed resistance to Portuguese 'pacification' efforts in Guinea came to a close by 1936, the colonial order still required several measures of coercion for its maintenance. These included the establishment of an administrative and legal structure as well as the imposition of Portuguese culture to create alienated individuals who would come to reject their own supposedly 'inferior' traditional values and institutions.

The *regime do indigenato* ('native' administration) was constructed to achieve these purposes, and it penetrated, to some degree, almost every *tabanca* (q.v.) to exercise tight control over the population subjugated by colonialism, especially as envisaged by the colonial architect António Enes. Briefly, the *indigenato* code was based on legal formulations began even before the *Estado Novo* of Portuguese fascism. It included the *Regulamento do Trabalho dos Indigenas* ('Native' Labor

Regulations) of 1899 and 1911 which legalized forced labor even though slavery (q.v.) had been officially abolished. It was justified that this measure would help to 'civilize' the 'natives.' The *Lei Organica da Administração Civil da Provincias Ultramarinas* (Civil Administration Law of Overseas Provinces) of 1914 stressed the importance of the *autoridades gentilicas* ('heathen authorities') in the colonial administration and proposed the establishment of a special judicial and political system for the so-called 'heathens' (*gentios*). The *Carta Organica da Guiné* (Organic Charter of Guinea) of 1917 formally divided the population of the territory into *indigenas* ('uncivilized natives') and *não-indigenas* ('civilized') peoples.

Regarding the *Carta Organica da Guiné*, it is interesting to note that in 1918 the colonial authorities set up an office of *Negócios Indigenas* (Native Affairs) in Bolama (q.v.), its first chief José Oliveira Ferreira Diniz, stressed that the new *politica indigena* (native policy), was designed to take advantage of the *'usos, costumes e instituções dos indigenas'* (practices, customs and institutions of the natives) and that the policy would be *'tutelar e benevolente'* (instructive and benevolent). It was also to be one of collaboration "since what the European lacks—physical resistance—is almost uniquely what the native can dispose"; one of a "policy of association, of the intelligence of the European who thinks and the hand of the native that executes" (Ferreira Diniz 1946, 4).

Later *Estado Novo* legislations like the *Estatuto Politico, Civil e Criminal dos Indigenas* (1929), the *Acto Colonial* (1930), the *Carta Organica do Império Colonial Português* (1933), and the *Reforma Administrativa Ultramarina* (1933), were all, in fact, consolidations of the previous regulations.

The *Indigenato* code was distinguishable from other colonial control mechanisms in that its provisions were applied administratively, without any recourse to a court of law. It was designed to punish swiftly and summarily, being devoid of any protracted procedures or appeals. Principally because of its simplicity and ease of application, it was indeed the control mechanism most often resorted to by the Portuguese colonial administrators in Guinea, Angola, and Mozambique. Although officially abolished in 1961, its demands and sanctions persisted until the last days of colonial rule, not to mention the brutal measures justified by counterinsurgency.

The operators of the *Regime do Indigenato* were the *administradores* and their immediate subordinates, the *chefes de posto*. These were the direct representatives of the Lisbon authorites on whom Portugal's colonial structure depended. To keep the *indigenas* under control, the use of pliable *regulos* (q.v.) and *chefes de tabancas* (village chiefs) was imperative. To enforce Portuguese authority in the administrative divisions termed the *circunscrições indigenas* (native circumscriptions), the *administradores* and the *chefes de postos* had at their disposal a brutal native police force known as the *cipaios*.

Usually each *chefe de posto* had at least two *cipaios* for his defense. These were often robust and ruthless African ex-soldiers in the Portuguese colonial army whose loyalty was measured by the zeal with which they could terrorize the subjugated into compliance. Under orders (and sometimes without) from their *chefes*, they would assault the *tabancas*, and arrest or severely punish the *gentios atrevidos* (bold natives), and seize livestock which would end up in the kitchens of the *posto*. Punishment was often carried out by means of the infamous *palmátoria* (q.v.), violently beaten on the hands and feet often until it bruised, drew blood, or broke bones.

The *regulos* and *chefes de tabancas* greatly facilitated the colonial state. These so-called *autoridades gentilicas* were, however, essentially auxiliary elements, because with colonial conquest and 'effective occupation,' there was only one effective authority in the *circunscrições indigenas* (and their subsections of *postos administrativos*), and that was Portuguese colonial authority itself.

REGULO. Paramount African chief, often incorporated into the system of colonial administration (*regime do indigenato*, q.v.). To a limited extent, *regulos* or *chefes de tabancas* (village chiefs) were inherited positions, but they were usually appointed by the colonial administration as civil servants, soldiers, police, or interpreters and were paid token salaries. They carried out the highly unpopular tasks of tax collection and labor recruitment and were assisted by armed police.

RELIGION. An estimated sixty to sixty-five percent of the population are animists, including Balantes, Pepels, Manjacos, Diolas, Bijagós, Nalus, Brames (qq.v.), and others. Most of the remainder are Muslim or have syncretic versions of Islam and African traditional religions, including the Fulas, Mandinkas, Beafadas, Susus (qq.v.), and several smaller groups. The Islamized sector is mostly located in the cattle-raising interior, while the animist groups are found more in the coastal regions and in certain parts of the interior. The Fula *jihads* were important in the introduction of Islam into Guinea-Bissau especially after the fall of Kaabu (q.v.).

There are a small number of Protestants and Catholics, but these are largely urban residents who had been exposed to Portuguese and Italian missionaries during the colonial period. Those Guineans of Cape Verdean extraction are almost all Catholics, as in the islands.

The government is particularly tolerant of the religious diversity in Guinea and takes care to allocate time on the national radio and in the national newspaper to a broad sector of religious offerings and regular programs. For example, on Sunday morning Catholic church services are often broadcast live on the radio, while on Fridays, the prayer services of the main Muslim mosque is also broadcast live. One also frequently finds large sections of the newspapers devoted to cultural or historical presentation of animist or Islamic traditions and practices. Unlike its largely Islamic neighbors to the north (Senegal, Mali [q.v.], and Mauretania), or a number of Catholic, Protestant, or animist-dominated West African nations to the south, no single religious grouping possesses special political or social power, so that all religions are treated in a balanced manner. Social or educational programs that are independent of the government, such as Islamic schools, animist ceremonies, Protestant or Catholic churches, and missionary societies are generally allowed to operate freely and without interference from the state. *See* GUINEA-BISSAU: FOREIGN RELATIONS.

RESISTANCE: TRADITIONS OF. Guinea-Bissau is famous for the successful armed liberation struggle (1963–1974) which its people, under the leadership of the legendary Amilcar Cabral, conducted against Portuguese colonial domination. This conflict was the culmination of a long tradition of resistance in the territory, a tradition which obviously did not start or end with Portuguese colonial conquest and domination.

Throughout the territory's history, the subject peoples offered active and passive opposition to injustice and oppression. Romantic interpretations of African history notwithstanding, most of the existing pre-colonial states and empires rested upon relationships of domination and exploitation. They were mainly polities in which the subjugated were sometimes the victims of heavy exactions, harsh oppression, and enslavement.

Guinean resistance to alien domination, whether African or

European, has been long-standing. Virtually all the people in the centralized and non-centralized polities, in the state and stateless societies, found themselves obliged to resist. On the one hand, the rulers and ruling classes felt the need to protect their power, privileges, and vital economic interests; on the other, their subjects, and the peoples of the chiefless and stateless societies, found it necessary to fight to prevent the expropriation of their land, labor, and wealth, the annihilation of their culture, and, *inter alia*, their enslavement. Indeed, the interrelated issues of freedom, independence, and sovereignty were the motive force behind the sometimes fierce armed confrontation to foreign domination.

However, the pattern of relationships between the invaded and the invaders did not tend inevitably towards armed confrontation. Collaboration with the foreigners was also principally prompted by the desire of the local ruling classes to safeguard their power and privileges, and on the other hand, the determination of the masses to escape from the despotism of local rulers and to be free from bondage and other forms of exploitative relationships. In this regard, such a strategy is clearly a form of resistance.

RESISTANCE: PRE-COLONIAL AFRICAN KINGDOMS. Even before the establishment of the Portuguese 'effective occupation' in the territory during the early years of the twentieth century, the numerous wars of conquest which resulted in the appearance and disappearance of various kingdoms and chieftaincies met with a complex variety of responses; these ranged from open confrontation to close collaboration.

Of the prominent pre-colonial polities, the most powerful and most durable was the Mandinka (q.v.) Kingdom of Kaabu (q.v.), founded in the mid-thirteenth century as a vassal state of the Mali (q.v.) Empire. With its capital at Kansala, in eastern Guinea-Bissau, it became an empire in its own right by the time of the fall of Mali in the sixteenth century. Exercising political control over a vast region which stretched from south of the river Gambia to parts of Guinea-Conakry, its influences affected, directly or indirectly, all the groups in Guinea-Bissau today.

Kaabu's strategies of expansion, effective domination, and economic survival, which included imposed overlordship, forced Islamization, and engagement in the slave trade, were much resisted by local groups like the Banyuns, Djolas, Pepels,

Manjacos, Mancanhas (also known as Brames), Beafadas and Balantas (qq.v.). While this resistance initially took the form of armed confrontation and migration to the littoral regions, it also entailed cooperation and collaboration.

Indeed, in the case of the Balantas, the largest ethnic group in the country, their stubborn resistance is implied in the name which the Mandinka rulers of Kaabu gave them: '*balanta*,' which, in the Mandinka language, means 'those who refuse.' That is to say, those who refused to be conquered militarily or to be dominated culturally.

The strategy of cooperation and collaboration adopted by some of these groups resulted sometimes in their extensive Mandinkanization. This is especially the case with the Beafadas, a group which has been particularly affected by Mandinka expansion and domination, to the extent that today it is almost totally 'Mandinkanized.' The Balantas offer yet another example. Although generally regarded by the Mandinkas as a 'stubborn' people, a significant number nevertheless cooperated and collaborated with the new imperial order, resulting in a 'Mandinkanized' sub-group known as the *Balanta-Mane*.

But the most formidable challenge to Mandinka dominance, besides the relentless internal power struggles among the ruling classes of Kaabu, remained that provided by the Fulas (q.v.), a pastoralist group whose presence in the territory (in appreciable numbers) is said to date back to the fifteenth century.

Arriving already differentiated into masters and slaves, cattle owners, craftsmen, and commoners, the new settlers readily submitted to the rules and demands of the Mandinka rulers. The *Fulbe-ribe*, or 'free-born' Fulas, promptly paid heavy tributes in goods, cattle and slaves. The treatment they received in return, however, was generally harsh and cruel, being subjected to extortionate payments of all sorts and often physically abused. Their prolonged indignation and anger erupted into revolts and rebellions in the nineteenth century, culminating in the establishment of such polities as Forrea (q.v.) in the southwestern corner of present-day Guinea-Bissau.

The establishment of Fula independence was achieved especially with the help of Fula slaves and former slaves, the *Fulbe-djiabe*, or 'captive' Fulas. Also crucial was the support rendered by Fula warlords from the Futa Jallon (q.v.) Confederation, a theocratic state established in the early nineteenth century as a result of the united front of Muslim Fula leaders in Futa Jallon (in the modern Republic of Guinea-Conakry) in the *jihad* waged against the 'infidels' of Kaabu. In Forrea, it particularly meant the displacement and dispossession of the local inhabitants and ruling classes, the Beafadas, together with their *protegées*, the Nalus.

With their growing power and the deep-rooted resentment of Mandinka dominance, the Fulas became increasingly bent on destroying Kaabu. Greatly weakened by the rebellions of provincial rulers, the downfall of the kingdom was only a matter of time. The decisive battle, in which the ruler of Kaabu, *Mansa* (King) Djanke Waali, faced with overwhelming defeat committed suicide, took place in Kansala, in 1867.

However, shortly after the establishment of Fula hegemony in Forrea, a civil war broke out between masters and slaves and former slaves, who were determined to shake off oppression and exploitation by any means necessary. As the ensuing bloody conflict raged furiously, from about 1878 to 1890, cooperation and collaboration with the aspiring Portuguese imperialists became a necessary means for emancipation.

Eager to bolster their weak position, the Portuguese promptly supported the *Fulbe-djiabe* in their revolt against the *Fulbe-ribe* dominance. However, both these group of Fulas, together with the Mandinkas, would later be valuable allies of Portugal (q.v.) in her desperate attempts to 'pacify' her proclaimed territory of *Guiné Portuguesa*.

RESISTANCE: ANTI-COLONIAL ROOTS. Regarding Luso-Guinean relations, at the heart of the dramatic encounter, which dates back to the arrival of the Portuguese in the fifteenth century, the inevitable conflict also revolved around the interrelated issues of sovereignty, and independence.

It was in 1444 that the Portuguese caravels under the command of Nuño Tristão (q.v.) on his third voyage of 'discovery,' reached modern Senegal or in the westernmost *'Terra dos Pretos'* (Land of the Blacks) in Portuguese, which was derived from the same but earlier Arabic reference to *'Bilad as Sudan'*. Two years later, on his fourth voyage, he and nineteen of his men were killed by some 'unfriendly natives' somewhere between the rivers Sine-Saloum (q.v.) (in Senegal) and Gambia (Teixeira da Mota 1946, 333). An enthusiastic slaver, who in Portuguese colonial parlance 'discovered' the territory today Guinea-Bissau, Tristão symbolizes that brand of adventurism which thenceforth descended upon the West African coast and gave rise to hostility and conflict between African and European, besides intensifying the exploitation of the masses.

From the time Portugal, anxious to monopolize the trade in slaves, gold, ivory and other valuable commodities, claimed exclusive rights over the region it designated '*Guiné de Cabo Verde*' (Guinea of Cape Verde), originally the coastal area between Senegal and Sierra Leone, but reduced over the centuries to roughly that of present-day Guinea-Bissau), the Portuguese and Africans found themselves locked in conflict. On the one hand, the local ruling classes fiercely resisted any encroachments on their land and their sovereign rights, while on the other, ordinary people found themselves having to resist enslavement and other forms of exploitation more than ever.

Indeed, from the arrival of the Portuguese in the fifteenth century to the dawn of the 'scramble' for colonies in Africa, the most important struggle in the country was that waged by the African masses against the transatlantic slave trade, which stimulated rivalry and competition between the local rulers and ruling classes. Resistance to the seemingly endless slave wars was widespread, in spite of the fact that the population of the territory was dispersed over vast rural areas, unorganized and divided not only by space but also by ethnicity, culture, and beliefs. The strategies adopted ranged from open conflicts (defensive and offensive postures) to flight and suicide.

Parallel to the struggles of the African masses against the slave trade was the stubborn resistance of local rulers against Portuguese attempts to undermine their sovereignties and independence and usurp their powers and privileges. The death of Nuño Tristão in 1446 should have left the Lisbon authorities with no doubt about the firm resolve of the Africans to resist hostile encroachments on their lands, but the Portuguese were determined to create at least an informal empire.

Placing greater emphasis on the use of diplomacy rather than warfare, Portugal was able to establish relations with a number of African potentates along the West African coast. This enabled Portuguese merchants from the Cape Verde Islands, 'discovered' in 1460 and settled forthwith, to conduct trade there.

However, in spite of the Portuguese Crown's pretensions, implied in the grand title of *Senhor do Comércio da Guiné* (Lord of the Guinea Trade) which Portugal's monarchs came to assume following the 'discoveries,' the trade was regulated by the African rulers, who levied *daxas* (a corruption of the Portuguese word *taxas*, meaning taxes) on the Cape Verdean traders, who, increasingly, flouted Lisbon's numerous commercial regulations concerning the 'Guinea trade.'

These Lisbon-branded 'illegal' traders were known as *lan-çados* (q.v.), apparently because they were 'thrown, or out-caste' among the native inhabitants of the mainland and, ac-cording to the accounts of an indignant Portuguese Jesuit in the early seventeenth century, became "as forgetful of God and their salvation as if they were the actual negroes and heathens of the land" (Guerreiro 1930, 400). They played a vital role in exploding the myth of Portugal's dominance in the region. Indeed, the very fact that these mainly white Portu-guese men had to 'go native' is evidence of the strength of African resistance. Regarded simply as *hospedes* (guests), they were obliged to respect the laws and customs of the societies which hosted them. Their flouting of Portugal's commercial laws was not so much lack of patriotism on their part, or uncontrollable greed for profits, as it was a reflection of the firm grip which the Africans had on their societies.

Yet the *lançados* were also instrumental in the establishment of a Portuguese foothold in Guinea-Bissau, by virtue of their intimate relationships with the indigenous people and the Afri-can environment. It was in Cacheu (q.v.) where the earliest Portuguese entrenchment efforts were made. In 1588 the *lan-çados* constructed a stockaded settlement which was encour-aged and supervised by the Portuguese Crown though its commercial representative, the *feitor* of the Cacheu/São Do-mingos river trade, Manuel Lopes Cardoso, who used clever subterfuges to get the authorization of King Chapala, the local ruler. Realizing that the 'fort' seriously compromised his kingdom's sovereignty and independence, the King mobilized his warriors and attacked it in 1590. The battle lasted three days and the angry *Buramos* (the Manjaco-Pepel-Mancanha people) apparently suffered heavy losses.

Nevertheless, the issue of forts remained highly sensitive and contentious. The local ruling classes were not slow to perceive that it undermined their power and authority and constituted a violation of their sovereignty. Consequently, they were quick to oppose all fortification attempts with all the means at their disposal, including both open conflict and pas-sive resistance. Among the strategies of non-violent resistance often resorted to were the denial of access to sources of fresh water and building materials, the closing of fairs and markets, and the refusal to permit the use of local labor.

Although by 1630 the Captaincy of Cacheu was already established and Captain-Majors (representatives of the Portu-guese Crown) began to be regularly appointed, Guinean resistance to Portuguese entrenchment efforts never ceased to manifest itself. Fundamentally, for centuries, the local rulers maintained their independence and sovereignty, demanding and receiving taxes and duties from their 'guests,' the Portuguese—in spite of the construction of forts and stockaded settlements.

In 1670, the myth of Portuguese sovereignty in the territory was exploded by a dejected *Conselho Ultramarino* (Overseas Council, a body which advised the Portuguese Crown) which noted that, somehow, the *Praça* (fortified settlement) of Cacheu had been 'miraculously' kept and that notwithstanding the Portuguese monarch's grand title of 'Lord of Guinea,' Portugal had nothing there more than 'a small piece of land,' maintained at a cost; that her flags were only allowed to fly over the settlement because she paid "a tribute or fee to a Negro King" (quoted in Silva Teixeira 1950, 103). One hundred and sixty years later, such sentiment was echoed by an equally despondent observer who stressed that the Pepels of Bissau had "neither respect nor fear" of the Portuguese, whose flag they allowed to fly over the *Praça* "because it is in their interest" (Chelmichi 1841, 122). Indeed, in spite of the imposing fort of *São José*, yet another disappointed observer noted that it was the Pepel King of Bissau (q.v.) "who makes the law in the settlement," who settled disputes and imposed fines, while the Portuguese Governor was "a mere spectator" (Pereira Barreto 1843,15).

The constant references, in Portuguese official reports, to the 'boldness' of the *gentios*, the 'insults' and 'injuries' they inflicted, and the 'decadence' of the *Praças* and *Presídios* reflect not only the fragile Portuguese position in the territory but also the effective Guinean challenge to Portugal's imperial ambitions.

The examples of 'boldness,' 'insults,' and 'injuries' consisted of actions taken by the local rulers and their subjects against the Portuguese presence in the *Praças* and *Presídios*, such as attacks, arrests, imprisonments, political assassinations, and open revolts. These include the arrest and imprisonment of the Captain-Major of Cacheu, José Gonçalves de Oliveira, in 1684; the arrest and death in custody of the Captain-Major of Bissau, José Pinheiro, in 1698; the assassination of a judge of the *Praça* of Bissau in 1842; the attacks on the *Praças* of Cacheu and Bissau by the Manjacos and Pepels respectively, in 1844; the revolt of the *grumetes* of the *Presídios* of Farim, in 1846; and the Geba (q.v.) trader revolt of

1853; the Manjaco attack on the *Praça* of Cacheu in 1856; widespread territorial uprisings in 1860; supression of Bissagos resistance and the joint Manjaco/Pepel assault on the *Praça* of Cacheu in 1861; the assassination of Governor Alvaro Teles Caldeira in 1871 which preceded a revolt; the 1874 Mandinka offensive led by Fodé Kaba in the Casamance; and the Felupe assault on the *Presídio* of Bolor in 1878.

The attack on Bolor prompted the dispatching of over 100 Portuguese soldiers and African auxiliaries and resulted in the 'disaster' of Bolor, with the massacre of the greater part of the expeditionary force. The immediate effect of the 'disaster' was the 'separation' of the territory from Cape Verde on 18 March 1879 and the adoption of a bold strategy of intervention in the internecine wars which raged in the newly proclaimed 'province' of *Guiné Portuguesa* among the Fulas and between these and other groups like the Beafadas and the Mandinkas. The new militancy actually succeeded in securing a large reservoir of African auxiliaries, indispensable in the intensified 'pacification' wars.

RESISTANCE: TO 'PACIFICATION'/'EFFECTIVE' OCCUPATION. A new military was inaugurated in 1879, on the eve of the partition of Africa, with naval bombardments of Pepel and Balanta (q.v.) settlements around Bissau, among other operations. Elated with the favorable outcome, the Portuguese seriously turned their attention to the question of 'pacifying' the whole territory. Between 1878 and 1886, a series of campaigns was launched against the Felupes, Manjacos, *Fulbe-ribe* of Gam-Suomo, the Beafadas of Jabada, the Nalus of Cadica, the *Fulbe-ribe* of Bolola, the Balantas of Nhacra and, *inter alia*, the Pepels of Bissau (Biombo) and Cacheu (Cacanda).

Nevertheless, despite the ruthlessness and brutality of the 'pacification' efforts, Portuguese military strength remained fundamentally weak. The spirit of resistance remained strong, and various acts of defiance continued to be registered, particularly among the Manjacos of Caio, the Beafadas of the Rio Grande de Buba, and the *Fulbe-djiabe* on the Rio Geba around Sambel Nhanta. In the *Praças* and *Presídios*, the 'colonial' army was kept in a permanent state of alert as the so-called *gentios* perpetrated various 'insults' and 'abuses.' Indeed, Portugal's imperial ambition was checkmated particularly by the territorial ambitions of African rulers like Musa Molo (q.v.).

Although in 1886 the Portuguese, with the help of rebellious

Fula warlords, scored a decisive victory against Musa Molo, the new militancy had already began to lose its impetus. The defiant inhabitants of the territory remained not only unsubmissive but actively hostile to the Portuguese presence. With the Berlin Conference declaration of 'effective occupation' as condition for recognition as colonial power, the desperate efforts which were made during the 1890's and early 1900's were riddled with more tragedies than triumphs. Most of the 'pacification' campaigns launched during this period ended frustrated or 'disastrous.'

In 1890, the campaign against the rebellious ruler, Moli Boia, was frustrated when this Fula warlord escaped to neighboring territory. The following year, the offensive against the Pepels of Bissau (Intim) ended disastrously for the Portuguese, with the deaths of four white officers (including the Commandant of the garrison of *São José*, Captain Joaquim António do Carmo Azevedo), three sergeants, forty-one soldiers, and an undisclosed number of African auxiliaries. Six months after the 'disaster' of Intim, a punitive campaign was again waged against Moli Bioa, and once again it was frustrated with the desertion, after a few encounters, of a substantial number of African auxiliaries. In 1891 a campaign was launched against the Balantas, and almost continuous battles took place against the Pepels who blocked the Cacheu river. In November 1894, a joint Pepel/Balanta assault on the *Praça* of Bissau was only prevented from overwhelming the settlement by the superior firepower of three gunboats anchored off the port. The punitive/'pacification' campaign which was launched the following year failed in its objective of capturing the Pepel stronghold of Antula, notwithstanding the signing of a 'Treaty of Submission,' on 22 July 1894, with bold conditions which included the payment of a poll tax (unprecedented in the territory) as 'tribute of submission' and the surrender of all weapons. The conditions were never observed.

The requirement of a poll tax was one of the main causes of the disastrous Portuguese encounter with the inhabitants of the region of Oio in 1897. A few months before the 'disaster' of Oio, the campaign to oblige the Manjacos of Caio to stop demanding the payment of *daxas* from traders and vessels passing through their territory ended up frustrated by the guerrilla tactics of the Manjaco warriors.

As the twentieth century dawned and *Guiné Portuguesa* remained ineffectively occupied and only 'Portuguese' in name, the Portuguese became increasingly desperate. In 1900, the determination to oblige the Bijagos of Canhabaque island to recognize Portuguese authority failed with the hasty withdrawal of the expeditionary force only a week after it disembarked. The following year, the attempt to avenge the 'disaster' of Bolor and 'pacify' the region also failed to oblige the Felupes to recognize Portuguese authority. In 1902, the brutal campaign to avenge the 'disaster' of Oio and 'pacify' the region nevertheless left the inhabitants with their familiar defiant posture and Portuguese sovereignty yet to be established.

The introduction of the *imposto de palhota* (hut tax) in 1903 and the determination to enforce its payment—the success of which would give at least the impression that Portuguese sovereignty had been established—provoked a number of uprisings: the Manjacos of Churo (1904); the Bijagós of Formosa island (1906). In 1907 the Beafadas led by Infali Sonco revolted in the Geba (q.v.) region, thus cutting off the coast from the interior towns of Bafatá and Gabú (qq.v.). Fulas in Cuor revolted from 1907 to 1908 requiring two reinforced Portuguese columns to put down the insurgents. Revolts of the Beafadas of Chime, Badora, and Quinara took place in 1908 as did those of the Felupes of Varela, the Balantas around Gole, and the Pepels of Bissau. The rebellion of the Beafada warlord and ruler of Cuor, Infali Sonco, in 1907 and 1908, was apparently motivated by his desire to free his realm of the *imposto de palhota*.

The proclamation of a Portuguese Republic in 1910 brought no change in Portugal's self-assigned, but much frustrated mission to 'civilize' the *gentios*. The determination to 'pacify' the territory and fulfill the condition of 'effective occupation' not only remained strong but would be given new impetus with the arrival of Captain João Teixeira Pinto.

When Teixeira Pinto arrived in the territory in 1912, he immediately noted that Portuguese authority was 'purely nominal' in the regions of the Balantas, the Manjacos, the Mancanhas/Brames, the Pepels and the 'Oincas.' Determined to 'pacify' those regions at all costs, he enlisted the support of the infamous Senegalese fugitive Abdul Injai (q.v., also known as Abdul Ndaiye), whose ruthless band of mercenaries (consisting mainly of wanted criminals, draft dodgers and colonial army deserters particularly from Senegal and Guinea-Conakry) was crucial in reversing Portugal's long series of military defeats and 'disasters' in the territory. In three years (1913–1915) and four very bloody 'pacification' campaigns, Abdul Injai's large and well-equipped phalanx (some 1,600 men at its peak), supported by hundreds of auxiliaries led mainly by Mandinka and Fula warlords from other parts of the territory, as well as a small but also well-armed Portuguese combat unit commanded by Teixeira Pinto himself, broke the stiff resistances of the 'Oincas' (1913); the Manjacos and Mancanhas/Brames (1914); the Balantas (1914); and the Pepels (1915). These wars were characterized by orgies of atrocities and a level of violence which, even in the context of 'pacification' campaigns in Africa, amounted to excessive cruelty and gross carnage.

With the defeats of the resisters on the mainland, the Portuguese concentrated their efforts on 'pacifying' the Bijagos archipelago in order to satisfy the condition of 'effective occupation.' Yet, in spite of easy access to the latest weapons, the use of air power, and a large number of African auxiliaries at their disposal, this took three major campaigns, in 1917, 1925, and 1935 to 1936, at the end of which the Portuguese themselves had to admit that the task was no simple police operation.

The devastating defeats of the territory's defiant but disunited peoples was due largely to the invading column's possession of superior weapons, including machine guns and artillery. To the overwhelming superiority in firepower was added a superiority in numbers, as each demonstration of the effectiveness of the invaders' weapons made African auxiliaries, attracted by the promise of wealth from the booty taken in conquest, easily recruited. In contrast, the invaded could only count on their physical bravery and, in most cases, their homemade flintlock muskets (known as *longas*), given the centuries-old Portuguese policy of arms embargo to the territory now given new impetus by the pronouncements of the Brussels Conference in 1890 banning the sale of firearms to Africans. The enormous disadvantage of the muzzleloading musket, which took time to reload after each round had been fired, is quite obvious. Furthermore, the absence of multi-ethnic unity and consciousness of a common struggle against a common enemy among the invaded, meant the absence of alliances which would have obliged the invaders to fight on several fronts at the same time. Nevertheless, notwithstanding the tremendous odds which weighed heavily against them, the success of the resistances of the Guineans lies in the very fact that the Portuguese and their allies, in spite of their technical superiority, not only did not always win the battles, but indeed took so long to conquer them.

RESISTANCE, PASSIVE ANTI-COLONIAL. Though finally subjugated, the spirit of defiance of the conquered remained. Passive resistance became the response to colonial domination. Throughout the brief period of colonial rule (less than sixty years in the case of the mainland and forty years in the case of the Bijagós archipelago), the colonized Guineans struggled ceaselessly against such impositions as *autoridades gentilicas* (native authorities), forced labor and forced cultivation of cash crops, hut and poll taxes, military service, and miserable wages and work conditions.

The most pervasive passive resistance was that against the myriad colonial taxes. Aside from 'hut' taxes, there were charges placed on burials, palm trees, livestock, censuses, and a wide variety of fines for petty colonial infractions. During the early phase of colonial rule, mass cross-regional and cross-border withdrawals and the burning of huts to avoid registration for tax payment were the dominant forms of protest. Emigration and evasion were also the most common modes of revolt against forced labor, as well as the extortions and violence of the local colonial officials and the imposed 'native authorities.' Tax revolts erupted in the Bijagós in 1917, and despite a declaration of their defeat more tax revolts took place in 1924 and 1925. Likewise, in the 1930's in the Bijagós a fresh wave of tax revolts sprang up, most notable the 1936 revolt.

With regards to forced cultivation of cash crops, in particular the cultivation of peanuts, resistance clearly manifested itself by the constant official references to the people as *indolentes* ('lazy-bones'), when such fact was itself clearly contradicted by the large seasonal exodus to neighboring territories to cultivate the very crops they would not cultivate in their homelands. Groups like the Felupes (q.v.) stubbornly refused to be engaged in peanut production. In response to low wages and terrible working conditions, Guinean workers also resisted exploitation as best they could, including feigning illness, working as slowly as possible, and terminating employment before end of contracts. Although strikes were rare, being illegal, disgruntled sailors and dockworkers at the port of Pijiguiti in Bissau (q.v.) nevertheless effected a brief work stoppage in 1956, which resulted in wage increases, followed three years later with a full scale strike (3 August 1959). Viewed with the greatest contempt by the colonial authorities, it was brutally suppressed with numerous deaths and injuries.

RESISTANCE: NATIONAL LIBERATION STRUGGLE. The 'Pijiguiti (q.v.) Massacre,' like the famous 'Boston Massacre' in the United States of America, became a vital turning point. The *Partido Africano da Independência de Guiné e Cabo Verde*, PAIGC (q.v.), founded three years earlier, decided in a secret meeting held on 19 September 1959 that liberation from Portuguese colonial domination could only be achieved through armed struggle based in the countryside. Guinean resistance had thus returned to armed confrontation. Four years after the event, a protracted war of liberation started.

Although the *Frente de Luta Pela Independência Nacional da Guiné-Bissau*, FLING (q.v.), could claim that its members actually initiated the armed struggle with attacks on Portuguese posts in the northern towns of São Domingos, Susana, Varela, and Bigene in 1961, the fact remains that it was militarily ineffective, having won no major battles against the colonial forces or liberated any territory. On the other hand, the well-prepared guerilla operations launched by the PAIGC in the southern regions of the country, inaugurated by the attack on the Portuguese garrison at Tité on 23 January 1963, resulted not only in some major military victories (notably, the Battle of Como Island in 1964 and the capture of the Portuguese military base at Madina de Boé in 1969), but also in liberating about two-thirds of the territory and half the total population six years later and establishing, in those liberated areas, alternative and radically different political and administrative structures, as well as economic, educational, and judicial systems.

By the early 1970's, in spite of the swollen size of the Portuguese military (some 40,000 regular troops), its supremacy in the air, and its use of napalm and white phosphorous bombs, the PAIGC's military success was evidenced by the fact that the colonial army, which was confined to a few urban centers and fortified camps in the interior, was unable to regain lost territory. Guerilla units were boldly attacking principal towns like Farim, Bafatá (q.v.), and Bissau. The assassination of Amilcar Cabral on 20 January 1973, the movement's celebrated leader, only hastened the departure of the Portuguese, with an intensified campaign which resulted in the seizure of the large Portuguese garrison at Guiledge (q.v.), in the southern region of Tombali on 25 May 1973 and, with the acquisition of new anti-aircraft weapons, the downing of a significant number of warplanes. On 24 September 1973, the People's National Assembly which met in Medina do Boé formally proclaimed the Republic of Guinea-Bissau.

It should be noted that the protracted bloody struggle resulted not only in the declaration of an independent state of

Guinea-Bissau, but also contributed significantly to the downfall of the Fascist dictatorship in Portugal (q.v.) on 25 April 1974, the independence of Cape Verde on 5 July 1975, and the dismantling of the Portuguese Empire.

RESISTÊNCIA DA GUINÉ-BISSAU/MOVIMENTO BAFATA (RGB-MB). This new political party was founded on 27 July 1986 in Lisbon, Portugal (q.v.) and was legalized on 26 December 1991. The leader of the RGB-MB is Dr. Domingos Fernandes Gomes, a gastrointestinal specialist and former clinical director (1984–1986) of *Hospital Simões Mendes*, who resigned his post to protest the 1986 executions of the accused coupplotters (these included a close friend of his, Viriato Pan, who had served as a former Attorney General). The motto of the party is: 'Peace, Progress and Liberty.'

RICE (Arroz [Port.], Mancarra [Crioulo]). Rice (Oryza sp.) has long been an important staple in the agriculture (q.v.) of Sudanic regions, along with millet and sorghum. Both wild and cultivated forms may be found. *Oryza breviligulata* is considered to be the wild ancestor of *Oryza glaberrima* which is cultivated on the Middle Niger by Mandinka (q.v.) peoples and by the coastal Senegambians (q.v.). *O. glaberrima* may have been cultivated as early as 1500 BC. *Oryza sativa* is a much later Asiatic species which is widely cultivated today. Although regions as far north as Tekrur grew rice in the Middle Ages, it is grown more extensively as one moves south and toward the coastal wetlands inhabited by Mandinkas, Balantas, or Susus (qq.v.). In these wetter areas rice is the only suitable starch crop. Approximately thirty percent of the total cultivated acreage in Guinea-Bissau (q.v.) is devoted to rice farming. Rice is generally not grown in Cape Verde because of inadequate water and inappropriate soils.

This tall grass is grown as a grain crop in flooded paddies with extensive irrigation canals throughout much of coastal Guinea-Bissau. In some wet delta areas rice may grow wild and other species of upland rice will grow on dry land like other grains. Rice is commonly served with chicken or fish and with a palm oil sauce. Rice is known as *malu* in Balanta, *malo* in Wolof, *mano* in the Mande language, *maro* in Fula, and as *umane* in Manjaco or Brame.

Before the war, the colonial economy (q.v.) produced over 100,000 tons of rice annually. Not only did this meet domestic needs, but it generated sufficient surplus for export to Cape

Verde, Portugal, Gambia, Senegal, and Angola. In the mid–1960's rice production fell to about 30,000 tons per year, and by 1967 production reached only 19,000 tons. As the liberated zones expanded the Portuguese were finally forced to begin to import rice. Just before independence in 1974 the colonial imports to Guinea-Bissau reached 35,000 tons. By 1976 a small rice surplus was already being generated, and imports had been substantially reduced, but the 1977–1980 drought devastated rice production, forcing the government to rely increasingly on rice imports which amounted to 13,000 tons in 1977, 30,000 tons in 1978, and 82,000 tons for 1981. Normal rainfall in 1982 and 1983 lessened rice imports in those years, but drought in 1983 forced the government to import 42,000 tons.

S

SADI. *See* ABDUL RAHMAN AL-SADI.

SALAZAR, DR. ANTÓNIO DE OLIVEIRA (1889–27 July 1970). Salazar was the Prime Minister of Portugal (q.v.) from 1932 until 1968, when he was incapacitated by a stroke. Following the overthrow of the Portuguese Crown in 1910 and instability of the Republican government which led to the 1926 coup, Salazar came to be the Finance Minister from 1926 to 1932, when he became the Prime Minister of Portugal. In 1933, Salazar and Dr. Marcelo Caetano (q.v.) were the chief architects of the absolutist Portuguese constitution and of the *Estado Novo* policy which maintained Fascist control of industry, labor, and the press in Portugal and in their African colonies.

SALOUM (SALUM). This Serer (q.v.) kingdom in Senegal is linked to the Gelwar (Gelewar) matrilineage of Kaabu (q.v.). While relatively small in extent, it was economically strong through the slave trade. The French Governor of Senegal, Faidherbe (q.v.), made some effort to control Saloum in 1859, but the movement of Islamic revivalism led by Al-Haj Umar Tall (q.v.) and his local followers was strong in Saloum; it was not until 1898 that it was brought fully under French colonial rule.

The allied kingdom of Sine (Sin) was perhaps founded by Maisa Wali Jon, who was also related to the Gelwar lineage of fifteenth century Kaabu. Sine on the right bank of the Saloum river was originally an area of Jolof strength, but this was steadily eroded from as early as the eleventh or twelveth century with Serer immigration from Futa Toro (q.v.). Serer immigrants increased substantially as refugees from wars with Coli Tenguella (q.v.) in the late fifteenth century. By the eighteenth and nineteenth centuries, if not before, Sine and Saloum were closely linked by Serer culture and by slave trading along the Upper Guinea coast.

While the former territories of Sine and Saloum do not overlap with the present borders of Guinea-Bissau, the earlier fifteenth and sixteenth century Portuguese *lançados* (q.v.) in Senegambia relied on these two kingdoms to produce slaves. Their linkage to Kaabu also gives them relevance to Guinea-Bissau.

SAMA KOLI (KALEMANKOTO BAA SAANE). The first King of the Mandinka state of Kaabu (qq.v.), Sama Koli was either the son or grandson of Tiramakhan Traore (q.v.), a general of Sundiata of Mali (q.v.). Sama Koli married Nyaaling of Bonje and continued the matrilineal line of Kaabu Kings with their son Saarafa Nyaaling Jeenung, his son Kuntinka Sira Bula Jeenung, and his son, Saamanka Dala Jeenung.

SÃO TIAGO. (15° 5'N, 23° 38'W). The largest island (851 sq. km.) of the Cape Verdean archipelago. This island is rocky and mountainous with some permanent sources of fresh water. The present capital is Praia (25,000 population) on a beach from which it draws its name. The former capital was at Ribeira Grande now known as the ruined city and fort of Cidade Velha.

São Tiago was first noted by the Portuguese in May 1460 by the ships of António De Noli and Diogo Gomes (qq.v.). Within a few years the first permanent settlers from the Algarve went to São Tiago and founded Ribeira Grande as the first capital. A commerce in slaves from Guinea grew to develop the island and to become an important export. By 1466 settlers and *lançados* (q.v.) traded freely in African slaves and products, soon resulting in the *Crioulo* (q.v.) population characteristic of the islands. As a consequence of this long history, São Tiago is considered to have the most African population of the archipelago. As an example of the scale of the trade, between 1514 and 1516 almost 3,000 slaves were landed at Ribeira Grande. The relative prosperity and autonomy of the Captaincies on São Tiago resulted, in 1564, in the rule reverting back to the Crown for a fuller monopolization of island and coastal trade. This oscillation and competition between island autonomy and colonial monopolies remained a central theme through most of Cape Verdean history.

Ribeira Grande reached a permanent population of 1,500 by 1572, although the interior town of Santa Catarina was already larger by this time. The slave plantation system was deeply entrenched, with a few dozen 'whites' and 'mestiços' in full authority using a small group of 'free Africans' as overseers who regulated some ninety percent of the African slaves population.

Aside from the central role of slavery (q.v.) in the economy, São Tiago was also a common stopping place for fresh water for ships going to South America or down the West African coast. Local production of livestock and plant dyes such as urzella and indigo (q.v.) were sometimes important. São Tiago horses were much prized for riding and in slave exchange. Given the long and late importance of slavery to Cape Verde, it is ironic that Matthew Perry's anti-slavery 'African Squadron' (q.v.) was based in São Tiago in the 1840's through the late 1850's.

SÃO TOMÉ. Discovered in 1471, the 'Cacao Islands' of São Tomé and Príncipe in the Gulf of Guinea were administered as one colony by the Portuguese, who set up a plantation economy on the two islands using laborers contracted primarily from Angola and the Cape Verde Islands. Conditions on these coffee and cacao-producing islands were so poor and the means of recruitment so coercive that the labor migrations to São Tomé and Príncipe did not differ much from the system of slavery (q.v.) which preceded it. With the official emancipation of slavery in 1869 the contract labor system emerged and continued well into the 1950's. Forced emigration to 'the south,' as the *Crioulos* (q.v.) termed it, was a desperate and despised alternative to the threat of famine. The laborers worked exhausting hours routinely suffering the abuses of torture, beatings, and chains. Disease was also rampant. This form of recruitment was prohibited in the Barlavento Islands so that the bulk of the workers came from the *badius* (q.v.) of the islands of São Tiago (q.v.) and Fogo.

SARACOTES (Saracole). This very small group of the Soninke (q.v.) branch of the Mande stock may be found in small clusters between Gabú (Nova Lamego, [q.v.]) and Bafatá.

SENEGAL. *See* GUINEA BISSAU: FOREIGN RELATIONS; SALOUM.

SENEGAMBIANS. This large cluster of the coastal, Atlantic stock of the Niger-Congo (or Nigritic) peoples includes virtually all of those people of Guinea-Bissau who are of neither Fula nor Mandinka (q.v.) stocks. The Senegambians include the Balantas, Banyuns, Biafadas, Bijagós, Diolas, Nalus, Pepels, Brames/Mankanyas, Manjacos, Serer (qq.v.), and Wolof. Senegambian peoples were found as far north as Mauretania until the eleventh-century expansion of the Berbers, when they were pushed back southward. They extended eastward through most of present Guinea-Bissau until the creation of Kaabu (q.v.) and of the secondary Mandinka (q.v.) kingdoms pushed them westward toward the coast. The southward spread of the Senegambians was similarly checked by the consolidation of power in the Guinea highlands at Futa Jallon (q.v.) and with the expansion of the Susu (q.v.) kingdom. At an early date the Senegambians incorporated the Sundanic food complex and added rice farming as a local speciality. The numerous small Senegambian groups represent the shattering effect from the pressure on all sides by more powerful centralized hierarchies. The Senegambians are either acephalous or only slightly centralized and are mostly animist, except for more recent Islamization among some. Sometimes Senegambians are known as 'Semi-Bantu' peoples of the Guinea Littoral. *See* ETHNIC GROUPS.

SERER. This Senegambian (q.v.) group is mainly located in southeastern Senegal but is related to the Diola (q.v.) of Guinea-Bissau and to the small, stratified Sine and Saloum (q.v.) kingdoms which were tributary states of Mali (q.v.) between the thirteenth and fifteenth centuries. The Serer represent almost one fifth of the population of Senegal. They were early migrants into Senegal from political upheavals from the eleventh to fifteenth centuries of the Fula in Futa Toro (qq.v.) in the Senegal River valley, and from pressures of expanding Kaabu (q.v.) in the fourteenth to eighteenth centuries.

SILA, ERNESTINA (? –1973). This exemplary woman (q.v.) militant and member of the Conselho Superior da Luta, CSL (q.v.), of the *Partido Africano da Independência de Guiné e Cabo Verde*, PAIGC (q.v.), was born in the Tombali region of Guinea-Bissau. In 1962 she contacted the Party as a teenager and then left home to dedicate herself to the nationalist struggle. Her main assignment was Public Health (q.v.) work in the liberated zones of the northern region. Her active work did not prevent her from marrying and raising children. On January 31, 1973, she was killed in combat on the Farim River (q.v.) on the way to the funeral for Amilcar Cabral (q.v.) in neighboring Guinea-Conakry. In March of 1977 the 'Titina' Sila Juice Factory was opened in Bolama (q.v.) in her memory. Her remains have now been buried in the military museum in Bissau (q.v.) near the mausoleum of Cabral.

SINE (SIN). *See* SALOUM.

SINTRA, PEDRO DA. Portuguese navigator who sailed off the coast of Guinea-Bissau in 1460 to reach Sierra Leone.

SLAVERY. The Portuguese first captured African slaves in the early 1440's on the Moroccan coast, especially at Arguim. Until the discovery of the New World, slaves were used as domestic servants in Europe and on sugar plantations in the various Atlantic islands. Domestic slavery in Cape Verde began in the fifteenth and lasted at a rather steady level until the ninteenth century. Parallel to this was a continual and significant import/export business through the 19th century.

Guinea-Bissau itself did not use the slave plantation system to any degree, but was chiefly an exporter. During the fifteenth century the export of slaves from Africa did not exceed 1,000 annually, but this was a uniquely Portuguese enterprise and occurred primarily on the upper reaches of the West African coast. This was at a time when the kingdom of Kaabu (q.v.) was being formed, and it was central in raiding Senegambian (q.v.) people to be sold to the Dyulas and *lançados* for export to Portugal (qq.v), the Cape Verde Islands, and the Canaries.

The slave trade in the sixteenth century was still monopolized by Portugal, but Spanish and English slavers began to erode the monopoly in the late sixteenth century. Cape Verdeans and *lançados* were directly involved in the trade along the coast which depended upon slave wars waged in the interior. Cape Verdean *panos* (q.v.), horses, and salt were brought from the islands to trade along the coast. The majority of African slaves were brought from Guinea and Senegambia in general. The pace of slaving increased through the century, reaching a height of some 5,000 slaves annually by the 1570's. Most of these slaves went to the New World, especially to the

Caribbean and to Brazil, although a small trickle still went to the Cape Verde Islands and to Europe.

Throughout the seventeenth century the Portuguese slave trade in Senegambia and Guinea-Bissau declined in both absolute and relative terms. On the one hand, more European powers were involved and Portuguese slavers became more active further down the coast in Angola and Mozambique. In the first half of the seventeenth century the portion of slaves from Guinea and Senegambia fell to about six percent of the total number of slaves from Africa, where it had been as much as seventy-five percent in the century before. Likewise, the numbers of slaves fell from previous highs of about 5,000 per year to a range of 1,000 to a high of 3,500 per year. The earlier figures related to the continuing wars of the now independent state of Kaabu in Guinea-Bissau, which generated large numbers of slaves for trade and export. In the seventeenth century, Kaabu became less dynamic and more stable, thus slowing the production of slave captives. The early seventeenth century saw renewed efforts by other European powers to engage in West African slavery; the real heyday of competitive and aggressive slaving had begun. The English Royal African Company averaged some 10,000 slaves each year in the area between Senegal and Sierra Leone in the late seventeenth century, but this large figure represented only twelve percent of their total slave trade from Africa at the time. At about the same period two Portuguese companies were established as slave trade monopolies at Cacheu (q.v.) in Guinea-Bissau. With a marked growth in the New World plantation system the demand was high, and insecurity prevailed among peoples of the coast and the interior as all of the major Sudanic states in the West African savanna had come to an end. The portion of slaving done by Portuguese vessels or with Portuguese traders continued to fall. Indeed, the coastal *lançados* and Dyula traders had almost free reign on trading in the context of virtual anarchy of slave commerce at this time.

By the eighteenth century slaves were being drawn from peoples located further within the interior as the various Fula (q.v.) wars of Islamic revival generated a high degree of insecurity at this period. In 1753 a Brazilian slave trade *companhia* (q.v.) was given monopoly rights at Bissau to acquire slaves for the Brazilian states of *Maranhão* and *Grão Pará* that Portuguese Prime Minister Pombal (q.v.) was seeking to develop. This accounted for a local resurgence in slaving, as slave exports from Bissau and Cacheu (qq.v.) rose to an average of some 700 per year in the late eighteenth century. Many of these slaves were generated from the incessant wars between the Mandinka (q.v.) state of Kaabu and the Fula people of Labé Province of Futa Jallon (q.v.).

The early nineteenth century saw the start of European abolition when it was realized that a cash economy (rather than slave barter) and industrial exports on a massive scale would be better served by 'free labor' which could purchase European goods and enter a system of colonial taxation in which unpaid slaves could not 'participate.' The wage-slave system began to cut away at the older system of chattel slavery. As a poor European nation, Portugal (q.v.) was slow to make this transition, and slavery lingered on into the nineteenth century. To a limited extent there was even some slight increase in the slave trade at this time in Guinea-Bissau, as the abolition and anti-slavery patrols had resulted in a relative scarcity of the slave supply, thus temporarily forcing an increased demand. On the other hand, the slave trade in the Upper Guinea coast in the early decades of the nineteenth century was only about ten to twelve percent of the total trade which had mostly drifted down to the Lower Guinea coast and Angola for the South Atlantic-Southern Brazilian slave trade.

For Guinea-Bissau the slaves were received from inland wars at collecting centers at Bissau, Cacheu, and Bolama, which were under Portuguese economic, political, and military protection. There was a mixture of slaves and legitimate trade, but the profits for slaves were still so great that if at all possible slaves were still sold cheaply on the coast and at rate three to five times higher in the Caribbean. Some slave shippers would take slaves belonging to various owners on the same shipment. Consequently, the owners sometimes branded their slaves for positive identification at the point of sale. At this point, the decentralized coastal peoples were again raided by the Portuguese *lançado* traders or, more often, by their allies and by some Africans such as the Bijagós, especially from Canhabaque. As the century wore on, there were some numbers of slaves from the Mandinka-related peoples when the Fulas continued to press their attacks on Kaabu in eastern Guinea-Bissau. With such interior pressures, the Fula war captives from the interior and from the coastal groups such as Nalus and Bagas (q.v.) were common victims in the 1820's, but by the 1840's and 1850's the trade was largely underground and even smaller scale. As the trade declined, the trade in hides, ivory, wax, and peanuts grew.

Despite the rather rapid spread of the official abolition movement led by the English in the early nineteenth century, Portugal was more often in violation of the restrictions and agreements to limit the trade. Brazilian slavers still kept interest in Bissau from which they took a significant portion of their slaves, but the annual numbers were usually only a few hundred per year. Some years did see higher numbers of slave exports almost equal to that of the eighteenth century, but this was not the norm. The British, and especially American, efforts to stop Brazilian or Portuguese slaving were half-hearted in the case of the 'African Squadron' (q.v.) based in Cape Verde, and because Britain and Portugal were key allies since 1386. This relationship was maintained in the several Anglo-Portuguese treaties of 1643, 1654, 1660, 1661, 1703, 1810, 1815, 1817, and 1842, but each only put more pressure on the Portuguese toward abolition, with several loopholes or failed provisions in each case.

The independence of Brazil from Portugal in 1822 and the Emancipation Proclamation in the United States in 1863 provided a formal basis for the sharp decline and ultimate extinction of the trade in Guinea-Bissau by the third quarter of the nineteenth century. At the close of the nineteenth century and into most of the twentieth century of open Portuguese colonialism, a system of contract labor replaced slavery, although the life of a 'contratado' was only a slight improvement, as wages were pitifully low and the conditions of employment were most oppressive. The contract labor system was particularly important to the economy of Cape Verde, which has long had great difficulty in supporting its own population by island agriculture because of prolonged droughts, gross colonial mismanagement, and backward systems of land ownership. Some Africans had short-term, personal benefits from the slave trade, but the protracted brutality associated with this commerce in human beings certainly stands as one of the most exploitative and inhuman epochs in human history. Also, most Europeans in Europe or in the New World did not benefit either; not only was there chronic insecurity and anxiety under the slave system, but only the small European class of slave owners and traders were the true 'beneficiaries' of this launching of the great African diaspora. See BADIUS; GOMES, D.; GONÇALVES, A.; GORÉE; GRUMETES; HAWKINS, J.; PANOS; SALOUM; SÃO TIAGO; SÃO TOMÉ; TANGO-MÃOS; TRISTÃO, N.

SONGHAI. Songhai was a major Sudanic state and became dominant on the Middle Niger after the slow disintegration of Mali (q.v.), although Songhai had been first established as a small Niger River state in 1504. Sonni Ali Ber (b. 1443?, d. 1492) is considered to be the founder of the Empire of Songhai as a result of his military campaigns in the 1460's which led to the capture of Timbuktu in 1469. Timbuktu had already fallen away from Mali in 1433, when it was seized by Tuareg invaders. After a long siege at Jenne this also fell to Songhai in 1473. The reign of Songhai was punctuated with military conflict with the Fula (q.v.), who put up strong resistance. In 1492 Sunni Ali was replaced by his Soninke general, Askia Muhammad, who had a colorful reign until 1528. From 1496 to 1498 Askia Muhammad undertook a celebrated pilgrimage *haj* to Mecca, and in 1512 he carried out military expeditions against Coli Tenguella (q.v.). Niani, a capital town of Mali, fell to Songhai in 1546, but in 1591 the Askia dynasty of Songhai came to an end with the conquest by Moroccan troops. The influence of Songhai was not as forcefully felt in Guinea-Bissau as was that of Mali, but it did have the effect of pushing various ethnic groups toward the coast and disrupting those already living along the coastal areas.

SONINKE. The Soninke are members of the Nuclear Mande stock of the Niger-Congo language family, but they speak a distinct dialect of the Mandinka (q.v.) language. While the Soninke are found in eastern Senegal and Western Mali, they are related to the Susus and the Dyula (qq.v.) traders of Guinea-Bissau. The most notable achievement of the Soninke people is their founding of the Sudanic empire of Ghana (literally, in Soninke, 'war chief'). The Soninke include a mixture from the Mandinka, Fula, Bambara, and especially the Berber people. From the neighboring Tukulor (q.v.) the Soninke received Islam. The Soninke have both class stratification and traditional hierarchies of nobility.

In 990 AD the Empire of Ghana seized Awdoghast and established its maximum control of trans-Saharan trade. By 1054 the Almoravids captured Awdoghast from Ghana, and in 1076 the sometime capital of Ghana at Kumbi Saleh also fell to the Almoravids. The Dyula branch of the Soninke was central in the trade and Islamization of the Upper and Middle Niger, which led to the formation of the state of Mali (q.v.). During the rule of Askia Mohammad (1493–1529) in the Empire of

Songhai (q.v.), the Soninke scholar Alfa (q.v.) Mahmoud Kati lived in Timbuktu and wrote the important *Tarikh al-Fettash*.

SONKO, *See* **INFALI SONKO.**

SPÍNOLA, GENERAL ANTÓNIO SEBASTIÃO RIBEIRO DE. (b. April 11, 1910). Born in Estremoz, Portugal (q.v.), Spínola received a strict military education and was a noted horseman. With his family close to the ruling circles of the Portuguese government and the powerful Champalimaud (q.v.) banking group he was long a prominent military officer. In the Second World War, Spínola was invited by Hitler to inspect conquered areas of the Soviet Union and is reported to have visited the German Sixth Army during its unsuccessful attempt to seize Stalingrad.

Spínola served as the military governor of Guinea-Bissau during the later years of the national liberation struggle led by the *Partido Africano da Independência de Guiné e Cabo Verde*, PAIGC (q.v.). He was implicated in the assassination of the PAIGC leader Amilcar Cabral (q.v.). Spinola's book *Portugal e o Futuro* was a model of a neo-colonial relationship for Portugal in its former colonies. Spínola was a central actor in the turbulent political scene in Lisbon in 1974 and 1975 when he served as the first President of Portugal in the post-*Estado Novo* period. During these heady days of transition to independence, Spínola tried, but failed, to keep both Portugal and Cape Verde under closer control and to resist the more radical movements of the time.

SUNDIATA KEITA. *See* **MALI; SUSUS.**

SUSUS (SOUSSOUS, SOSSOS, SOSOS). This Mande derived group is found in the extreme south of Guinea-Bissau's coastal areas and in Guinea-Conakry and Sierra Leone. In Guinea-Bissau they are concentrated around Catio and Cacine. The Susus are related to the Dyulas and Soninke (qq.v.), who were the chief founders of the Empire of Ghana. With the fall of Kumbi Saleh (the capital of Ghana near Walata) in 1076, the Susu branch of the Soninke fled to the south, away from the Almoravids. In the flight to the south, the Susus spread the main crops of the Sudanic agricultural (q.v.) complex to new areas. Later, on the coast and in the coastal interior of today's Guinea-Conakry, the Islamized paramount Chiefs blocked further southward expansion of the Senegambians.

In about 1200 one Susu state called Kaniaga emerged and was able to gain enough strength to reconquer Kumbi Saleh in 1203, thus ruling southern Soninke groups and northern Mandinkas (q.v.). The head of this Susu state was Sumaguru (Soumaora, Sumawuru), Kante (Konteh) of a Tekrur (q.v.) dynasty. Sumaguru's rule at Kumbi Saleh was considered harsh and oppressive and helped to precipitate the final decline of ancient Ghana. In 1230 Sumaguru extended his empire with the conquest of Kangaba near the important Wangara gold mines which he ruled along with Diara as Susu States. During the rule of Sumaguru, he killed eleven of the local Mandinka Kings, sparing the life of only one, a cripple named Sundiata Keita, who was later to become the powerful founder of the major state of Mali (q.v.). Even before the actual defeat of Sumaguru, the growing trade at Walata had already eclipsed that of Kumbi Saleh.

Further expansion of the Susu states was halted by the growth of Mali under Sundiata. At the battle of Kirina in 1235 Sundiata's forces defeated the army of Sumaguru. By 1240 Sundiata occupied the remaining remnants of Ghana and founded the Keita dynasty of Mali. The Susus moved back south to Futa Jallon (q.v.) where they stayed until the period of the Fula (q.v.) *jihads* in the late eighteenth century, which reduced them to slaves or drove them to the coast of Guinea-Conakry and southern Guinea-Bissau. On the coast the Susus acquired local customs and, to a certain extent, brought the Islam they had obtained from Futa Jallon. Today the coastal Susu play an important role in commerce, and Susu is spoken widely in the area.

T

TABANCA COMMITTEES. These committees were formed by the *Partido Africano da Independência de Guiné e Cabo Verde*, PAIGC (q.v.), in villages throughout the liberated zones during the nationalist struggle; they served to link the PAIGC with the peasantry. Since independence, tabanca committees have been expanded throughout most of the countryside as well as in neighborhoods in the cities, comprising an estimated total of 3,600 committees. They are theoretically each composed of three men and two women (q.v.) who are elected by the villagers; their official responsibilities included tax collection, helping to implement health (q.v.) programs, monitoring outsiders, and arranging meetings between party officials and villagers. In actual practice the committees vary greatly, but very few include women members, many consist of just one or two village leaders, and difficulties in communication and transport between the countryside and the Bissau-based Party have prevented the committees from carrying out their duties in many cases.

In early Portuguese accounts, the term 'tabanca' often refered to fortified or walled villages. In Cape Verde, the term 'tabanca' refers to aspects of the musical and folklife of the *badius* (q.v.).

TALL, AL-HAJ AL-IMAMI UMAR(U) (b. 1794–7, d. 1864). Al-Haj Umar is one of the famed Fula (q.v.) leaders of the nineteenth century who revitalized Islam in a region from Futa Jallon to Futa Toro (qq.v.). Tall was born in a Torobe clan near Podor (or Halwar) in Tekrur (q.v.), which had come to replace the previous Denianke dynasty of Tekrur. His father Osman Muktar was known for his piety typical of the *marabout* tradition. Osman had been among those Torobe who had displaced the earlier Denianke dynasty of Tekrur founded by Coli Tenguella (q.v.) in the closing of the fifteenth century.

Umar Tall pursued religious studies within the theological framework of the *Tijaniya tariqa* at Walata as a student of Abdel Karim. From about 1825 to 1827 he undertook a pilgrimage to Mecca traveling to the Hausa Sultanate of Sokoto in Nigeria and on to Arabia. In the decades just before Umar Tall's visit, northern Nigeria had been the setting for the great Fulani *jihad* of Usman dan Fodio. Clearly this was an important influence which Umar Tall considered on his *haj* which allowed him to continue his studies with a learned community of Muslim scholars. Indeed he became known as the *Khalifa* (legitimate successor) of Sheikh Tijani for the Bilad as-Sudan (Land of the Blacks). He returned to Sokoto, Nigeria where he stayed from 1832 to 1838 and became closely associated with its Khalifa, Muhammad Bello. Al-Haj Umar was actually married into the Bello family, but after Bello's death in 1837, Al-Haj Umar went on to Mali stopping at Macina and briefly in Futa Toro. In Segou he was confined by the Bambara; this was not to be forgotten.

At last, he applied his inspired religious teachings to become a politico-religious leader in Futa Jallon. He was received at Timbo, which served as his administrative and *Tijaniya* religious center in Futa Jallon. From there he went to other major towns at Kankan and Dinguiray where he spread his teaching and mission by building a school and large mosque. From 1846 to 1852 Umar Tall was trading slave captives on a wide stretch of the Upper Guinea coast for firearms to prepare for his *jihad* and the creation of a new Islamic state launched from his interior base at Dinguiray. He broke with the existing Al-Imami of the area in 1848 to prepare for his forced exile or *hejira*, as did the Prophet Muhammad.

On 21 May 1854 he left Dinguiray with his devoted army to carry his *jihad* to Macina and Segou, where he had been mistreated by those people who he considered were not practicing Islam in the 'correct' fashion. By April 1855 he seized the goldfields at Bambuk and Bure. This move provoked the French to attack, fearing that they would lose their control of this important source of gold. The French under Faidhérbe (q.v.), who were backing Tall's rival, Samballa Diallo, launched their counterattack in 1857, and drove him away on 18 July. Tall organized a major recruitment to his army in 1858 and 1859 to block the French and their Senegalese allies. In 1861 Tall withdrew to the southeast just east of Gambia and Guinea and fell upon the Bambara of Segou, where he installed his son Ahmed as ruler in 1861. He then seized Macina in 1862 and battled the French colonialist Faidhérbe in 1863. A power struggle for Islamic legitimacy, coupled with the colonial intrusion, caused most of Umar Tall's efforts to vanish after his death in February 1864, when he was replaced by Abdul Bokar Kan.

While Al-Imami Umar may not have entered into Guinea-Bissau his 'long march' and *jihad* on the Upper Niger directly precipitated the increasing Fula attacks led by Alfa Molo (q.v.) on Kaabu (q.v.) in the 1850's and 1860's and the fall of Kansala in 1867. Similarly, the penetration of the French colonial military into the southeast part of Senegal was to lead to an intensification of French claims in the Casamance (q.v.), especially in Ziguinchor, which had formerly seen a notable Portuguese presence. Thus, Tall's spirit of refortified Islam was not especially lasting, but the regional expansion of the Fula and the formation of Franco-Portuguese borders has an influence in Guinea-Bissau persisting to the present.

TANDAS (TENDAS). This small concentration of some 30,000 Senegambian (q.v.) people is found to the northeast of Gadamael near the southern frontier with Guinea-Conakry. As with many Senegambians, they were far more widespread but were heavily raided by Mali (q.v.) and later by the *jihads* waged from Futa Jallon (q.v.) during the time of slavery (q.v.). Their survival depended upon their retreat to coastal estuary enclaves or sparsely populated hill country.

TANGOMÃOS, TANGOMAUS. This term seems to be derived from the Arabic word 'targama,' to translate. In the trade of slaves from a wide diversity of language groups it was critical to have slave traders skilled in a variety of local languages. The Portuguese *lançados* (q.v.) or *tangomãos* and their African 'wives' produced mixed offspring who were natural linguists in this respect. André Donelha also used the Senegambian (q.v.) term *chalona* for linguists playing this commercial role at this time. Some sources indicate that the term *tangomãos* meant 'tattooed or scarified men,' which may refer to a Portuguese maritime custom to use tattoos or to African cicatrice designs.

As such the *tangomãos* were independent-minded Luso-African or African merchant slavers, often allied with *grumetes* (q.v.), who were all acculturated to the *lançado* lifestyle and *Crioulo* (q.v.) language. In the sixteenth and seventeenth centuries both terms were widely used among the Portuguese present on the Upper Guinea coast and in the Cape Verde Islands, as they moved between the two places. Both terms, often used as synonyms, are archaic, since the region and nature of their activity has ceased.

TARRAFAL. A notorious political prison located on the northern end of São Tiago in the Cape Verde archipelago. This prison camp was begun during the Portuguese Fascist era in 1936 to house Communist Party members and their sympathizers who were opposed to the rule of Salazar. As the nationalist wars began, the camp was filled with Africans as well. Tarrafal had a particularly nasty reputation for torture, brutality, and death. Its extremely isolated location made escape virtually impossible. In 1971 more than 100 agents of the *Policia Internacional para Defesa do Estado*, PIDE (q.v.), arrived in Cape Verde and Guinea-Bissau. There they infiltrated and arrested the nationalists who were confined at the Tarrafal *concelho* prison or the work camp of Chão Bom. Although politically important, the overall prison staff consisted of about a dozen guards and administrators. In Guinea-Bissau the military fortress of D'Amura in Bissau played the same role.

TEKRUR (TUKOLOR). One of the earliest Islamized states of the western Sudan from which the Fulas (q.v.) of Guinea-

Bissau have originated. Tekrur (Senegal) appeared at, or about, the time of ancient Ghana as early as the third century AD and certainly no later than the sixth century. Tekrur was likely an area of Serer people before the 'red' Fula entered to create Tekrur's first Jaogo dynasty. The Tekrur (Tukulor) farmers and the Fula herders are closely related by both being Fulbe-speaking members of the Atlantic sub-family of the Niger-Congo language stock. Tekrur was based on a trading and bureaucratic superstructure built from traditional settled village political systems and subsistence agriculture. Its location in the Sahel was an ideal southern terminus for trans-Saharan trade, or for trade moving east and west across the savanna.

In the eighth and nineth centuries Tekrur experienced significant growth, and until the end of the tenth century Tekrur was a fully autonomous state on the middle Senegal River valley and was about the equal of Ghana. The Tukulor peoples of Tekrur actively competed with Ghana for control of the trans-Saharan trade.

However, in 990 AD Ghana conquered the Berber trade center at Awdoghast and then forced Tekrur into a tributary status, probably led by the Manna dynasty. Between the late tenth century and the mid-eleventh century Islamized Berber traders entered Tekrur, where they settled, married local women, and acquired slaves.

The admixture of Berber and Tukulor elements resulted in the emergence of the Fula peoples who spread throughout most of the sub-Saharan Sahel and savanna regions. The sedentary farmers and traders of Tukulor stock became devout Muslims while the cattle-herding Fula resulting from the Berber-Tukulor merger were somewhat less Islamized, although they had a more North African appearance. When the Almoravids sought to restore their control of the trade lost to Ghana and avenge their loss of Awdoghast, the leaders of Tekrur made an alliance with them in order to aid in the defeat of Ghana in 1076, thus permitting Tekrur to return to its independent status until the late thirteenth century when it became a tributary state of expanding Mali. The Muslim geographer and historian, Al-Idrisi visited Tekrur in 1153 and 1154 and described it as a place of active trade. During its height, Tekrur was linked to Marrakesh by an overland trade route about 200 miles inland from the Atlantic Coast.

Although the first Muslims of Tekrur were the traders and their slaves, the eleventh century saw the incorporation of Islam as the court religion of the Tekrur ruling class. Many neighboring and subordinated peoples remained animists and even anti-Islamic, including some of the early cattle-herding Fulas. The formative Empire of Mali (1230–1546, [q.v.]) was first converted to Islam at a later period than Tekrur; this is generally considered to have occurred in 1050, when Barmandana of Mali accepted this faith and established the Keita dynasty. In fact, Islam was spread to and through Mali by Dyula peoples (a Soninke group, [q.v.]) who conducted east-west trade from Tekrur under the Denianke dynastic line. This east-west trade became especially important in the twelveth and thirteenth centuries when Mali experienced its greatest growth. A new Soninke ruling class came to power in Tekrur in about 1250, briefly permitting Tekrur to control Senegal until 1285 when it was brought under the authority of the Malian ruler Sakura. Tekrur was only under the direct control of Mali until 1350, when the Malian representatives were deposed by the Wolof, thus taking this state beyond the frontiers of Mali once again. Tekrur, or more properly, Futa Toro, regained an independent status in 1520 at the time of Coli Tenguella (q.v.); the Denianke line he established endured until 1775. In the nineteenth century Tekrur fell under the control of Al-Imami Umar Tall (q.v.) until it was subjugated by the French.

TENGUELLA (BA) (TEENGALA, TENGELLA, TEMALA), COLI (KOOLI, KOLY). Given very different origins and very different dates, this work assumes that the name Coli Tenguella actually represents at least two different Fula (q.v.) leaders of the same name who led, respectively, the Fula occupation of Futa Toro (q.v.) in the late fifteenth century and the Fula occupation of Futa Jallon (q.v.) in the first quarter of the sixteenth century.

Apparently Coli Tenguella (I) came from Termes, Mauretania at the end of an early period of Fula migration. In the 1490's he defeated neighboring Senegalese Wolof kingdoms and western portions of the Empire of Mali (q.v.), thereby establishing the Denianke (Denaanke) dynasty (1490's–1775) in the Futa Toro plateau of Senegal. Once he and his followers occupied the fertile flood plain of the upper Senegal River he was proclaimed as the Sitatigui (leader of the way) of the Futa Toro Denianke. The existence of Futa Toro cut the western trade and communication links of the Empire of Mali, which had become important to the Portuguese as a source of gold and slaves.

The visit of a Portuguese emissary of King João II (q.v.) in about 1494 prompted Mali's Mansa (Emperor) Mamudi I to complain about the attacks of Tenguella. Conflict was inevitable over such a strategic piece of territory with access to the gold routes to Bure and Bambuk. Coli Tenguella was finally forced out of Futa Toro and retreated to the southern plateau region of Futa Jallon in Guinea Conakry, which was also part of a generally declining Malian Empire. Futa Jallon had been occupied by Dialonke, Susu, and various Mandinka (qq.v.) peoples as well as by some Fula before Coli Tenguella arrived, but it was he who merged these various peoples into a new state which was opposed to the rule of Mali (although one of his several wives was from the Malian ruling class). Tenguella organized local resistance to Mali in the late fifteenth century, and in 1510 he and his followers returned to Futa Toro to rule over local Wolof. In 1511 Coli Tenguella was killed in a battle at Amar by a general of Askia Muhammad of Songhai. The Fula warrior bands had acculturated and assimilated sufficient Mandinka peoples, including some from Guinea-Bissau, so that the Denianke dynasty continued until 1775.

It was presumably his son, Coli Tenguella (II) (ca. 1512–1537), who led the army after his father's death and continued to re-establish and expand Futa Toro rule at the expense of the neighboring Soninke and Wolof of Senegal, although an effort to expand in Guinea-Bissau was successfully resisted by the Beafadas and Susus (qq.v.). With Fula pressure on the east and *lançado* (q.v.) pressure on the west, the small-scale Senegambian (q.v.) peoples were trapped between two greater and better armed powers. This vulnerability made the coastal people the most common victims in the slave trade. Their position was further weakened by European rivalries on the coast which required an endless search for slaves and persistent inter-ethnic warfare to produce slave-captives for centuries. It was in this context that Tenguella II was active. His attempt to take over the Bambuk goldfields failed in 1534, and three years later Tenguella (II) was killed. The Denianke followers, however, proceeded to enlarge their control in an area between the Sahel and Futa Jallon.

The lineage of Coli Tenguella has not yet been fully unraveled by historians, who offer varied interpretations of this man and his successors. There may have been a Coli Tenguella (III), who in alliance with Mandinka fragments overthrew the Soninke chiefs of Futa Toro in 1559 to perpetuate the Denianke line. In any case, this early Denianke period saw the emergence of sedentary Fula who began to dominate those Fula who remained as pastoralists.

The 1625 description of Guinea derived from André Donelha's interviews with old Fula slaves in Cape Verde who still kept memories of 'Dulo Demba' (possibly Coli Tenguella) alive. Donelha learned of Tenguella's great military sweep from Futa Toro across Guinea after crossing the Upper Senegal in canoes to enter Jalof and Mandinka territory as far west as 140 leagues from the mouth of the Gambia. According to Donelha, the forces of Tenguella reached the Beafada (q.v.) territory at Guinala (q.v.) on the Rio Grande, where he met the Beafada King Famena, who had himself tried to conquer the Bijagós. The Beafada and Fula had a great battle in which the cavalry forces of Tenguella were driven back. With such a large number of dead on both sides a memorial was built of the bones at Guinala. Donelha visited this site in 1581 and found bones still plentiful as well as a type of horse which arrived with the Fula attack.

During the Tenguella periods the Fula followers often crossed over or disrupted portions of eastern Guinea-Bissau and brought in new Fula people. Under the influence of the Tenguellas the Fulas were stimulated to build up more permanent settlements. As a result of these movements of the Fula, a population of semi-sedentary cattle herders was generated from Fula and Mandinka peoples already living in the Kaabu kingdom of Guinea-Bissau. In the eighteenth and nineteenth centuries the Fulacunda population of Guinea-Bissau increased considerably.

TIMENES. This very small Senegambian (q.v.) group has some representatives located south of Gabú (q.v.) and was isolated from other Senegambians after Mandinka (q.v.) expansion. Mostly they are found in Sierra Leone and Liberia.

TIRAMAKHAN (TIRAMANG) TRAORE. A general of Sundiata Keita (d. 1255 AD) of Mali (q.v.). Tiramakhan entered the Senegambian (q.v.) region to crush the revolt of a Wolof King against Sundiata and to strengthen the control of Mali after it defeated the Susu (q.v.) people under Sumaguru in 1235. Thus, at some time in the mid-thirteenth century, Tiramakhan's control was consolidated, and he married Nyaaling, who was perhaps a member of a local Beafada (q.v.) ruling lineage before the arrival of Tiramakhan's forces. His presence laid the foundation for the Mandinka state of Kaabu (q.v.) (ca. 1250–1867). Sources are unclear as to the exact genealogical relationship between Tiramakhan and the first Kaabu King,

Sama Koli (q.v.) (Kelemankoto Baa Saane), but it appears that he was either the son or grandson of Tiramakhan in a royal line of matrilineal descent.

TOMAS. This very small Senegambian (q.v.) group is located just east of Gabú (q.v.).

TOURÉ, AL-IMAMI SAMORI. Although Touré's political domain was largely in adjacent Guinea-Conakry, his influence reached deeply inside Guinea-Bissau in the nineteenth century in the regional Islamization movement and in his stalwart resistance to colonialism during the period 1882–1898. Touré was born in about 1830 in the Upper Niger valley. His father, Lanfia, was a regional Dyula (q.v.) cloth merchant. His context was one of regional upheaval because of the slave wars and the power vacuum caused by the collapse of Songhai and the Denianke dynasty of Futa Toro (q.v.). Ahmadou Tall, the son of Umar Tall (q.v.), was also active in the region in these years. The destabilized region allowed for the kidnapping of his mother by regional warlords. He offered himself as a hostage. This was clearly an important formative life event.

In the early 1880's Touré had established his power base over a large area of Futa Jallon (q.v.) and adjacent territories including parts of Ivory Coast, Liberia, Sierra Leone, Guinea, Mali, and Burkina Faso to fill the power vacuum and to resist the French, who termed him the 'Bonaparte of the Sudan.' In April 1883 his forces battled at Bamako, and in 1884 he proclaimed himself as the Imami of the region. As early as 1886 his rule was considered to be modelled after an Islamic state. To slow his spread the French signed peace treaties with Touré in 1886, 1887, and 1889. Touré considered that they did not live up to the terms of these treaties, and from 1891 to 1893 he resumed combat with the French forces in several major towns of Futa Jallon. In 1898 the French Colonial Minister Andre Lebon launched his final attack against the forces of Touré, and Toure was finally halted. Toure himself was arrested on 29 September 1898 and sent into exile in Gabon where he died on 2 June 1900.

TRAORE. See TIRAMAKHAN TRAORE.

TRISTÃO, NUÑO. Portuguese navigator and captain of an armed caravel who, along with Antão Gonçalves, captured a dozen Africans (Moors) at Cape Blanc (north coast of Mauretania) in 1441 and returned to Portugal (q.v.) with them and a cargo of gold dust. Tristão directly and personally engaged in slave-capturing and the killing of those who resisted. One of the twelve captives was of noble birth. From 1443 to 1444 Tristão reached Arguim, seizing twenty-nine men and women. Merchants soon grasped the idea of large and easy profits. In 1444 Tristão decided to outfit a major raiding expedition of six ships under Lançarote and Gil Eannes, thus initiating one of the earliest European-inspired slave raids on the African coast. In the same year Tristão became the first European to venture beyond the Mauretanian desert, as he reached the mouths of the Senegal, Gambia, and Saloum (q.v.) rivers, thinking they were branches of the Nile. In 1446 Tristão reached an undetermined area along the Upper Guinea coast, perhaps the Gambia river. In the following year his aggressive exploits came to an end when he was killed by Africans defending their lands against his incursions. Although often portrayed as the 'discoverer' of Guinea-Bissau, Tristão never reached the modern territory of this nation.

U

UNIÃO CABOVERDEANA PARA A INDEPENDÊNCIA E DEMOCRACIA (UCID). Founded in 1981 in Cape Verdean emigrant communities, the UCID is a right of center opposition group based in Lisbon and Cape Verdean diaspora communities. The evolution of many of its leaders was in an earlier group called the *União Democratica de Caboverde*, UDC (q.v.). It has strongly opposed the *Partido Africano da Independência de Cabo Verde*, PAICV (q.v.), on many foreign and domestic polices, such as agrarian and land reform and relations with the Socialist nations and especially on its links with Guinea-Bissau. In the 1975 elections, UCID was excluded, and in the 1991 elections UCID was unable to field a candidate amidst its internal divisions over leadership. It offered Celso Celestino as its Presidential candidate in 1995, but he was not able to gain a single seat.

UNIÃO DAS POPULAÇÕES DAS ILHAS DE CABO VERDE (UPICV). The UPICV was led by José Leitão da Graça and his wife Maria Querido, who was named its Secretary General. The UPICV sought to preserve the Cape Verdean 'personality' in its program of limited social transformation. Apparently the

UPICV was first formed in 1959 in the United States. Following the Lisbon coup the UPICV supported the *União Democrática de Cabo Verde*, UDCV (q.v.), position of a referendum on unity with Guinea-Bissau, charging that the PAIGC would make Cape Verde 'a Soviet military base.' In the mid–1970's the UPICV sprouted certain Maoist terminology and on May 23, 1975, renamed itself the Peoples Liberation Front of Cape Verde. Following the independence of Cape Verde on July 5, 1975, the central leaders of the UPICV were exiled to Portugal, although the UPICV claimed responsibility for a small anti-PAIGC disturbance in São Vicente in August 1975. In the 1990's the UPICV still survives as a tiny ineffective political party in Cape Verde.

UNIÃO DEMOCRÁTICA DA GUINÉ (UDG). This small group emerged in the late 1950's and briefly merged with the *União Democrática de Cabo Verde*, UDCV (q.v.), to form the *Mouvement de Liberátion de la Guinée "Portugaise" et des Îles du Cap Vert*, MLGCV (q.v.), of Dakar in 1959. Apparently, this was a small-scale and short-lived effort to build a more conservative party which could rival the rapidly growing *Partido Africano da Independência de Guiné e Cabo Verde*, PAIGC (q.v.). It was from the MLGCV that the *Frente de Luta Pela Independência Nacional da Guiné-Bissau*, FLING (q.v.), a long-term PAIGC opponent, emerged in 1962.

UNIÃO DEMOCRÁTICA DAS MULHERES (da Guiné e Cabo Verde). UDEMU was created by the *Partido Africano da Independência de Guiné e Cabo Verde*, PAIGC (q.v.), in mid–1960 to officially represent the issues pertinent to women (q.v.) within the anti-colonial framework of the PAIGC.

UNIÃO DOS NATURAIS DA GUINÉ PORTUGUESA (UNGP). Sought independence without revolution.UNGP leader Benjamin Pinto Bull (q.v.) went to Lisbon in July 1963 for negotiations which failed and prompted UNGP unity with the *Frente de Luta Pela Independência Nacional da Guiné-Bissau*, FLING (q.v.), a year after its formation. Benjamin Pinto Bull's brother, Jaime Bull (q.v.), was made Vice President of the UNGP and was made FLING President after 1966.

UNIÃO GERAL DOS ESTUDIANTES DA AFRICA NEGRA (UGEAN). The UGEAN was formed in Europe for militant African nationalist students by the *Partido Africano da Inde-*

pendência de Guiné e Cabo Verde, PAIGC (q.v.), and the MPLA in Angola.

UNIÃO GERAL DOS TRABALHADORES DA GUINÉ-BIS-SAU (UGTGB). The UGTGB emerged in 1963 in association with the *Frente de Luta Pela Independência Nacional da Guiné-Bissau*, FLING (q.v.), and was a rival of the *Partido Africano da Independência de Guiné e Cabo Verde*, PAIGC (q.v.), workers' affiliate, the *União Nacional dos Trabalhadores da Guiné*, UNTG (q.v.), which had been secretly formed in 1959.

UNIÃO NACIONAL DOS TRABALHADORES DA GUINÉ (UNTG). Founded in 1959 around the time of the Pijiguiti (q.v.) strike. It was affiliated with the *Partido Africano da Independência de Guiné e Cabo Verde*, PAIGC (q.v.), as a party organization. In 1961 its first statutes were drafted with Luís Cabral (q.v.) acting as the Secretary General. The UNTG serves to organize the working class of Guinea and during the war sought to organize the working class of Cape Verde. On May 1, 1976 (May Day), the *Comissão Organizadora dos Sindicatos Caboverdeanos* (COSC, the Organizing Commission of Cape Verdeans Unionists) was formed as the complement and parallel body of the UNTG in the Cape Verde Islands.

UNIÃO POPULAR PARA LIBERTAÇÃO DA GUINÉ (UPLG). The UPLG was formed in 1961 and then quickly merged with the *Frente de Luta Pela Independência Nacional da Guiné-Bissau*, FLING (q.v.) in 1962.

UNION DES RESSORTISSANTS DE LA GUINÉE PORTU-GAISE (URGP). The URGP was formed in 1963 and became aligned with *Frente de Luta Pela Independência Nacional da Guiné-Bissau*, FLING (q.v.), in 1964.

UNITED NATIONS. International organization formed in 1945 for humanitarian and peace-keeping purposes. On December 14, 1960, the 1514th meeting of the General Assembly passed a resolution on global decolonization which gave great support to the anti-colonial and nationalist movements in Africa. In 1961 the *Partido Africano da Independência de Guiné e Cabo Verde*, PAIGC (q.v.), submitted considerable documentation to the United Nations regarding the effects of Portuguese colonialism. On April 2–8, 1972, a special United Nations team entered Guinea-Bissau as guest of the PAIGC. As the intended consequence of this trip the Special Committee on Decolonization announced on April 13, 1972 that the PAIGC "is the only and authentic representative" of the people of Guinea. Subsequent resolutions in the UN General Assembly and the UN Security Council reaffirmed the "right of self-determination and independence" in November 1972, thus weakening Portugal's position and substantially strengthening the PAIGC. After the PAIGC declared the independence of Guinea in September 1973 the UN General Assembly adopted a resolution on October 22, 1973 condemning Portugal's continued occupation and then gave its recognition to the new Republic of Guinea-Bissau on November 2, 1973. The Republic was admitted to the United Nations as a full member on September 17, 1974 following the April coup in Lisbon. These events preceded the negotiated independence for Cape Verde. Just prior to its full freedom, the UN Special Committee on Decolonization undertook a fact-finding mission in the islands to determine its health, financial, educational, and developmental needs. The Republic of Cape Verde officially joined the UN on September 17, 1975.

UNITED STATES. *See* GUINEA-BISSAU: FOREIGN RELATIONS; GUINEA-BISSAU: AMERICAN (U.S.A.) RELATIONS

URZELLA. *See* INDIGO, PANOS

V

VEIGA, CARLOS ALBERTO WAHNON DE CARVALHO (21 October 1949–). Veiga is a lawyer by training and is the leading member of the PAICV breakaway Movement for Democracy (MpD) (q.v.) in Cape Verde which won the elections in January 1991, ousting the PAICV (q.v.). Previously, during the one-party state period, Veiga had served in the PAIGC/PAICV government as Director of Internal Administration (1975–78) and as its Attorney General from 1979 to 1980 until breaking with it on issues of party democracy and economic policy. He then entered a private legal practice but stayed in public service by his work of the Cape Verdean Constitutional Commission from 1985 to 1990. In early 1990 he began to formulate a rival democracy movement which in November of 1990 emerged as the MpD party (which nominated him as its candidate for Prime Minister).

In the 1991 elections he scored a very strong victory over his PAICV opponent Pedro Pires (q.v.). Since February 1991 Veiga has served as the Prime Minister of Cape Verde. He seeks to expand the free market political economy and end the fifteen years of a Socialist/statist economy system. He seeks a mixed economy guided by private initiative and an irreversible multi-party democracy guaranteeing human rights. Veiga continues to be the Prime Minister of Cape Verde following his second electoral victory in 1995 which has almost identical percentages over the PAICV as in the 1991 elections.

VIEIRA, JOÃO BERNARDO 'NINO' (1939–). President of the country's highest political organs since the 1980 coup d'état, including the Council of State (formerly the Revolutionary Council) and the *Partido Africano da Independência de Guiné e Cabo Verde*, PAIGC (q.v.), Politburo, as well as Commander in Chief of the Armed Forces and Secretary General of the PAIGC. Vieira was born in Bissau (q.v) and was an electrician by trade. He joined the PAIGC in 1960 and in the following year attended the Party school in Conakry led by Amilcar Cabral (q.v.). From 1961 to 1964 Vieira was the Political Commissioner in the Catio region in southern Guinea-Bissau. Having received advanced military training in Nanking, China, Vieira was made military head of the entire Southern Front in 1964, when he was also made a member of the PAIGC Political Bureau as a result of the First Party Congress in that year. In 1965 he became the Vice President of the War Council, and he continued his work as military head of the Southern Front. From 1967 to 1970 he was the ranking member of the Political Bureau assigned to the Southern Front, and after 1970 he held full national responsibility for military operations of the War Council. In 1971 he became a member of the CEL and subsequently was the Secretary for the PAIGC Permanent Secretariat. Following independence he became the Commander-in-Chief of the Armed Forces as well as presiding over the People's National Assembly. In August 1978, Vieira was appointed Prime Minister of Guinea-Bissau following the death of Francisco Mendes (q.v.) in July of that year. On 14 November 1980 Vieira overthrew President Luís Cabral (q.v.) in a coup to become the President of the Republic, Chair of the Revolutionary Council, and Secretary General of the PAIGC in the first extraordinary Congress of the party in 1981.Following the 1984 elections and the adoption of a new Constitution, Vieira became the Chairman of the Council of State. Vieira increasingly consolidated his rule between 1981 and 1986 and was promoted to the rank of Brigadier General in 1983. In 1992 he was promoted to the rank of four-star General.

Through the 1990's Vieira has presided over many fundamental changes in Guinea-Bissau's foreign relations (q.v.); structural adjustments in the field of economics (q.v.); and has allowed a major political transition (q.v.) which has led to plural Democracy and elections (q.v.). On 14 May 1994, he retired from the Army, in order to be eligible to run for President as the PAIGC candidate in the 1994 elections. First round election results did not give Vieira the required majority in July 1994, but in a hotly contested second round he was able to defeat a much underrated challenge by Kumba Yala of the *Partido Renovação Social*, PRS (q.v.). The scenario of the MpD and PAICV which played out in Cape Verde was thereby approximated in Guinea-Bissau but was instead narrowly averted to keep the ruling party in power. President Vieira thus becomes the first democratically elected president in multiparty elections.

VIEIRA, OSVALDO. Vieira was a famous guerrilla commander of the northern and eastern fronts during the protracted armed liberation struggle, as well as a member of the Conselho Executivo (q.v.) of the *Partido Africano da Independência de Guiné e Cabo Verde*, PAIGC (q.v.). He was born in Bissau (q.v.) in 1939 of humble parents, and he joined the PAIGC as a teenager. After a period of mobilization work, he initiated the PAIGC war in the north by boldly attacking a Portuguese detachment near Morés on 7 July 1963. The success of this attack greatly impressed the local inhabitants and helped to win them over to the liberation cause.

Vieira went on to receive further military training in the People's Republic of China at the Nanking Military Academy in 1964. Upon his return, he assumed command of the northern front, with an operational base at Morés, in the legendary forests of Oio which had for centuries been famous as a center of resistance against the Portuguese. Here, with political commissar Francisco 'Chico Te' Mendes (q.v.) and young field commanders like António N'Bana and Inocêncio Kani (q.v.), the later assassin of Amilcar Cabral (q.v.), Osvaldo launched a number of successful operations against the Portuguese colonial forces in 1964 and 1966, thereby greatly expanding the liberated area in that region.

With the death of Domingos Ramos (q.v.) in November 1966, he took over command of the eastern front, aided by Pedro Pires (q.v.), both of whom were members of the newly created eight-member Conselho de Guerra (q.v.) which included Amilcar Cabral, Aristides Pereira, Luís Cabral, Francisco Mendes, and João Vieira (qq.v.). Osvaldo Vieira died on 31 March 1974 in the PAIGC hospital at Kundara, just over the southern border with Guinea-Conakry, apparently after an operation for an illness. He is remembered in Guinea-Bissau by, among other things, a boarding school in Morés and the international airport near Bissau.

VILLAGE COMMITTEES. *See* TABANCA COMMITTEES.

W–Z

WEST AFRICAN CROPS. *See* AGRICULTURE; INDIGO; RICE.

WOMEN. The *Partido Africano da Independência de Guiné e Cabo Verde*, PAIGC (q.v.), has from its inception to the present time put forth the full liberation of women as one of its central goals. A number of women were incorporated into leadership positions within the PAIGC's fighting forces during the nationalist armed struggle, and the Party insisted that at least two of the members of *tabanca* committees be women. Also, the Democratic Union of Guinean and Cape Verdean Women, UDEMU (q.v.), was formed by the PAIGC in the mid–1960's and remains active today in promoting women's issues. However, the Party has not yet succeeded in placing more than a tiny handful of women into leadership posts in the Party and government. Also, while educational opportunities for women have been expanded since independence, the male-dominated nature of the social and familial structure has not been seriously challenged, and very few women are able to pursue economic independence.

There are no formal restrictions for women being in the PAIGC, except that officially neither a woman nor a man in a polygynous union is permitted. Even though polygamy is not favored by the PAIGC, it is clear that there are a number of violations of this postion. During the growth of the PAIGC's liberated zones, divorce was made easier for women, especially those of Muslim unions who had rather limited rights to divorce. Marriages are only permitted by joint consent and forced marriage or child marriage is opposed. The institution of bridewealth is also curbed. In general the position of women has been improved, given the predominant traditions which were widely based on male supremacy. Now the rights of women are legally protected. For example, children born out of wedlock must be supported by their fathers, and the status of 'illegitimacy' has been legally abolished. The numbers of women in industry are increasing, even though the overall numbers of industrial jobs are few. Since independence, March 8, International Women's Day, is now observed.

Within the PAIGC about twelve percent of the regular members are women, and there is one woman member in the Politburo and many women members in the Central Committee and in the Popular National Assembly. Women are commonly found in the health and educational services where such possibilities were limited during colonial rule. During the armed struggle UDEMU was created to assist in the mobilization of women for the war effort. UDEMU was replaced by the Commissão Feminina (Female Commission) toward the close of the war, but the preoccupation with military affairs and resistance to change by male chauvinists ultimately resulted in the failure of the Commissão Feminina under the leadership of Carmen Pereira (q.v.). There is also a Ministry for the Promotion of Women headed by Francisca Pereira, a veteran of the liberation struggle.

Since independence, efforts to organize women have continued under the Commissão Organização das Mulheres (Commission [of the] Organization of Women, COM) to address special needs of women and to incorporate them more fully into national reconstruction. A number of women made distinguished contributions during the nationalist war; among them are Dr. Maria Boal, Director of the Pilot School and Friendship Institute, Carmen Pereira, the highest ranking woman in the PAIGC, and Ernestina Silla, exemplary heroine. Articles thirteen, sixteen, and twenty-five of the Constitution of the Republic of Guinea-Bissau provide for the legal, social, and electoral equality of men and women. *See* DUARTE, D.; GOMES, I.; GUERRA, S.; SILA, E.

ZIGUINCHOR. The town of Ziguinchor was founded around 1645 by the Portuguese Captain-Major of Cacheu (q.v.), Gonçalo Gamboa de Ayala, who apparently convinced a number of Cape Verdeans from São Filipe, Fogo, to settle there. Situated on the south bank of the River Casamance (q.v.) between the island of Karabane (at the mouth of the river) and the town of Sédhiou (some 100 kilometers upriver), it was, as a *presídio*, a dependency of Cacheu dominated by 'Portuguese' *mestiços, lançados,* and *grumetes* (qq.v.), who were very active in the local trade in slaves. Indeed, a local legend holds that the settlement is a corruption of the Portuguese expression 'Cheguei, choram,' meaning 'I arrived, they cry,' an allusion, no doubt, to the arrival of the Portuguese slave traders and the inevitable weeping which followed.

It is not clear when the *presídio* of Ziguinchor was established. However, when André Brue, director of the Gorée-based *Compagnie de Sénégal* visited the place in 1700, he found a Portuguese fort equipped with a few pieces of artillery. Nevertheless, it was a relatively unimportant outpost controlled by Luso-African families, one of the most powerful and influential being the Carvalho Alvarenga family. In 1766, Carlos Carvalho Alvarenga was the *Capitão-cabo*, the highest ranking official of the Portuguese Crown in the *presídio*, while some seventy years later, when the French raised their flag over the island of Karabane, Portugal's representative was Manuel Carvalho Alvarenga from the same family, whose superior in Guinea was Honório Pereira Barreto (q.v.), his nephew. (The *Capitão-Cabo*'s sister, Rosa Carvalho Alvarenga, was the mother of Honório Pereira Barreto).

Ineffectively controlled by Guinea, Cape Verde, and Portugal, the *presídio* of Ziguinchor was left to manage its own affairs until the advancing French brought it under their sphere of influence, with loud cries of '*usurpação*' ('usurpation') from especially the Portuguese in Cacheu. Indeed, the uneventful French occupation of the island of Karabane in 1836, after their acquisition eight years earlier of the adjacent island of Joque (known to the Portuguese as *Ilheu dos Mosquitos,* or Mosquito Island), was quickly followed by yet another uneventful hoisting of the *tricolore* flag of France at the upriver settlement of Sédhiou. It was now only a matter of time before the whole Casamance region, including the long-proclaimed Portuguese 'possession' of Ziguinchor, became part of the expanding French Empire.

Upon assuming office as Governor of Guinea in 1837, Honório Pereira Barreto wasted no time launching a protracted and bitter war of words against the French '*usurpadores*.' When the French built a fort in Karabane and obliged the Portuguese to pay custom duties there, while they, on their way upriver, would bluntly refuse to do likewise at Ziguinchor, Barreto tried frantically to dislodge them by sending numerous dispatches to Cape Verde and Portugal, pleading passionately that something be done about the 'usurpation.' Furthermore, he protested strongly to the French authorities at Gorée and, invoking the Anglo-Portuguese Alliance which dated back to 1373, asked the English in Bathurst (Banjul) Gambia and Freetown, Sierra Leone for a warship to be sent to the river Casamance "to defend the integrity of Portugal and her dominions" (cited in Walter 1947, 165).

But it was all in vain. Most disappointing for the Governor of Guinea was the fact that the urgent dispatches to his superiors in Praia and Lisbon met with no response. Frustrated and perplexed, he wondered whether it was because he was "a negro" and so did "not deserve consideration." Greatly disillusioned, he proposed that the *presídio* of Ziguinchor be sold or ceded to salvage the *dignidade nacional* (national dignity) of Portugal. Barreto died a disappointed man in 1859.

With the death of Barreto, the lone voice of protest against the entrenchment of the French in Casamance was silenced. It would appear that Portugal, still recovering from a bloody civil war (1826–1834) which further weakened her politically and economically and having 'lost' Brazil, the most prized 'possession', in 1822, was much more preoccupied with her renewed colonization efforts in Angola and Mozambique and much less concerned with defending her centuries-old pretentions about the right of 'discovery,' occupation, conquest, and colonization.

Therefore, when on 12 May 1886 a Luso-French Treaty was signed in Paris to delimit the respective 'possessions' of Portugal and France in the region, neither the Portuguese themselves, nor the people on either side of the new border (if they were aware), could have been greatly surprised.

Ziguinchor, and the Casamance region in general, partly because of the long 'Portuguese' presence and influence, reflected in the existence of a Portuguese *Crioulo* language, continues to have close ties with Guinea-Bissau. However, the cultural unity between them can be attributed more to the six centuries of domination by the Mandinkas of the Empires of Mali and Kaabu (qq.v.). It remains to be seen whether this fact can be used to help efforts at regional or subregional integration.

Today Ziguinchor is the regional capital of the troublesome Senegalese province of Casamance, which has seen armed conflict between Senegalese troops and soldiers of the Mouvement Des Force Démocratiques de la Casamance (MFDC) (q.v.). Efforts to resolve the Casamance conflict have resulted in an important conference at Cacheu which resulted in a cease-fire between the conflicting parties.

Bibliography

Introduction

The purpose of this bibliography is to provide a substantive listing of some of the principal works about Guinea-Bissau, thereby laying the groundwork for further research and reading. By no means do we claim to be all-inclusive: our focus is on the more significant and accessible publications. In this vein, we made a particular effort to include English-language entries, as these are likely to be the most useful to the majority of readers. While this means that numerous sources in foreign languages have been omitted, we did include many foreign language references to aid the multilingual researcher in a more thorough search of the literature, and because a number of significant aspects of Guinea-Bissau have only been discussed or referred to in those languages (usually Portuguese or French). The relative lack of English language studies on the history of Guinea-Bissau is in part a consequence of the purposeful effort of the Portuguese to restrict non-Lusophone contact with their colonies, except regarding slavery and certain aspects of foreign trade in which relations with the non-Lusophone world were selectively encouraged. The successful nationalist war for independence and the internationally acclaimed writings and speeches of Amilcar Cabral, the leader of the independence struggle, generated a much greater volume of English language publications. Today the majority of works about Guinea-Bissau continue to be published in Portuguese and French, but there is an expanding literature in English reflecting widening academic, journalistic, diplomatic, economic, and cultural exchanges between Guineans and Anglophones.

The organization of the bibliography is as follows:

1. Bibliographies
2. Periodicals Relating to Guinea-Bissau

1. Bibliographies

Bell, Aubrey F.G. *Portuguese Bibliography*. Oxford: Oxford University Press, 1922.

Berman, Sanford. "African Liberation Movements: A Preliminary Bibliography." *Ufahamu*, III, 1 (Spring), 1972.

Bibliografia Cient'fica da Junta de Investigações do Ultramar. Lisbon, 1980.

Boletim de Bibliografia Portuguesa. Lisbon: Biblioteca Nacional.

Cahen, Michel. "Bibliographie" [of relations between Portugal and Luso-African countries], *Afrique Contemporaine*, 137 (January–February–March 1986): 45–55.

Chabal, Patrick. "Bibliography" [of works by or concerning Amilcar Cabral] in *Amilcar Cabral: Revolutionary Leadership and People's War*, 241–269. Edited by P. Chabal, Cambridge: Cambridge University Press, 1983.

Chilcote, Ronald H. "Amilcar Cabral: A Bio-Bibliography of His Life and Thought, 1925–1973." *Africana Journal*, V. 4 (1974): 289–307.

———. *Emerging Nationalism in Portuguese Africa: A Bibliography of Documentary Ephemera Through 1965*. Stanford, CA: Hoover Institution, 1969.

Duignan, Peter, editor. *Guide to Research and Reference Works on Sub-Sahara Africa*. Stanford, California: Hoover Institution Press, 1972.

———, and L.H. Gann. *Vol. 5 of Colonialism in Africa 1870–1960. A Bibliographical Guide to Colonialism in Sub-Saharan Africa*. London: Cambridge University Press, 1973.

Figueiredo, Jaime de. "Bibliografia Caboverdeana: Subsidios para uma Ordenação Sistematica." *Cabo Verde: Boletim de Propaganda e Informação*. V (49)31; (50)31; (54)31; (56)37; 1953–4.

Flores, Michel. "A Bibliographic Contribution to the Study of Portuguese Africa (1965–1972)." *Current Bibliography on African Affairs*, VII, 2 (1974): 116–37.

Gibson, Mary Jane. *Portuguese Africa: A Guide to Official Publications.* Washington, D.C.: Library of Congress, Reference Department, 1967.

Gonçalves, José Júlio. "Bibliografia Antropológica do Ultramar Português." *Boletim Geral das Colonias.* 281–90, 335–41, 431–71, 483–501, 1961.

Gupta, Anirudha. "African Liberation Movements: A Bibliographical Survey." *Africa Quarterly*, X: 52–60, April–June 1970.

Kornegay, Francis A., Jr. "A Bibliographic Memorial to Amilcar Cabral: Selected Survey of Resources on the Struggle in Guinea-Bissau." *Ufahamu*, III, 3: 152–159, Winter 1973.

Lopes, Carlos. *1100 Referências para a Pesquisa em Ciências Sociais na Guiné-Bissau*, 2e Edição. Geneva: Centre de Documentation, Institut Universitaire d'Etudes du Développement, 1985.

McCarthy, Joseph M. *Guinea-Bissau and Cape Verde Islands: A Comprehensive Bibliography.* New York: Garland, 1977.

Matthews, Daniel G. "African Bibliography Today: Selected and Current Bibliographical Tools for African Studies, 1967–1968." *Current Bibliography on African Affairs* , November 1968.

Rogers, Francis Millet and David T. Haberly. *Brazil, Portugal and Other Portuguese-Speaking Lands: A List of Books Primarily in English.* Cambridge, MA: Harvard University Press, 1968.

Ryder, A.F.C. *Materials for West African History in Portuguese Archives.* London: Athlone Press, 1965.

Rydings, H.A. *The Bibliographies of West Africa.* Ibadan: Ibadan University Press, 1961.

Tenreiro, Francisco. "Bibliográfia Geográfica da Guiné." *Garcia de Orta*, II, 1 (1954): 97–134.

United States Library of Congress. *A List of References on the Portuguese Colonies in Africa (Angola, Cape Verde Islands, Mozambique, Portuguese Guinea, São Tomé and Principe).* Washington, D.C., 1942.

2. Periodicals Relating to Guinea-Bissau

Acta. Conselho do Govêrno da Guiné Portuguesa, Bissau, 1919+.

Actas do sessões. Conselho Legislativo. Bissau, 1925+.

Africa. Lisbon.

Africa Confidential. London.

Africa. Literatura—Arte e Cultura. Triannual review focusing on the Luso-African countries. Lisbon.

Africa News. A twice-weekly service for broadcast and print. Durham, N.C.

Africa Report. Rutgers University: New Brunswick, New Jersey.

Afrique Asie. Paris.

Ba-Fatâ: Boletim Informativo. Official publication of the Resistência da Guiné-Bissau/Movimento Ba-Fatâ (Guinea-Bissau Resistance/Ba-Fatâ Movement), Loures/Portugal, since December 1992.

Baguera. Monthly. Official publication of the Partido da Convergência Democrática (Democratic Convergence Party). Bissau, since May 1992

Bantaba. Journal of the secondary school, Kwame N'Krumah. Bissau.

Blufo. Mimeographed journal for the liberated areas. PAIGC:Conakry.

Boletim Arquivo Histórico Colonial. Lisbon.

Boletim Cultural da Guiné Portuguesa. Organ of the Centro de Estudos da Guiné Portuguesa. 1946 +. Lisbon.

Boletim da Sociedade de Geográfia de Lisbõa. Lisbon.

Boletim de Informação Cientifica e Técnica. Quarterly. Published by the Centro de Estudos de Técnologia Apropriada (Centre for the Study of Appropriate Technology) of the Instituto Nacional de Estudos e Pesquisa (National Institute of Studies and Research). Bissau, since January 1988.

Boletim de Informação Sindical. União Nacional de Trabalhadores da Guiné-Bissau.

Boletim de Informação Sócio-económicos. Quarterly. Published by the Centre de Estudos Sócio-económicos (Centre of Socio-Economic Studies) of the *Instituto Nacional de Estudos e Pesquisa* (INEP). Bissau, since November 1985.

Boletim Geral das Colónias. Lisbon.

Boletim Oficial da Guiné Portuguesa. Weekly, 1880 +. Bolama & Bissau.

Boletim Trissemanal da Agência Noticiosa da Guiné-Bissau (A.N.G.).

Cabo Verde; Boletim de propaganda e informação. Monthly, 1949– 1964. Praia.

Comunitário. Monthly. Official publication of the Ministério da Informação e Telecomunicações (Ministry of Information and Telecommunications), Bissau, since 1989.

Corubal. Fortnightly. Official publication of the *Resistência da Guiné-Bissau/Movimento Bâ-Fatâ* (Guinea-Bissau Resistance/Ba-Fata Movement), Bissau, since 1988.

Decisão. Conakry: PAIGC, August 30, 1970.

Diario de Noticias. Lisbon.

Ecos da Guiné: Boletim de informação e de estatística. Bissau, 1951 +.

Expresso Bissau. Independent weekly newspaper. Bissau, since 7 July 1992.

Facts and Reports. Press cuttings on Angola, Mozambique, Guinea-Bissau, Portugal, and Southern Africa, edited by the Angola Comité. Amsterdam.

Feretcha. Folheto Informatívo. Weekly. Official publication of the Partido da Convergência Democrática, Bissau, Since 1993?.

Ganga Real. Official publication of the Frente Democrática (Democratic Front Party). Bissau, since 1991.

Garcia de Orta. Lisbon.

Le Soleil. Senegal.

Libertação. Mimeographed journal for the liberated areas. PAIGC: Conakry.

O Militante. Publication of the Secretariat of the Central Committee of the PAIGC. Bissau.

Mato Malgos: Revista de Educação Ambiental. Fortnightly. Published by the Guinean environmentalist NGO, Tiniguena (a Felupe expression meaning "This land is ours"). Bissau, since January 1993.

Mundo Português. Lisbon.

Nô Pintcha. Official PAIGC publication in Guinea-Bissau since independence. Three times weekly.

Nôs Luta. Orgão de informação da Radio Voz de S. Vincente.

Nubedade: Boletim de Novidades da Biblioteca Pública. Quarterly. Published by the *Instituto Nacional de Estudos e Pesquisa,* (INEP). Bissau, since 1987.

O Democrata. Monthly. Official publication of the *Partido Democrático do Progresso,* Bissau, since March 1993.

Objective: Justice. Quarterly magazine covering United Nations activity against apartheid, racial discrimination, and colonialism. New York: United Nations Office of Public Information.

PAIGC (Partido Africano da Independência da Guiné e Cabo Verde). Edição dos Serviços Cultarais do Conselho Superior da Luta.

PAIGC Actualidades. Boletim Informativo do Comité Central do PAIGC. Monthly.

PAIGC Actualités. Bulletin d'Information édité par la Commission d'Information et Propagande du Comité Central du PAIGC. Monthly, 1969–1974. Conakry.

PAIGC Actualités. LSM Information Center, Richmond, B.C., Canada; quarterly english edition.

PAIGC Actualités: La vie et la lutte en Guinée et Cap-Vert. Monthly; nos. 21–36, 38 (17 numbers in all); September, 1970–February, 1972. Conakry.

Ponto de Encontro. Quarterly. Published by the SOLIDAMI (Solidaridade e Amizade, an organization which coordinates the activities of all the NGOs in the country). Bissau, since January 1989.

Portugal. Anglo-Portuguese Publications.

Portugal em Africa. Lisbon.

Portuguese and Colonial Bulletin. Anti-colonial bulletin published by K. Shingler, London (during the colonial wars).

Présence Africaine. Paris.

Relatório Anual de Actividades do INEP (Annual Report of the Activities of INEP). Published annually by INEP, Bissau, since October 1985.

Revista Militar. Lisbon.

Revista Portugal em Africa. Lisbon.

Soronda. Review of Guinean Students. Published by the National Institute of Studies and Research (INEP) as of April 1986. Bissau.

Soronda. Revista de Estudos Guinéense (Review of Guinean Studies). Bi-yearly. Published by INEP, Bissau, since January 1986.

Southern Africa. New York.

Terceiro Mundo. Lisbon.

Tricontinental Bulletin. Published in Spanish, English, and French by the Executive Secretariat of the Organization of Solidarity of the Peoples of Africa, Asia, and Latin America. Havana, Cuba.

Ufahamu. Berkeley, California.

West Africa. London.

3. General References: Statístical

Anuário da Guiné Portuguesa. Lisbon: Sociedade Industrial de Tipografia, 1946 + .

Anuário estatístico. Annuaire statistique. Lisbon: Tipografia Portuguesa, 1947 + .

Anuário estatístico. II. Províncias ultramarinas, 1969. Lisbon: Instituto Nacional de Estatística, 1971.

Banco Central da Guiné-Bissau. Situação Econômica e Financeira, Bissau, 1992.

Brito, Eduíno. "Guiné Portuguesa—Censo da População Não Civilizada de 1950." *Boletim Cultural da Guiné Portuguesa*, VII, 28 (October 1952): 725–56.

Curtin, Philip D. *The Atlantic Slave Trade: A Census*. Madison, Wis.: University of Wisconsin Press, 1969.

General Inventory of Animal Husbandry. Bissau: General Bureau of Statistics and Planning, State Commission of Economic Development and Planning, 1975.

Heisel, Donald Francis. "The Demography of the Portuguese Territories: Angola, Mozambique and Portuguese Guinea." In W.I. Brass et. al. (eds.), *The Demography of Tropical Africa*, edited by W. I. Brass et. al., 440–465. Princeton, NJ: Princeton University Press, 1968.

Lima, José Joaquim Lopes de. *Prospecto estatístico-econômico da Província de Cabo Verde.* Lisbon, 1875.

————. "Sobre a Statística das Ilhas de Cabo Verde e suas Dependências na Guiné Portuguesa." In José Lima (ed.). *Ensaios Sobre a Statística das Possessões Portuguesas,* vol. 1. Lisbon, 1844.

Macedo, Zeferino Monteiro de. *A Estat'stica ante o Movimento Comercial da Prov'ncia noPeriodo de 1939–1961.* Bissau: Repartição Provincial dos Serviços de Economica e Estatística Geral, 1961.

PAIGC. "La République de Guinée-Bissau en Chiffres." Conakry: Commissariat d'Etat à l'Economie et aux Finances, 1974.

PAIGC. "Sur la Création de l'Assemblée Nationale Populaire en Guinée (Bissau). Résultats et Bases des Elections Générales Réalisés dans les Regions Libérées en 1972." Conakry, 1973.

Província da Guiné—Censo da população de 1950, 2 vols. Bissau: Imprensa Nacional, 1951.

Províncias Ultramarinas Portuguesas: Dados Informativos. Lisbon: Agência Geral do Ultramar, 1962–66.

Recenseamento Geral da População e da Habitação. 16 de Abril de 1979. Bissau: Ministério da Coordenação Econômica e Plano, August 1981.

Resumo Estatístico Aduaneiro—Província da Guiné no Ano de 1914. Lisbon: Ministério das Colônias, Imprensa Nacional, 1916.

Resumo Estatístico Aduaneiro—Província da Guiné no Ano de 1917. Lisbon: Ministério das Colônias, Imprensa Nacional, 1918.

Vieira, Ruy Alvaro. "Alguns Aspectos Demográficos dos Bijagós da Guiné." *Boletim Cultural da Guiné Portuguesa,* X(1955): 23–34.

World Bank. *The World Bank Atlas.* Washington: The World Bank, 1991.

————. *World Tables.* Washington: The World Bank, 1991.

————. *World Debt Tables: External Debt of Developing Countries.* Vol. 2, Washington, 1991.

4. General References: Historical/Legal/Political

Abshire, David M. and Michael A. Samuels, *Portuguese Africa: A Handbook.* New York: Praeger, 1969.

Agência Geral do Ultramar. *Estatuto dos Indígenas Portugueses das Províncias da Guiné, Angola e Mozambique.* Lisbon, 1954

Ajayi, J. F. A., and Crowder, Michael. *History of West Africa,* 2 vols. Columbia University Press: New York, 1972.

Alexis de Saint-Lô. *Relation du voyage au Cap Verd.* Paris: 1637.

Almeida, Pedro Ramos de. *História do Colonialismo Português em*

Africa (Cronológia, do sec. XV a XX). Lisbon: Editorial Estampa, 1979.

Angola Comité. *Portugal and NATO,* 3rd edition. Amsterdam, 1972.

Anon. *Liberation Struggle in Portuguese Colonies.* New Delhi: Peoples Publishing House, 1970.

Axelson, Eric. *Congo to Cape: Early Portuguese Explorers.* New York: Barnes and Noble, 1973.

———. *Portugal and the Scramble for Africa, 1875–1891.* Johannesburg: Witwatersrand University Press, 1967.

Barros, Simão. *Origens da Colónia de Cabo Verde.* Lisbon: n.d.

Beazley, Charles Raymond. *Prince Henry the Navigator (1394–1460).* New York: G.P. Putnam, 1895.

Bennett, Norman, and George E. Brooks. *New England Merchants in Africa.* Boston: Boston University Press, 1965.

Blake, J. W. *Europeans in West Africa 1460–1560,* 2 vols. 1942.

Blake, John W. *European Beginnings in West Africa, 1454–1578.* The Hakluyt Society: London, 1937.

Boulegue, Jean. *Les Luso-Africains de Senegambie.* Lisboa: Ministério da Educação , 1989.

Bovill, Edward William. *The Golden Trade of the Moors: West African Kingdoms in the Fourteenth Century.* Princeton: Marcus Weiner, 1995

Boxer, Charles R. *Race Relations in the Portuguese Colonial Empire 1415–1825.* Oxford: Oxford University Press, 1963.

———. *Portuguese Society in the Tropics.* Madison and Milwaukee, Wisconsin: University of Wisconsin Press, 1965.

———. *The Portuguese Seaborne Empire 1415–1825.* London: Hutchinson, 1969.

———. *Four Centuries of Portuguese Expansion, 1415–1825.* Berkeley and Los Angeles, California: University of California Press, 1972.

Brooks, George E. Jr. *Luso-African Commerce and Settlement in the Gambia and Guinea-Bissau Region.* Boston University, African Studies Center, Working Papers Number 24, 1980

———. *Yankee Traders, Old Coasters and African Middlemen: A History of American Legitimate Trade with West Africa in the Nineteenth Century.* Boston: Boston University Press, 1970.

———. *Kola Trade and State-Building: Upper Guinea Coast and Senegambia, 15th to 17th Centuries.* Boston University, African Studies Center, Working Papers Number 38, 1980.

———. *Landlords and Strangers: Ecology, Society, and Trade in Western Africa, 1000–1630.* Boulder: Westview Press, 1993.

Cadamosto, Luís de. *Viagens de Luís de Cadamosto e de Pedro de Sintra.* Pref. por Damião Peres. Lisboa: Academia Portuguesa da História, 1948.

Caetano, Marcello. *Colonizing Traditions, Principles and Methods of the Portuguese.* Lisbon: Agência Geral do Ultramar, 1951.

————. *Portugal's Reasons for Remaining in the Overseas Provinces*. Lisbon: Agência Geral do Ultramar, 1970.

Carreira, António. *Formação e Extinção de Uma Sociedad Escravocrata (1460–1878)*. Praia: Instituto Cabo-Verdeano de Livro, 1983.

Carson, Patricia. *Materials for West African History in the Archives of Belgium and Holland*. London: Athlone Press, 1962.

Castro, Armando. *O Sistema Colonial Português em Africa (Meados do SéculoXX)*. Lisbon: Editorial Caminho, 1979.

Chilcote, Ronald H. *Emerging Nationalism in Portuguese Africa: Documents*. Stanford, CA: Hoover Institution, 1972.

————. *Portuguese Africa*. Englewood Cliffs, NJ: Prentice-Hall, 1967.

Cipolla, C.M. *Guns and Sails in the Early Phase of European Expansion (1400–1700)*. London, 1965.

Colvin, Lucie Gallistel. *The Uprooted of the Sahel: Migrants' Quest for Cashin the Senegambia*. New York: Praeger, 1981.

Corpo de Polícia de Segurança Pública. *Regulamento, 1956 maio 12*. Praia: Imprensa Nacional, 1956.

Corrêa, António A. Mendes. *Ultramar Português. II. Ilhas de Cabo Verde*. Lisbon: Agência Geral do Ultramar, 1954.

Cortesão, Jaime. *Os Portuguêses em Africa*. Lisbon: Portugália Editora, 1968.

Cortesão, Jaime. *Os Descobrimentos Portuguêses*. 6 vols., 1980 (vols. 1 e 2, 3.); 1975 (vol 4); 1976 (vol. 5); 1978 (vol. 6). Lisboa: Livros Horizonte.

Crone, G. R. trans. and ed. *The Voyages of Cadamosto and Other Document on Western Africa in the Second Half of the Fifteenth Century*. London: The Hakluyt Society, 1937.

Cultru, P. *Premier Voyage du Sieur de La Courbe Fait à la Coste d'Afrique en 1685*. Paris: Champion and Larose, reprinted 1973.

Curtin, Philip D. *Economic Change in Pre-Colonial Africa*. 2 vols., Madison: University of Wisconsin Press, 1976.

Davies, Oliver. *West Africa Before the Europeans*. Metheun: London, 1967.

De Pina, Marie Paule. *Les Îles du Cap Vert*. Paris: Karthala, 1987.

Duffy, James. *Shipwreck and Empire: Being an Account of Portuguese Maritime Disasters in a Century of Decline*. Cambridge: Harvard University Press, 1955.

————. *Portuguese Africa*. Cambridge: Harvard University Press, 1961.

————. "Portugal in Africa." *Foreign Affairs*, XXXIX: 481–493, April 1961.

————. *Portugal in Africa*. Baltimore: Penguin Books, 1962.

Dumont, René and Marie France Mottin. *L'Afrique Etranglée*. Paris: Seuil, 1982.

Duncan, T. Bentley. *Atlantic Islands: Madeira, the Azores, and the Cape Verdes in Seventeenth-Century Commerce and Navigation.* Chicago: University of Chicago, 1972.

Dunn, John. *West African States: Failure and Promise.* Cambridge: Cambridge University Press, 1978.

Durieux, A. "Essai sur le Statut des Indigènes Portugais de la Guinée, de l'Angola et du Mozambique." *Mémoires de l'Académie Royale des Sciences Coloniales—8,* V, 3 (1955).

Ellis, Alfred Burdon. *West African Islands.* London: Chapman and Hall, 1885.

Eltis, David. *Economic Growth and the Ending of the Transatlantic Slave Trade.* Oxford University Press: New York, 1987

Fage, J.D. "Slavery and the Slave Trade in the Context of West African History." *Journal of African History,* 3 (1969).

Fernandez-Armesto, Felipe. *Before Columbus: Exploration and Colonisation from the Mediterranean to the Atlantic, 1229–1492.* London: Macmillan Education Ltd, 1987.

Ferreira, Eduarto de Sousa. *Portuguese Colonialism from South Africa to Europe.* Germany: Druckerei Horst Ahlbrecht, 1972.

———. *Portuguese Colonialism in Africa: The End of an Era.* Paris: Unesco Press, 1974.

Garfield, Robert. *A History of São Tomé Island, 1470–1655.* Mellen Press: Lewiston, NY, 1992.

Gomez, Michael. *Pragmatism in the Age of Jihad: The Precolonial State of Bundu.* Cambridge University Press: New York, 1992 .

Guerreiro, Padre Fernão. *Relação Anual das Coisas que Fizeram os Padres da Companhia de Jesus nas suas Missões, nos Annos de 1600 a 1609.* Imprensa da Universidad, Coimbra, 1930.

Hair, P.E.H., and J. D. Alsop. *English Seamen and Traders in Guinea 1553–1565.* Lewiston, NY: Mellen Press, 1992

Hakluyt, Richard. *Voyages and Discoveries.* Baltimore: Penguin Books, 1972 (first published in 1589.)

Hamdun, Said and Noël King. *Ibn Battuta in Black Africa.* Princeton: Marcus Weiner Publishers, 1994.

Hammond, Richard J. *Portugal and Africa, 1815–1910: A Study in Uneconomic Imperialism.* Stanford, CA: Standord University Press, 1966.

———. "Race Attitudes and Policies in Portuguese Africa in the Nineteenth and Twentieth Centuries." *Race* January 1968.

Hawkins, John. *A True Declaration of the Troublesome Voyage to the Parts of Guinea and the West Indies in 1567 and 1568.* London, 1569.

Herbert, Eugenia W. "Portuguese Adaptation to Trade Patterns: Guiné to Angola (1443–1640)." *African Studies Review,* XVII 1974: 411–423.

Humbaraci, Arslan, and Nicole Muchnik. *Portugal's African Wars.* New York: Third World Press, 1973.

Ibn Battuta. *Travels in Asia and Africa, 1325–54.* Translated by H. A. Gibb. London: Routledge, 1929

Krueger, Hilmar C. "Genoese Trade with Northwest Africa in the Twelfth Century." *Speculum,* 8 1933: 377–395.

Lavradio, Marques do. *Portugal em Africa Depois de 1851.* Lisbon: Agência Geral das Colonias, 1936.

Lawrence, Arnold W. *Trade Castles and Forts of West Africa.* Stanford, California: Stanford University Press, 1964.

Levtzion, Nehemiah. *Ancient Ghana and Mali.* London: Methuen, 1973.

Livermore, Harold. *A New History of Portugal.* Cambridge, 1966.

Lopes, Edmundo Armenio Correia. *A Escravatura: Subsídios para a sua História.* Lisbon: 1944.

Luttrel, A. "Slavery and Slaving in the Portuguese Atlantic to about 1500." *In The Trans-Atlantic Slave Trade from West Africa.* Edinburgh: Centre of African Studies, University of Edinburgh, 1965.

Lyall, Archibald. *Black and White Make Brown: An Account of a Journey to the Cape Verde Islands and Portuguese Guinea.* London: Heinemann, 1938.

Markov, P. "West African History in German Archives." *Journal of the Historical Society of Nigeria.* December 1963.

Marques, António Henrique de Oliveira. *História de Portugal. Desde os Tempos mais Antigos até à Presidência do Sr. General Eanes.* 3 vols. Lisboa: Palas Editores, 1982 (vol. 1, 9. ed.); 1983 (vol. 2, 10. ed.); 1981 (vol. 3, 6. ed.).

———. *History of Portugal.* 2nd ed. 2 vols. New York: Columbia University Press, 1976.

Marques, João Martins de Silva. *Descrobrimentos Portugueses: Documentos para a Sua historia.* 2 vols., Lisboa: Institute para a Alta Cultura, 1944.

Marupa, M.A. *Portuguese Africa in Perspective: The Making of a Multi-Racial State.* 1973.

Mello, Guedes Brandão de. *Relatório do Governor Geral da Província de Cabo Verde, 1890.* Lisbon: Imprensa Nacional, 1891.

Minter, William. *Portuguese Africa and the West.* Baltimore: Penguin Books, 1972.

Monteiro, Júlio, Jr. "Achegas para a História de Cabo Verde." *Cabo Verde: Boletim de Propaganda e Informção,* I, 12 (1949–50): 23.

Moore, Francis. *Travels into the Inland Parts of Africa.* London: Edward Cave, 1738.

Moreira, Adriano. "As 'Elites' das Províncias Portuguesas de Indígenato (Guiné, Angola, Moçambique)." *Garcia de Orta* 4, 2: 159–189, 1956.

———. *Portugal's Stand in Africa.* New York: University Publishers, 1962.

Nielson, Waldemar A. *African Battleline: American Policy Choices in Southern Africa.* New York: Harper and Row, 1965.

Nogueira, Franco. *The United Nations and Portugal. A Study of Anti-Colonialism*. London: Tandem, 1964.

Nunez, Benjamin. *Dictionary of Portuguese African Civilization*, 2 vols., Amsterdam: Hans Zell, 1992.

Park, Mungo. *Travels in the Interior Districts of Africa*. London: G. & W. Nicol, 1799.

Pereira, Duarte Pacheco. *Esmeraldo de Situ Orbis*. Translated and edited by George Kimble. London: Hakluyt Society, 1937.

Peres, Damião. *História dos Descobrimentos Portugueses*. 3rd. ed. Porto: Vertente, 1983.

Prestage, E. *The Portuguese Pioneers*. New York: Barnes and Noble, 1967.

Reade, Winwood. *The African Sketch Book*, 2 vols. London: Smith, 1873.

Roberts, George. *The Four Voyages of Captain George Roberts; Being a Seriesof Uncommon Events, Which Befell Him in a Voyage to the Islands of the Canaries, Cape de Verde, and Barbadoes, from which He Was Bound to the Coast Guinéy*. London: A. Bettenworth, 1726.

Robinson, R. *Contemporary Portugal*. London: George Allen and Unwin, 1979.

Rodney, Walter. *A History of the Upper Guinea Coast, 1545 to 1800*. London: Oxford University Press, 1970.

Salazar, António de Oliveira. *H.E. Professor Oliveira Salazar. Prime Minister of Portugal, Broadcast on 12 August, 1963, Déclaration on Overseas Policy* Lisbon: Secretariado Nacional da Informação, 1960.

———. "Policy in Africa." *Vital Speeches*, XXXIV (March 15, 1968): 325–28.

Santarém, Visconde de. *Recherches sur la Priorité de la Découverte des Pays Situés sur la Côte Ocidentale d'Afrique, au-dela du Cap Bojador, et sur les Progrés de la Science Geographique, aprés les Navigations des Portugais, au XV siecle*. Paris: Librairie Orientale de V Dondey-Dupré, 1842.

Saunders, A.C. de C.M., *A Social History of Black Slaves and Freemen in Portugal 1441–1555*. Cambridge: Cambridge University Press, 1982.

Serrão, Joaquim V. *História Breve da Históriografic Portuguesa*. Lisbon: 1962.

Serrão, Joel (ed.). *Dicionário de História de Portugal*, 4 vols. Lisbon, 1963–70.

Smith, William. *A New Voyage to Guinea*. London: Frank Cass, 1967 (1744).

Sp'nola, António de. *Portugal e o Futuro*. Lisbon: Arcadia, 1974.

Steeber, Horst. "The European Slave Trade and the Feudal Mode of Production on the West African Slave Coast." *Ethnographische-Archaeologische Zeitschrift*, #4, (1969).

Valdearan, Marcos. "De los Antigos Reinos al Domínio Português." *Revista Africa Hoy* (Madrid), 4, 1980.

Vasconceios, Ernesto Júlio de Carvalho. *As Colónias Portuguesas*, 2d edition. Lisbon, 1904.

Venter, Al J. *Africa at War*. Old Greenwich, CT: The Devin-Adair Company, 1974.

Vogt, John. *Portuguese Rule on the Gold Coast, 1469–1682*. Athens Georgia: University of Georgia Press, 1979.

Anon. *War on Three Fronts: The Fight Against Portuguese Colonialism*. Committee for Freedom in Mozambique, Angola and Guinea, 1971.

Whitaker, Paul M. "The Revolutions of 'Portuguese' Africa." *Journal of Modern African Studies*, VIII, 1: 15–35, April 1970.

5. History of Guinea-Bissau

Agência Geral do Ultramar. *Estatuto da Província da Guiné*. Lisbon: 1955.

――――. *Guiné: pequena monografia*. Lisbon, 1961.

――――. *Estatuto político-administrativa da Guiné*. Lisbon, 1963.

――――. *Estatuto político-administrativa da Guiné*. Lisbon, 1964.

――――. *Guiné*. Lisbon, 1967.

――――. *Estatuto político-administrativa da Prov'ncia da Guiné, 542/72*. Lisbon, 1972.

――――. *Estatuto político-administrativa da Guiné*. Lisbon, 1973.

Almeida, Francisco de. "O Antigo Testamento e a Guiné Portuguesa (Alguns Confrontos Ergalogicsos)." Dissertation, Lisboa: Biblioteca do Instituto Técnica, 1971.

Almeida, J.B.P. *Exploração da Senegambia Portuguesa*. Lisbon: 1878.

Alves, Frederico. *Romance da Conquista da Guiné*. Lisbon: 1944.

Andrade, António Alberto de. "História Breve da Guiné Portugesa." *Ultramar*, VII, 4 (April–June) 7–56, 1968.

Andrade Elisa. *The Cape Verde Islands from Slavery to Modern Times*. Dakar: U.N. African Institute for Economic Development and Planning, May 1973.

Andrews, Kenneth R. *Elizabethan Privateering: English Privateering During the Spanish War, 1585–1603*. Cambridge: Cambridge University Press, 1964.

Anon. "A Guiné Portuguesa em Ruínas." *As Colónias Portuguesas*, 1887, 5(17,18): 99–100.

Anon. "Sur le Rio Cacheoó l'Esclavage en Guinée Portuguesa—Moussa Molo." *Bulletinde la Société de Geographie de Lille*. 19, 6, 1893.

Azurara, Gomes Eannes. *Discovery and Conquest of Guiné*, 2 vols. Ed. and Trans. E. Porestage and London: C.R. Beazley, 1896–99.

Barbosa, Honório José. *O Processo Criminal e Civil no Julgado Instructor e no Tribunal Privativo dos Ind'genas.* Bissau: Imprensa Nacional, 1947.

Barcellos, Christiano José de Senna. *Subsídios para a História de Cabo Verde e Guiné,* 7 vols. Lisbon: 1899–1913.

Barreto, Honório Pereira. *Memória sobre o Estado Actual de Senegâmbia Portugueza, Causas de sua Decadencia, e Meios de a Fazer Prosperar.* Lisbon, 1843. Reprint ed., Bissau, 1947.

Barreto, João. *História da Guiné, 1418–1918.* Lisbon: 1938.

Barros, João de. *Chronicles of the Voyages of Cadamosto.* Lisbon: 1937.

Beaver, P. *African Memoranda. Relative to an Attempt to Establish a British Settlement on the Island of Bulama, on the Western Coast of Africa, 1792,* London, 1805 (New York: Humanities Press), 1968.

Bénézet, A. *Relation de la Côte de la Guinée,* 4th ed. London: 1788.

Biker, Joaquim Pedro Vieira Judice. "Relatório sobre a Pacificação da Guiné." Province of Guiné, October 1903.

Boléu, José de Oliveira. *"Viagens de Descobrimento e Exploração Nas Costas da Guiné." Boletim Cultural da Guiné Portuguesa,* Bissau, vol. 1, n. 4. 1946, 713–728.

Boone, Catherine. *Merchant Capital and the Roots of State Power in Senegal:1930–1985.* New York: Cambridge University Press: 1992.

Boulegue, Jean. "Contribution a la Chronologie du Royaume du Saloum." *Bulletin de l'Institut Fondamental d'Afrique Noire,* Dakar, 28, Serie B, 1966, pps. 657–62.

Bernatzik, Hugo Adolf. *Aethiopien des Westens Forshungscreisen in Portugiesisch-Guinea.* 1933

Brazao, Arnaldo. "A Vida Administrativa da Colônia da Guiné." *Boletim Cultural da Guiné Portuguesa.* 7 (July): 751–782, 1947.

Brooks, Geroge E. "Bolama as a Prospective Site for American Colonization in the 1820s and 1830s." *Boletim Cultural da Guiné Portuguesa,* XXVIII (January 1973): 5–22.

Brosselard, le Capitaine H. "Voyage dans la Senegambie et la Guiné Portuguaise." *Le Tour du Monde—Nouveau Journal des Voyages* (Paris), LVII: 97–144, 1889.

Campos, Valentim da Fonseca. *Guiné à Saque—Documentos e Factos para a História.* Lisbon, 1912.

Caroço, Jorge F. Velez. *Relatório Anual do Governador da Guiné,* 1921–1922. Coimbra, 1923.

Carreira, António Augusto Peixoto. *Guiné Portuguesa,* 2 vols. Lisbon, 1954.

———. "Aspectos Históricos da Evolução do Islamismo na Guiné Portuguesa." *Boletim Cultural da Guiné Portuguesa,* XXI: 405–56, 1966.

———. *As Companhias Pombalinas de Navagação.* Lisbon: 1969.

――――. "Alguns Aspectos da Administração Publica em Cabo Verde no Século XVIII." *Boletim Cultural da Guiné Portuguesa*, XXVII, 105 (January): 123–204, 1972.

――――. *Documentos Para a História das Ilhas de Cabo Verde e "Rios de Guiné."* Lisbon, 1983.

――――. *Cabo Verde: Formaçao e Extinção de uma Sociedade Escravocrata (1460–1878).* Praia: Instituto Cabo-Verdeano do Livro, 1983.

――――. *Os Portugueses nos Rios de Guiné (1500–1900).* Lisbon, 1984.

Casimiro, Augusto. *A Ocupação Militar da Guiné.* In *História da Expansão Portuguesa no Mundo.* Lisboa: Editorial Atica, 1940; vol. 3, 359–370.

Castro, Armando Augusto Gonçalves de Moraes. *Memória da Província da Guiné.* Bolama, 1925.

Chagas, C.I.R. das. *Escoberta e ocupação da Guiné só pelos portuguesas.* Lisbon, 1840.

Chelmicki, José Conrado Carlos de. *Corografia Cabo-Verdiana ou Descripção Geografico-Historica da Provincia da Ilhas de Cabo-Verde e Guiné.* Tomes I and II, Lisbon, 1841.

Coelho, Francisco de Lemos. *Duas descrições seiscentistas da Guiné.* Damião Peres (ed.). Lisbon: Academia Portuguesa da História, 1669 [1953].

Conselho de Inspecção de Produtos de Exportação. *Regulamento. Aprovado por Portaria numero 139, de 23 de dezembro de 1935.* Bolama: Imprensa Nacional, 1936.

Congresso Comemorativo do Quinto Centanário do Descobrimento da Guiné, 2 vols. Lisbon, 1946.

Corbeil, R., R. Mauny and J. Charbonnier. "Préhistoire et Protohistoire de la Presqu'île du Cap-Vert et de l'Extrême Ouest Africain." *Bulletin, Institut Français d'Afrique Noire*, X(1948): 378–460.

Cortesão, Armando Zuzarte. "Subsídios para a História do Descobrimento da Guiné e Cabo Verde." *Boletim Geral das Colónias.* LXXVI, 1(1931): 2–39.

Costa, Abel Fontoura da. *Cartas das ilhas de Cabo Verde de Valentim Fernandes, 1506–1508.* Lisbon: Agência Geral do Ultramar, 1939.

Cunha, Amadeu. *Quinto centenário da descoberta da Guiné, 1446–1946.* Bissau: 1946.

Da Mota, Avelino Teixeira. "A Descoberta da Guiné." *Boletim Cultural da Guiné Portuguesa.* I, 1: 11–68 (January); 2: 273–326 (April); 3: 457–509 (July), 1946.

――――. "O Problema da Descoberta da Guiné Portuguesa." In *Congresso Comemorativo do Quinto Centenário do Descobrimento da Guiné.* vol. 1, p. 333–338, Lisboa: Sociedade de Geográfia de Lisboa, 1946.

———. "Chronologia e Ambito das Viagens Portuguesas de Descoberta da Africa Occidental, de 1445 a 1462." *Boletim Cultural da Guiné Portuguesa*. II, 6: 315–341 (April), 1947.

———."Notas sobre a Historiográfia da Expansão Portuguesa e as Modernas Correntes da Investigação Africana." *Anais do Clube Militar e Naval*. LXXIX, 7–9: 229–294 (July–September), 1949.

———. "Fernao Vaz, Explorador Ignorado do Golfo da Guiné." *Boletim Cultural da Guiné Portuguesa*, 379–384, 1951.

———. *Guiné Portuguesa*, 2 vols. Lisboa: Agencia-Geral do Ultramar, 1954.

———. "O Centenário da Morte de Honório Barreto." *Boletim Cultural da Guiné Portuguesa*. XIII, 50 (April): 195–202, 1958.

———."Descoberta de Bronzes Antigos na Guiné Portuguesa." *Boletim Cultural da Guiné Portuguesa*. XV, 59 (July): 625–34, 1960.

———. "Un Document Nouveau pour l'Historie des Peuls au Senegal Pendant les XVeme et XVIéme Siecles." *Boletim Cultural da Guiné Portuguesa*. XXIV: 782–860, 1969.

———. *As Viagens do Bispo D. Frei Vitoriano Portuênse a Guiné e a Cristianização dos Reis de Bissau*. Lisboa: Centro de Estudos de Cartografia Antiga, 1974.

Da Silva, Francisco Teixeira. *Relatório do Govêrno da Província da Guiné Portuguesa com Referência a 1887–1888*. Lisboa: Tipografia Minerva Central, 1889.

Da Silva, Maria da Graca Garcia Nolasco. "Subsídios para o Estudo dos 'Lançados' na Guiné." *Boletim Cultural da Guiné Portuguesa*. Vol. 25, nos. 97–100, 1970.

Da Silva, Viriato Lopes Ramos. "Subsídios para a História Militar da Ocupação da Província da Guiné." *Boletim da Sociedade de Geográfia de Lisbôa*. XXXIII, 9–10, (September–October): 33–50, 1915.

De Almada, André Alvares. *Relação ou Descripção de Guinée*. Lisbon: 1733.

———. "Tratado Breve dos Rios de Guiné de Cabo Verde ate os Baixos de Santa Ana." In Africa Ocidental (1570–1600). Edited by A. Brasio. Vol. III, *Monumentos Missionaria Africana*. Lisboa: Agencia-Geral do Ultramar, 1964, (first published in 1594, then 1841).

De Gouveia, Pedro Inácio. *Relatório do Governador da Província da Guiné Portuguesa*. 1882.

Dinis, Antonio J. Dias. "A Influência de Cabo Verde na Colonização da Guiné." *Boletim da Sociedade de Geografia de Lisbôa*, 57–64, 1943.

———. *O Quinto Centenário do Descobrimento da Guiné Portuguesa à Luz da Crítica Histórica, 1446–1946*. Braga, 1946.

———. "Guiné Portuguesa. A Influência Política, Social e Económica dos Regimentos na Formação da Colonia." *Boletim Cultural da Guiné Portuguesa*, V, 18 (April): 225–256, 1950.

————. "O Descobrimento da Guiné—Aires Tinoco—Um Héroi Ignorado." *Boletim Cultural da Guiné Portuguesa*. VII, 27 (July 1952): 645–56.

Donelha, André. *Descrição da Serra Leoa e dos Rios de Guiné do Cabo Verde(1625) [An account of Sierra Leone and the Rivers of Guinea of Cape Verde (1625)]*. Edição do texto português, introdução, notas e apêndice por Avelino Teixeira da Mota. Notas e tradução inglesa por P. E. H. Hair. Lisboa: Junta de Investigações Científicas do Ultramar, 1977.

————. "Os Rios da Guiné no livro do geógrafo flamengo D. O' Dapper. Descrição da Africa. Séc.XVII." *Boletim Cultural da Guiné Portuguesa*, Bissau. vol. 6, n. 23, 1951, p: 711–743.

————. "A Guiné ou Senegâmbia Portuguesa. No tempo do Governador Pedro Inácio de Gouveia." *Boletim Cultural da Guiné Portuguesa*, Bissau, vol. 7, n. 26, 1952, p. 403–476.

Duarte, Fausto Castilho. *Anuário da Guiné Portuguesa, 1946–1948*. Lisbon: Agência Geral das Colonias, 1948.

————. "Os Caboverdeanos na Colonização da Guiné." *Cabo Verde: Boletim de Propaganda e Informação*. I, 2(13), 1949–50.

————. "A Libertação de Guiné Portuguesa pela Carta de Lei de 1879." *Boletim Cultural da Guiné Portuguesa*, VII, 28 (October): 789–832, 1952.

————. "A Organização Administrativa da Guiné de 1615 a 1676." *Boletim Cultural da Guiné Portugesa*. XIV, 53 (January: 97–122, 1959.

Esteves, Maria Luísa. *A Questão Do Casamansa E A Delimitação das Fronteiras da Guiné*. Bissau: Instituto Nacional de Estudos e Pesquisa, 1988.

Fargues, G. "Guinée-Bissao et Archipels Portugais." in *Année Africaine, 1968*, 259–60. Paris: A. Pédone, 1970.

Faro, Jorge. "Duas Expedições Enviades a Guiné Anteriormente a 1474 e Custeadas pela Fazenda de D. Afonso V." *Boletim Cultural da Guiné Portugesa*, XII, 45 (January): 47–104, 1957.

————. "Os Problemas de Bissau, Cacheu e suas Dependencias Visitos em 1831 por Manuel António Martins." *Boletim Cultural da Guiné Portuguesa*. XIII, 50 (April): 203–18, 1958.

————."O Movimento Comercial do Porto de Bissau de 1788 a 1794." *Boletim Cultural da Guiné Portuguesa*. XIV, 54 (April): 231–60, 1959.

Ferreira Diniz, José. de Oliveira. "A Política Indígena na Guiné Portuguesa," in, *Congresso do V Centenário do Descobrimento da Guiné*, Vol. 1, 2–20. Lisboa: Bertrand, 1946.

Fonseca, Alfredo Loureiro da. "As Relações do Descobrimento da Guiné e das Ilhas dos Açores, Madeira e Cabo Verde." *Boletim da Sociedade de Geografia de Lisbôa*. XIV, 5: 267–93, 1898–1899

————. *Guiné. Alguns Aspectos Ineditos da Actual Situação da Colônia*. Lisbon: Sociedade de Geografia de Lisboa, 1915.

Galvão, Henrique. *Outras Terras, Outras Gentes*, vol. 1. Lisbon: 1944.
———. *Portuguese Guinea*. London: His Majesty's Stationery Office, 1920.
Gomes, Diogo. *De la Première Découverte de la Guinée*. Centro de Estudos da Guiné Portuguesa, Publication 21, Bissau, 1959.
Hawkins, Joye Bowman. "Conflict, Interaction, and Change in Guinea-Bissau: Fulbe Expansion and Its Impact, 1850–1900." Ph.D. Dissertation, UCLA, Los Angeles, 1980.
Innes, Gordon. *Kaabu and Fuladu; Historical Narratives of the Gambian Mandinka*. London: School of Oriental and African Studies, University of London, 1976.
Keymis, Lawrence. *A Relation of the Second Voyage to Guinea, Performed and Written in the Year 1596*. London, 1596.
Lança, Joaquim da Graça Correia. *Relatório da Província da Guiné Portuguesa Referido ao Anno Económica de 1888–1889*. Lisbon: Imprensa Nacional, 1890.
Leary, Frances A. *Gabu in the Nineteenth Century: A Study of Futa Jalon-Firdu-French Relations*. London: Conference on Manding Studies, University of London, 1972.
Leite, Duarte. "Do Livro Inédito: 'Acerca da Crónica da Guiné.' " *O Diabo*. III, 142, (March), 1937.
———. *Acerca da "Crônica dos Feitos de Guiné."* Lisboa: Bertrand, 1941.
———. "Um Crítico da Crônica da Guiné." *Revista de Universidade de Coimbra* XIV, 1942.
———. "O Cinco Centenário do Descobrimento da Guiné Portuguesa à Luz da Crítica Histórica." *Seara Nova* , October, 122–30, 1946.
Lereno, Alvaro de Paiva de Almeida. *Subsídios para a História da Moeda em Cabo Verde, 1460–1940*. Lisbon: Agência Geral das Colonias, 1942.
———. "A Política Ultramarina Portuguesa no Seculo XVIII." *Ultramar, 30,* 1967.
Lobato, Alexandre. "A Expansão Ultramarina Portuguesa nos Séculos XVI e XVII." *Ultramar, 29,* 1967.
———. "As Fontes e as Formas da Reorganização Ultramarina Portuguesa no Século XIX." *Ultramar, 30,* 1967.
Lopes, Carlos. *Mansas, Escravos, Grumetes E Gentio: Cacheu na encruzilhada de civilizaçoes*. Bissau: Institute Nacional de Estudos e Pesquisa, 1993.
Lyall, Archibald. *Black and White make Brown*. A Study of Portuguese Guinea and Cape Verde. London, Heinemann, 1936.
Manding Studies Conference. London, School of Oriental and African Studies, 1972.
Marinho, Joaquim Pereira. *Primera Parte do Relatório de Alguns Accon-*

tecimentos Notaveis em Cabo Verde, Reposta a Differentes Acusações Feitas Contra O Brigadeiro. Lisbon, 1838.

Martins, Alfredo Cardoso de Soveral. *Relatório do Governador da Guiné.* Bolama: 1903.

Mauny, Raymond. "Navigations et Découvertes Portugaises sur les Côtes Ouest-Africaines." *Boletim Cultural da Guiné Portuguesa.* VII, 27(July 1952): 515–24.

Mauro, Frédéric. *Le Portugal et l'Atlantique au XVIIeme Siècle, 1570–1670. Etude Économique.* Paris: Ecole Pratique des Hautes Études, 1960.

Mees, Jules. "Les Manuscrits de la Crônica do Descobrimento e Conquista de Guiné par Gomes Eannes de Azurara et les Sources de João de Barros." *Revista Portuguesa Colonial e Maritima.* IX, 50: 50–62, 1901.

Mendy, Peter Karibe. "The Problems and Prospects of Liberation Education in Guinea-Bissau." Master of Social Science Dissertation, University of Birmingham , England, 1980.

———. "A Economia Colonial da Guiné-Bissau: Nacionalização e Exploração, 1915–1959."in, *Soronda, Revista de Estudos Guinéense.* No. 9: 25–51. INEP, Bissau., Jan. 1990.

———. *Colonialismo Português em Africa: A Tradição de Resistência na Guiné-Bissau, (1879–1959).* Bissau: Instituto Nacional de Estudos e Pesquisa, 1994.

Miguéis, João José de Melo. "*Ocupação Militar da Guiné.* Resumo Histórico extraído dum trabalho inédito." *In Exposição Histórica da Ocupação. Principais factos da ocupação ultramarina (Séculos XIX e XX, até à Grande Guerra).* Lisboa: Agência-Geral das Colónias, 1937: 5–29.

Monod, T., Avelino Teixeira da Mota and R. Mauny. *Description de la côte occidentale d'Afrique par Valentim Fernandes (1506–1510).* 1951

Nazareth, Ilido Marinho Falcao de Castro. *Projecto de Ocupação da Província da Guiné e sua Organização Militar.* Lisbon: Imprensa Nacional, 1911.

Negociações Relativas à Delimitação das Possessões Portuguesas e Francesas na Africa Ocidental. Documentos apresentados às Cortes na Sessão Legislativa de 1887 pelo Ministro e Secretário de Estado dos Negócios Estrangeiros. 2 vols. Lisboa: Imprensa Nacional, 1887.

Nolasco Da Silva, Maria G. G. "Subsídios para o Estudo dos Lançados da Guiné." *Boletim Cultural da Guiné Portuguesa*, Bissau, 25: 25–40, 217–32, 397–420, 1970.

Oliveira, José Marques de. "Honório Barreto e os Interesses Portugueses em Africa." *Cabo Verde: Boletim de Propaganda e Informação.* XI, 123(1959–60): 13.

PAIGC. *História da Guiné e Ilhas de Cabo Verde.* Porto: 1974.

Pattee, Richard. "Portuguese Guinea: A Microcosm of a Plural Society in Africa." *Plural Societies*. IV, 4: 57–64, Winter 1973.

Pélissier, René. *Naissance de la Guiné: Portugais et Africains en Sénégambie (1841–1936)*, Orgeval, France: Pélissier Montamets, 1989.

Pereira, Pachecho. *Esmeraldu de Situ Orbis*. 1937.

Pimpão, Alvaro Júlio da Costa. "A 'Crônica da Guiné' de Gomes Eanes da Zurara." *Biblos* XVII (1926): 374–89, 595–607, 647–87.

Pinto, João Teixeira da. *A Ocupação Militar da Guiné*. Lisbon: Agência Geral das Colonias, 1936.

Quinn, Charlotte A. *Mandingo Kingdoms of the Senegambia*. Evanston, Illinois: Northwestern University Press, 1972.

———. "A 19th Century Fulbe State." *Journal of African History*. XII (1971): 427–40.

Ravenstein, E.G. "The Voyages of Diogo Cão and Bartolomeu Dias, 1482–88." *Geographical Journal*, 625–55, 1900.

Rema, Henrique Pinto. "As Primeiras Missões da Costa da Guiné (1533–1640)." Separata do *Boletim Cultural da Guiné Portuguesa*. 22, 87/88: 225–268, 1967.

Rocha, Carlos Ayala Vieira da. *João Teixeira Pinto. Uma Vida Dedicava a Ultramar*. 1971.

Schoenmakers, Hans. "The Establishment of the Colonial Economy in Guinea Bissau." *Les Cahiers du CEDAF*. Brussels, 2–3–4: 3–29, June–July 1986.

Sidibe, Bakary K. *The Story of Kaabu: Its Extent and People*. London: Conference on Manding Studies, University of London, SOAS, 1972.

Roche, Christian. "Ziguinchor et son Passé (1645–1920)." *Boletim Cultural da Guiné Portuguesa.*, vol. 28, 109: 35–59, 1973.

Rodrigues, Manuel M. Sarmento. *No Governo da Guiné. Discursos e Afirmações*. Lisbon: Agência Geral do Ultramar, 1949.

———. *The Portuguese Overseas Province*. Lisboa: Agência Geral do Ultramar, 1954.

———. *No governo da Guiné*. Lisboa: Agência Geral do Ultramar, 1954

Silva, Joaquim Duarte. *Honório Pereira Barreto. (Notas para uma Biografia)*. Lisboa: Agência-Geral das Colónias, (Col. Pelo Império, N. 52), 1939.

Smith, William. *A New Voyage to Guinea* . London: John Nourse, 1744.

Snelgrave, William. *Nouvelle Relation de quelques Endroits de Guinée et du Commerce d'Esclaves qu'on y fait*. Amsterdam: 1735.

Teague, Michael. "Bulama in the Eighteenth Century." *Boletim Cultural da Guiné Portuguesa* XIII, 50: 175–194, April 1958.

Teixeira, Cândido da Silva. "Companhia de Cacheu, Rios e Comércio da Guiné (Documentos para a sua História)." *Boletim do Arquivo Histórico Colonial* I, 85–521, 1950.

Trigo, António B. Morais. "A Morte de Nuno Tristão." *Boletim Cultural da Guiné Portuguesa*. II, 5, 189–92: January 1947.

União Nacional de Guiné. *Guiné—Ano XVI da Revolução Nacional.* Bissau, 1943.

United States. Department of State. *Portuguese Guinea.* Washington, D. C., 1966.

Vasconceios, Ernesto Júlio de Carvalho e. *Guiné Portuguesa.* Lisbon: Tipografia da Cooperativa Militar, 1917.

Viegas, Luís António de Carvalho. *Guiné Portuguesa*, 3 vols. Lisbon: Sociedade de Geografia de Lisbōa, 1936–40.

———. *Ilha de Canhabaque. Relatório das Operações Militares em 1935–36 pelo Governador Major de Cavalaria.* Bolama: Imprensa Nacional, 1937.

———. "História Militar da Guiné na sua História Geral." *Revista Militar,* 1946.

Walter, Jaime, ed. *Honório Pereira Barreto: Biografia, Documentes. Memória sobre o Estado Actual da Senegâmbia Portuguesa.* Bissau: Centro de Estudos da Guiné Portuguesa, Públication 5, 1947.

Wren, Walter. *The Voyage of Mr. George Fenner to Guiné, and the Islands of Cape Verde, in the Year of 1566.* London: J.M. Dent, 1927.

Zurara, Gomes Eanes da. *The Chronicle of the Discovery and Conquest of Guinea.* 2 vols. London: Hakluyt Society, 1896–9. First published in 1452.

———. *Crônica do Descobrimento e Conquista da Guiné.* Segundo o manuscrito da Biblioteca Nacional de Paris. Introdução de José de Bragança. 2 vols. Porto: Livraria Civilização, Editora, 1937.

———. *Crônica dos feitos de Guiné.* 2 vols. Lisbon, 1949.

6. Physical Features, Geography, Flora and Fauna

Brito, Raquel Soeiro de. *Guiné, Cabo Verde e São Tomé e Príncipe, Alguns Aspectos da Terra e dos Homens.* Lisbon: 1966.

Cabral, Rego, and J.M. Seguro. "Pequeno Estudo Sobre os Pavimentos Terreos da Guiné e o Endurecimento das Ruas de Bissau." *Boletim Cultural da Guiné Portuguesa.* IV, 14: 265–72, April 1949.

Carvalho, José A.T., and Fernando J.S. de F.P. Nunes. *Contribuição para o Estudo do Problema Florestal da Guiné Portuguesa.* Lisbon: Junta de Investigações do Ultramar, 1956.

Castel-Branco, Armando J.F. "Entomofauna da Guiné Portuguesa e S. Tomé e Príncipe: *Hemípteros* e *Himenópteros.*" *Boletim Cultural da Guiné Portuguesa.* XI, 44: 67–86, October 1956.

Church, R. J. Harrison. *West Africa. A Study of the Environment and of Man's Use of it.* New York: John Wiley, 1961.

Cortesão, Armando. *Cartografia e Cartografos Portuguesas dos Seculos XV e XVI*. 2 vols. Lisboa: Edição da Seara Nova, 1935.

Costa, João Carrington S. da. *Fisiografia e Geologia da Província da Guiné*. Porto: Imprensa Moderna, 1946.

Crespo, Manuel Pereira. *Trabalhos da Missão Geo-hidrográfica da Guiné, 1948–55*. Bissau: Centro de Estudos da Guiné Portuguesa, Publication 18, 1955.

Ferreira, Fernando Simoes da Cruz. "A Guiné-Suas Características e Alguns Problemas." *Boletim Geral das Colónias*. XXVI, 306: 9–27, December 1950.

Guerra, Manuel dos Santos. *Terras da Guiné e Cabo Verde*. Lisbon: 1956.

Guimarães, C. "As Chuvas na Guiné Portuguesa." *Boletim Cultural da Guiné Portuguesa*, XII, 47: 315–32, July 1957.

———. "O clima da Guiné Portuguesa." *Boletim Cultural da Guiné Portuguesa*. XIV, 55: 295–358, July 1959.

Henriques, Fernando Pinto de Almeida. " 'Secas' e 'Crises' no Arquipélago de Cabo Verde." *Cabo Verde: Boletim de Propaganda e Informação*. XII, 143, 35, 1960–1961.

Mota, Avelino Teixeira da. *Toponimos de Origem Portuguesa na Costa Ocidental de Africa desde o Cabo Bojador ao Cabo de Santa Caterina*. Bissau: Centro de Estudos da Guiné Portuguesa, publication 14, 1947.

Stallibrass, Edward. "The Bijonga or Bissagos Islands." *Proceedings of the Royal Geographical Society*. XI, 595–601, 1889.

Teixeira, A. J. da Silva. *Os Solos da Guiné Portuguesa*. Lisbon, 1962.

United States. Department of the Interior. Army Map Service. Geographic Names Division. *Portuguese Guinea: Official Standard Names Approved by the U.S. Board on Geographic Names*. Washington, D.C.: U.S. Government Printing Office, 1968.

Vasconcelos, Ernesto Julio de Carvalho e. *Colónias Portuguesas: Estudo Elementar de Geografia Física, Económica e política. Guiné Portuguesa*. Lisboa, 1917.

7. Anthropology and Ethnology

Ameida, António de. "Das Etnonomias da Guiné Portuguesa, do Arquipélago de Cabo Verde e das Ilhas de São Tomé e Príncipe." *Boletim Geral das Colónias*. LIV, 109–48, 1938.

———. "Sobre e Etno-economia da Guiné Portuguesa." *Boletim Geral das Colónias*. LV, 166–167, 22–32, 1939.

Anon. "Les Traditions Orales du Gabu." *Actes du Colloque Interna-*

tional sur les Traditions Orales du Gabu," *Ethiopiques* (Dakar), No. 28, Special Issue (October 1981).

Atkins, Guy, ed. *Manding: Focus on an African Civilization*. School of Oriental and African Studies: London, 1972.

Barbosa, Honório. "Os Indígenas da Guiné Perante a Lei Portuguesa". *Boletim Cultural da Guiné Portuguesa*. 2 (6) 1947: 343–362.

Barbosa, Octávio C. Gomes. "Breve Notícia dos Caracteres Étnicos dos Indígenas da Tribo Beafada." *Boletim Cultural da Guiné Portuguesa*. I, 2: 205–71, April 1946.

————. "Contribuição para o Estudo dos Biafadas." Disertação, Instituto Superior de Ciências e Política Ultramarina, Universidade Técnica, Lisbon, n.d. [c. 1968].

Barros, Augusto de. "A Invasão Fula da Circunscrição de Bafata. Queda dos Beafadas e Mandingas. Tribos 'Gabungabé.' " *Boletim Cultural da Guiné Portuguesa*. II, 7: 737–43, July 1947.

Barros, Luis Frederico de. *Senegambia Portuguesa ou Notícia Descriptiva das Diferentes Tribus que Habitam a Senegambia Meridional*. Lisbon: Matos Moreira, 1878.

Bérenger-Féraud, L.J.B. *Les Peuplades de la Sénégambie*. Paris: 1879.

Bernatzik, H. A. *Aethiopien des Westens*. 2 vols. Vienna: 1933.

Bertrand-Bocande, M. "Notes sur la Guinée-Portugaise ou Senegambie Meridinale." *Bulletin de la Societie de Geographie*, Ser. 3, XI 1849: 265–350; XII: 56–93.

Brito, Edúino. "A Poligamia e a Natalidade entre os Grupos Étnicos Manjaco, Balanta e Brâme." *Boletim Cultural da Guiné Portuguesa*, VII, 25: 161–179, January 1952.

————. "Aspectos Demográficos dos Balantas e Brâmes do Território de Bula." *Boletim Cultural da Guiné Portuguesa*. VIII, 31: 417–470, July 1953.

————. "Onomástica Fula e os Graus de Parentesco." *Boletim Cultural da Guiné Portuguesa*. 599–616, 1955.

————. "Festas Religiosas do Islamismo Fula." *Boletim Cultural da Guiné Portuguesa*, XI, 41: 91–106, January 1956.

————. "Notas sobre a Vida Religiosa dos Fulas e Mandingas." *Boletim Cultural da Guiné Portuguesa*. XII, 46: 149–190, April 1957.

————. "Notas sobre a Vida Familiar e Jurídica da Tribo Fula. Instituições Civis. I. A Família." *Boletim Cultural da Guiné Portuguesa*. XII, 47: 301–314, July 1957.

————. "Notas sobre a Vida Familiar e Jurídica da Tribo Fula. Instituições Civis. II. O Casamento." *Boletim Cultural da Guiné Portuguesa*, XIII, 49: 7–24, January 1958.

————. "O Direito Costumeiro e o Conceito Espécial de Personalidad." *Boletim Cultural da Guiné Portuguesa*. XX, 79: 213–234, July 1968.

Bull, Jaime Pinto. "Balantas de Mansoa." *Inquerito Etnografico*, Bissau, 1947.

————. "Subsídios para o Estudo da Circumcisão entre os Balantas." *Boletim Cultural da Guiné Portuguesa*. VI, 24: 947–954, October 1951.

Cardoso, Carlos. "Ki-Yang-Yang: Uma Nova Religiäo dos Balantas?" *Soronda*. No. 10, 3–15, July 1990.

————. *Religion und Gesellschaftliche Reproduktion: Über die Struktur und Funktionsweise der Balantareligion* (Religion and Social Reproduction: About the Structure and Functioning of Balanta Religion), PhD Thesis, Friedrich-Schiller University, Jena, Germany, 1991.

————. *Mythos, Religion und Philosophisches Denken in Guinea-Bissau*. Cuba: CEAMO, n.d.

Caroço, Jorge Vellez. *Monjur, O Gabú e A Sua História*. Centro de Estudos da Guiné Portuguesa, No. 8, 1948.

Carreira, António Augusto Peixoto. *Vida, Religião e Morte dos Mandingos*. Lisbon: 1938.

————. "Alguns Aspectos do Regime Jurídico da Propriedade Imobiliária dos Manjacos." *Boletim Cultural da guiné Portuguesa*. I, 4 (October 1946): 707–12.

————. "Aspectos Históricos da Evolução do Islamismo na Guiné Portuguesa." *Boletim Cultural da Guiné Portuguesa*, Separata do No. 84: 405–437, 1946.

————. "A Etnonímia dos Povos de entre o Gâmbia e o Estuario do Geba." *Boletim Cultural da Guiné Portuguesa*. XIX: 233–276, 1946.

————. *Vida Social dos Manjacos*. Centro de Estudos da Guiné Portuguesa, No. 1, 1946.

————. *Mandingas da Guiné Portuguesa*. Centro de Estudos da Guiné Portuguesa, No. 4, 1947.

————. *Fulas do Gabú*. Bissau: Centro de Estudos da Guiné Portuguesa, 1948.

————. *Mutilações Corporais e Pinturas Cutaneas Rituais dos Negros da Guiné Portuguesa*. 51 pp. Bissau: Centro de Estudos da Guiné Portuguesa, publication 12, 1950.

————. "A Poligamia entre os Grupos Étnicos da Guiné Portuguesa." *Boletim Cultural da Guiné Portuguesa*. VI, 24: 924–925, October 1951.

————. "O Levirato no Grupo Étnico Manjaco." *Boletim Cultural da Guiné Portuguesa*. VIII, 29: 107–112, January 1953.

————. "Região dos Manjacos e dos Brâmes." *Boletim Cultural da Guiné Portuguesa*. XV, 60: 735–784, October 1960.

————. "Organização Social e Economica dos Povos da Guiné Portuguesa." *Boletim Cultural da Guiné Portuguesa*. XVI, 64: 641–736, October 1961.

————. *O Fundamento dos Etnónimos na Guiné Portuguesa*. Bissau: Centro de Estudos da Guiné Portuguesa, 1962.

————. "Social and Economic Organization of the People of Portuguese Guinea." *Translations on Africa*, 1–99, 5 October 1962.

————. "Aspectos da Influência da Cultura Portuguesa na Area Compreendide entre o Rio Senegal e o Norte da Serra Leõa (Subsídio para o seo Estudo)." *Boletim Cultural da Guiné Portuguesa*, XIX: 373–416, 1964.

————. "As Primeiras Referências Escritas à Excisão Clitoridiana no Ocidente Africano." *Boletim Cultural da Guiné Portuguesa*. XX, 147–150, 1965.

————. "Manjacos-Brames e Balantas." *Boletim Cultural da Guiné Portuguesa*. 22, 85/86: 41–62, 1967.

————. *Panaria Cabo Verde-Guinéense Aspectos Históricos e socioeconómicos*. Lisbon: Museu de Etnologia do Ultramar, 1968.

Carreira, António Augusto Peixoto and A. Martins de Meireles. "Notas sobre os Movimentos Migratórios da População Natural da Guiné Portuguesa." *Boletim Cultural da Guiné Portuguesa*. XIV, 53, January 1959.

Carreira, António Augusto Peixoto and J. Basso Marques. *Subsídios para a Estudo da Lingua Manjaca*. Centro de Estudos da Guiné Portuguesa, No. 3 , 1946.

Carvalho, Joaquim Pereira Garcia. "Nota sobre a Distribuição e História das Populações do Posto de Bedanda." *Boletim Cultural da Guiné Portuguesa*. IV: 307–318, April 1949.

Castro, Armando Augusto Gonçalves de Morais e. "Etnografia da Colónia da Guiné." *Mensario Administrativo*. VII: 27–30, April 1948.

Cesar, Amandio. *Em 'Chao Papel' na Terra da Guiné*. Lisbon: 1967.

Charry, Eric. *Musical Thought, History, and Practice among the Mande of West Africa*. Ph.D. Dissertation, Princeton University, 1992.

Cisse, Nouha. *La Fin du Kaabu et les Débuts du Royaume du Fuladu*. Mémoire de Maítrise, Université de Dakar, 1977–78.

Conduto, João Eleuterio. *Influência do Islamismo na Vida Económica dos Fulas*. Lisbon: 1965.

Corrêa, António A. Mendes. *Études Anthropologiques sur les Populations de l'Archipel de Cap Vert et de la Guinée Portugaise* vol. 2. Dakar: Institut Français d'Afrique Noire, 1950–51.

————. "Movimentos de Populações na Guiné Portuguesa." *Actas y Memorias. Sociedad Española de Anthropologia, Etnografia y Pre-História*. XXII, 1/4: 179–196, 1947.

————. *Raças do Império*. Lisbon: 1943.

————. *Uma jornada científica na Guiné Portuguesa*. Lisbon: Agência Geral das Colonias, 1947.

————. and Alfredo Ataíde. "Contribution à l'Antropologie de la Guinée Portugaise." In, *Quinzième Congrès International d'Antropologie et d'Archéologie Préhistorique*. Porto: 1930.

Correia, Carlos Bento. *Oamendoim na Guiné Portuguesa*. Lisbon: 1965.

Coutouly, Gustave de. "Les Populations de l'Archipel des Bissagos." *Revue d'Etnographie et des Traditions Populaires*. I: 22–25, 1921.

Crawley, Eve. "Análise de uma Infelicidade: Religiäo e Interpretaçöes Pessoalistas." *Soronda*. No. 3: 112–126, January 1987.

Cunha Taborde, A. de. "Apontamentos Etnográficos sobre as Felupes de Suzana." *Boletim Cultural da Guiné Portuguesa*, 5: 187–223, 1950.

Da Mota, Avelino Teixeira. "Etnográfica." *Boletim Cultural da Guiné Portuguesa*. I, 1: 183–290, January 1946.

————. *Inquérito Etnográfico Organizado pelo Governo da Colónia no Ano de 1946*. Bissau: Publicação Comemorativa do Quinto Centenário da Descoberta da Guiné, 1947.

————. "A Secunda Conferência Internacional dos Africanistas Ocidentais." *Boletim Cultural da Guiné Portuguesa*. III, 9: 13–74, January 1948.

————. "A Agricultura de Brâmes e Balantas vista Através da Fotografia Aéra." *Boletim Cultural da Guiné Portuguesa*. V, 18: 131–172, April 1950.

————. "Notas sobre o Povoamento e a Agricultura Indígena na Guiné Portuguesa." *Boletim Cultural da Guiné Portuguesa*. VI, 23: 657–680, July 1951.

————. "Contactos Culturais Luso-Africanos na 'Guiné do Cabo Verde.' " *Boletim da Sociedade de Geografia de Lisbôa*. LXIX, 11–12: 659, November–December 1951.

————. *As Viagens do Bispo D. Frei Vitoriano Portuênse A Guiné E A Cristianização dos Reis de Bissau*. Lisboa: Junta De Investigações Cientificas do Ultramar, Centro de Estudos de Cartografia Antiga, 1974.

Da Mota, A. Teixeira, and Mario G. Ventim Neves. *A Hábitação Indígena na Guiné Portuguesa*. Bissau: Centro de Estudos da Guiné Portuguesa, Publication 7, 1948.

Diagne, Ahmadou Mapaté. "Contribution à l'Étude des Balantes de Sédhiou." *Outre-Mer*. V, 1: 16–42, March 1933.

Dias, José Manuel de Braga. "Mudança Socio-cultural na Guiné Portuguesa." Disertação, Instituto Superior de Ciências Sociais a Política Ultramarino, Universidade de Lisbôa, Lisbon, 1974.

Dinis, António Joaquim Dias. "As Tribos da Guiné Portuguesa na História." *Portugal em Africa*. 2 ser., III, 16: 206–15, July–August 1946.

————. "As Tribos da Guiné Portuguesa na História (Algumas Notas)." *Congresso Comemorativo do Quinto Centenário do Descobrimento da Guiné*. vol. 1, Lisbon, 241–271, 1946.

Ethnological Studies on Portuguese Guinea. *Translations on Africa*. 137: 1–55, December 3, 1964.

Fernandes, Raul M. "Le Problematique du Changement de la Structure Familiale chez les Bidjogos." Masters Thesis, Université de Paris VIII, Paris, 1984.

———. "O Espaco e o Tempo no Sistema Politica Bidjogó." *Soronda*, No. 8: 5–23, July 1989.

Fiel, Conde de Castillo. "Geografia Humana de la Guiné Portuguesa: Impresiones de un Viage de Estudos à travers del Africa Occidental." *Archivos del Instituto de Estudios Africanos.* II, 4, June 1948.

Fonseca, A. H. Vasconcelos da. "Questionário de Inquérito sobre as Raças da Guiné e seus Caracteres Étnicos." *Boletim Oficial da Colónia da Guiné.* suplemento ao 17 Abril, 1927.

Gomes, Barbosa O. C. "Breve Notícia dos Caracteres Étnicos dos Indígenas da Tribo Biafada." *Boletim Cultural da Guiné Portuguesa.* 1: 205–274, 1946.

Gonçalves. José Júlio. "A Cultura dos Bijagós." *Cabo Verde: Boletim de Propaganda e Informação.* X, 117, 1958–59.

———. "O Islamismo na Guiné Portuguesa." *Boletim Cultural da Guiné Portuguesa.* XIII, 52: 397–470, October 1958.

Handem, Diana L. *Nature et Fonctionnement de Pouvoir Chez les Balanta-Brassa*, Ph.D. Dissertation, School of Higher Studies of the Social Sciences, Paris, 1985.

Hawkins, Joye Bowman. *Conflict, Interaction, and Change in Guinea-Bissau: Fulbe Expansion and Its Impact, 1850–1900*, Ph.D. Dissertation, UCLA, Los Angeles, 1980.

Henry, Christine. "Marinheiros Bidjogós: Passado e Presente." *Soronda.* No. 8: 25–46, July 1989.

Hopkins, Nicholas. "Mandinka Social Organization." In *Papers on the Manding*, edited by C. T. Hodge. Indiana University Press: Indiana, Bloomington; 1971.

João, Mamadú. "Aspectos da Vida Social dos Mancanhas: A Cerimónia do Ulém." *Soronda.* No. 13: 59–66, January 1991.

Lampreia, José D. "Catalogo-Universitário da Secção de Etnografia do Museu da Guiné Portuguesa." Lisbon: 1962.

———. "Etno-História dos Bahuns da Guiné Portuguesa." *Garcia de Orta.* #4 , 1966.

Leprince, M. "Notes sur les Mancagnes ou Brames." *Antropologie* 16: 57–65, 1905.

Lima, Augusto J. Santos. *Organização Economica e Social dos Bijagós.* Centro de Estudos da Guiné Portuguesa, No. 2, 1946.

Lima, J.A. Peres de and Constâncio Mascarenhas. "Populações Indí-ʹgenas da Guiné Portuguesa." *Arquivo de Anatomia e Antropologia.* XIII, 4: 595–618, 1929–30.

Linares, Olga F. *Prayer, Power and Production; the Jola of Casamance, Senegal.* New York: Cambridge University Press, 1992.

Lopes, Carlos. *Etnia, Estado e Relações de Poder na Guiné-Bissau.* Lisbon: Edições 70, 1983.

Lopes, Edmundo Armenio Correia. "Antecedentes da Aculturação dos

Povos da Guiné Portuguesa." *Mundo Português*. XI, 124: 135, April 1944.

Mané, Mamadou. *Contribution à l'Histoire du Kaabu, des Origines au XIXe siècle*. Dakar: IFAN, 1979.

Mark, Peter Allen. *The Wild Bull and the Sacred Forest: Form, Meaning and Change in Senegambian Initiation Masks of the Diola*. New York: Cambridge University Press, 1992.

Marques, José Eduardo A. da Silva. "A Gerontocracia na Organização Social dos Bijagós." *Boletim Cultural da Guiné Portuguesa*. X (1955): 293–300.

Mateus, Amílcar de Magalhaes. "Acerca da Pre-História da Guiné." *Boletim Cultural da Guiné Portuguesa*. IX, 35: 457–472, July 1954.

———. "Estudo da População da Guiné Portuguesa. Relato Preliminar da Primeira Campanha da Missão Etnológica e Antropologica da Guiné." *Anais. Junta de Missões Geograficas e de Investigações do Ultrama.*, I: 243–260, 1946.

Meireles, Artur Martins de. "Baiu (Gentes de Kaiu). I. Generalidades." *Boletim Cultural da Guiné Portuguesa*. III, 11: 607–638, July 1948.

———. *Mutilações Etnicas dos Manjacos*. Bissau: Centro de Estudos da Guiné Portuguesa, Publication 22, 1960.

McCullough, Charles Ross. "The State of Prehistoric Archaeology in Morocco, Spanish Sahara, Mauritania, Mali, Gambia, Portuguese Guinea and Senegal." Master's Thesis, University of Pennsylvania, 1969.

Montenegro, Teresa. "Kasisas: Marginais deste e do Outro Mundo." *Soronda*, No. 13: 67–84, January 1991.

Moreira, José Mendes. "Breve Ensaio Etnográfico acerca dos Bijagós." *Boletim Cultural da Guiné Portuguesa,* 69–115, January 1946.

———. *Fulas do Gabu*. Bissau: Centro de Estudos da Guiné Portuguesa, Publication 6, 1948.

———. "Da Ergologia dos Fulas da Guiné Portuguesa." *Boletim Cultural da Guiné Portuguesa*. XXVI: 101–102, January–April 1971.

———. "Os Fulas da Guiné Portuguesa na Panoramica Geral do Mundo Fula." *Boletim Cultural da Guiné Portuguesa*. 19, 75, 76: 289–432, 1964

Murdock, George Peter. *Africa: Its People and Their Culture and History*. New York: McGraw-Hill Book Co., 1959.

Nogueira, Amadeu I. P. "Monografia sobre a Tribo Banhum." *Boletim Cultural da Guiné Portuguesa*, II, 8: 973–1008, October 1947.

Oliveira, Armindo Estrela de. "Estudo Geográfico da Guiné: O Povo Balanta." Disertação, Lisbon, 1970.

Pereira, A. Gomes. "Contos Fulas." *Boletim Cultural da Guiné Portuguesa*, III, 10: 445–452, April 1948.

Pereira, F. Alves. "Utensílios da Época da Pedra na Guiné Portuguesa." *O Archéologo Portugueses*. XIII , 1918.

———. "No Segredo das Crencas. Das Instituições Religiosas na Guiné Portuguesa." *Boletim Cultural da Guiné Portuguesa*. IV 15: 419–488, July 1949; 16: 687–721, October 1949.

Quinn, Charlotte. *Mandingo Kingdoms of the Senegambia: Traditionalism, Islam, and European Expansion*. Evanston, Illinois: Northwestern University Press, 1972.

Quintino, Gernando R. Rogado. "Os Povos da Guiné." *Boletim Cultural da Guiné Portuguesa*. XXII, 85–86, January–April 1967.

———. "Totemism in Portuguese Guinea." *Translations on Africa*. #271: 20–41, 1965.

Santos, Eduardo dos. "Catolicismo, Protestantismo, e Islamismo na Guiné Portuguesa." *Ultramar*. VIII, 4: 112–124, April–June 1968.

Santos Lima, A.J. "Organização Económica e Social dos Bijagós." *Centro de Estudos da Guiné Portuguesa*. 2: 1–154, 1947.

Scantamburlo, Luigi. *Etnologia dos Bijagós da Ilha de Bubaque*. Bissau, INEP, 1991.

Shaw, Thomas M. *The Fulani Matrix of Beauty and Art in the Djolof Region of Senegal*. Lewiston, N.Y.: The Edwin Mellen Press, Vol. 34, 1994.

Silva, Artur Augusto da. "Considerações sobre os Direitos de Família e Propriedade entre os Fulas da Guiné Portuguesa e suas Recentes Transformações." Extraito do *Boletim Cultural da Guiné Portuguesa*. 31: 405–415, 1953.

———. "Usos e Costumes Jurídicos dos Felupes da Guiné." *Boletim Cultural da Guiné Portuguesa*. XV, 57: 7–52, January 1960.

———. *Usos e Costumes Jurídicos do Fulas da Guiné Portuguesa*. Bissau: Centro de Estudos da Guiné Portuguêsa, 1958.

———. "Usos e Costumes Jurídicos dos Mandingas." *Boletim Cultural da Guiné Portuguesa*. XXIII, 90–91, April–July 1968; XXIV, 93, January 1969.

Taborda, António da Cunha. "Apontamentos Etnográficos sobre os Felupes de Suzana." *Boletim Cultural da Guiné Portuguesa*. V, 18: 187–224, April 1959; 20: 511–561, October 1950.

Tadeu, Viriato Ã. *Contos do Caramô, Lendas e Fabulas Mandingas da Guiné Portuguesa*. Lisbon: Agência Geral das Colónias, 1945.

Valoura, Francisco. "O Balanta e a Bolanha." *Boletim Cultural da Guiné Portuguesa*. XXV: 561–568, 1970).

Viegas, Luís António de Carvalho. "Os Diferentes Nucleos Populacionais da Guiné Portuguesa e seu Estado de Civilização na Vida Familiar." *Conferéncia Internacional dos Africanistas Ocidentais*. vol. 5: 333–346, 1947.

8. Language; Arts, Music, and Literature

Language

Anon. "Les Langues Ethniques de Guinée-Bissau: le Créole et le Portugais." *RéalitiesAfricaines et Langue Française*. II: 8–42, June 1979.

Barbosa, Alexandre. *Guinéus: Contos, Narrativos, Crônícas*. Agencia Geral do Lisboa, Ultamar:1967.

Barbosa, Jorge Morais. "Cabo Verde, Guiné e São Tomé e Príncipe: Situação Lingúistica." Lisbon: Instituto Superior de Ciências Sociais e Política Ultramarina. 1966.

———. *Crioulos: Estudos Lingúisticos*. Lisbon: Academia Internacional da Cultura Portuguesa, 1967.

Bella, L. De Sousa. "Apontamentos sobre a Língua dos Balantas de Jabadá." *Boletim Cultural da GuinéPortuguesa*. I, 4: 729–765, October 1946.

Bocandé, Bertrand de. "De la Langue Créole de la Guinée Portugaise. Notes sur la Guinée Portugaise ou Sénégambie Meridionale." *Bulletin de la Société de Géographie de Paris*. ser. III, XI (1849): 265–350; XII, 57–93.

Buis, Pierre. *Essai sur la Langue Manjako de la Zone de Bassarel*. Bissau: INEP Colecção Kacu Martel, No. 8, 1990.

Bull, Benjamin Pinto. *Le Créole da la Guinée Bissau. Structures Grammaticales Philosophie et Sagesse à travers ses Surnoms, ses Verbes et ses Expressions*. Dakar: Faculté des Lettres et Sciences Humaines, 1975.

———. *O Crioulo da Guiné-Bissau: Filosofia e Sabedoria*. Lisboa and Bissau: ICALP/INEP, 1989.

Cardoso, Henrique Lopes. "Pequeno Vocabulário do Dialecto Pepel." *Boletim da Sociedade de Geografia de Lisbôa*. XX, 10 (1902): 121–28.

Carreira, António Augusto Peixoto. "Alguns Aspectos da Influéncia da Língua Mandinga na Pajadinca." *Boletim Cultural da Guiné Portuguesa*. XVIII, 71: 345–384, July 1963.

——— and João Basso Marques. *Subsídios para o Estudo da Língua Manjaca*. Bissau: Centro de Estudos da Guiné Portuguesa, 1947.

Couto, Hildo Honório do. "As Consoantes Pré-nasalizadas do Crioulo da Guiné-Bissau." *Soronda*, No. 14: 97–105, July 1992.

Da Silva, Viriato Lopes Ramos. "Pequeno Vocabulário Português-Mandinga." *Boletim da Sociedade de Geografia de Lisbôa*. XLVII, 3–4: 98–108, March–April 1929; 5–6: 142–151, May–June 1929.

Djalo, Ibrahima. "Contribuição para uma Reflexão-educação: Multilinguismo e Unidade Nacional." *Soronda*. No. 3: 101–111, January 1987.

Kihm, Alain. "La Situation Linguistique en Casamance et en Guinée-Bissau." *Cahiers d'Etudes Africaines*. Vol. 20, No. 3: 369–386, 1979.

––––––. "Nasality in Kriol: the Marked Case?" *Journal of Pidgin and Creoles Languages.* Vol. 1, No. 1: 81–107, 1986.

Klingenheben, August. "Die Permutationen des Biafada und des Ful." *Zeitschrift fur Eingebornen-Sprachen.* XV 3: 180–213, 1924; 4: 266–272, 1925.

Lopes, Edmundo Armenio Correia. "O Dinheiro nas Línguas da Guiné." *Mundo Português.* XII: 139, 1945.

––––––. "Manjacos. Língua." *Mundo Português*, X: 113–114, 1943.

Macedo, Francisco. "O Problema das Línguas na Guiné-Bissau," *Humanidades.* No. 22: 33–38, 1989.

Marques, João Basso. "Aspectos do Problema da Semelhança da Língua dos Papéis, Manjacos e Brâmes." *Boletim Cultural da Guiné Portuguesa.* II, 5: 77–109, January 1947.

Mbodj, Cherif. *Phonologie du créole de Guinée-Bissau.* Dakar: Centre de Linguistique Appliquée, 1979.

Montenegro, Teresa, and Carlos de Morais. "Uma Primeira Interrogação em Crioulo a Cultural Popular Oral." *Africa. Literature-Arte e Cultura.* 2, 6: 25–32, October–December 1979.

N'Diaye-Correard, Geneviève. *Etudes FCA ou Balante (Dialecte Ganja).* Paris: SELAF, 1970.

Quintino, Fernando R. Rogado. "Algumas Notas sobre a Gramática Balanta." *Boletim Cultural da Guiné Portuguesa.* VI, 21: 1–52, January 1951.

––––––. "Conhecimento da Língua Balanta, através da sua Estrutura Vocabular." *Boletim Cultural da Guiné Portuguesa.* XVI, 64: 737–768. October 1961.

Rougé, Jean-Louis. "Uma Hipótese sobre a Formação do Crioulo da Guiné-Bissau e da Casamansa," *Soronda.* No. 2: 28–49, July 1986.

––––––. *Petit Dictionnaire Etymologique du Kriol de Guinée-Bissau et Casamance.* Bissau: INEP, Colecção 'Kacu Martel' No. 5, 1988.

Scantamburlo, Luigi. *Gramática e Dicionário da Lingua Criol da Guiné-Bissau.* Bologna, Italy: Editrice Missionaria Italiana, 1981.

Tenreiro, Francisco. "Acerca de Arquipélagos Crioulos." *Cabo Verde: Boletim de Propaganda e Informação.* XII, 137: 31, 1960–61.

Westermann, Diedrich and M. A. Bryan. *Languages of West Africa.* Oxford University Press, 1952.

Wilson, W. A. A. "Uma Volta Lingúistica na Guiné." *Boletim Cultural da Guiné Portuguesa.* vol. XIV, No. 56: 569–601, 1959.

Wilson, William Andre Auquier. *The Crioulo of Guiné.* Johannesburg: Witwatersrand University Press, 1962.

Arts, Music, and Literature

Amado, Leopoldo. "A Literatura Colonial Guinéense." *Soronda.* No. 9: 73–93, January 1990.

Andrade, M. de. *Antologia de Poesia Negra de Expressão Portuguesa.* Lisbon, 1956.

———. "Guiné-Bissau. Seminário sobre a Metodologia da Recolha das Tradições Orais." *Africa. Literatura-Arte e Cultura.* 1, 3: 300–305, January–March 1979.

———. *Literatura Africana de Expressão Portuguesa.* Lisbon, 1967.

Anon. "João de Barrosóum Pintor Guinéense." *Africa. Literatura-Arte e Cultura.* 1, 1: 40–42, July 1978.

Anon. *Junbai, Storias de Bolama e do Outro Mundo.* Bolama, Guiné-Bissau: Imprensa Nacional, 1979.

Anon. *Matenhas Para Quem Luta!* Bissau: Conselho Nacional de Cultura, 1979.

Anon. *Os Continuadores da Revolução e a Recordação do Passado Recente.* Bolama, Guinea-Bissau: Imprensa Nacional, n.d. [c. 1981].

Antologia dos Jovens Poetas. Mementos Primeiros da Construção. Bissau: Conselho Nacional de Cultura, 1978.

Barbosa, Alexandre. *Guinéus: Contos, Narrativas, Crônicas.* Lisbon: Agência Geral do Ultramar, 1967.

Belchior, Manuel Dias. *Contos Mandingas.* Porto: Portucalense Editora, 1968.

———. *Grandeza Africana: Lendas da Guiné Portuguesa.* 1963.

Brocado, Maria Teresa. "Os 10 Poemas de Vasco Cabral—Uma Leitura." *Africa. Literatura-Arte e Cultura.* 2, 8: 367–376, April–June 1980.

Cabral, Vasco. "10 Poemas de Vasco Cabral." *Africa. Literatura-Arte e Cultura,* 1, 5: 525–534, July–September 1979.

———. *A Luta é a Minha Primavera.* Lisbon: Africa Editora, 1981.

Cesar, Amandio. *Contos Portugueses do Ultramar. I. Cabo Verde, Guiné e S. Tomé e Príncipe.* Porto: Portucalense Editora, 1969.

Conduto, João Eleuterio. "Contos Bijagós." *Boletim Cultural da Guiné Portuguesa.* X: 489–506, 1955.

Cooperativa Domingos Badinga. *'N sta li, 'n sta la.* Bolama: Imprensa Nacional da Guiné-Bissau, 1979.

D'Almada, Carlos. "3 Poemas." *Africa. Literatura-Arts e Cultura.* 2, 10: 610–611, October–December 1980.

De Pina, F. Conduto. *Grandessa di no Tchon.* Lisbon: Author's edition, 1978.

Dickinson, Margaret. *When Bullets Begin to Flower: Poems of Resistance from Angola, Mozambiqueand Guiné.* Nairobi: East Africa Publishing House, 1973.

Ferreira, João. "Dois Capítulos do Romance Inedito 'UANA.' " *Africa. Literatura-Arte e Cultura.* 1, 3: 280–288, January–March 1979.

Ferreira, Ondina. "Djidius—Pequena Mongrafia." *Africa. Literatura-Arte e Cultura.* 1, 3: 263–267, January–March 1979.

————. "Fiju di Mandipole." *Africa. Literatura-Arte e Cultura*. 2, 9: 454–458, July–September 1980.

Filipe, Daniel. *O Manuscrito na Garráia*. Lisbon: Guimaraes, 1960.

Gomes, A. "Notas sobre a Música Indígena da Guiné." *Boletim Cultural da Guiné Portuguesa*. V. 19: 411–424, July 1950.

Guisti, Emilio. *Contes Créoles de Guinée-Bissau*. Paris: EDICEF/Conseil International de Langue Française, 1981.

Hamilton, Russell G. *Voices From an Empire: A History of Afro-Portuguese Literature*. Minneapolis, Minnesota: University of Minnesota Press, 1975.

Horton, Christian Dowu. "Indigenous Music of Sierra Leone: An Analysis of Resources and Educational Implications." Ph.D. Dissertation, UCLA, 1979.

Jessup, Lynne. *The Mandinka Balafon: An Introduction with Notation for Teaching*. USA: Xylo Publications, 1983.

Knight, Roderic. "Music of the Mande." (Video) Program notes. Original Music OMV 006, 1992.

————. "Jali Nyama Suso: Kora Player of the Gambia." (Video) Program notes.

Lopes, Norberto. *Terra Ardentes: Narrativas da Guiné*. Lisbon: Editora Maritimo Colonial, 1947.

Martinho, Fernando J.B. "A Nova Poesia da Guiné-Bissau." *Africa. Literatura-Arte e Cultura*, 1, 2: 157–163, October–December 1978.

Montenegro, Teresa e Carlos Morais. "Três Provérbios em Crioulo—Uma Approximação à Universalidade dos Ditos." *Africa. Literatura-Arte e Culture*. 3, 11: 19–26, January–June 1981.

————. "Uma Primeira Interrogação em Crioulo a Cultura Popular Oral." *Africa. Literatura-Arte e Cultura*. 2, 6: 3–13, October–December 1979.

Moser, Gerald M. "The Poet Amílcar Cabral." *Research in African Literature*. 9, 2: 176–197, 1978.

————. *A Tentative Portuguese-African Bibliography: Portuguese Literature in Africa and African Literature in the Portuguese Language*. University Park, PA: Pennsylvania State University Press, 1970.

Proenca, Helder. "5 Poemas." *Africa. Literature-Arte e Cultura*. 2,6: 26–32, October–December 1979.

————. *Näo Posso Adiar a Palavra, Sa da Costa*. Lisboa, 1982.

————. "A Pintura e a Escultura na Guiné Portuguesa." *Boletim Cultural da Guiné Portuguesa*, XIX: 277–288, 1964.

Quintino, Fernando R. Rogado. "Música e Dança na Guiné Portuguesa." *Boletim Cultural da Guiné Portuguesa*, XVIII, 72: 551–570, October 1963.

Sequeira, José Pedro Lopes. "Uma Palavra Humana Ligada ao Trabalho Proficuo de Cada um." *Africa. Literatura-Arte e Cultura*. 1, 4: 439–441, April–June 1979.

Simoes, João Gaspar. "A Antologia da Ficção Cabo-verdeana." *Diário de Notícias*: 13–15, January 1, 1961.
So, Abdul Carimo. "Presença dos Novos Poemas e prosas de Abdul Carimo So." *Africa. Literatura-Arte e Cultura*. 2, 13: 65–66, April–June 1986.
Torrado, António. "A Propósito de um Livro de Histórias." *Africa. Literatura-Arte e Cultura*. 1, 4: 467–469, April–June 1979.

Health and Education

Anon. *A Educação na Guiné-Bissau*. Comissariado de Estado da Educação Nacional, Bissau: Imprensa Nacional, 1978.
Anon. "Education and Production in Guinea-Bissau." *Development and Dialogue*. 2: 51–57, 1978.
Anon. *Child Mortality in Guinea-Bissau: Malnutrition or Overcrowding?* Report of MISAS/SAREC team on project of child health and nutrition, October 1978–April 1980. Copenhagen, Denmark: Institute of Anthropology, 1983.
Almeida, Fernando C.M. Tavares. "Serviços de Saúde e Assistência na Guiné Portuguesa." *Ultramar*. VIII, 4: 165–175, April–June 1968.
Brandao, J. da Costa. "O Ensino na Guiné Portuguesa." *Ultramar.*, VII, 4: 146–164, April–June 1968.
Brener-Suarez, Angela. "Toxic Terrorism." *Third World First* 1(2): 31–37, 1990.
Da Mota, Avelino Teixeira. "O Centro de Estudos da Guiné Portuguesa." *Boletim Cultural da Guiné Portuguesa*. VIII: 609–650, 1953; X: 641–655, 1955.
De Costa, Damasceno Isaac. *Relatório do Servico da Delegação de Saúde da vila de Bissau, Respectivo ao ano de 1884*. Lisbon: Typografia Guinéense, 1887.
De Oliveira, Darcy. "Guinée-Bissau: Education et Processus Révolutionnaire." *l'Homme et la Société*. 197–217, 1978.
De Oliveira, Darcy. "Guinée-Bissau: Education et Processus Révolutionnaire." *l'Homme et la Société*. 197–217, 1978.
De Oliveira, Rosiska e Miguel Darcy. *Guiné Bissau: Reinventar a Educação*. Lisbon: Colecção Cadernos Livros, 1978.
Ferreira, Fernando S. da C. *As Tripanosomiases nos Territórios Africanos Portuguêses*. Centro de Estudos da Guiné Portuguesa, Publicação 9, 1948.
Freire, Paulo. *Pedagogy in Process. The Letters to Guinea-Bissau*. New York: The Seabury Press, 1978.
Furtado, Alexandre. "Investigação sobre a História do Ensino na Guiné-Bissau." *Soronda*. No. 1: 125–142, January 1986.

Instituto Nacional de Estudos e Pesquisa. *ANO 1. Relatório Anual de Actividades*. Bissau: INEP, 1985.

Lepri, Jean-Pierre. "Formaçäo de Professores, Locais, Materiais Escolares e Insucesso Escolar na Guiné-Bissau." *Soronda*. No. 5: 83–92, January 1988.

Lopes, Carlos. *Guiné-Bissau Alfabeto*. Bologna, 1984.

Macedo, Francisco de. *A Educação na República da Guiné-Bissau*. Braga: Editorial Franciscana, 1978.

Mendy, P. Karibe. *"The Problems and Prospects of 'Liberation Education' in Guinea-Bissau."* Masters Dissertation, Centre of West African Studies. University of Birmingham, Birmingham, England, 1980.

PAIGC. *Programa do Ensino para as Escolas das Regioes Libertadas*. Conakry: PAIGC, n.d.

PAIGC. *Regulamento das Escolas do Partido*. Conakry: PAIGC, September 19, 1966.

Rosa, M. F. "Ensino Rudimentar para Indígenas em Angola e na Guiné Portuguesa," *Boletim Cultural da Guiné Portuguesa*. Vol. VI, 24: 805–884, 1951.

Sena, Luiz de and Marie Claude Lambers. *L'Education en Guinée-Bissau: Situation et Perspectives*. Paris: IRFED, 1977.

Tavares, Estevao. l'*Enseignement en Guinée 'Portugaise.'* Conakry: PAIGC, June 1962.

Tendeiro, João. *Actualidade Veternária da Guiné Portuguesa*. Bissau: Centro de Estudos da Guiné Portuguesa, Publication 15, 1951.

———. *Tripanosomiases Animais da Guiné Portuguesa*. Bissau: Centro de Estudos da Guiné Portuguesa, Publication 110, 1949.

Varela, João Manuel. "Para uma Universidade da Guiné-Bissau/Capo Verde." *Africa. Literatura-Arte e Cultura*. 1, 1: 57–64, July 1978.

10. Agriculture, Economics, Development

Aguilar, R, & Zeján, M. *Guinea-Bissau: A Fresh Start?* SIDA, Stockholm: SIDA Macroeconomics Studies Series No. 17, 1991.

———. *Guinée-Bissau: Getting Off the Track*. Stockholm: SIDA Macroeconomics Studies Series No. 5, 1992.

Almeyra, Guillermo M. "Development as an Act of Culture: A First-Hand report on the Experience of Guinea-Bissau." *CERES*. 11, 1: 23–28, 1978.

Alvesson, M. & Zejan, M. "Guiné-Bissau: o Impacto do Programa de Adjustamento Estrutural sobre o Bem-estar dos Pequenos Proprietarios Rurais." *Soronda*. No. 11, January 1991.

Andreini, Jean-Claude, and Marie-Claude Lambert. *La Guinée-Bissau d'Amílcar Cabral à la Reconstruction Nationale*. Paris: Editions l'Harmattan, 1978.

Anon. "La République de Guinée-Bissau: Quelques Données de Base." *Marchés Tropicaux et Mediterranéens*, 1741: 733–735, March 1979.

Anon. *Introdução à Geografia Económica da Guiné-Bissau*. Bissau: Commissariat of Economic Coordination and Planning, 1980.

Anon. Centre de Recherches en Aménagement et en Développement (CRAD). *Développement Intègre de la Zone IV [Guinea-Bissau]. Région de Bolama. Rapport de la Phase I*. Québec, Canada: Université Laval/Montréal: Service Universitaire Canadien Outre-mer (SUCO), 1981.

Areal, Joaquim A. "Possibilidades Industriais da Guiné." *Boletim Cultural da Guiné Portuguesa*. IX, 36: 707–770, October 1954.

Atchinger, Gertrud. "Efeitos do Programa de Adjustamento Estrutural sobre as Condiçöes Economicas e Sociais das Mulheres da Zona Rural," *Soronda*. No. 14: 65–82, July 1992.

Baptista, Manuel Martins. "Agricultura da Colónia da Guiné." *Boletim Geral das Colónias*. L: 49–64, February 1934.

Bollinger, Virginia L. *Development Strategy's Impact on Ethnically-Based Political Violence: A Theoretical Framework with Comparative Applications to Zambia, Guiné-Bissau and Mozambique*. Ph.D. Dissertation., University of Colorado at Boulder, 1984.

Cabral, Amílcar. "Para o Conhecimento do Problema da Erosão do Solo na Guiné, I. Sobre o Conceito de Erosão." *Boletim Cultural da Guiné Portuguesa*. IX, 33:163–194, January 1954.

———. "A Propósito de Mecanização da Agricultura na Guiné Portuguesa." *Boletim Cultural da Guiné Portuguesa*. IX, 389–400, April 1954.

———. "Acerca da Utilização da Terra na Africa Negra." *Boletim Cultural da Guiné Portuguesa*. IX, 34: 401–416, April 1954.

———. "Queimados e Pousios na Circunscrição de Fulacunda em 1953." *Boletim Cultural da Guiné Portuguesa*. IX, 35: 627–646, July 1954.

———. "Acerca da Contribuição dos 'Povos' Guinéenses para a Produção Agrícola da Guiné." *Boletim Cultural da Guiné Portuguesa*. IX, 36: 771–778, October 1954.

———. "Recenseamento Agrícola da Guiné: Estimativa em 1953." *Boletim Cultural da Guiné Portuguesa*. XI, 43: 7–243, July 1956.

———. "A Propos du Cycle Cultural Achide-Mils en Guinée Portugaise." *Boletim Cultrual da Guiné Portuguesa*. XIII, 50: 146–156, April 1958.

———. "Feux de Brousse et Jachères dans le Cycle Cultural Arachide-Mils," *Boletim Cultural da Guiné Portuguesa*. XIII, 51: 257–268, July 1958.

Cabral, Maria H. and Amílcar Lopes Cabral. "Breves Notas acerca da Razão de Ser, Objectivos e Processo de Execução do Recenseamento Agrícola da Guiné." *Boletim Cultural da Guiné Portuguesa*, IX, 33, 195–204, January 1954.

Cabral, Vasco. "Nécessités Sociales et Développement Économique Planifié." *Studia Diplomatica*. 31, 2: 153–170, 1978.

Commissariado de Estado de Coordenação Econômica e Plano (CECEP), *Introdução a Geografia Econômica da Guiné Bissau*, 1980.

Dos Santos, Jesus Nunes. "Alguns Aspectos da Economia da Guiné." *Boletim da Sociedade de Geografia de Lisbôa*. LXV, 1–2: 49–71, January–February 1947.

Dumont, René. "La Guinée-Bissau Peut Encore Echapper au Sous-développement." *Le Monde Diplomatique*. July 1979.

Felkai, Istvan. "Tenir la promesse faite aux paysans." *Le Monde Diplomatique*. April 1983.

Ficheiro Nacional de Tabancas, Monografia do Sector de Biombo, Região de Biombo. Bissau: Department of Regional Development, State Commission on Economic Coordination and Planning, 1980.

Fonseca, Jorge P. Concela de. "Alguns Aspectos da Colheita, Armazenamento e Transporte do Amendoim (mancarra) na Guiné Portuguesa." *Garcia de Orta*. 2, 3: 287–309, 1954.

Food and Agriculture Organization (FAO). *Guinea-Bissau: Agricultural Sector Review*. Rome: FAO/World Bank Cooperative Program, 1983.

Funk, Ursula. "Land Tenure, Agriculture, and Gender in Guinea-Bissau." In *Agriculture, Women, and Land: The African Experience*. Edited by Jean Davison, pps. 33–58, Boulder, Colorado: Westview Press, 1988.

Galli, Rosemary. "Liberalisation is Not Enough: Structural Adjustment and Peasants in Guinea-Bissau." *Review of African Political Economy*. No. 49: 53–68, 1990.

Geisslhofer, Hans. *Planification Villageoise en Guinée-Bissau*. Dakar: ENDA, 1981.

Goulet, Denis. *Looking at Guinea-Bissau: a New Nation's Development Strategy*. Washington, D.C.: Overseas Development Council, 1978.

———. "Political Will: The Key to Guinea-Bissau's Alternative Development Strategy." *International Development Review*. 19, 4: 2–9, April 1977.

Handem, Diana Lima. "Desenvolvimento na Base e Participação Popular: Uma Alternativa?," *Soronda*. No. 12: 27–44, July 1991.

Harrell-Bond, Barbara. "Guinea-Bissau: Part III: Independent Development." American University Field Staff Report No. 22, 1981.

Henkes, William C. *Mineral Industry of Angola, Mozambique and Portuguese Guinea*. Washington, D. C.: U.S. Bureau of Mines, 1966.

Hocket, Anne-Marie. "Analyse Socio-Économique d'une Tabanca de la Région de Bafata." Bissau, 1977.

————. *Etude des Habitudes de Consommation et des Besoins en Produits d'Importation des Populations Rurales de Guinée-Bissau.* Bissau: Ministry of Economic Coordination and Planning, 1981.

————. *Etudes Socio-Économiques de Base sur la Guinée-Bissau.* 5 vols. Bissau: Ministry of Economic Coordination and Planning, 1979.

————. *Paysanneries en Attente Guinée-Bissau.* Dakar: ENDA, 1983.

————. and Seco Uldely. *Les Ex-Royaumes Pepel du Tor et du Biombo: Zones d'Emigration Temporaire: Situation Socio-économique.* Bissau: Commissariat of Economic Coordination and Planning, 1980.

Horta, C. A. Picado. *Análise Estructural e Conjuntural de Ecónomia da Guiné.* Bissau, 1965.

Imbali, Faustino. *L'impact de la Participation de la Population au Developpement, Etude de Cas: Village de Cantone et Mato-Farroba au Sud de la Guinée-Bissau.* Masters Thesis, Université de Bourdeaux II, Bourdeaux, France, 1987.

————. "O Estado e os Camponeses Perante o Constrangimento do Desenvolvimento." *Soronda.* No. 8 (July 1989): 63–86.

International Labour Office. *Portugal, Portuguese Guinea, Legislative Decrees: Native Labour.* Geneva: 1938.

Junta de Investigações do Ultramar (JIU). *Prospectiva do Desenvolvimento Economico e Social da Guiné.* Lisboa, 1972.

Makedowsky, Eric. "Les Insufficances et les Erreurs de la Politique Économique." *L'Année Politique et Économique Africaine.* Société Africaine d'Edition, 1981.

Marini, Emilio. "Desenvolvimento Agrícola da Guiné Portuguesa." *Boletim Geral do Ultramar.* Ano 36, 422–23: 285–289, 1960.

Mehretu, A. *Regional Disparity in Sub-Saharan Africa: Structural Readjustment of Uneven Development.* Boulder, Colorado: Westview Press, 1989.

Mendes, José-Luis Morais Ferreira. "Considerações sobre a Problemática da Planificação e do Desenvolvimento Agrícola na Guiné." *Boletim Cultural da Guiné Portuguesa.* 26, 101: 217–223, 1971.

————. "Inquérito Agrícola—Região do Gabu." *Boletim Cultural da Guiné Portuguesa.* 26, 104: 785–799, 1971.

————. *Problemas e Perspectivas do Desenvolvimento Rural da Guiné.* Lisbon: 1968.

Mendomça, Pio Coelho de. "Elevação do Nível de Vida do Trabalhador na Guiné Portuguesa." *Boletim Cultural da Guiné Portuguesa.* XI, 42: 111–130, April 1956.

Mendy, Peter Karibe. "A Economia Colonial da Guiné-Bissau: 'Nacionalização' e Exploração, 1915–1959," *Soronda.* No. 9: 23–51, January 1990.

Ministério do Ultramar. "Missão de Inquérito Agrícolas de Cabo Verde, Guiné, São Tomé e Príncipe." *Recenseamento Agrícola da Guiné, 1960–61.* Lisbon: Imprensa Nacional, 1963.

Padovani, Fernando, "O Programa de Adjustamento na Guiné-Bissau e a Discussão de um Modelo," *Soronda*. No. 11, January 1991.

Pereira, Luísa Teotónio and Luís Moita. *Guiné-Bissau: 3 Anos de Independência*. Lisbon: CIDA-C 1976.

Projecto do IV Plano de Fomento. II. Ultramar. Lisbon: Imprensa Nacional, Casa de Moeda, 1973.

Quina, Carolina. "Guinée-Bissau. Les Enjeux du Développement Économique." *Afrique Asie*. 1013, 378: 30–31, July 27, 1986.

Quintino, Fernando R. Rogado. "Das Possibilidades do Aumento da Produção na Guiné."*Boletim Cultural da Guiné Portuguesa*. VI, 22: 365–370, April 1951.

Recenseamento Agrícola da Guiné, 1960–61. Lisbon: Comissão para os Inquéritos Agrícolas no Ultramar, 1963.

Rudebeck, Lars. "The Effects of Structural Adjustment in Kandjadja, Guinea-Bissau." in *Review of African Political Economy*. No. 49:34–51, 1990.

———. "Conditions of Development and Actual Development: Strategy in Guinea-Bissau." in *Problems of Socialist Orientations in Africa*. Mai Palmberg. Edited by Uppsala: Scandanavian Institute of African Studies, 1978.

———. "Development and Class Struggle in Guinea-Bissau." *Monthly Review*. 30, 8: 14–32, January 1979.

———. *Problèmes de Pouvoir Populaire et de Développement: Transition Difficile en Guinée-Bissau*. Research Report no. 63. Uppsala, Sweden: Scandanavian Institute of African Studies, 1982.

Rudebeck, L. and K. Hermele. "Structural Adjustment in a West African Village." in *At the Crossroads: Political Alliances and Structural Adjustment: Two Essays on Angola, Guinea-Bissau, and Mozambique*. pps. 5–71, edited by AKUT (No. 41), University of Uppsala, AKUT Series No. 41, Uppsala, 1989.

Sampaio, Mario. "The New Guinea Bissau: How Long Will It Live?" *African Development:* 11–13, March 1974.

Santareno, José Alberto Lemos Martins. "A Agricultura na Guiné Portuguesa." *Boletim Cultural da Guiné Portuguesa*. XII, 47: 355–384, July 1957.

Sardhina, Raul M. De Albuquerque and C. A. Picado Horta. "Perspectivas da Agricultura, Silvicultura e Pecuária na Guiné." *Boletim Cultural da Guiné Portuguesa*. XXI, 81: 24–306, January 1966.

Schissel, Howard. "Guinea-Bissau/Cape Verde. Now the Boat's Come in." *West Africa*. 3455: 2510–12, October 31, 1983.

———. "Improving Productivity [in Guinea-Bissau]." *West Africa*. 3405: 2883–87, 8 November 1982.

Silá, Abdulai. "Estratégias de Desenvolvimento e Alternativas Tecnológicas: um Estudo de Caso (Guiné-Bissau)," *Soronda*, No. 13: 3–40, January 1992.

Silva, Artur Augusto da. "Ensaio de Estudo da Introdução na Guiné Portuguesa, das Cooperatives Agrícolas." *Boletim Cultural da Guiné Portuguesa.* IX, 34: 417–430, April 1954.

Soler, Anita. "Guinée-Bissau: l'Irréparable?" *Afrique Asie.* 1013, 381: 34, September 7, 1986.

Sumo, Honore de. "La Guinée-Bissau s'Amare a l'Occident." *Jeune Afrique.* 1351:36, November 26, 1986.

Tall, Moktar Matar. *Rapport de Mission (31 Aout–9 Septembre 1983) Valuation du Potentiel Scientifique et Technique de la Guinée-Bissau.* Dakar: Centre de Recherches pour le Développement International, 1983.

Tvedten, Inger. "Programas de Adjustamento Estrutural e Implicações Locais: O Caso dos Pescadores Artesanais na Guiné-Bissau," *Soronda.* No. 11, January 1991.

U.S. Bureau of Labor Statistics. Office of Foreign Labor and Trade. *Labor Conditions in Portuguese Guinea.* Washington, D.C.: Government Printing Office, 1966.

Van Den Reysen, Placca Bagirishya. *Rapport de Mission en Guinée Bissau et aux Îles du Cap-Vert.* Addis Ababa; United Nations, FAO/CEA, 1978.

Veiga, Aguinaldo, and L. Patrício Ribas. "Alguns Aspectos da Estrutura Económica da Guiné." *Boletim Cultural da Guiné Portuguesa.* IV, 14: 289–305, April 1949.

11A. By Amílcar Lopes Cabral (See Also His Writings on Agriculture, 1954–1958)

1960

Cabral, Amílcar Lopes. *Memorandum Enviado ao Govérno Português pelo Partido Africano da Independência.* Conakry: PAIGC, December 1, 1960.

1961

———. *Discurso Proferido pelo Delegado da Guiné 'Portuguesa' e das Ilhas da Cabo Verde,* Cairo: PAIGC, March 25–31, 1961.

———. "The Death Pangs of Imperialism." In *Rapport Général sur la Lutte de Libération Nationale.* Conakry: PAIGC, July 1961.

———. *Memorandum à Assembleia Geral da Organização das Nações Unidas.* Conakry: PAIGC, September 26, 1961.

———. "Une Crise de Connaissance." *Third Conference of African People.* (Cairo). 1961.

———. (Under pseudonym Abel Djassi). *The Facts About Portugal's African Colonies*. Introduction by Basil Davidson. London: Union of Democratic Control, 1961.

———. *Un Crime de Colonialisme (Fondements Juridiques de notre Lutte Armée de Libération Nationale)*. *Extrait du Rapport Présenté par le Camarade Amílcar Cabral, au Comité Spécial de l'ONU pour les Territoires Administrés par le Portugal*. Conakry: PAIGC, 1961.

———. *Note Ouverte au Gouvernement Portugais*. Conakry: PAIGC, 1961.

1962

———. *Déclaration sur la Situation Actuelle de Lutte de Libération en Guinée 'Portugaise' et aux Îles du Cap Vert*. Conakry: PAIGC, January 20, 1962.

———. "Liberation Movement in Portuguese Guinea." *Voice of Africa*. II: 32, March 1962.

———. "La Guinée Portugaise et les Îles du Cap-Vert." *Voice of Africa*. II: 37–39, May 1962.

———. *Le Peuple de la Guinée "Portugaise" devant l'Organisation des Nations Unies: Présentée au Comité Spécial de l'ONU pour les Territories Administrés par le Portugal*. Conakry: PAIGC, June 1962.

———. "Guinée, Cap-Vert, Face au Colonialisme Portugais." *Partisans*. II, 7: 80–91, November–December 1962.

———. *Déclaration à l'Occasion du Anniversaire des Grèves de Bissao et du Massacre de Pigiuti*. Conakry: PAIGC, 1962.

———. *Déclaration Faite par M. Amílcar Cabral du Parti Africaine de l'Indépendance de la Guinée et du Cap-Vert (PAIGC) lors de la 142Oème Séance de la Quatrième Commission de 12 Décembre 1962*. New York: PAIGC, 1962.

———. *Discours Prononcé par Chef de la Délégation de la Guinée "Portugaise" et des Îles du Cap-Vert, Secrétaire Générale du PAIGC*. Conakry: PAIGC, 1962.

———. *La Lutte de Llibération Nationale en Guinée Portugaise et aux Îles du Cap-Vert*. Conakry: PAIGC, 1962.

———. *Rapport aux Etats-Unis*. Conakry: PAIGC, 1962.

1963

———. *Déclaration du PAIGC sur l'Évacuation par les Autorités Portugaises des Civils Européens du Sud*. Paris: Comité de Soutien à l'Angola et aux Peuples des Colonies Portugaises, February 1963.

———. "Solução Pacifica para Guiné e Cabo Verde." *Portugal Democrático*, VII: 6, February–March 1963.

———. *Nous Avons Lutté par des Moyens Pacifiques. Nous n'avons eu que les Massacres et le Génocide.* Addis Ababa: PAIGC, May 1963.

———. *Pourquoi Nous Avons Pris les Armes pour Libérer Notre Pays.* Addis Ababa: PAIGC, May 1963.

———. "The War in Portuguese Guinea." *African Revolution.* I: 103–108, June 1963.

———. "A Guerra na Guiné." *Portugal Democrático.* VIII: 3, October 1963.

———. "O PAIGC Pede à ONU Auxílio Concreto." *Portugal Democrático.* VIII:4, December 1963.

1964

———. "The Struggle in Guinea." *International Socialist Journal.* I: 428–446, August 1964.

———. "The Struggle of Portuguese Guinea." *Translations on Africa.* 77: 29–40, 1964.

1965

———. *Le Développement de la Lutte Nationale en Guinée "Portugaise" et aux Îles du Cap Vert en 1964.* Conakry: February 1965.

———. "La Lutte du PAIGC." *Remarques Africaines.* VII: 19–22, May 26, 1965.

———. "Liberating Portuguese Guinea from Within." *The New African,* IV: 85, June 1965.

———. "Contra a Guerra Colonial: Mensagem de Amílcar Cabral ao Povo da Guiné e de Cabo Verde." *FPLN Boletim,* 14–15, August 1965.

1966

———. *Intervention Faite à la Première Conférence de la Solidarité des Peuples d'Afrique, d'Asie et d'Amérique Latine.* Havana: January 1966.

———. "The Social Structure of Portuguese Guinea and its Meaning for the Struggle for National Liberation." *Translations on Africa,* 420, 37–48, August 24, 1966.

———. "Portuguese Colonial Policy." *Africa Quarterly,* V, 4: 287–299, 1966.

———. *Fondements et Objectifs de la Libération Nationale sur la Domination Impérialiste.* Conakry: PAIGC, 1966.

———. "l'Arme de la Théorie." *Partisans,* 26–27, 1966.

1967

————. "Combattre et Bâtir." *La Nouvelle Revue Internationale*, February 1967.

————. "Breve Análisis de la Estructura Social de la Guinea 'Portuguesa.' " *Pensamiento Crítico*, 2–3: 24–48, March–April 1967.

————. "Mankind's Path to Progress." *World Marxist Review*, X: 88–89, November 1967.

1968

————. "Determined to Resist." *Tricontinental Magazine*, 8: 114–126, September–October 1968.

————. "National Liberation and Social Structure." in, *Guerrilla Warfare and Marxism: A Collection of Writings from Karl Marx to the Present on Armed Struggles for Liberation and Socialism*, William J. Pomeroy, (ed.), New York: International Publishers, 1968.

1969

————. "Guinea (B): Political and Military Situation." *Tricontinental*, 37: 25–34, April 1969.

————. "Guinea: The Power of Arms." *Tricontinental Magazine*, 12: 5–16, May–June 1969.

————. *The Struggle in Guinea*. Cambridge: Africa Research Group, 1969.

————. *Revolution in Guinea: An African People's Struggle*, London: Stage 1 Books, 1969.

1970

————. *National Liberation and Culture*. Speech Delivered at Syracuse University under the Auspices of The Program of Eastern African Studies of the Maxwell School of Citizenship and Public Affairs. February 20, 1970.

————. "Report on Portuguese Guinea and the Liberation Movement," Hearing before the Subcommittee on Africa of the Committee on Foreign Affairs, *House of Representatives, 91st Congress*, Second Session, Thursday, February 26. Washington, D.C.: United States Government Printing Office, 1970.

————. "Our Army is our Whole People." *Newsweek*, LXXV: 38–39, March 9, 1970.

————. "PAIGC: Optimistic and a Fighter." *Tricontinental Magazine*, 19,20" 167–174, July–October 1970.

——. "Report on Portuguese Guinea and the Liberation Movement." *Ufahamu*, I, 2: 69–103, Fall 1970.

——. *Sur les Lois Portugaises de Domination Coloniale.* Conakry: PAIGC, 1970.

——. *Sur la Situation de Notre Lutte Armée de Libération Nationale,.* Janvier-Septembre, Conakry: PAIGC, 1970.

——. *Libération Nationale et Culture.* Conakry: PAIGC, 1970.

——. *Guinée "Portugaise:" le Pouvoir des Armes.* Paris: François Maspero, 1970.

——. *Message to the People on the Occasion of the Fourteenth Anniversary of the Foundation of the PAIGC.* Conakry: PAIGC, 1970.

——. *Revolution in Guinea.* New York: Monthly Review Press, 1970.

1971

——. *The Eighth Year of Our Armed Struggle for National Liberation.* Conakry: PAIGC, 1971.

——. *A Brief Report on the Situation of the Struggle* (January–August), Conakry: PAIGC, 1971.

——. *Sobre a Situação da Luta. Sobre Alguns Problemas Práticos da Nossa Vida e da Nossa Luta*, Conakry: PAIGC, August 9–16, 1971.

——. *A Consciência Nova que a Luta Forjou nos Homens e Mulheres da Nossa Terra éa Arma Mais Poderosa do Nosso Povo contra os Criminosos Colonialistas Portuguesas.* Conakry: PAIGC, September 1971.

——. "PAIGC Attacks." *Tricontinental*, 68: 38–39, November 1971.

——. "A Brief Report on the Situation of the Struggle, January–August 1971." *Ufahamu*, II, 3 (Winter): 5–28, 1972.

——. *Our People Are Our Mountains: Amílcar Cabral on the Guinean Revolution.* Introduction by Basil Davidson. London: Committee for Freedom in Mozambique, Angola and Guiné, 1971.

1972

——. *New Year's Address to the People of Guinea and Cape Verde.* January, PAIGC: Conakry, 1972.

——. "PAIGC's Denuciation." *Tricontinental Bulletin*, 71 (February 1972): 44.

——. *Speech Given at the 32nd Session of the United Nations Security Council*, Addis Ababa. February 1972.

——. "Frutos de una Lucha." *Tricontinental* 31: 61–77, July–August 1972.

——. *The People of Guinea and the Cape Verde Islands in Front of the United Nations*, Speech at the 27th Session of the United Nations General Assembly. October 1972.

———. "Identity and Dignity in Struggle." *Southern Africa*, V, 9: 4–8, November 1972.

———. "Identity and Dignity in the National Liberation Struggle." *Africa Today*, (Fall): 39–47, 1972.

———. "Interview." in, *NLF: National Liberation Fronts, 1960/1970*, Donald C. Hughes and Robert E. A. Shanab, (eds.) , pp. 156–70, New York: Morrow, 1972.

———. *Rapport Bref sur la Lutte en 1971*. Conakry: PAIGC, 1972.

———. *Establishment of the Peoples National Assembly and the 1972 Election Results*, January 8, 1972.

1973

———. *Mensagem do Ano Novo*. Conakry: PAIGC, January 1973.

———. "Support for the People's Legitimate Aspirations to Freedom, Independence and Progress." *Objective: Justice*, V:4–7, January–March 1973.

[A. Cabral was assassinated in Conakry on 20 January 1973]

———. "An Informal Talk by A. Cabral." *Southern Africa*, VI, 2: 6–9, February 1973.

———. "Cinquante Ans de Lutte pour la Libération Nationale." *Questions Actuelles du Socialisme/Socialist Thought and Practice*, 98–110, March–April 1973.

———. "The Struggle Has Taken Root." *Tricontinental*, 84: 41–49, 1973. Press Conference in Conakry in September 1972.

———. "Realidades." *Tricontinental*, 33: 97–109, 1973). (Interview).

———. "Original Writings of Amílcar Cabral." *Ufahamu*, III, 3: 31–42, Winter 1973.

———. *Return to the Source: Selected Speeches of Amílcar Cabral*. New York: African Information Service and PAIGC, 1973.

———. *Cabral on Nkrumah*. Newark, NJ. PAIGC, 1973.

———. *Revolutsiya v Guinée*. Moscow: Glavnaya Redaktsva Vostochnoi Literaturi, 1973.

1974

———. "National Liberation and Culture." *Transition*, IX, 45: 12–17, 1974.

———. *Alguns Princípios do Partido*. Lisbon: Seara Nova, 1974.

1975

———. *Unité et Lutte*. vol. I: *L'Arme de la Théorie*; vol. II: *La Pratique Révolutionnaire*. Paris: Maspéro, 1975.

1980

――――. *Unity and Struggle: Speeches and Writings of Amílcar Cabral.* New York: Monthly Review Press, 1980; and London: Heinemann Educational Books, 1980.

1983

――――. "Princípios do Partido e a Prática Política." in, *Cabral ka Muri.* Portugal: Department of Information, Propaganda and Culture of the Central Committee of the PAIGC, 1983.

1988

――――. *Estudos Agrários de Amílcar Cabral,* Instituto de Investigação Científica Tropical IICT/INEP, Lisboa/Bissau, 1988.

11B. About Amílcar Cabral

Ahmed, Feroz. "Amílcar Cabral: Editorial and Interview." *Pakistan Forum*, III, 4: 3–4, January 1973.

Andelman, David A. "Profile: Amílcar Cabral. Pragmatic Revolutionary Shows How an African Guerrilla War Can be Successful." *Africa Report*, XV, 5: 18–19, May 1970.

Andreini, Jean-Claude, and Marie-Laure, Lambert. *La Guinée-Bissau: d'Amílcar Cabral a la Reconstruction Nationale.* Paris: Harmattan, 1978.

Anon. "Without Cabral." *Economist*, CSLVI: 29, January 1973.

Anon. "Tributes to Amílcar Cabral." *Ufahamu*, III, 3: 11–29, Winter 1973.

Anon. *La Pensée Politique d'Amílcar Cabral.* Montreal: SUCO, 1978.

Anon. "Palavras de Ordem Gerais do Camarada Amílcar Cabral aos Responsaveis do Partido, November de 1965." PAIGC: Conakry, 1969.

――――. "Amílcar Cabral: O Homen e a sua Obra." Conakry, PAIGC July 1973.

Benot, Yves. "Amílcar Cabral and the International Working Class Movement." *Latin American Perspectives.* 11, 2:81–96, 1984.

Bessis, Sophie. "Qui a Tué Amílcar Cabral?" *Jeune Afrique*, 1193: 53–56,61, November 16, 1983.

Bienen, Henry. "State and Revolution, the Work of Amílcar Cabral." *Journal of Modern African Studies*, XII: 191–210, June 1974.

Bockel, Alain. "Amílcar Cabral, Marxiste Africain." *Ethiopiques*, 5: 35–39, January 1976.

Cabral, Vasco. *Intervention du Camarade Vasco Cabral, Membre du Comité Executif de la Lutte de PAIGC, au Symposium en Mémoire d'Amílcar Cabral.* Conakry: PAIGC, January 1973.

Cardoso, Carlos. "Os Fundamentos do Conteúdo e dos Objectivos da Libertação Nacional no Pensamento de A. Cabral." *Conferência Internacional sobre a Personalidade de A. Cabral,* December 1984.

Chabal, Patrick. "Amílcar Cabral as Revolutionary Leader." Ph.D. Dissertation, Trinity College, University of Cambridge, August 1980.

Chabal, Patrick. *Amílcar Cabral: Revolutionary Leadership and People's War,* Cambridge: Cambridge University Press, 1983.

————. "The Social and Political Thought of Amílcar Cabral: A Reassessment. *Journal of Modern African Studies,* 19, 1: 31–56, 1981.

Chaliand, Gérard. "The Legacy of Amílcar Cabral." *Ramparts,* 17–20, April 1973.

————. "The PAIGC without Cabral: An Assessment." *Ufahamu,* III, 3: 87–95, Winter 1973.

Chilcote, Ronald H. "African Ephemeral Material: Portuguese African Nationalist Movements." *Africana Newsletter,* I: 9–17, Winter 1963.

————. "The Political Thought of Amílcar Cabral." *Journal of Modern African Studies,* VI, 3: 378–388, October 1968.

————. "Amílcar Cabral: A Bibliography of His Life and Thought, 1925–1973." *Africana Library Journal,* 5, 4: 289–307, Winter 1974.

————. "The Theory and Practice of Amílcar Cabral: Revolutionary Implications for the Third World." *Latin American Perspectives.* 11, 2: 3–14, 1984.

————. *Amílcar Cabral's Révolutionary Theory and Practice: A Critical Guide.* Lynne Rienner Publishers, Boulder & London, 1991.

Clapham, Christopher. "The Context of African Political Thought." *Journal of Modern African Studies,* 8, 1: 1–13, 1970.

Crimi, Bruno. "Amílcar Cabral Prêt pour l'Independance." *Jeune Afrique* 619: 12–16, November 18, 1972.

————. "Les Assassins de Cabral." *Jeune Afrique,* 8–12, February 3, 1973.

————. "Autopsie d'un Assassinat Politique." *Jeune Afrique,* 604: 36–39, August 5, 1972.

————. "La Vérite sur l'Assassinat d'Amílcar Cabral." *Jeune Afrique,* 734: 18–21, 31 January 1975.

Dadoo, Yusuf. "Amílcar Cabral—Outstanding Leader of Africa's Liberation Movements." *African Communist* 53, 2: 38–73, 1973.

Davidson, Basil. "Profile of Amílcar Cabral." *West Africa,* XXVII, April 1964.

————. "Amílcar Cabral—Death of an African Educationist." *Times Educational Supplement,* 3009: 6, January 26, 1973.

————. "On Revolutionary Nationalism: The Legacy of Cabral." *Latin American Perspectives.* 11, 2: 15–42, 1984.

De Andrade, Mário. "Amílcar Cabral: Profil d'un Revolutionnaire Africain." *Presence Africaine*, 86, 2: 3–19, 1973.

———. "Amílcar Cabral et la Guerre du Peuple." *Afrique-Asie* 66, vii, 23 September–4 October 1974.

———. "L'oeuvre de Cabral." *Afrique-Asie*, 75: 14–15, 27 January 1975.

———. and Arnaldo Franca. "A Cultura na Problemática da Libertação Nacional e do Desenvolvimento a Luz do Pensamento Político de Amílcar Cabral." *Raizes*, I, 1: 3–19, January–April 1977.

———. *Amílcar Cabral. Essai de Biographie Politique.* Maspero: Paris, 1980.

De Bragança, Aquino. *Amílcar Cabral.* Lisbon: Initiativas Editoriais, 1976.

———. "L'Assassinat de Cabral." *Afrique-Asie*, XXIV, 8–15, February 19–March 4, 1973): 8–15.

———. "The Plot Against Cabral." *Southern Africa*, 4–8, May 1973.

———. "Cabral is Assassinated by Portuguese Agents." *African World*, 1–16, February 3, 1973.

De Figueiredo, A. "Amílcar Cabral." *Race Today*, 40, February 1973.

Ferreira, Eduardo de Sousa. "Amílcar Cabral: Theory of Revolution and Background to his Assassination." *Ufahamu*, III, 3: 49–68, Winter 1973.

Hill, Sylvia. "International Solidarity: Cabral's Legacy to the African-American Community." *Latin American Perspective.* 11, 2: 67–80.

Hubbard, Maryinez L. "Culture and History in a Revolutionary Context: Approaches to Amílcar Cabral." *Ufahamu*, III, 3: 69–86, Winter 1973.

Ignatiev, Oleg. *Amílcar Cabral: Filho de Africa.* Lisbon: Prelo Editora, 1975.

———. *Três Tiros da PIDE. Quem, Porque e Como Mataram Amílcar Cabral.* Lisbon: Prelo Editora, 1975.

Intelligence Report. *Amílcar Cabral: a Commentary*, Lisbon: Overseas Companies of Portugal, 1973.

Jinadu, L. A. "Some African Theorists of Culture and Modernization: Fanon, Cabral and Some Others." *African Studies Review*, 21, 1: 121–138, April 1978.

Kravcova, T. I. "Amilkar Kabral (1924–1973)." *Narodny Azil Afriki*, 3: 76–87, 1974.

Lopes, Carlos. "As Dominantes Teóricas no Pensamento de Amílcar Cabral." *Revista Internacional de Estudos Africanos*, 2: 63–92, June–December 1984.

Magubane, Bernard. "Amílcar Cabral: Evolution of Revolutionary Thought." *Ufahamu*, II, 2: 71–87, Fall 1971.

Marcum, John A. "Guinea Bissau: Amílcar Cabral, The Meaning of an Assassination." *Africa Report*, 18: 21–23, March 1973.

McCollester, Charles. "The Political Thought of Amílcar Cabral." *Monthly Review*, 24, 10: 10–21, March 1973.

Morgado, Michael S. "Amílcar Cabral's Theory of Cultural Revolution." *Black Images*, III, 2: 3–16, 1974.

Moser, G. M. "The Poet Amílcar Cabral." *Research in African Literature*, 9, 2: 176–97, 1978.

Nyang, S. "The Political Thought of Amílcar Cabral: a Synthesis." *Odu*, 13: 3–20, January 1976.

Nzongola-Ntalaja. "Amílcar Cabral and the Theory of the National Liberation Struggle, *Latin American Perspectives*, 11, 2: 43–54, 1984.

Opuku, K. "Cabral and the African Revolution." *Présence Africaine*, 105–6: 45–60, 1978.

Reed, Rick. "A Song of World Revolution: In Tribute to Amílcar Cabral." *Institute of the Black World Monthly Report*, February 1973.

Ribeiro, Sérgio. *Sobre a Unidade no Pensamento de Amílcar Cabral.* Tricontinental Editora, Colecção Terceiro Mundo, Lisboa, 1983.

Segal, Aaron. "Amílcar Cabral: In Memoriam." *Third World*, 2, 4: 7–8, April 1973.

Vieyra, Justin. "Amílcar Cabral: Liberté pour 350,000 Guinéens." *Jeune Afrique*, 230: 23, May 1, 1965.

12. On National Liberation

Amadou, Fode. "Cette Année, un Nouvel Etat Souverain." *Afrique-Asie*, 36: 31–32, August 6, 1973.

Anderson, P. "Portugal and the End of Ultra-Colonialism." *New Left Review*, 15/16, 2 parts, n.d.

Anon. "Le Problème des Réfugiés de la Guinée-Bissau en Casamance." *Sénégal d'Aujourd'hui*, 12: 11–17, October 1964.

Anon. "The Situation of Portuguese Guinea Refugees in the Casamance Region of Senegal." *Translations on Africa*, 108: 17–21, 1964.

Anon. *La Lutte Continue, Janvier-Avril, 1964.* Paris: Comité de Soutien à l'Angola et aux Peuples des Colonies Portugaises 1964.

Anon. "Liberation Movements in Portuguese Guinea: (PAIGC) Totes Up 1964 Achievements." *Translations on Africa*, 220: 5–10, 1964.

Anon. *Guinée "Portugaise" et Îles du Cap-Vert, L'An Deux de la Guerre de Guinée*, Janvier–Décembre 1964 Paris: Comité de Soutien à l'Angola et aux Peuples des Colonies Portugaises, 1965.

Anon. "Portuguese Guinea: More War Than Most." *Africa Confidential*, 3, February 2, 1968.

Anon. *A Profile of PAIGC*. Program to Combat Racism. Geneva: World Council of Churches, 1970.

Anon. "Allies in Empire: The U.S. and Portugal in Africa." *Africa Today*, 17, 4, July–August 1970.

Anon. *Guinée e Cap-Vert. Libération des Colonies Portugaises*. Algiers: Information CONCP (Conférence des Organisations Nationales des Colonies Portugaises), 1970.

Anon. "Guinea-Bissau's Liberation Struggle." *Race Today*, III, 11: 375–377, November 1971.

Anon. *Portuguese Colonies: Victory or Death*. Havana, Cuba: Tricontinental, 1971.

Anon. *Report of a Visit to the Liberated Areas of Guinea-Bissau*. Helsinki: National Union of Finnish Students, 1971.

Anon. "Guinea-Bissau: Along the People's Paths." *Tricontinental Bulletin*, 70: 43–47, January 1972.

Anon. "Portugal's African Wars." *Conflict Studies* 34 , March, 1973.

Anon. "Guinea-Bissau: La Victoire Reconnue." *Afrique Asie*, 65: 22–23, 9–22 September 1974.

Anon. "Guerre et Paix en Guinée-Bissau: Naissance d'une Nation." *Afrique-Asie*, 66, September 23 to October 6, 1974.

Anon. "La Politique Étrangère de Guinée-Bissau." *La Révolution Africaine*, October 1974.

Anon. *Guinea-Bissau: Toward Final Victory. Selected Speeches and Documents from the PAIGC*. Richmond, B.C., Canada: LSM Press, 1974.

Anon. *Sun of Our Freedom: The Independence of Guinea Bissau*. Chicago: Chicago Committee for the Liberation of Angola, Mozambique and Guinea, 1974.

Anon. "Naissance d'un Nouvel État Africain: la République de Guinée-Bissau." *Présence Africaine*, IV: 248–301, 1974.

Anon. "L'Independence du Cap-Vert: Un Nouveau Pays vers l'Unité avec la Guinée-Bissau." *Afrique-Asie*, 86, 1975.

Beetz, Dietmar. *Visite in Guiné-Bissau*. Berlin: Podium, 1975.

Belchior, Manuel. *Os Congressos do Povo da Guiné*. Lisbon: Editora Arcadia, 1973.

Bender, Gerald J. "Portugal and her Colonies Join the Twentieth Century." *Ufahamu*, IV, 3: 121–162, 1974.

Bergersol, J. "Guinea-Bissau Begins to Reconstruct." *African Development*, 18–19, October 1974.

Biggs-Davison, John. *Portuguese-Guinea: Nailing a Lie*. London: Congo Africa Publications, 1970.

Bigman, Laura. *Revolutionary Democracy in Guinea-Bissau*. Master's Thesis, Howard University, December 1980.

Bosgra, S. J. and C. Van Krimpen. *Portugal and NATO*. Amsterdam: Angola Comité, 1970.

Bouabid, M. "Guinée Bissau: I'Heure de la Reconstruction." *Révolution Africaine*, 555, 11–17: 20–27, October 1974.

Cabral, Vasco. "Foreign Capitalist Interests in the So-Called Portuguese Guinea and the Islands of the Green Cape." in *Peace and Socialism—Al Tali'a Seminar: Africa; National and Social Revolution*, (Cairo, October 24–29), II, 36, 1966.

———. "Guinea-Bissau." *World Problems of Marxism, Peace and Socialism Review*, 113–116, February 1974.

———. "Speech of the Delegation of 'Portuguese' Guinea." in *Peace and Socialism—Al Tali'a Seminar: Africa; National and Social Revolution*, II, 42, Cairo, October 24–29, 1966.

Campbell, Bonnie. *Libération Nationale et Construction du Socialisme en Afrique (Angola, Guinée-Bissau et Mozambique)*. Montréal: Editions Nouvelles Optique, 1977.

Cesar, Armandio. *Guiné 1965: Contra-Ataque*. Braga: Editoria Pax, 1965.

Chabal, Patrick. "National Liberation in Portuguese Guinea, 1956–1974." *African Affairs*, 80, 318: 75–99, January 1981.

———. "Guinée-Bissau, Cap Vert: Histoire et Politique." *Le Mois en Afrique: Revue d'Études Politiques et Économiques Africaines*, 190/191: 119–131, October–November 1981.

———. "Party, State and Socialism in Guinea-Bissau." *Canadian Journal of African Studies*. 17, 2: 189–210, 1983.

———. "Revolutionary Democracy in Guinea-Bissau," in P. Chabal (ed.), *Political Domination in Africa: Reflections on the Limits of Power*, Cambridge: Cambridge University Press, 1986.

Chaliand, Gérard. *Armed Struggle in Africa: With the Guerrillas in "Portuguese Guinea."* New York: Monthly Review Press, 1969.

———. *Guinée "Portugaise" et Cap Vert en Lutte pour leur Indé-'pendance*. Paris: François Maspero, 1964.

Chilcote, Ronald H. "Development and Nationalism in Brazil and Portuguese Africa." *Comparative Political Studies*, January 1969.

———. "Guiné-Bissau's Struggle: Past and Present." *Africa Today*, 24, 1, January–March 1977.

———. "Nationalist Documents on Portuguese Guinea and Cape Verde Islands and Mozambique." *African Studies Bulletin*, X, 1: 22–42, April 1967.

———. "Struggle in Guinea-Bissau." *Africa Today*, 21: 57–62, Winter 1974.

Cornwall, Barbara. *The Bush Rebels: A Personal Account of Black Revolt in Africa*. New York: Holt, Rinehart and Winston, 1972.

Crimi, Bruno. "Guinée-Bissau: Naissance d'un État." *Jeune Afrique*, 666: 24–28, 13 October 1973.

Da Cruz, Luís Fernando Diaz Correia. "Alguns Aspectos da Subversão na Província Portuguesa da Guiné." *Ultramar*, VIII, 4: 125–147, April–June 1968.

Davidson, Basil. "Revolt of 'Portuguese' Guinea." *Tricontinental Magazine*, 8: 88–91, September–October 1968.

———. *The Liberation of Guiné: Aspects of an African Revolution.* Harmondsworth: Penguin, 1969.

———. "Liberation Struggles in Angola and 'Portuguese' Guinea." *Africa Quarterly*, X, 1: 25–31, April–June 1970.

———. "An Independent Guinea-Bissau: Political Foundations." *West Africa*, January 29, 1973.

———. "Guinea-Bissau Builds for Independence." *New World Review*, XLI, 2: 36–42, 1973.

———. "The Prospect for Guinea-Bissau." *Third World* , 3–6, April 1973.

———. "A Report on the Further Liberation of Guinea." *The Socialist Register*, 283–301, 1973.

———. "Guinea-Bissau and the Cape Verde Islands: The Transition from War to Independence." *Africa Today* , XXI: 5–22, Fall 1974.

———. "Guinée-Bissau: Naissance d'une Démocratie Africaine." *Le Monde Diplomatique*, 247: 34–36, October 1974.

———. "Notes on a Liberation Struggle." *Transition*, IX, 45: 10–21, 1974.

———. *Growing from Grass Roots. The State of Guinea Bissau.* London: Committee for Freedom in Mozambique, Angola and Guiné, n.d.

———. *No Fist Is Big Enough to Hide the Sky. The Liberation of Guinea-Bissau and Cape Verde.* London: Zed Press, 1981.

———. "Practice and Theory: Guinea-Bissau and Cape Verde." in Barry Munslow, ed., *Africa. Problems in the Transition to Socialism.* London: Zed Books, 1986; 95–113.

Davis, Jennifer. *The Republic of Guinea-Bissau: Triumph Over Colonialism.* New York: The Africa Fund, n.d.

De Andrade, F. J. H. Rebelo. "Armed Forces Activities in Portuguese Guinea." *Ultramar*, VII, 4: 176–200, April–June 1968.

De Andrade, Mario. "*A Guerra do Povo na Guiné-Bissau.* Lisbõa: Livraria Sa da Costa Editoria, 1975.

———. "Colonialisme, Culture et Revolution." in *Colonias Portugaise: la Victoire ou la Mort.* Havana: Tricontinental, 39–53, 1970.

De Bragança, Aquino. "Eloge d'une Bourgeoisie Africaine (l'Experience Révolutionnaire de Guinée-Bissau)." in *Problèmes Actuels de l'Unité Africaine.* Algiers: SNED, 512–524, 1973.

———. "Guinée-Bissau: les Vérités sur les Négociations." *Afrique-Asie* 58: 16–18, June 10, 1974.

———. "La Longue Marche d'un Révolutionnaire Africain." *Afrique-Asie*, XXIII, 5: 12–20, February 18, 1973.

Dhada, Mustafa, *Warriors at Work: How Guinea Was Really Set Free.* Niwot: University Press of Colorado, 1993.

Dias, H. " 'Portuguese' Guinea." *Portuguese and Colonial Bulletin*, V, 6: 300, December 1965–January 1966.

Dias, José Manuel de Braga. *Mudança Sócio-Cultural na Guiné Portuguesa*. Disertação, Universidade Técnica de Lisboa, Instituto Superior de Ciências Sociais e Política Ultramarina, Lisbon, 1974.

Diggs, Charles C., Jr. "Text of the Proclamation of the State of Guinea-Bissau by the people's National Assembly." *Issue; a Quarterly Journal of Africanist Opinion*, 3, 3: 28–32, 1973.

Duarte, Abílio Monteiro. "Aiding the Struggle in 'Portuguese' Guinea." *Revolution*, I: 44–47, August–September 1963.

————. " 'Portuguese' Guinea." *Information Bulletin (World Marxist Review)*, 42: 53–54, May 13, 1965.

————. "On the Question of Territories under Portuguese Domination." United Nations General Assembly Document A/AC.109/PV.966, March 29, 1974.

Duarte, Dulce Amada. "The Cultural Dimension in the Strategy for National Liberation: the Cultural Bases of the Unification between Cape Verde and Guinea-Bissau. *Latin American Perspectives*, 11(2): 55–66, 1984.

Ehhmark, Anders and Per Wastberg. *Angola and Mozambique: The Case Against Portugal*. New York: Roy Publishers, 1963.

Felgas, Helio. *A Luta na Guiné*. Lisbon: 1970.

————. *Os Movimentos Terroristas de Angola, Guiné, Moçambique (Influencia externa)*. Lisbon: 1966.

Ferreira, E. *Portuguese Colonialism in Africa: The End of an Era*. Paris: UNESCO Press, 1974

Fernandez, Gil. "Talk with a Guinean Revolutionary." *Ufahamu*, I, 1: 6–21, Spring 1970.

————. "We Are Anonymous Soldiers of U.N." *Objective: Justice*, IV, 1: 48, January–March 1972.

First, Ruth. *Portugal's Wars in Africa*. London: Christian Action Publications Ltd., 1972.

Frente de Libertação da Guiné e Cabo Verde. *Message to the Portuguese Colonists in Guiné and Cape Verde,* Partido Africano da Independência, Conakry: October 1960.

Frente de Luta pela Independência National de Guiné Bissau. *Charte Préambule*. Dakar, 1962.

Galtung, Ingegerd. *Reports from So-called Liberated Portuguese Guinea-Bissau*. Morgenbladet, Oslo, n.d.

Gibson, Richard. *African Liberation Movements. Contemporary Struggles Against White Minority Rule*, London: Oxford University Press, 1972.

Guinée, Peter. *Portugal and the EEC*. Amsterdam: Angola Comité in Cooperation with the Programme to Combat Racism of the World Council of Churches, Geneva, 1973.

Hadjor, Kofi B. "The Revolution in Guinea-Bissau." *Africa*, 12–14, April 1974.

Henrikson, Thomas. "People's war in Angola, Mozambique, and Guinea-Bissau." *Journal of Modern African Studies*, 14, 3: 377–399, 1976.

Hoti, Ukson. "The Liberation Struggle in the Portuguese Colonies." *Review of International Affairs*, 30–31, November 5–20, 1972.

Ignatyev, Oleg Konstantinovich. *Along the Paths of War: War Diaries from Three Fronts of Guinea*. Moscow: Political Literature Publications, 1972.

Infante, M. "La Guinée-Bissau al l'Ora del l'Independenza." *Politica Internazionale*, 10: 54–56, October 1973.

Ivekovic, I. "Guinée-Bissau: Naissance d'une Indépendance." *Questions Actuelles du Socialisme*, 25, 7–8: 141–156, July–August 1975.

Lawrence, Ken. "PIDE and SDECE: Plotting in Guinea." In *Dirty Work: the CIA in Africa*. Edited by Ellen Ray et al., 140–145, London: Zed Press, 1980.

Lefort, René. "Avec les Nationalistes de Guinée Portugaise." *Le Monde*, 6–7, November 1970.

Lipinska, Suzanne. "Deux Semaines dans le Maquis de la Guinée-Bissao." *Africasia*, 16–18, 1970.

Lobban, Richard A. "Cape Verde Islands: Portugal's Atlantic Colony" *Africa Magazine*, 36–39, May 1973.

———. "The Fall of Guiledge." *Africa Magazine*, 24, August 1973. (Paris).

———. "The Progress of the War in Guinea-Bissau." *Southern Africa*, August 1973, (New York).

———. "Guinea-Bissau: 24 September and Beyond." *Africa Today* 21, 1: 15–24 , 1974.

———. "The Cape Verde Islands: Colonialism on the Wane" *Southern Africa*, VIII:4–7, January 1975

———. "Guinea-Bissau: A New Era." *New World Review*, January–February 1975.

———. "Interview with President Luís Cabral." *Southern Africa*, VIII, 9: 12–14, 1975.

Lopes, Carlos. *Etnia, Estado e Relações de Poder na Guiné-Bissau*. Lisbon: Edições 70, 1982.

———. *Guinea Bissau: From Liberation Struggle to Independent Statehood*. London: Zed Press, and Boulder: Westview Press.

———. *A Transição Histórica na Guiné-Bissau; do Movimento de Libertação Nacional aoEstado*. Mémoire. Geneva: Institute Universitaire d'Etudes du Développement, November 1982.

Makedonsky, Jeanne. "L'Épineuse Décolonisation de la Guinée-Bissau." *Revue Française d'Etudes Politiques Africaines*, 9, 105: 43–55, September 1974.

Makedowsky, Eric. "Le PAIGC Seul Maitre à Bord." *Afrique et Monde,* August 13, 1974.

Malatu, G. "Viva Guinea Bissau." *Africa,* 38: 11–16, October 1974.

Marcum, John A. "Three Revolutions." *Africa Report,* 12: 6, November 1967.

———. *The Politics of Indifference: Portugal and Africa, A Case Study in American Foreign Policy.* Syracuse, N.Y.: Syracuse University: Program of Eastern African Studies, 1972.

Marcus, J. "A New Departure in Luso-America Relations." *Africa Today,* 16, 1, February–March 1969.

Margarido, Alfredo. "Les Partis Politiques en Guinée Portugaise, en Angola, et aux Îles du Cap Vert." *Mois en Afrique,* 9, July 1966.

———. "Partis Politiques Africains sous Domination Portugaise." *Revue Française d'Etudes Politiques Africaines ,* 44–68, July 1968.

———. "Guinée et Guinée-Bissau: Bilan Provisoire de la Tentative d'Invasion de Novembre." *Revue Française d'Etudes Politiques Africaines,* 63: 18–20, March 1971.

Maria, Victor. "La Guinée 'Portugaise.' " *Voices of Africa,* II: 34–35, March 1962.

Martelli, George. "Progress in Portuguese Guinea." *Geographical Magazine.* 128–137, June 1967.

Matteos, Salahudin Omawale. "The Cape Verdeans and the PAIGC Struggle for National Liberation." *Ufahamu,* III, 3: 43–48, Winter 1973.

McCollester, Charles. "The Political Thought of Amílcar Cabral." *Monthly Review,* XXIV, 10: 10–21, March 1973.

Mendy, Justin. "The Struggle Goes On." *Africa Report .* 24, March–April 1973.

Miranda, Nuño de. "Defesa de Portugal." *Cabo Verde: Boletim de Propaganda e Informação,* XIII, 147: 6, 1961.

Moolman, J. H. "Portuguese Guinea: The Untenable War." *Africa Institute Bulletin,* XII, 6: 243–260, 1974.

Neto João Baptista Nunes Pereira. "Movimentos Subversivos da Guiné, Cabo Verde e São Tomé e Príncipe." *Cabo Verde, Guiné, São Tomé e Príncipe.* Lisbon: 1966.

Ngwube, Douglas. "Guinea-Bissau: Decisive Phase." *Africa,* 23–24, June 1974.

O'Brien, Jay. "Tribe, Class, Nation: Revolution and the Weapon of Theory in Guinea-Bissau." *Race and Class,* 19, 1: 1–18, 1977.

Ogawa, Tadahiro. *Nô Pintcha.* Tokyo: Taimatsu-Sha, 1972.

PAIGC. *Estatutos dos Pioneiros do Partido.* Conakry, n.d.

———. *Proclamação.* Movimento de Libertação da Guiné e Cabo Verde. Conakry: November 1960.

———. *Statuts et Programme.* Conakry, 1962.

————. *Communique: Le Peuple de la Guinée 'Portugaise' devant l'ONU.* New York, 1962.

————. *Communique: Extraits de Quelques Articles de L'Organe du PAIGC.* Conakry, April 1963.

————. *Communique: Développement de la Lutte de Libération Nationale: l'Action du PAIGC.* Algiers, 1963.

————. *Communique: Le Développement de la Lutte de Libération Nationale en Guinée 'Portugaise' et aux Îles du Cap Vert en 1964.* Conakry, 1964.

————. *Communique: Le PAIGC à la Conférence des Chefs d'État et de Gouvernement des Pays Non-alignés, le Caire, Octobre 1964.* Conakry, 1965.

————. *Lei da Justiça Militar de 19 de Setembro de 1966, com as Modificações Introduzidas pelo Bureau Político do Partido, na Reunião de 20 a 23 de dezembro de 1966.* Conakry, 1966.

————. *Statuts de l'Institut Amitié.* Conakry, 1969.

————. *Regulamento de Disciplina Interna.* Quembra, 1970.

————. *Regulamento Interno dos Internatos das Regiões Libertades,* Conakry, September 1971.

————. *Manual Político.* Vol. 1. Conakry, 1972.

————. *O Nosso Livro, Primeira Classe.* Uppsala, 1970.

————. *O Nosso Livro, Quarta Classe.* Uppsala, 1972.

————. *Projecto da Revisão de Lei da Justiça Militar.* Conakry, 1972.

————. [and United Nations]. *Resolution Adoptée par le Comité Spécial à sa 854ème Séance, le* 13 Avril 1972 à Conakry (Guinée). AF/109/63, 1972.

————. *Message du Comité Exécutif de la Lutte du PAIGC.* Conakry, January 1973.

————. *Biographies Sommaires des Membres du Secrétariat Permanent du Comité Exécutif de* la Lutte, Conakry, July 24, 1973.

————. *Proclamação do Estado da Guiné-Bissau,* Adopted by the Peoples National Assembly, 24 September 1973. Boé, Guiné-Bissau, 1973.

————. *Sobre a Situação em Cabo Verde.* Lisbõa, 1974.

————. *Report of the Supreme Council of the Struggle to the Third Congress of the PAIGC, State Papers and Party Proceedings Series 1, No. 3,* MAGIC (Mozambique, Angola and Guinea Information Center). London: 1978.

Pereira, Aristides. *Communiqué.* Conakry: PAIGC, October 2, 1972.

————. "Guinée 'Portugaise': Dernier Quart d'Heure?" *Révolution Africaine,* 99: 7, 19 December 1962.

Pineau, Guy. *Le PAIGC et la Lutte de Libération Nationale en Guinée Bissau et aux Îles du Cap Vert.* Mémoire. Université de Paris, October 1972.

Pinto, Cruz. "Guinea-Bissau's Liberation Struggle Against Portuguese Colonialism." *Freedomways*, 3, 1972.

Rodrigues, Manuel M. Sarmento. *A Nossa Guiné*. Lisbon: 1972.

Rodrigues, Paulo Madeira. *4 Paises Libertados. Portugal, Guiné-Bissau, Angola, Moçambique*. Lisbon: Livraria Bertrand, 1975.

Rubio Garcia, L. "El Caso de Guinea-Bissau: uma Descolonizacion Vista como Fenômeno Cultural." *Revista de Política Internacional*, 139: 169–190, May–June 1975.

Rudebeck, Lars. *Guinea-Bissau: A Study of Political Mobilization*. Uppsala: Scandanavian Institute of African Studies, 1974.

———. "Political Mobilisation for Development in Guinea-Bissau." *Journal of Modern African Studies*, 10, 1: 1–18, 1972.

Rurihose, N. "La Reconnaissance de la Guinée-Bissau et le Droit International." *Etude Zairoises*, 3: 73–89, December 1973.

Sampaio, Mário. "The New Guinea-Bissau: How Will It Survive?" *African Development*, 11–13, March 1974.

Schilling, Barbara (ed). *Angola, Guinea, Mozambique. Dokumente und Materialien des Befreiungskampfes des Volker Angolas, Guinea und Mozambique*. Frankfurt-am-Main: Verlag Marxistische Blatter, 1971.

Sevilla-Borja, H. et. al. "U.N. General Mission to Guinea (Bissau)." *Objective: Justice*, 4: 4–15, July–September 1972.

Spínola, António de. *Por uma Guiné Melhor*. Lisbon: Agência Geral do Ultramar, 1970.

———. *Portugal e o Futuro*. Lisbôa: Arcadia, 1974.

———. *O Problema da Guiné*. Lisbon: Agência Geral do Ultramar, 1970.

Tavares, Estevão et. al. *Déposition des Ex-détenus par la Police Politique Portugaise (PIDE)* à Bissau, en Guinée "Portugaise." Conakry: PAIGC, 1962.

União Democrática das Mulheres da Guiné e Cabo Verde. *Estatutos*. Conakry, n.d.

União Nacional dos Trabalhadores da Guiné. *Estatutos*. Conakry: August 1962.

United Nations. "Security Council's Attention Drawn to Situtation in Portuguese Territories, with Resolution." *United Nations Review*, X: 9–11, April 1963.

———. "Questions Relating to Africa: Communications Concerning Portuguese Guinea." *Yearbook of the United Nations*, 120–121, 1964.

———. "Statement on Territories Under Portuguese Administration." *U.N. Monthly Chronicle*. V: 32–42, July 1968.

———. "Adoption of General Assembly Resolution on Territories Under Portuguese Administration." *U.N. Monthly Chronicle*, VI: 23–33, December 1969.

———. "Security Council Condemns Portugal and Demands Compensation." *U.N. Monthly Chronicle*, VI: 3–19, January 1971.

———. "Report of the U.N. Special Mission to Guinea (Bissau)." *Objective: Justice*, September 1972.

———. "U.N. Special Mission to Guinea-Bissau." *Third World*, 2, 4: 9–19, April 1973.

———. "Working Paper on Guinea (Bissau) and Cape Verde, Special Committee on the Situation with Regard to the Implementation of the Declaration on the Granting of Independence to Colonial Countries and Peoples." *United Nations General Assembly*, 24 May 1973.

———. "Statement of the President of the U.N. General Assembly on the Implementation of the Declaration on the Granting of Independence to Colonial Countries and Peoples." *United Nations General Assembly*, 29th session, October 3, 1974.

United States Congress. House Committee on Foreign Affairs, Subcommittee on Africa. *Report on Portuguese Guinea and the Liberation Movement*. Washington, D.C.: Government Printing Office, 1970.

Urdang, Stephanie. *Fighting Two Colonialisms: Women in Guinea-Bissau*. New York: Monthly Review Press.

———. *A Revolution Within a Revolution: Women in Guinea-Bissau*. Somerville, Massachusetts: New England Free Press, n.d.

———. "Towards a Successful Revolution: The Struggle in Guinea-Bissau." *Objective: Justice* 11–17, January–March 1975.

Valimamad, E. D. *Nationalist Politics, War and Statehood: Guinea-Bissau, 1953–1973*. Ph.D. Dissertation, Oxford: St. Catherine's College, 1984.

Venter, Al J. *Portugal's Guerrilla War: The Campaign for Africa*. Cape Town: John Malherbe Pty. Ltd., 1973.

———. "Portugal's War in Guinea-Bissau." *Munger Africana Library Notes*, California Institute of Technology, April 1973.

Wallerstein, Immanuel. "The Lessons of the PAIGC." *Africa Today*, 62–68, July 1971.

Zartman, I. William. "Guinea: The Quiet War Goes On." *Africa Report*, XII, 8: 67–72, November 1967.

13. Post-Independence Politics

Aaby, Peter. *The State of Guinea-Bissau. African Socialism or Socialism in Africa?* Uppsala: Scandanavian Institute of African Studies, 1978.

Aguilar, R. & Zeján, M. *Guinea-Bissau: A Fresh Start?* SIDA Macroeconomic Studies Series No. 17, Stockholm, 1991.

Aguilar, R. & Zeján, M. *Guinea-Bissau: Getting off the Track*. SIDA Macroeconomic Studies Series 25, Stockholm, 1992.

Almeyro, Guillermo. "Sobre el Caracter del Estado en Guinea Bissau y Mozambique." *Revista Coyocan*, 87–111, 1978.

Alves, Fernando. "Lionel Vieira: um Embaixador Pouco Diplomatica." *Africa* (Portugal), June 6, 1986.

Andreini, Jean-Claude and Marie-Claude Lambert. *La Guinée Bissau d'Amílcar Cabral à la Reconstruction Nationale.* Paris: l'Harmattan, 1978.

Anon. "Trouble à la Frontière entre le Sénégal et la Guinée-Bissau." *La Presse* (Tunisia) March 14, 1973.

Anon. "Sowing the First Harvest: National Reconstruction in Guinea-Bissau." Liberation Support Movement: Oakland, CA, 1978.

Anon. "Guinée-Bissau: Deux Ans Déjà." *L'Observateur*, 123: 7–54, October 1975.

Anon. "La Guinée-Bissau: le Démarrage du Nouvel Etat." *Afrique Contemporaine*, 86: 11–17, July–August 1976.

Anon. *Guiné-Bissau: 3 Anos de Independência.* Lisbon: Africa in Struggle Series, Anti-Colonial Center for Information and Documentation, CIDA-C, 1976.

Anon. "Guinea-Bissau: Reality and Ideology." *Africa*, 70: 62–63, June 1977.

Anon. "Guinea-Bissau Premier Said to Stage Coup." *The New York Times*, November 16, 1980.

Anon. "Guinea-Bissau Coup: Cabral Out." *Guardian* (New York), November 16, 1980.

Anon. "Events in Guinea-Bissau: A Chronology." *People's Power*, 16–23, Spring 1981.

Anon. "Spécial Guinée-Bissau: Ier Congrès Extraordinaire du PAIGC 6–14 November 1981." *ECO Magazine*, Mensuel Africain d'Information et Politique (Bénin), 42: 17–24, December 1981.

Anon. "Guinea Bissau. Party Congress Evokes Diverse Reaction." *Africa News*, 28, 3: 8–9, January 18, 1982.

Anon. "Another Purge of the Left." *West Africa*, 3389. July 19, 1982.

Anon. "Guinea-Bissau. Constitution Revision Panel." *West Africa*, 3421: 631, March 7, 1983.

Anon. "Guinea-Bissau. Death Sentences of 38 Commuted." *West Africa*, 3431, May 16, 1983.

Anon. "Guinea-Bissau: Ministers Out." *West Africa*, 3446: 2030, August 29, 1983.

Anon. "Guinea-Bissau: Another Cabinet Reshuffle." *West Africa*, 3450, September 26, 1983.

Anon. "Guinea-Bissau: Top Party Cadres Expelled." *West Africa*, 3454: 2478, October 24, 1983.

Anon. "Vitor Saude Maria Saiu da Embaixada." *Diário de Notícias*, March 27, 1984.

Anon. "Eleições Locais na Guiné-Bissau." *Diário de Notícias,* April 1, 1984.

Anon. "Guinea-Bissau. Foreign Minister Dropped in Reshuffle." *West Africa,* 3493: 1550, July 30, 1984.

Anon. "Guinea-Bissau. The Tale of Another Plot." *West Africa,* 3650:2406, November 18, 1985.

Anon. "Six are Executed in Guinea-Bissau." *The New York Times ,* July 22, 1986.

Anon. *Guinea-Bissau: A Prescription for Comprehensive Adjustment.* Washington, D.C. World Bank, 1987

Autra, Traore Ray. "Comment les Soussou du Sénégal Appellent les Ressortissants de la Guinée Bissau et des Îles du Cap Verts." *Notes Africaines,* 162: 42–44, Abril 1979.

Benoist, Joseph-Roger de. "Guinée-Bissau, le Socialisme du Bon Sens." *Croissance des Jeunes Nations,* 168: 14–18, February 1976.

Bollinger, Virginia L. *Development Strategy's Impact on Ethnically-Based Political Violence: A Theoretical Framework With Comparative Applications to Zambia, Guinea-Bissau and Moçambique.* Dissertation, University of Colorado at Boulder, 1984.

Cabral, Luís. "Ha Medo na Guiné-Bissau." *Africa* (Portugal), June 11, 1986.

Chabal, Patrick. "Party Politics behind Cabral Coup." *West Africa,* 2554–2556, December 1980.

———. "The PAIGC: the Dilemmas of Continuity." *West Africa,* 2593–2594, December 1980.

———. "Coup for Continuity?" *West Africa* 62–63, January 1981.

———. "Party, State and Socialism in Guinea-Bissau." *Canadian Journal of African Studies,* 17, 2: 189–210, 1983.

Chazan, N. *"Patterns of State-Society Incorporation and Disengagement in Africa,"* in *The Precarious Balance: State and Society in Africa,* Edited by D. Rothchild and N. Chazan, Boulder: Westview Press, 1988.

Conchiglia, Augusta. "Bissau: un Sommet pour Cinq." *Afrique-Asie,* 313: 40, January 16–29, 1984.

Cunningham, James. *Nationalist Development in Guinea-Bissau.* Ph.D. Dissertation, School of Oriental and African Studies, London.

Dash, Leon. "Guinea-Bissau's Leftist Leaders Seek New, Pragmatic Directions." *Washington Post,* 14–15, June 6, 1981.

Da Silva, Baptista. "Guiné-Bissau. O Instável Poder." *Terceiro Mundo,* 84: 32–35, December 1985.

Davidson, Basil. "Guinea-Bissau's People's Election." *People's Power,* 6: 27–31, January–February 1977.

Decreane, Philippe. "Guinée-Bissau: La Mobilisation Permanente." *Le Monde,* April 13/14, 1976.

Dia, Mam Less. "Guinée Bissau: Les Difficultés de L'Indépendance." *Le Soleil* (Senegal), July 11, 1975.

Dianoux, Huges Jean de. "La Guinée-Bissau et les Îles du Cap Vert." *Afrique Contemporaine*, 107: 1–17, January–February 1980.

Fauvet, Gil. "Cabral Displeased with Deputies." *New African*, 22–23, August 1979.

Felkai, Istvan. "Tenir la Promesse Faite aux Paysans." *Le Monde Diplomatique*, April 1983.

Forrest, Joshua B. "Guinea-Bissau Since Independence: A Decade of Domestic Power Struggles." *The Journal of Modern African Studies*, 25, 1, March 1987.

———. *State, Peasantry and National-level Power Struggles in Post-Independence Guinea-Bissau*. Ph.D. Dissertation, University of Wisconsin–Madison, 1987.

———. *Guinea-Bissau: Power, Conflict, and Renewal in a West African Nation*. Boulder: Westview, 1992.

Foy, Colm. " 'Nino' Affirms the Revolution." *West Africa*, 3497: 1723, August 27, 1984.

Gacha, Manuele. "Eveil de la Conscience Nationale et Stratégie Révolutionnaire chez Amílcar Cabral." *Revue Française d'Études Politiques Africaines*, 129: 69–84, July 1976.

Galli, Rosemary E. "The Political Economy of Guinea-Bissau: Second thoughts." *Africa* 59, 3: 371–380, 1989.

———. "Liberalization is Not Enough: Structural Adjustment and Peasants in Guinea-Bissau," *Review of African Political Economy*, 49: 52–68, 1990.

———. "The Absence of Agrarian Capitalism in Guinea-Bissau during the Estado Novo Regime," Paper presented to the *Second International Conference on Social Science in Portuguese-Speaking Africa*, Bissau, November 19–25, 1990.

Galli, Rosemary, and J. Jones. *Guinea-Bissau: Politics, Economics and Society*. London: Frances Pinter Publishers and Boulder: Lynne Rienner Publishers, 1987

Gasper, Fernando. "Um Reporter na Zona Proibida." *Presso*, June 13, 1986.

Gjerstad, Ole and Chantal Sarrazin. *Sowing the First Harvest. National Reconstruction in Guinea-Bissau*. Oakland, CA: LSM Press, 1974.

Harrell-Bond, Barbara. *Guinea-Bissau: Part III: Independent Development*. American University Field Staff Report 22, 1981.

Jegou, Jacques. "L'Afrique Lusophone Dix Ans après la Mort d'Amílcar Cabral." *Afrique Contemporaine*, 28–33, July–September 1983.

Jones, Jocelyn. *The Party, State and Peasantry in Guinea-Bissau*. Ph.D. Dissertation. Oxford: St. Hilda's College, 1987.

Lavrencic, Karl. "New Routes in Guinea-Bissau." *West Africa* 3479: 880, April 23, 1984.

Lopes, Carlos. *Etnia, Estado e Relações de Poder na Guiné-Bissau*. Lisbon: Edições 70, 1982.

———. *A Transição Histórica na Guiné-Bissau; do Movimento de Libertação Nacional ao Estado*. Mémoire. Geneva: Institut Universitaire d'Etudes du Développement. November 1982.

———. *Guinea-Bissau: From Liberation Struggle to Independent Statehood*, Zed Books/London and Westview Press/Boulder, Colorado, 1987.

———. *Para uma Leitura Sociológica da Guiné-Bissau*. Bissau: INEP, 1988.

Makedonsky, Jeanne. "Guinée-Bissau: Premières Élections du temps de Paix." *Africa*, 86: 49–54, 89, December 1976.

Makedowsky, Eric. Untitled section on Guinea-Bissau. in *L'Année Politique et Economique Africaine Edition*. Société Africaine d'Edition, 51, 149–151. 1981.

Moita, Luís. *Os Congressos da FRELIMO, do PAIGC e do MPLA: uma Análise Comparativa*. Lisbon: CIDA-C & Ulmeiro, 1979.

Munslow, Barry. "The 1980 Coup in Guinea Bissau." *Review of African Political Economy*. 109–113, May–September 1981.

Obichere, B. "Reconstruction in Guinea-Bissau: from Revolutionaries and Guerillas to Bureaucrats and Politicians." *Current Bibliography on African Affairs*, 8, 3: 204–219, 1975.

Odou, René. "Guinée-Bissau: un Coup d'État pour Rien." *Afrique Nouvelle*, 1637: 6–7, November 19–25, 1980.

PAIGC. "Constitution de la République de Guinée-Bissau." *Présence Africaine*, 88, 4: 302–309, 1973.

———. "Ante-Projecto dos Estatutos dos PAIGC," Cadernos para o III Congresso. Bissau: Edição do Serviço de Informação e Propaganda do Secretariado-Geral do PAIGC, October 7, 1977.

———. "Teses para o III Congresso do PAIGC." Bissau: Secretariado do PAIGC, October 21, 1977.

———. "III Congresso do PAIGC, Documentos do Trabalho." Bissau: November 15–20, 1977.

———. "Relatório do C.S.L." III Congresso do PAIGC. Bissau: Conselho Superior da Luta, November 15–20, 1977.

———. "Programa do Partido." Bissau: INACEP, 1979.

———. "Mensagem sobre o Estado da Nação." President Luís Cabral. Bissau: INGB, May 1979.

———. "Programa do Governo Provisório." Bissau: Conselho da Revolução, July 3, 1981.

———. "Programa Bienal 1980–1981." *Revista ANG*. Bissau: Comissariado de Informação e Cultura, 1981.

———. "Anteprojecto do Programa e Estatutos do PAIGC." Cadernos do lo Congresso Extraordinário. Bissau: Secção de Informação, Propaganda e Cultura do Secretariado do CNG do PAIGC, November 8–14, 1981.

Pereira, Luísa Teotonio and Luís Moita. *Guiné Bissau 3 Anos de Independência*. Lisbon: CIDA-C, 1976.

Rudebeck, Lars. *Guinea-Bissau: Folket, Partiet och Staten*. Uppsala: Scandinavian Institute of African Studies, 1977.

————. *Guinea-Bissau: Difficulties and Possibilities of Socialist Orientation*. Uppsala: Scandinavian Institute of African Studies, 1978.

————. "Development and Class Struggle in Guinea-Bissau." *Monthly Review*, 30, 8, January 1979.

————. *Problèmes de Pouvoir Populaire et de Développement. Transition Difficile en Guinée-Bissau*. Uppsala: Scandanavian Institute of African Studies, 1982.

Sarrazin, Chantal and Ole Gjerstad. *Sowing the First Harvest: National Reconstruction in Guinea-Bissau*. Oakland, California: LSM Information Press, 1978.

Sigrist, Christian. "Probleme des Demokratischen Neuaufbaus in Guiné-Bissau und den Kapverden." *Revue de la Société Amílcar Cabral*, (Université de Bielefeld), 2, 1977.

Soler, Anita. "Guinée-Bissau: l'Irréparable?" *Afrique Asie*, 1013, 381:34, September 7, 1986.

Sumo, Honore de. "La Guinée-Bissau s'Amare a l'Occident; le Congrès du PAIGC Confirme l'Orientation Libérale et Ramanie les Instances Dirigeantes du Parti." *Jeune Afrique*, 1351:36, November 26, 1986.

Vasconcellos, Tania. "Bissau: la Chute de Saude." *Afrique-Asie*, 1013, 319: 28, April 9 to 23, 1984.

————. "Guinée-Bissau: Épuration au Parti." *Afrique Asie*, 1013, 326: 32, July 29, 1984.

Vieira, João Bernardo, [President]. Speech , in *O Militante*, Publication of the Secretariat of the Central Comittee of the PAIGC, Special/ Congress, Bissau, November–December 1981.

Washington, Shirley. *Some Aspects of Post-War Reconstruction in Guinea-Bissau*. Ph.D. Dissertation, Political Science, Howard University, 1978.

Appendices

Contents

Appendix A
The PAIGC Program

I. *Immediate and Total Independence*
1. Immediate winning, by all necessary means of the total and unconditional national independence of the people of Guinea and the Cape Verde Islands.
2. Taking over of power, in Guinea by the Guinean people, and in the Cape Verde Islands by the people of Cape Verde.
3. Elimination of all relationships of a colonialist and imperialist nature; ending all Portuguese and foreign prerogatives over the popular masses; revision or revocation of all agreements, treaties, alliances, concessions made by the Portuguese colonialists affecting Guinea and the Cape Verde Islands.
4. National and international sovereignty of Guinea and the Cape Verde Islands. Economic, political, diplomatic, military, and cultural independence.
5. Permanent vigilance, based on the will of the people, to avoid or destroy all attempts of imperialism and colonialism to reestablish themselves in new forms in Guinea and the Cape Verde Islands.

II. *Unity of the Nation in Guinea and the Cape Verde Islands*
1. Equal rights and duties, firm unity and fraternal collaboration between citizens, whether considered as individuals, social groups or as ethnic groups. Prohibition and elimination of all attempts to divide the people.
2. Economic, political, social and cultural unity. In Guinea this unity will take into consideration the characteristics of the various ethnic groups at the social and cultural levels, regardless of the population in these groups. In the Cape Verde Islands, each island or group of identical and close islands will be able to have certain

autonomy at the administrative level, while remaining within the framework of national unity and solidarity.

3. The return to Guinea of all emigrés who wish to return to their country. The return to the Cape Verde Islands of all emigrés or transported workers who wish to return to their country. Free circulation for citizens throughout the national territory.

III. *Unity of the Peoples of Guinea and the Cape Verde Islands*

1. After the winning of national independence in Guinea and the Cape Verde Islands, unity of the peoples of these countries for the construction of a strong and progressive African nation, on the basis of suitably consulted popular will.

2. The form of unity between these two peoples to be established by their legitimate and freely elected representatives.

3. Equal rights and duties, solid unity and fraternal collaboration between Guineans and Cape Verdeans. Prohibition of all attempts to divide these two peoples.

IV. *African Unity*

1. After the winning of national independence and on the basis of freely manifested popular will, to struggle for the unity of the African peoples, as a whole or by regions of the continent, always respecting the freedom, dignity and right to political, economic, social and cultural progress of these peoples.

2. To struggle against any attempts at annexation or pressure on the peoples of Guinea and the Cape Verde Islands, on the part of any country.

3. Defense of the political, economic, social and cultural rights and gains of the popular masses of Guinea and the Cape Verde Islands is the fundamental condition for the realization of unity with other African peoples.

V. *Democratic, Anti-Colonialist, Anti-Imperialist Government*

1. Republican, democratic, lay, anti-colonialist and anti-imperialist government.

2. Establishment of fundamental freedoms, respects for the rights of man and guarantees for the exercise of these freedoms and rights.

3. Equality of citizens before the law, without distinction

of nationality or ethnic group, sex, social origin, cultural level, profession, position, wealth, religious belief or philosophical conviction. Men and women will have the same status with regard to family, work and public activities.

4. All individuals or groups of individuals who by their action or behavior favor imperialism, colonialism or the destruction of the unity of the people will be deprived by every available means of fundamental freedoms.

5. General and free elections of the organizations in power, based on direct, secret, universal voting.

6. Total elimination of the colonial administrative structure and establishment of a national and democratic structure for the internal administration of the country.

7. Personal protection of all foreigners living and working in Guinea and the Cape Verde Islands who respect the prevailing laws.

VI. *Economic Independence, Structuring the Economy and Developing Production*

1. Elimination of all relationships of a colonialist and imperialist nature. Winning of economic independence in Guinea and the Cape Verde Islands.

2. Planning and harmonious development of the economy. Economic activity will be governed by the principles of democratic socialism.

3. Four types of property: state, cooperative, private and personal. Natural resources, the principle means of production, of communication and social security, radio and other means of dissemination of information and culture will be considered as national property in Guinea and the Cape Verde Islands, and will be exploited according to the needs of rapid economic development. Cooperative exploitation on the basis of free consent will cover the land and agricultural production, the production of consumer goods and artisan articles. Private exploitation will be allowed to develop according to the needs of progress, on the condition that it is useful in the rapid development of the economy of Guinea and the Cape Verde Islands. Personal property—in particular individual consumption goods, family houses and savings resulting from work done—will be inviolable.

4. Development and modernization of agriculture. Trans-

formation of the system of cultivating the soil to put an end to monocultivation and the obligatory nature of the cultivation of groundnuts in Guinea, and of maize in the Cape Verde Islands. Struggle against agricultural crises, drought, glut and famine.

5. Agrarian reform in the Cape Verde Islands. Limitation of the extension of private rural property in order that all peasants may have enough land to cultivate. In Guinea, taking advantage of the traditional agrarian structures and creating new structures so that the exploitation of the land may benefit the maximum number of people.

6. Both in Guinea and in the Cape Verde Islands, confiscation of the land and other goods belonging to proven enemies of the freedom of the people and of national independence.

7. Development of industry and commerce along modern lines. Progressive establishment of state commercial and industrial enterprises. Development of African crafts. State control of foreign commerce and co-ordination of internal trade. Adjustment and stablization of prices. Elimination of speculation and unfair profits. Harmony between the economic activities of town and countryside.

8. Budgetary balance. Creation of a new fiscal system. Creation of a national currency, stablized and free from inflation.

VII. *Justice and Progress for All*
  a. **On the Social Level**
    1. Progressive elimination of exploitation of many by man, of all forms of subordination of the human individual to degrading interests, to the profit of individuals, groups or classes. Elimination of poverty, ignorance, fear, prostitution and alcoholism.

    2. Protection of the rights of workers and guaranteed employment for all those capable of work. Abolition of forced labor in Guinea and of the exporting of forced or "contract" labor from the Cape Verde Islands.

    3. Fair salaries and appointments on the basis of equal pay for equal work. Positive emulation in work. Limitation of daily working hours according to the needs of progress and the interests of the workers. Progressive elimi-

nation of the differences existing between workers in the towns and those in the countryside.

4. Trade union freedoms and guarantees for their effective exercise. Effective participation and creative initiative of the popular masses at every level of the nation's leadership. Encouragement and support for mass organizations in the countryside and in the towns, mainly those for women, young people and students.

5. Social assistance for all citizens who need it for reasons beyond their control, because of unemployment, disability or sickness. All public health and hygiene organizations will be run or controlled by the state.

6. Creation of welfare organizations connected with productive activity. Protection of pregnant women and children. Protection of old people. Rest, recreation and culture for all workers, manual, intellectual and agricultural.

7. Assistance for victims of the national liberation struggle and their families.

b. **On the Level of Education and Culture**

1. Teaching centers and technical institutes will be considered as national property and as such run or controlled by the state. Reform of teaching, development of secondary and technical education, creation of university education and scientific and technical institutes.

2. Rapid elimination of illiteracy. Obligatory and free primary education. Urgent training and perfection of technical and professional cadres.

3. Total elimination of the complexes created by colonialism, and of the consequences of colonialist culture and exploitation.

4. In Guinea development of autochthonous languages and of the Creole dialect, creation of a written form for these languages. In Cape Verde development of a written form for the Creole dialect. Development of the cultures of the various ethnic groups and of the Cape Verde people. Protection and development of national literature and arts.

5. Utilization of all the values and advances of human and universal culture in the service of the progress of the peoples of Guinea and Cape Verde. Contribution by the culture of these peoples to the progress of humanity in general.

6. Support and development of physical education and sport for all citizens of Guinea and the Cape Verde Islands. Creation of institutions for physical education and sport.
7. Religious freedom: freedom to have or not to have a religion. Protection of churches and mosques, of holy places and objects, of legal religious institutions. National independence for religious professionals.

VIII. *Effective National Defense Linked to the People*
1. Creation of the necessary means of effective national defense: army, navy and air force, linked to the people and directed by national citizens. Those fighting for independence will form the nucleus of national defense.
2. Democratic government within the armed forces. Close collaboration between the armed forces and the political leadership. Discipline.
3. The whole people will have to participate in vigilance and defense against colonialism, imperialism and the enemies of its unity and progress.
4. Complete ban on foreign military bases on the national territory.

IX. *Proper International Policy in the Interests of the Nation, of Africa and of the Peace and Progress of Humanity*
1. Peaceful collaboration with all the peoples of the world, on the basis of principles of mutual respect, national sovereignty, territorial integrity, non-aggression and non-interference in internal affairs, equality and reciprocity of advantages, and peaceful co-existence. Development of economic and cultural relations with all peoples whose governments accept and respect these principles.
2. Respect for the principles of the UN Charter.
3. Non-adhesion to military blocs.
4. Protection for Guinean and Cape Verdean nationals resident abroad.

Appendix B.1
Government Officials of Guinea-Bissau
(as of 25 October 1992)

President of the Republic and Council of State:
Gen. João Bernardo Vieira
First Vice President of the Council of State:
Brig. Iafai Camara
Second Vice President of the Council of State:
Vasco Cabral

Ministers of State:
Prime Minister:	Carlos Correia
Cooperation and Foreign Affairs	Bernardino Cardoso
Justice:	Mamadou Djalo Pires
Territorial Administration:	Manuel Mane
Finance:	Filinto Barros
Agriculture:	Mario Cabral
Fisheries:	Eduardo Fernandes
Natural Resources:	João Cardoso
Commerce and Industry:	Ansumane Mane
Culture and Education:	Fernando Da Silva
Social Affairs/Promotion of Women:	Francisca Pereira
Health:	Henriqueta G. Gomes

Public Works, Construction, and Urbanization:
Alberto Lima Gomes
Transport: Luis Oliveira Sanca
Labor, Civil Service, Administrative Reform:
Malam Bacai Sanha
Defense: Samba Lamine Mane
Interior: Abubacar Baldé

Secretary of State for:
Foreign Affairs:	Marcelino Lima
Economic Planning:	Nelson Dias

Treasury: Rui dias de Sousa
(the following are as of July 1986)
Resident: Northern Province: Mario Cabral
Resident: Southern Province: Luisa Oliveira Sanca
Resident for the Eastern Province: Malam Bacai Sanha
Presidency: Benardino Cardoso
Fisheries: Abubacar Baldé
Information: Agnelo Regalla
Natural Resources: Pio Correira
Tourism and Handicrafts: Alberto Lima Gomes
Transport: Mario Ribeiro
Education: Manuel R. Barcelos
War Veterans: Joaquim Furtado

Other Important Officials:
Governor of the National Bank: Pedro Godinho Gomes
President of the Supreme Court: Rui das Merces Barreto
Commander of the Police: Lourenço Gomes
Secretary General, Women's Union: Francisca Pereira
Armed Forces Chief of Staff: José Marc Vieira
President, National Assembly: Carmen Pereira

Appendix B.2
Government Officials of Guinea-Bissau:
(as of 31 July 1993)

NOTE: Shortly after the Fifth Congress of the ruling PAIGC, which took place at the Air Force Base near Bissau between 15 and 23 December 1991, and much to the surprise of most Guineans, President João Bernardo Vieira announced a government reshuffle aimed, he declared, at tackling the "new challenges of the socio-political democratization of the country" (*Nô Pintcha*, 22/1/92,3). Headed by a Prime Minister (an office abolished since 1984), the war veteran and former Minister of Rural Development and Agriculture, Carlos Correia, the restructured executive was the result of the dismissal of four ministers and two Secretaries of State, a reshuffling exercise and the appointment of a few trusted "outsiders." It would appear that the dismissed ministers, Carmen Pereira (Social Affairs), Mussa Djassi (Information and Telecommunications), Iafai Camara (Armed Forces), and Vasco Cabral (Justice), were the victims of the President's belated campaign against the "errors and irresponsibilities of ministers" who, he pointed out, not only exercised little or no control over their subordinate functionaries but shut their eyes to the obvious "anomalies," and in the process, allowed the cohabitation of "God and the Devil" (ibid.).

Less than a year later, on 25 October 1992, and without much surprise to most Guineans, President Vieira announced yet another much-speculated and long-awaited government reshuffle, promised in a speech celebrating nineteen years of Independence (24 September 1992); an exercise which was promptly characterized as an effort at "ethnic equilibrium," an allusion to the numbers of Crioulos in the previous government. This latest reorganization finished with the system of resident ministers and brought in relatively young and highly educated people with a view to giving the new administration a "technical edge." The balancing act resulted in the dropping off of some notable long serving ministers such as Manuel "Manecas" dos Santos (Information and Telecommunications, Transport, Social Infrastructure, Commerce and Tourism, Economy and Finance, Natural Resources and Industry); Victor Freire Monteiro (Minister-Governor of the National Bank, Finance, Fisheries); and Julio Semedo (Foreign Affairs). On 12 May 1993, in a most unusual act, Alexandre Furtado, Minister of National Education (since 1991) resigned his post, "in virtue of the leadership of the Government having meddled in his competences" (*Nô Pintcha*,12/5/93, 3). He was replaced by the Secretary of State for Culture, Youth and Sports, Fernando Delfim da Silva.

On 17 March 1993, an alleged coup d'etat (or mutiny or shuffle) by elements of the Forças da Intervenção Rapida (Rapid Intervention Force), led by Sergeant Amadu Mané, and implicating the leader of the Partido da Renovação e Desenvoliemento (Renovation and Development Party), João da Costa, as well as militants of other opposition parties, ended in the death of the commander of that elite force, Major Robalo Gomes da Pina. The alleged conspirators, some of whom (particularly members of the opposition, including João da Costa) have now been released from detention, have yet to be tried, and a new commander yet to be appointed.

The Officials (as of 31 July 1993):

The Presidency
Head of State and of the Government, President of the Council of State and Commander-in-Chief of the Armed Forces:
João Bernardo Vierira
First Vice President of the Council of State: Iafai Camara
Second Vice President of the Council of State: Vasco Cabral
Minister-Director, The Presidency: Flavio Proença

The Legislature
President of the Popular National Assembly: Tiago Aleluia Lopes

The Government
Prime Minister: Carlos Correia
Foreign Affairs and International Cooperation:
Bernardino Cardosa
Justice: Mamadu Saliu Djalo Pires
Territorial Administration: Alhadji Manuel Mané
Finance: Filinto Barros
Rural Development and Agriculture: Mário Cabral
Fisheries: Eduardo Fernandes
Natural Resources: João Gomes Cardosa

Commerce and Industry: Ansumane Mané
Public Health: Henriqueta Godhino Gomes
National Education: Fernando Delfim Da Silva
Social Affairs and Women's Promotion: Francisca Pereira
Public Works: Alberto Lima Gomes
Transport and Communications: Luís Oliveira Sanca
Administrative Reform, Civil Service and Labor:
Malam Bacai Sanha
Governor of the Central Bank: Luís Candido Ribeiro
Defence: Samba Lamine Mané
Interior: Abubacar Baldé

Secretaries of State

Foreign Affairs: Marcelino Lima
Planning: Nelson Dias
Treasury: Rui Diu Da Sousa
Veterans of the Liberation War: Mário Mendes
Tourism and Handicrafts: Zeca Martins
Culture, Youth and Sports: Not yet appointed
Information: Califa Seidi

Other Important Officials

President of the Supreme Court of Justice: Daniel Ferreira
Commander of the Police: Eduardo Pinto
Chief of State Security: João António Monteiro
Chief of Staff of the Armed Forces: Lt. Col. Saco Cassama
Commander of the Rapid Intervention Force: Not yet appointed
National Secretary of the Union of the Women of Guiné-Bissau:
Francisca Pereira
National Secretary of the Amilcar Cabral African Youth:
Amaro Correia
Mayor of the City of Bissau: Manuel Saturnino Da Costa
President of the Guinean League for Human Rights:
Fernando Gomes

Appendix C
Governors of Guinea (and Cape Verde) residing in Ribeira Grande, São Tiago.

NOTE: The amount of the coast under Portuguese control declined over the centuries. These data are adapted from the works of António Carreira and expanded with additional data. Note that the *capitania* system in Cacheu was begun in 1588, but was subordinate to the Governor of Cape Verde.

1592	Duarte Lobo da Gama
1595	Bras Soares de Melo
1597	Francisco Lobo da Gama
1603	Fernando da Mesquita e Brito
1606	Francisco Correa da Silva
1611–1612	Francisco Martins de Sequeira
1614	Nicolau de Castilho
1618	Francisco de Moura
1622	Francisco Rolim
1622–1628	Francisco de Vasconcelos da Cunha
1628	João Pereira Corte-Real
1632	Francisco Cristovão Cabral
1636–1638	Jorge de Castilho
1639–1640	Jeronimo Cavalcanti de Albuquerque
1640–1642	João Serrão da Cunha
1642	Jorge de Araujo
1642–1648	Roque de Barros Rego
1650	Gonçalo de Gamboa Ayala
1650	Pedro Semedo Cardoso
1651	Jorge de Mesquita Castelo-Branco
1651–1658	Pedro Ferreira Barreto
1658–1663	Francisco de Figueira
1663–1667	António Galvão
1667–1671	Manuel da Costa Pessoa
1671–1676	Manuel Pacheco de Melo
	João Cardoso Pissaro

1676–1682	Manuel da Costa Pessoa
1685	Ignácio de Franca Barbosa
1687	Verissimo de Carvalho da Costa
1690–1691	Diogo Ramires
1692–1696	Manuel António Pinheiro da Camara
	António Gomes Mena
1698	António Salgado
1702–1707	Gonçalo de Lemos Mascarenhas
	Rodrigo de Oliveira da Fonseca
1711	João Pinheiro da Camara
1715	Manuel Pereira Calheiros
1715–1718	Serafim Teixeira Sarmento de Sá
1720	António Vieira
1726	Francisco Miguel da Nobrega
1728	Francisco de Oliveira Grans
1733	Bento Gomes Coelho
1737–1738	José da Fonseca Barbosa
1738–1748	João Zuzarte de Santa Maria
1751	António José d'Eca e Faria
1751–1762	Luís António da Cunha d'Eca
1757	Manuel António de Sousa e Menezes
1761	Marcelino Pereira d'Avila
1764–1767	Bartolomeu de Sousa e Brito Tigre
	João Jacome de Brito Baena

Governors of Guinea and Cape Verde Residing in Praia, São Tiago

1769–1776	Joaquim Salema Saldanha Lobo
1777	António do Vale de Sousa e Menezes
1781	Duarte de Melo da Silva e Castro
1782	Bishop D. Frei Francisco de S. Simâo
1782–1784	António Machado de Faria e Maia
1789	Francisco José Teixeira Carneiro
1793	Francisco da Silva Maldonado d'Eca
1796	Marcelino António Basto
1803	António Coutinho de Lencastre
1818	António Pusich
1821	Luís Ignacio Xavier Palmeirim
1822	João da Mata Chapuzet
1826	Caetano Procopio Godinho Vasconcelos
1830	Duarte de Mesquitela da Costa Sousa de Macedo
1833	José Coutinho de Lencastre (never took office)

1834	Manuel António Martins
1835–1838	Joaquim Pereira Marinho
1836	Domingos Correia Arouça
1837	Joaquim Pereira Marinho
1839	João de Fontes Pereira de Melo
1842	Francisco de Paula Bastos
1845–1848	José Miguel de Noronha
1848–1851	João de Fontes Pereira de Melo
1851–1854	Fortunato José Barreiros
1854–1858	António Maria Barreiros Arrobas
1858–1860	Sebastião José Calheiros Menezes (later Governor of Angola)
1860–1861	Januário Correia de Almeida (temporary)
1861–1864	Carlos Augusto Franco
1864–1869	José Guedes Carvalho e Menezes
1869–1870	Caetano Alexandre de Almeida e Albuquerque
1870	José Maria Pinto Mota (for a few months)
1870–1876	Caetano Alexandre de Almeida e Albuquerque
1876	Guilherme Quintino Lopes Macedo (for a few months)
1876–1878	Vasco Guedes de Carvalho e Menezes (later Governor of Angola)
1878–1881	António de Nascimento Pereira de Sampaio

District Governors of Guiné Portuguesa

1758	Sebastião da Cunha Soto Maior
1837–1871	Honório Pereira Barreto
	Telles Caldeira

Governors of Guiné Portuguesa

NOTE: In 1879 the administration of Guinea Portuguesa is separated from the authority of the Governor of Cape Verde

1879–	Agostinho Coehlo
1881–	Pedro Inácio Gouveia
1885–1886	Francisco Paula Gomes Barbosa
1886–1887	José Eduardo de Brito
1887–1888	Eusébio Castelo do Vale
1888–	Francisco Teixeira da Silva
1891–	Luís Augusto de Vasconcelos e Sá

1895–	Eduardo João da Costa Oliveira
1921–1926	Jorge Frederico De Vellez Caroco
1947–48	Manuel Maria Sarmento Rodrigues

Appendix D
United States Consuls in Cape Verde (and Guinea)

Dates	Consuls
1818–1827	Samuel Hodges, Jr. (of Taunton)
1827–1836	William G. Merrill
1837–1847	Ferdinard E. Gardner
1847–1848	William Peixoto
1848–	Montgomery D. Parker
1853	John G. Forney (only from Feb. to Aug.)
1855	N. A. Haven
1857–1866	William H. Morse
1864	E. F. Wallace
1867–1869	Benjamin Tripp, Jr. (of New Bedford)
1869–	Clarimundo Martins (of Boa Vista)
1871–	A. L. Onderdonk
1873–1876	Hanibal J. Silva
1873–	Joseph Hester
1876–	Thomas M. Terry (of Benton Harbor, Mich.)
1889–1892	Henry Pease (service dates are greater)
–1898	Bartleman
1898–	Ernest Beaumont
1916–	Will L. Lowrie

Appendix E
Cape Verdean Slave Registries, 1856

The study of slavery in Cape Verde is fragmentary, however the 1856 slave registries in the National Archive give very detailed accounts of slave origins, prices, occupations, age, sex, and body characteristics, all broken down by owner and island. In reviewing these summary observations it should be noted that the categories and numbers vary in earlier historical periods.

Number of slave owners in Islands:	1,358
Number of female slaves:	2,442
Number of male slaves:	2,300
Total number of slaves:	5,180
Average number of slaves per owner:	
All Islands	3.81
São Tiago	4.41
Fogo	4.37
Sal	4.28
Boa Vista	3.35
São Nicolau	2.54
Santo Antão	2.46
São Vicente	2.28
Brava	1.95

Praia *conselho* slave population
1,519 (M = 771; F = 748)

Slave Prices by Occupations:

Herders	35–160 escudos
Weavers	25–140 escudos
Cooks (m)	75–120 escudos
Cooks (f)	25–130 escudos
Carpenters	35–160 escudos
Stoneworkers(m)	35–160 escudos
Stoneworkers(f)	25–130 escudos

Seamstresses	25–130 escudos
Washers	25–115 escudos

Slave Prices by Age:

10–15 years	65–100 escudos
15–20 years	100–140 escudos
20–40 years	115–200 escudos
40–50 years	90–140 escudos
50–60 years	70–90 escudos
60–70 years	40–70 escudos
70 plus	20–35 escudos

Group of Cape Verdean Slaves with Known Origins (n = 2,871):

Same Island as Owner	74.5%
Other Cape Verde Island	9.0%
Africa	16.4%

African Ethnic Origins: (most common first)

Mandingo, Bissagos, Balantas, Guinea?, Fula, Felupe, Quissi, Banyun, Bambara, Talibanca, Manjaco, Beafada.

Appendix F
Facts and Figures on Guinea-Bissau
(Source: World Bank, 1991)

GNP	$176 million (USD)
Real Growth Rate (1980–90)	3.7% p.a.
Population (1989)	960,000
Population (1990)	981,000
Population Growth Rate (1980–90)	1.9% p.a.
GNP/capita (1990)	$180
Agricultural Share of GDP (1970)	47%
Agricultural Share of GDP (1990)	46%
Daily calories/capita	2,690
Life expectancy at birth (1970)	36 years
Life expectancy at birth (1990)	40 years
Fertility (total births/woman, 1970)	5.9
Fertility (total births/woman, 1990)	6.0
School enrollment (1970)	29%
School enrollment (1990)	35%
Percent Illiterate (1985)	69%
One US Dollar (July 1991)	3,335 Guinean pesos
One US Dollar (July 1993)	10,000 Guinean pesos

Appendix G
Economic Data on Guinea-Bissau

TABLE I
Trade Deficits of Guinea-Bissau, 1975–1990 (US$ millions)

Year	Exports	Imports	Deficit	Exp/Imp Ratio
1975	7.1	38.0	30.9	19
1976	6.2	36.6	30.1	17
1977	12.7	36.8	24.1	34
1978	12.1	49.3	37.2	25
1979	14.1	75.5	61.4	19
1980	11.3	61.1	49.8	18
1981	13.9	52.0	38.1	27
1982	11.8	69.4	57.6	17
1983	15.5	58.4	42.9	27
1984	17.4	60.1	42.7	29
1985	11.6	63.0	51.4	18
1986	9.7	51.2	41.5	19
1987	15.4	44.7	29.3	34
1988	15.9	58.9	43.0	27
1989	14.2	68.9	54.7	21
1990	19.2	58.0	48.8	33

Source: World Bank, World Tables, 1991; BCG, 1992.

TABLE II
Foreign Public Debt of Guinea-Bissau (US$ millions), 1975–1990

	1975	1980	1985	1986	1987	1988	1989	1990
GNP	181.6	104.8	155.9	124.6	160.1	151.0	167.0	184.5
Total Debt	7.0	134.1	307.8	336.0	437.5	455.0	498.4	592.8
Long-term Debt:	7.0	127.6	263.9	310.6	402.4	416.7	460.5	544.3
Short-term Debt:	—	5.1	40.8	23.1	30.6	35.4	32.9	43.1
IMF Credit:	—	1.4	3.1	2.3	4.5	3.0	4.9	5.3
Debt Service	—	4.6	9.0	6.0	10.2	7.2	12.2	8.7
TD/GNP (%)	3.8	127.9	197.4	269.4	273.2	301.3	298.4	321.3
DS/GNP (%)	—	4.4	5.8	4.8	6.8	4.8	7.3	4.8

Source: World Bank, World Debt Tables, 1991, 166–169.

TABLE III
Origin of Imports of Guinea-Bissau (Percentage Total)

	1978	1979	1980	1986	1987	1988	1989	1990
EUROPE	81.8	85.1	78.7	76.5	74.2	79.2	80.9	88.9
France	4.6	8.8	11.4	2.9	8.1	0.8	0.7	2.3
Germany	4.1	11.1	2.0	8.3	1.4	3.0	3.8	3.1
Portugal	20.5	26.7	31.3	29.8	25.5	37.1	38.5	56.6
Sweden	10.6	9.7	8.4	8.3	4.7	0.7	0.8	0.0
USSR	0.6	8.8	7.0	2.8	2.9	6.3	4.4	0.4
Others	41.4	20.0	18.6	24.4	31.6	31.8	32.6	25.7
AFRICA	2.8	4.0	6.3	15.6	18.2	15.4	15.0	9.0
Cape Verde	0.2	0.4	0.7	0.1	0.0	0.0	0.0	1.7
Senegal	1.4	2.8	4.1	9.6	15.4	14.6	14.5	5.2
Others	1.2	0.8	1.5	5.9	2.8	0.8	0.5	2.1
ASIA	2.1	4.3	9.3	5.4	2.6	3.6	1.7	0.7
China	1.9	0.4	1.2	2.8	0.1	0.4	0.7	0.2
Pakistan	—	1.1	1.4	0.0	0.0	3.1	1.0	0.0
Others	0.2	2.8	6.7	2.6	2.5	0.0	0.0	0.0
AMERICAS	10.2	1.1	0.5	2.5	5.0	1.8	2.5	1.4
Total	100.0	100.0	100.0	100.0	100.0	100.0	100.0	100.0

Source: FAO, 1983; BCG, 1992.

TABLE IV
Destination of Exports of Guinea-Bissau (Percentage of Total)

	1978	1979	1980	1986	1987	1988	1989	1990
EUROPE	54.9	66.6	79.9	65.4	56.0	52.8	45.9	77.6
France	2.3	1.7	0.2	8.5	7.0	10.3	0.5	4.8
Portugal	20.6	38.1	26.5	49.4	35.0	32.5	35.4	45.3
Spain	18.3	20.8	24.9	5.0	6.0	4.6	4.1	13.6
Others	13.7	16.0	28.3	2.5	8.0	5.4	5.9	13.9
AFRICA	45.1	32.2	16.3	11.0	43.0	47.2	21.5	6.0
Angola	34.9	23.4	—	—	—	—	—	—
Cape Verde	1.6	2.1	6.0	1.0	9.0	0.8	0.6	2.4
Gambia	1.6	0.5	0.9	2.0	8.0	13.4	13.8	0.0
Guinée								
Conakry	5.1	0.0	—	2.5	5.0	0.9	0.0	0.0
Nigeria	—	—	—	1.5	0.0	6.5	0.0	0.0
Senegal	1.9	6.0	1.4	3.0	20.0	21.9	8.5	0.3
Others	—	—	—	1.0	1.0	3.7	8.5	3.3
ASIA	—	1.2	3.8	23.6	1.0	0.0	32.6	16.4
China	—	1.2	3.8	18.0	1.0	0.0	0.0	0.0
India	—	—	—	5.6	0.0	0.0	32.6	16.4
AMERICAS	—	—	—	—	—	—	—	—
Total	100.0	100.0	100.0	100.0	100.0	100.0	100.0	100.0

Source: FAO, 1983; BCG, 1992.

TABLE V
Debt Burdens of Members of ECOWAS (US$ millions), 1990

Country	GNP	TED	TDS	TED/GNP(%)	TED/XGS(%)
Benin	1,845	1,427	15	77.4	6.5
Burkina Faso	3,164	834	34	26.4	6.4
Cape Verde	376	152	5	40.4	3.8
Ivory Coast	8,806	17,956	1421	203.9	38.6
Gambia	242	352	47	193.5	26.0
Ghana	6,157	3,498	345	56.8	34.9
Guinée	2,784	2,497	72	89.7	8.3
Guinea-Bissau	185	593	9	321.3	45.1
Liberia	—	1,870	1	—	—
Mali	2,421	2,433	65	100.5	11.5
Mauritania	983	2,277	69	226.7	13.9
Niger	2,485	1,829	95	73.6	24.8
Nigeria	30,585	36,068	3014	110.9	20.3
Senegal	5,631	3,745	323	66.5	22.9
Sierra Leone	814	1,189	24	146.2	—
Togo	1,583	1,296	86	81.8	14.1

Note: TED = Total External Debt; TDS = Total Debt Service; EGS = Export of Goods and Services. Source: World Bank, World Debt Tables, 1991.

Appendix H
Culturo-Linguistic Groups of Guinea-Bissau

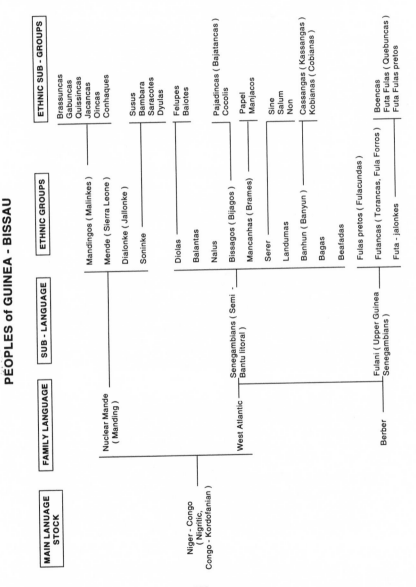

PEOPLES of GUINEA - BISSAU

MAIN LANUAGE STOCK	FAMILY LANGUAGE	SUB - LANGUAGE	ETHNIC GROUPS	ETHNIC SUB - GROUPS
Niger - Congo (Nigritic, Congo - Kordofanian)	Nuclear Mande (Manding)		Mandingos (Malinkes)	Brassuncas Gabuncas Quissincas Jacancas Oincas Conhaques
			Mende (Sierra Leone)	
			Dialonke (Jallonke)	
			Soninke	Susus Bambara Saracotes Dyulas
	West Atlantic	Senegambians (Semi - Bantu litoral)	Diolas	Felupes Baiotes
			Balantas	
			Nalus	Pajadincas (Bajatancas) Cocolis
			Bissagos (Bijagos)	
			Mancanhas (Brames)	Papel Manjacos
			Serer	Sine Salum Non
			Landumas	
			Banhun (Banyun)	Cassangas (Kassangas) Kobianas (Cobianas)
			Bagas	
			Beafadas	
		Fulani (Upper Guinea Senegambians)	Fulas pretos (Fulacundas)	
	Berber		Futancas (Torancas, Fula Forros)	Boencas Futa Fulas (Quebuncas) Futa Fulas pretos
			Futa - jalonkes	

Appendix I
Evolution of Crioulo Culture

I. AFRICAN GROUPS:

A. Sometime slave sources

Fulas (Futa Toro, Futa Jallon, Firdu) ···>
Mandinkas (Bambara, Kissi, Kaabuncas) ·······································>
Wolof, Serer, (Sine/Salum) ···>

B. Usual slave sources:

Senegambians (Balantas, Brames, Banyun,
Beafadas, Felupes, Manjacos, Papeis, Nalus)······························>

ESCRAVOS

C. Non-Slave African groups:

African and Luso-African Traders (e.g. Bissagos,
Dyulas, Tangomãos, Grumêtes, Senhores) ······························>

II. EUROPEAN GROUPS:

A. **European Traders:** Portuguese, English,
French, Americans, Lebanese ·····················>

B. **Portuguese Officials:** Feitores,
Ouvidores, Padres, Soldiers, Capitãos,
Fidalgos ··>

C. **Exiles:** Lançados, Sephardic Jews,
Degredados ·····························>

III. CRIOULO POPULATION <·····································
By "Race": Mestiços, Mulatões, Mistos
By Socio-Political Status: Assimilados
By Socio-economic status: Badius, Rendeiros,
Contratados

(SEE: *Historical Dictionary of Cape Verde, 3rd Edition*)

About the Authors

Richard Lobban (Ph.D, Anthropology, Northwestern University, 1973) is a Professor of Anthropology and the Director of the Program of African and Afro-American Studies at Rhode Island College. Since Rhode Island has a notable Cape Verdean and West African population he is active with local groups from these places, and he often teaches on West Africa and Cape Verde.

Lobban has worked with Mozambican refugees in 1964; written on Portuguese Africa since 1965; crossed Guinea-Bissau on foot and canoe during wartime with the nationalist guerrillas in 1973. After independence in 1975 he returned to Guinea-Bissau and Cape Verde to witness the very last days of colonialism and the start of independence. With these long-standing contacts he revisited the Cape Verde islands in 1992 while writing a book on contemporary Cape Verde, which focuses on the rise of plural democracy in the islands. In 1993 he participated in the celebrations of the 20th anniversary of independence in Guinea-Bissau.

Lobban's African research also focuses extensively on social and economic issues in Egypt, the Sudan, and Tunisia. He also has special interests in the ancient civilizations of those nations. He was a founder and first President of the Sudan Studies Association and published numerous articles, chapters, and books on those lands, including the *Historical Dictionary of the Sudan* (Scarecrow Press, 1992) with his wife Carolyn Fluehr-Lobban and John Voll.

Peter Karibe Mendy (Ph.D, Political Science, Birmingham University, England, 1987) is currently Deputy Director of Guinea-Bissau's *Instituto Nacional de Estudos e Pesquisa* (National Institute of Studies and Research), Senior Researcher, and Coordinator of its Center for the Study of Contemporary History. He has taught Political Science in England (Caulden College, Stoke-on-Trent) and Social Studies in the Boston area of the United States. He has published articles in Guinean and Portuguese academic journals on the history of resistance in Guinea-Bissau. He conducted research for his doctoral thesis in Guinea-Bissau and is the author of a forthcoming book entitled *Guiné-Bissau: Colonialismo Português e a Resistência Africana, 1879–1959*.

Dr. Mendy is presently conducting research on the emergence of political pluralism in Guinea-Bissau, and is a member of the National Core Team of the UNDP-sponsored National Long-Term Perspective Study (NLTPS) for this country. He is also interested in West Africa regional and sub-regional integration and has actively participated in international conferences on the subject.

Susan Hurley-Glowa (M.M., University of Louisville; M.A. and A.B.D, Brown University) is a Doctoral Candidate at Brown University in ethnomusicology and is writing on the musical traditions of São Tiago, Cape Verde. She has studied and played with Crioulo musicians in New England and has recorded with Norberto Tavares. From 1992 to 1993 she conducted doctoral field research in Cape Verde under a Fulbright grant. Hurley-Glowa lives in Idaho and is also a professional french horn player.